Archaeology and the
New Testament

ARCHAEOLOGY
AND THE
NEW TESTAMENT

A Companion Volume to
ARCHAEOLOGY AND THE OLD TESTAMENT

by
MERRILL F. UNGER, Th.D., Ph.D.

ZONDERVAN
PUBLISHING HOUSE
OF THE ZONDERVAN CORPORATION
GRAND RAPIDS, MICHIGAN 49506

ARCHAEOLOGY AND THE NEW TESTAMENT
Copyright 1962 by
Zondervan Publishing House
Grand Rapids, Michigan

ISBN 0-310-33380-6

Library of Congress Catalog Card No. 62-7371

Twenty-first printing 1982

Printed in the United States of America

CONTENTS

1. THE ROLE OF ARCHAEOLOGY IN THE STUDY OF THE NEW TESTAMENT 13

2. FROM ALEXANDER THE GREAT TO HEROD THE GREAT — THE FOUNDATIONS OF NEW TESTAMENT POLITICAL AND CULTURAL HISTORY 27

3. PALESTINE AND THE ROMAN WORLD AT THE TIME OF CHRIST 50

4. THE DEAD SEA SCROLLS AND THE MINISTRY OF JOHN AND JESUS 75

5. PLACES WHERE JESUS WALKED AND WORKED IN JUDAEA AND THE JORDAN VALLEY.......................... 95

6. PLACES WHERE JESUS WALKED AND WORKED IN NORTHERN AND CENTRAL PALESTINE 118

7. CHRISTIANITY IS BORN AND EXTENDS BEYOND JUDAEA...... 146

8. ANTIOCH, THE BIRTHPLACE OF CHRISTIAN MISSIONS....... 170

9. THE CITIES OF PAUL'S FIRST MISSIONARY TOUR.......... 181

10. CHRISTIANITY PREPARED FOR WORLD-WIDE PROCLAMATION..201

11. THE CHURCHES OF MACEDONIA....................... 216

12. THE GOSPEL AND THE GLORY OF ANCIENT GREECE........ 232

13. TRIBULATIONS AND TRIUMPHS IN EPHESUS.............. 248

14. GOSPEL PROGRESS AND THE CITIES OF THE LYCUS VALLEY...264

15. GOSPEL PROGRESS IN OTHER CITIES OF PROCONSULAR ASIA..274

16. PAUL'S LAST JOURNEY TO JERUSALEM AND THE END OF HIS THIRD MISSIONARY TOUR.................... 287

17. PAUL THE PRISONER OF ROME....................... 297

18. ARCHAEOLOGY AND THE NEW TESTAMENT AS LITERATURE..324

Bibliography 338

Index 343

ACKNOWLEDGMENTS

The author is indebted to Mr. Alan Marshall and Mr. Robert Ramey for the artwork, including the numerous line drawings and maps scattered throughout the book. Dr. W. F. Albright, chairman of the Editorial Committee of the American Schools of Oriental Research, kindly granted permission for the artist's reproduction of the Triumphal Arch of Gerasa and the Temple of Zeus. Mr. Cornelius Zylstra, editor at Baker Book House, granted permission to use reproductions of various coins in Ramsay's *The Cities of St. Paul* from the reprint edition. To many others the author is indebted for help and suggestions, especially to his beloved wife for constant encouragement and for typing the final manuscript. Grateful thanks is also accorded the Zondervan Publishing House for many courtesies and for its efforts to make *Archaeology and the New Testament* a distinctive publication.

LIST OF ILLUSTRATIONS

Breasted's Fertile Crescent, 14

The New Testament World, 14

The Emperor Vespasian, 24

Bronze Coin From Persian Period, 28

Persian Gold Daric, 28

Alexander's Route of Conquest, 29

One of Alexander's "Hele-poleis" (siege towers), 30

Alexander's Causeway to Tyre, 30

Tetradrachma Coin With Name of Alexander, 31

Silver Shekel of Year 1 of the First Revolt, 31

The Hellenistic World, 36

Ptolemy I, 37

Tetradrachma Coin of Ptolemy I, 37

Antiochus III the Great, 41

Coin of Antiochus III, 41

The Maccabean Kingdom, 42

Coin of John Hyrcanus I, 45

Coin of Alexander Jannaeus, 45

Handwashing Among the Jews, 46

Eagle Drawn From Tetradrachma Coin, 49

Coin of Antigonus, 50

Coin of Alexander Jannaeus, 50

The Roman Empire, 44 B.C. to 234 A.D., 52

Palestine Under Herod the Great, 54

Romans Commemorating the Peace of Augustus, 55

Statue of the God Hadad, 56

Fragment of Nabataean Pottery, 56

Myrrh, 57

Frankincense, 57

Ruins of the Herodium at Bethlehem, 59

Coin of Herod the Great, 61

Bethlehem Today, 62

Shepherds Field Outside Bethlehem, 62

The Emperor Augustus, 66

The Emperor Tiberius, 66

Denarius With Head of Tiberius Caesar, 67

Palestine During Jesus' Ministry, 68

Bronze Coin From Procuratorship of Pilate, 70

The Dead Sea From the Dead Sea Hotel, 79

Coin Showing Judaea Guarded by Soldier, 82

Bronze Coin From Second Revolt, 82

Ruins at Qumran, 84

Jerusalem in New Testament Times, 96

Jewish Ossuary, 97

The Wailing Wall, Jerusalem, 98

Coin of Herod the Great Inscribed Around Wreath, 99

Roman Siege Procedures, 100

Ground Plan of the Herodian Temple, 101

Seven Branched Candlestick, 102

The Ecce-Homo Arch, 104

Street in Old Jerusalem, 104

Traditional Site of Golgotha, 105

Traditional Garden Tomb, 105

The Tower of Antonia at Jerusalem, 106

Jerusalem Today, 107

Mt. of Olives Seen From the Dome of the Rock, 108

Branch of Olives, 109

Mustard Plant, 109

Palestinian Olive Press, 110

The Garden of Gethsemane, 111

Oriental House, 113

Ancient Palestinian Well, 114

Yoke of Oxen, 114

The Jordan River As It Leaves the Sea of Galilee, 116

The Valley of Megiddo (Plain of Esdraelon), 120

"Lilies of the Field," 121

Tares (Darnel), 121

Palestinian Synagogue of 1st or 2nd Century, 122

Palestinian Water Jar, 123

Grape Harvest, 124

Treading Grapes in 1st Century Palestine, 124

The Capernaum Synagogue, 3rd Century, 127

List of Illustrations

Carob Pods, 129

Tiberias and the Sea of Galilee, 131

Statue of Christ As the Good Shepherd, 132

Temple of Jupiter, Baalbek, 133

Altar Rock for God, Baalbek, 133

Mt. Hermon and the Lebanon Mountains, 135

Sidon—Harbor and Crusaders' Fort, 138

Temple of Zeus at Gerasa (Jerash), Floor Plan, 140

Ruins of the Theatre at Jerash, 140

Head of Hadrian Drawn From a Coin, 142

The Triumphal Arch at Gerasa (Jerash), 143

The Grape Vine in Bloom, 144

Mt. Gerizim Seen From Jacob's Well, 145

Coin of Herod the Great With Caduceus, 149

Ruins of Herod's Summer Palace, Samaria, 150

Modern Tarsus, 156

Coins From Tarsus, 157

Straight Street in Damascus, 160

Ruins of an Ancient Aqueduct to Caesarea, 165

Ruins of Caesarea, Palestine, 165

Palestine Under Herod Agrippa I, 167

Coin of Herod Agrippa I With Umbrella and Grain, 168

Modern Antioch on the Orontes, 175

The Chalice at Antioch (Artist's Sketch), 179

Paul's First and Second **Missionary** Journeys, 182

Island of Cyprus, 183

Asia Minor (Phrygia), 187

Coins From Antioch of Pisidia, 189

Remains of an Ancient Aqueduct at Pisidian Antioch, 193

Coins From Antioch of Pisidia, 194

Hellenized Native Hero Found at Iconium, 195

Coins From Iconium, 196

Coins From Lystra, 198

Coins From Derbe, 199

Map of the Growth of Christianity, 202

Asia Minor (Bethynia and Pontus), 213

Map of Paul's Journey Into Europe, 217

The Ruins of Philippi, 224

Temple of Theseus, Athens, 235

Interior of the Parthenon, Athens, 235

The Parthenon, Athens, 239

The Erechtheum, Athens, 239

The Acropolis, Athens, 239

Modern Canal Across the Isthmus of Corinth, 241

Ruins of the Lechaeum Road, Corinth, 241

Ruins of the Temple of Apollo, Corinth, 246

Remains of an Arch, Corinth, 246

Temple of Artemis (Diana), Ephesus, 251

Map of Ancient Ephesus, 254

Ruins of the Amphitheatre, Ephesus, 255

The Arkadiane, Ephesus, 255

Palestine at the Time of Herod Agrippa II, 300

Cornucopia From Time of Herod Agrippa II, 302

Coin From Time of Herod Agrippa II, 302

Palestine at the Time of the Jewish Roman War, 303

Paul's Third Journey and Journey to Rome, 304

War Galley of the 1st Century A.D., 309

Women's Hair Styles of the Graeco-Roman World, 312

The Emperor Nero, 312

The Appian Way Today, 314

Section of a Roman Road, 314

The Arch of Titus, Rome, 315

Roman Coins (A.D. 30), 316

Map of Rome, 317

The Colosseum, Rome, 318

A View Among the Ruins of Ancient Rome, 318

Roman Table for Reclining at Meals, 318

Ruins of the Roman Forum, 320

Modern Sign on the Mamertine Prison, Rome, 322

Archaeology and the New Testament

Chapter 1

THE ROLE OF ARCHAEOLOGY IN THE STUDY
OF THE NEW TESTAMENT

Archaeology (from the Greek *archaios,* "old," "ancient" and *logos,* "word," "treatise," "study") is a science devoted to the recovery of the remains of ancient civilizations with a view to reconstructing the story of their rise, progress, and fall. Considered in this aspect, archaeology is the handmaid of history, particularly of ancient history. It is the research department of all branches of learning that seek to expand man's knowledge of the past.

General archaeology undertakes the excavation, decipherment, and critical evaluation of the remains of ancient human life wherever found on this planet. The more circumscribed field of biblical archaeology confines itself to the study of the material remains of those lands and peoples that directly or indirectly affect the language and literature of the Bible, as well as its message and meaning. For the Old Testament the geographical area of interest centers in James Breasted's famous "fertile crescent," with one tip touching Palestine and the other tip extending to lower Iraq and the Persian Gulf, with the body of the moon comprising the Middle and Lower basin of the Euphrates and Tigris Rivers. For the New Testament, the focus of activity falls in Palestine and fans out into the Graeco-Roman culture of the Mediterranean world of the first century A.D.[1]

The fascination of biblical archaeology for the student interested in expanding the scientific aspects of the study of the Bible is immense. No realm of research has offered more thrilling rewards or afforded greater promise of continued progress.

There are, however, certain essential differences in the results of the application of archaeological research to the Old Testament as over against the New Testament. In the Old Testament the impact has been much more obvious, because ancient Bible history previous to the fifth century B.C. was much less known than the later Graeco-

[1]See map on page 14.

13

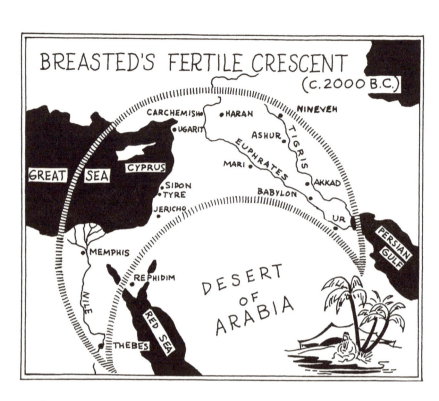

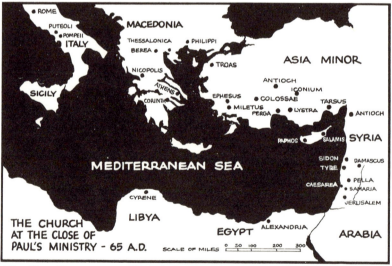

The New Testament world with focus of activity in Palestine and extending westward to the Graeco-Roman civilization of the Mediterranean area

Roman period of Mediterranean history that underlies the New Testament. Old Testament archaeology has rediscovered whole nations, resurrected important peoples, and in a most astonishing manner filled in historical gaps, adding immeasurably to the knowledge of biblical backgrounds.[2]

Although New Testament archaeology has not been called upon to perform such sensational feats, its importance is no less far-reaching and is becoming more significant each year. Dealing with a much shorter span of history (a bare century in contrast to several millennia of the Old Testament world), and concerned largely with smaller groups of individuals united by spiritual ties rather than with a whole nation like Israel, held together by political bonds, archaeological data have been more difficult to apply to the New Testament than the Old, but scarcely have they been less important or exciting.

I. WHAT THE NEW TESTAMENT IS

Before considering the service archaeology is rendering the study of the New Testament, it is well to pause a moment to inquire precisely what the New Testament is. Christians of various shades of theological persuasion naturally define it differently. But whatever the attitude or critical evaluation, the Greek New Testament as a historical document is of incalculable importance in the spiritual history and destiny of mankind and is so recognized by practically all Christians. Moreover, historic, spiritually vitalized Christianity has always defined it in the highest terms and reposed implicit faith in its message and redemptive efficacy.

1. *The New Testament Is the Inspired Revelation of God to Man*

While naturalistic negative criticism has from time to time sought to reduce the inspiration of the New Testament to a purely human level, denying divine intervention in any degree in the production of the New Testament documents, less radical views have allowed some measure of supernatural superintendence over the writing of these records of the origin of the Christian faith. Any view less than this can hardly present a rational explanation of the remarkable regenerative ministry of the New Testament nor avoid the bane of spiritual bankruptcy.

Mediating positions recognize the factor of divine intervention in inspiration, but posit that there were error and fallibility on the human plane, and that the reflection of these in the sacred writings is not inconsistent with the production of Holy Writ. These views, in vogue in recent decades, are an accommodation to the affirmed

[2]Cf. the author's *Archaeology and the Old Testament*, 3rd ed. (Grand Rapids, 1956), pp. 9-25.

findings of scientific research and the alleged assured results of modern criticism.[3] Although they represent a reaction against the crass naturalism of radical liberalism, and have fostered more constructive critical study of the Bible, they do not represent the historic, conservative belief of the church.

The orthodox opinion on biblical inspiration still remains that the New Testament (as well as the Old) is God-breathed and without error or mistake in the original autographs.[4] This conviction extends infallible inspiration not only to the thoughts of Scripture but also to the very words, and extends it equally and comprehensively to all of the canonical books of both Testaments. Thus Scripture, as the disclosure of the redemptive purposes and plans of God for the human race, is inspired in a unique way. The product itself is accordingly unique and on a different plane from any other writing, sacred or secular.

2. *The New Testament Is the Capstone and Consummation of Old Testament Revelation*

It is inseparably connected with the Old Testament as a tree is connected with its roots, as a house with its foundation, as a head with its body. Separated from its roots, a tree dies. Without a foundation, a house collapses. Cut off from its body, a head becomes lifeless. Without the Old Testament, there could have been no New Testament, and apart from it, the New Testament is pointless. One is the counterpart of the other. As Augustine maintained, the New Testament is enfolded in the Old and the Old is unfolded by the New.

To apply the results of archaeological research to the New Testament without recognizing its inseparable connection with the Old Testament as a fulfillment of all the redemptive plans and promises made there, has produced much confusion. For this reason historical and archaeological findings have frequently been misused. The result has been serious misunderstanding and misinterpretation.

As the consummation of Old Testament revelation, which was preparatory and introductory to it, the New Testament recounts the history of the incarnation, the earthly life, death, resurrection, and ascension of Christ and the founding of Christianity. In addition, it presents a systematic exposition of the doctrines of the Christian faith. As the capstone of all the redemptive plans and purposes for man

[3]Cf. Kenneth Kantzer, "Revelation and Inspiration in Neo-Orthodox Theology," *Bibliotheca Sacra*, April, 1958, pp. 120-127; July, 1958, pp. 218-228; Oct., 1958, pp. 302-312; Paul King Jewett, *Emil Brunner's Concept of Revelation* (London, 1954), pp. 118-120; 158-172; *Revelation and Inspiration* ed. by John F. Walvoord, (Grand Rapids, 1957), pp. 210-252.
[4]Laird Harris, *Inspiration and Canonicity of the Bible* (Grand Rapids, 1956); Wick Broomall, *Biblical Criticism* (Grand Rapids, 1957), pp. 11-84.

(and without detracting in the least from its inseparable unity with the Old Testament), the New Testament is beyond doubt the most important document in the world. It records God's full and final message for sinful man. It presents Him in history of whom the Old Testament speaks in symbol, type, and prophecy. In presenting Him it brings sinful humanity face to face with the One who alone can meet its deepest and most fundamental need of salvation from sin.

No other religious writings—the Vedas, the Koran, the sacred scriptures of Taoism, Confucianism, or Buddhism—can compare with the New Testament. It has a place apart because of the unique Person it presents and the unique work of salvation He accomplished by His sinless life, vicarious death, and glorious resurrection. His ascension to heaven from which He came, the consequent gift of the Holy Spirit and the establishment of the Church of Christ are all well-attested events of history unparalleled by the claims, much less by the facts, of any other religion.

Not only as authenticated history, but in the matter of prophecy, which is so frequently interwoven with history in the biblical revelation, the New Testament is unparalleled. It catalogues in detail the complex and minute fulfillment of Old Testament predictions concerning the first advent of the Messiah in suffering, rejection, and death. But it goes farther than this. It picks up the extensive theme of yet-unfulfilled Old Testament prophecy concerning the second advent of the Messiah in glory, and the establishment of the kingdom over Israel, and develops these far-reaching disclosures with added revelation in the great eschatological discourses of Jesus (Matthew 24:1-25:46), Paul (I Thessalonians 4:1-II Thessalonians 2:12), Peter (II Peter 2:1-12) and particularly John in the book of the Revelation.

Although, as history, the New Testament covers less than a single century, as prophecy, it spans the ages of time and plumbs eternity, past as well as future. Whatever naturalistic criticism may attempt to do with its miracles and its fulfilled prophecies, all the labors of form criticism to "demythologize" it still leaves its greatest wonders — the glorious Person of whom it tells and the great work of salvation He wrought — untouched and rationally inexplicable, except on the basis that He was what the New Testament declares He was—God in human flesh appearing—and He did what the New Testament asserts He did —died, rose again from the dead, ascended to heaven, and gave the gift of the Holy Spirit to call out His redeemed Church.

Moreover, if Christ is what the New Testament sets Him forth to be, and if He did what the New Testament says He did and what the subsequent facts of history and our experience of His salvation give us reliable reasons to be the case, then the New Testament which catalogues these tremendous truths and calls men from the sordidness of sin to God is indeed among God's very best gifts to man and one of man's most valuable treasures.

II. How Archaeology Facilitates the Study of the New Testament

If the New Testament is what it is herein defined to be, and what history, fulfilled prophecy, and the experience of redeemed humanity attest it to be, its own incalculable importance in degree attaches to every branch of research that can forward the study of it and contribute to its elucidation. In the forefront of such studies is the science of biblical archaeology. In the New Testament field this comparatively young science (about a century-and-a-half hold in its broadest limits, but only a youngster of less than a half-century in the sense of an exact science) is growing in significance year by year and constantly making new contributions to the better understanding of the New Testament on the human side.

1. *Archaeology Expedites the Scientific Study of the New Testament*

This is perhaps its most fundamentally significant contribution. The Bible has always had the student who studied it from the aspect of its spiritual message and meaning. But sacred Scripture in addition needs the technical expert—the trained linguist, grammarian, historian, geographer, and textual critic. In this list of specialists in various phases of biblical science, the archaeologist now takes a prominent and important place.

Without the consecrated labors of biblical technicians, knowledge of Scripture on the human plane (and the Bible is a human book as well as divine) would remain static or even suffer retrogression. This situation would soon affect the spiritual comprehension of Holy Writ, since the divine and human elements in Bible study interact and cannot be separated one from another or one be neglected without adverse effect upon the other.

An example of archaeology aiding the scientific study of the New Testament is furnished in the field of textual criticism. This fundamental area of research, which by the nature of the case is basic to all other study in this field, has been signally advanced during the past fifty years by new manuscript finds which have furnished technical scholars with added data for the evaluation and revision of the labors of textual critics, particularly the epochal work of Westcott and Hort.

Most recent official statistics on the number of witnesses to all or parts of the Greek New Testament list 2,440 minuscule manuscripts,

232 uncials, 1,678 lectionaries, 63 papyri and 25 ostraca (potsherds).[5] Particularly significant are the Chester Beatty Papyri from the third century, edited by Sir Frederic Kenyon in 1933-1937. From a papyrus codex which originally contained all four gospels and the Acts, six leaves of Mark, seven of Luke, and thirteen of Acts remain.[6] From a papyrus codex originally containing ten Pauline epistles, 86 leaves are extant, and from another papyrus codex originally of the book of Revelation, only the portion comprising chapters 9:10-17:2 has been preserved.

Of uncial manuscripts, among the most important ones discovered in the twentieth century are Codex W from the early fifth century and Codex Theta from the ninth century, both containing the four gospels. Of late other uncial manuscripts have also been recovered.[7]

A whole new field of scientific investigation of the New Testament in recent years has been opened up by the recognition of the value of the Greek lectionaries. These aids to the study of the original text, designed by their compilers to supply readings for the liturgical year of the church, contain most of the New Testament except the Revelation and a portion of the Acts. They are shedding much light on the history of the transmission of the New Testament text and furnish a valuable illustration of archaeology's ability to promote constructive scientific research of the Scriptures.[8]

In the area of ancient versions of late years, manuscript evidence has been supplemented making possible further progress in textual analysis. In addition, several versions not previously known have been brought to light.[9] Interesting and significant for textual criticism is the discovery at Dura on the Euphrates of a parchment fragment of the Diatessaron of Tatian in Greek, belonging to the period just prior to the Roman garrison city's fall to the Persians in A.D. 256-257. Published in 1935, this bit of evidence settles once and for all the long debate whether or not Tatian's Harmony ever existed in Greek.

These textual advances have made feasible a constant stream of revisions of the Bible in the common languages of the peoples of Europe and America, besides giving impetus to scores and scores of translations for the mission fields of the globe.

[5]Cf. Ernst von Dobschuetz in Eberhard Nestle's *Einfuehrung in das griechische Neue Testament* 4te Auf. 1923 and in *Zeitschrift fuer die neutestamentliche Wissenschaft* XIII, pp. 248-264; XXV, pp. 299-306; XXXII, pp. 185-206; Kurt Aland, *Theologische Literaturzeitung* (1953), pp. 465-496.
[6]See F. G. Kenyon, *The Text of the Greek Bible, a Students' Handbook,* 1937.
[7]B. M. Metzger, "Recently Published Greek Papyri of the New Testament," *Smithsonian Report for 1948,* pp. 439-452; G. Maldfeld and B. M. Metzger, *Journal of Biblical Literature,* LXVIII (1949), pp. 359-370.
[8]See chapter XVIII.
[9]See Bruce Metzger, "Bible Versions (Ancient)," *Twentieth Century Encyclopaedia* (1955), pp. 137-143.

Archaeology in giving valuable aid in establishing a critical text, opens up the way for profitable research on the part of the grammarian, the philologian and the lexicographer. The remarkable recovery of papyri since about 1890,[10] besides enabling scholars to evaluate the true character and literary nature of the language of the New Testament,[11] are immeasurably aiding the accurate understanding of the morphology (a study of the form of words), phonology (a study of their sound and pronunciation) and syntax (the relations of words to one another in the sentence) of the Greek in the New Testament. Moreover, in illustrating and thus elucidating the meaning of New Testament vocabulary in the light of the common language of the time, the papyri are rendering far-reaching service to the lexicographer, making possible great strides in this area.[12]

Of particular importance is the *Theologisches Woerterbuch zum Neuen Testament* by Gerhard Kittel. This magnificent work (based on the earlier work of H. Cremer, which was frequently revised since its appearance in 1866) promises to be a crowning achievement made possible by new archaeological discoveries expanding the horizons of biblical knowledge. The majority of its seven volumes have already appeared. Since the death of Gerhard Kittel in 1948, the work has been continued by Gerhard Friedrich. Dealing only with words of theological import, it, however, is able to treat them much more accurately and fully than any of its great predecessors because of modern advance in research.

Of first-rate importance also is the *Greek-English Lexicon of the New Testament and other Early Christian Literature*, translated and edited by Arndt and Gingrich and published by the University of Chicago (1958). This valuable work that employs the latest results of papyrological studies, renders obsolete such earlier lexicons as Thayer, Moulton and Milligan, and even Liddell and Scott.

2. Archaeology Acts As a Balance in the Critical Study of the New Testament

New Testament scholarship, like that of the Old Testament, has often been plagued with extremism. In the case of both Testaments, archaeology has frequently acted as a corrective and purge in showing the falsity of many erratic theories and false assumptions. This is true of the Old Testament to a larger degree perhaps than the New Testament. The simple reason for this is that incomparably less was known of Old Testament backgrounds than was true of the New Testament

[10]See Chapter 18.
[11]See Adolf Deissmann, *Light from the Ancient East*, 3rd ed., (1927).
[12]See Walter Gingrich, "Lexicons of the Greek New Testament," *Twentieth Century Encyclopaedia*, pp. 657-659.

before the advent of the science of biblical archaeology in the nineteenth century. This situation gave more radically inclined higher
critics greater range for extreme naturalistic views than was possible
in the New Testament where a great deal was already known about its
historical environment from abundant classical and other sources.[13]
Nevertheless, archaeological research has important bearings in balancing New Testament criticism.

To cite an example, the date of the gospel of John is a case in
point. According to the influential Tuebingen School, founded by F.
C. Baur, fewer than a half-dozen books of the New Testament were
written in the first century A.D. John's gospel was placed as late
as the second half of the second century, thus being effectually
removed from authentic apostolic tradition. Until recently it has been
popular in radical critical circles to posit a date for the fourth gospel
not earlier than the first half of the second century. The school of
form criticism since 1919[14] has carried on this unsound practice of
late-dating the gospels, particularly John, which is in a peculiarly
vulnerable position, and which is supposed by these scholars to be devoid of any original historical matter and to reflect the beliefs and
ideas of an early second-century Gnostic sect.

New archaeological finds are effectively countering these extreme views. A small papyrus fragment containing John 18:31-33,
37-38, published in 1935 and now in the John Rylands Library at Manchester, England, constitutes the oldest known fragment of the New
Testament. It is dated by competent palaeographers within the period
A.D. 100-150.[15] The evidence it furnishes at once exposes the un-
tenableness of the Tuebingen School and the contentions of many of
the form critics. Added to this, the Qumran Documents of the Dead
Sea Scrolls since 1947 show that the supposed second-century Gnostic
ideas of John's gospel are authentic to first-century Jewish sectarian
life and thought and substantiate the traditional first-century date of
John's gospel within the apostolic period. Likewise numerous geographical and topographical allusions in the fourth gospel[16] have been

[13]See the present author's *Archaeology and the Old Testament*, 3rd ed. (Grand
Rapids, 1957), pp. 14-25.
[14]Cf. M. Dibelius, *Formgeschichte des Evangeliums* 1919; 2nd ed., 1933; Engl.
Trans. *From Tradition to Gospel*, 1935; R. Bultmann, *Die Geschichte der synop-
tischen Tradition* 1921, 2nd ed., 1931; L. J. McGinley, *Form Criticism of the
Synoptic Healing Narratives*, 1944.
[15]So C. H. Roberts who published the fragment in 1935 and H. I. Bell, A. Deiss-
mann, W. H. P. Hatch, and F. G. Kenyon.
[16]See the present writer's *The Dead Sea Scrolls and Other Amazing Archaeological
Discoveries* 1957, pp. 1-50. F. F. Bruce, *Second Thoughts on the Dead Sea
Scrolls*, 1956. W. F. Albright, *The Bible After Twenty Years of Archaeology,
Religion in Life*, XXI, 4 (1952) pp. 547-550.

vindicated against the critical charge of adaptations or later pure inventions.[17]

The Bodmer Papyrus Manuscript of John (dating from about 200 A.D. and preserving most of the gospel of John) is another recent phenomenal discovery that bears on the date and text of the fourth gospel[18] and is as spectacular in its own right as the discoveries from Qumran and other places in the Dead Sea area. This early manuscript, for example, omits the account of the woman taken in adultery (John 7:53-8:11) as well as the troublesome incident of the moving of the waters at the pool of Bethesda (John 5:3b-4). There is, moreover, no mark or hint that either scribe or corrector knew of anything additional belonging at these two points in the text. Thus it apparently is growing increasingly evident that these two passages were not a part of the original writing. This manuscript also substantiates the reading God (theos) rather than Son (huios) in John 1:18.

Also of unparalleled significance is the Gospel According to Thomas included in the thirteen papyrus volumes discovered in 1945 in Upper Egypt. These have yielded the text of a new collection of the sayings attributed to Jesus and have been transmitted with a prologue by an editor named "Didimus Jude Thomas." This collection includes a number of completely new parables and shorter sayings of Jesus and promises to be of far reaching importance in the study of the sources of the gospels.[19]

Another example of archaeology's role in balancing New Testament criticism is the abandonment of the often-made claims that Christianity was highly influenced by the mystery religions. In the heyday of the religionsgeschichtliche Schule, this was a popular contention. However, discoveries of the past generation in Palestine, Syria, and Egypt have caused the pendulum to swing back to a more balanced position and have gone far to demonstrate the uniqueness of early Christianity as a historical phenomenon. Instead of Christianity turning out to be only one of many various sects of similar nature which professedly proliferated in the eastern part of the Roman Empire in the first century A.D., as was the contention in former decades, it appears as a unique historical phenomenon, like the religion of Israel which preceded it.

Excavations in Bible lands have uncovered no documents or buildings belonging to such alleged sects. Dura on the Euphrates has

---

[17]Cf. W. F. Albright, The Archaeology of Palestine, 1949, pp. 244-249.
[18]Papyrus Bodmer II, Victor Martin, Bodmer Library, Geneva, 1956, Supplement, 1958.
[19]The Gospel According to Thomas translated from the Coptic by A. Guillamont, Henri-Charles Puech, Gilles Quispel, Walter Till and Abd Al Masih (New York, 1959): see Chapter IV, pp. 92, 93 for a full discussion.

yielded heathen temples, a Christian chapel, a Jewish synagogue, a Mithraeum, as well as fragments of Jewish and Christian writings, but nothing has turned up belonging to any other comparable religious group. Numberless synagogues, churches, and pagan temples have been found in Syria and Palestine, but there is a conspicuous absence of other religious structures. Egypt has yielded early written evidence of Jewish, Christian, and pagan religion. It has preserved works of Manichaean and other Gnostic sects, but these are all considerably later than the rise of Christianity. The total array of archaeological evidence thus presents the Christian faith as unique as a historical phenomenon, like the faith of Israel that preceded it and formed the indispensable introduction to it.

3. *Archaeology Illustrates and Explains the New Testament*

Perhaps the most striking example of this contribution of archaeology again comes from the papyri. The great mass of documents in the vernacular Greek which has come to light in ever-increasing quantity, besides illustrating New Testament language and literature, expands the horizons of biblical history, furnishing vastly augmented knowledge of the life of the common people of the Hellenistic-Roman era in Egypt as well as elsewhere in the Graeco-Roman world. Economic, cultural and social conditions of the New Testament period are now much better understood.

Since 1930 exciting papyri finds from the second century A.D., including a whole library of lost Gnostic literature from the third and fourth centuries discovered since 1945 at Chenoboskion (Nag Hammadi) in Upper Egypt, supply invaluable information concerning Christianity. It is now evident that the Gnostics of the early Church had stranger and more pernicious doctrines than critical scholarship had formerly attributed to them. The new material shows how unsustained such criticism was in attempting to identify Gnostic tenets with the teachings of Jesus and the apostles. Besides it gives point to numerous solemn New Testament warnings against such dangerous doctrinal aberrations.

To cite other examples of archaeological illustration and elucidation, diggings at various places may be mentioned. Excavations at New Testament Jericho since 1950 have facilitated the understanding of the biblical references.[20] The forum of the Roman city with a grand facade facing the Wadi Quelt has been uncovered. At Delphi an inscription has been found which makes possible to date the arrival of the proconsul Gallio at Corinth in the summer of A.D. 51 and to conclude that Paul came to the city at the beginning of A.D. 50. The

[20]Cf. Matthew 20:29; Mark 10:46; Luke 10:30; 18:35; 19:1.

Rome of Paul's time has been revealed by excavation showing temples, theatres, forum, aqueducts and other sites doubtless familiar to the Apostle.

Corinth, Athens, Philippi, Ephesus and other cities evangelized by Paul are now much better known as a result of archaeological excavation. The Temple of Artemis at Ephesus (Acts 19:27) came to light after long search. The theatre is also now known, although the remains probably date later than Paul's time. Palestine of Christ and the whole Graeco-Roman world of Paul and the apostles are put in a new light by archaeological research and lend the evidence they furnish to the illustration and elucidation of the pages of the New Testament.

4. Archaeology Supplements the New Testament

An example is furnished by added light on the important era from the accession of Herod the Great (B.C. 37) to the fall of Jerusalem to the Romans (A.D. 70). This period is now far better known as a result of archaeological research than it was in the nineteenth century. Since then many gaps in our information have happily been filled in. Most significant of the discoveries affecting the environment of Jesus, John the Baptist and the early apostles are the dead Sea Scrolls. These valuable documents, especially the recovered literature of the Essene-type of sect which flourished at Qumran in the wilderness area near the Dead Sea southwest of Jericho since 1947, have revolutionized knowledge of sectarian Judaism of the time and have set forth in clear focus the pre-Gnostic milieu of thought and language in which Jesus and John the Baptist grew up.[21]

Another illustration of archaeology's ability to fill in gaps in historical knowledge is found in the evidence it affords of the thoroughness of the interruption not only of Jewish communal life in Pales-

The Emperor Vespasian. Artist's drawing from a coin of the period (69-79 A.D.)

[21]Cf. F. F. Bruce, Second Thoughts on the Dead Sea Scrolls (Grand Rapids, 1955), pp. 123-137.

tine as a result of the First Revolt of A.D. 66-70 but of the Christian communities as well. The completeness of the catastrophe involved in the destruction of Jerusalem is seen in the fact that not a single synagogue of the early Roman period has apparently survived. Known synagogues date to the end of the second century A.D. or later. Contrary to common contention, Jewish communal life was not resumed at Jerusalem. Not a single one of the numerous Jewish tombs in the region of Jerusalem can be dated to the period after A.D. 70. All inscribed ossuaries hitherto found in the vicinity of Jerusalem belong to the period 30 B.C. to 70 A.D.

Christians suffered even more than the rest of the Jewish population of Palestine, since they were indiscriminately treated as Jews by their pagan neighbors and persecuted by Jews as well. Before the last Roman invasion of Judaea, the Christian remnant fled from Jerusalem to Pella. Understanding the scope of the disaster that befell Jerusalem, which archaeology helps to make clear, has important bearings on New Testament criticism and on New Testament interpretation as well.[22]

5. *Archaeology Authenticates the New Testament*

Since the background of the New Testament is recorded in the contemporary history of the Graeco-Roman world, of which there exists a fair knowledge, classical historians and critics have always been tempted to measure swords with the New Testament in the matter of its historical, geographical, and literary authenticity. While difficulties still persist, archaeology has in numerous cases vindicated the New Testament, particularly Luke.[23] The Acts of the Apostles is now generally agreed in scholarly circles to be the work of Luke, to belong to the first century, and to involve the labors of a careful historian who was substantially accurate in his use of sources. Attempts to impugn Luke's reliability have constantly been made, but most of these have been rendered futile by light from the monuments of antiquity and the archaeologist's spade.[24]

The role which archaeology is performing in New Testament research (as well as that of the Old Testament) in expediting scientific study, balancing critical theory, illustrating, elucidating, supplementing and authenticating historical and cultural backgrounds, constitutes the one bright spot in the future of criticism of the Sacred

[22]Cf. W. F. Albright, *Archaeology of Palestine* (1949), p. 242.
[23]Cf. A. T. Robertson, *Luke the Historian in the Light of Research* (1920), pp. 1-241.
[24]Cf. the works of Sir William Ramsay, *St. Paul the Traveller and the Roman Citizen* (1897); *The Cities of St. Paul* (1907, reprint 1949), *The Bearing of Recent Discovery on the Trustworthiness of the New Testament* (4th ed. 1920; reprint 1953).

Oracles. The unanswerable evidence of the archaeologist's spade is bound not only to make Scripture better understood on the human plane, but also better respected on the same plane by scholars who will not recognize the supernatural in history and whose only creed is pure science.

LITERATURE ON THE ROLE OF ARCHAEOLOGY
IN THE STUDY OF THE NEW TESTAMENT

Cadbury, H. J., "The Present State of New Testament Studies" in *The Haverford Symposium in Archaeology and the Bible*, 1938, pp. 78-110.
————, "Current Issues in New Testament Studies" in *Harvard Divinity School Bulletin* (1954) 49-64.
Howard, W. F., "A Survey of New Testament Studies During Half a Century — 1901-1950" in *London Quarterly and Holborn Review* CLXXVII (1952), pp. 6-16.
Stauffer, Ethelbert, "Der Stand der Neutestamentlichen Forschung" in *Theologie und Liturgie*, 1952, pp. 35-105.
Sukenik, E. L., *The Earliest Records of Christianity*, 1947.
Kenyon, Sir Frederic, *Our Bible and the Ancient Manuscripts*, 1940.
Dalman, Gustav, *Sacred Sites and Ways*, 1935.
Styger, Paul, *Die Roemischen Katakomben*, 1933.
Crowfoot, J. W., *Early Churches in Palestine*, 1941.
Metzger, Bruce, *Annotated Bibliography of the Textual Criticism of the New Testament*, 1955.
Boulton, W. H., *Archaeology Explained* (London, 1952).

Chapter 2

From Alexander the Great to Herod the Great — The Foundations of New Testament Political and Cultural History

Shortly before 400 B.C. the Old Testament period ended. The four centuries intervening until the rise of the New Testament era are sometimes called the "Four Hundred Silent Years," since according to conservative criticism, divine inspiration was in abeyance and no canonical Scripture was produced. Liberal critics, on the other hand, commonly place Ezra, Nehemiah, and Chronicles about 250 B.C., many of the Psalms, Proverbs, and the book of Daniel in the Maccabean age, and Esther even later—about 125 B.C. Zechariah 9-14 is placed around 200 B.C., as well as Ecclesiastes, Canticles, and Jonah. The collection of Isaiah and the addition of "Second Isaiah" are put between 300-200 B.C. Spacious arguments are advanced for the late dating of these books, but unanswerable proof is lacking for placing any of them later than 400 B.C.[1]

Although this period under conservative criticism, constituted an extended hiatus as far as revelation and inspiration in the canonical sense are concerned, it nevertheless witnessed the rise of an important body of extra-canonical literature of vast importance to the background of the New Testament, called the Apocrypha and Pseudepigrapha. This body of literature furnishes an indispensable introduction to the understanding of the times and the advent of the New Testament era. The political, social, religious, and moral conditions that constitute the cultural background of New Testament history had their origin and development during these intertestamental centuries.

[1]For the late-date arguments see Bernhard W. Anderson, *Understanding the Old Testament* (Englewood Cliffs, N. J., 1957); Henry Pfeiffer, *Old Testament Introduction* (New York, 1941), pp. 812, 830, 765, 742. Frank Knight Sanders, *History of the Hebrews* (New York, 1928), pp. 310-317; J. Bewer, *The Literature of the Old Testament* (New York, 1933); Otto Eissfeldt, *Enleitung in das Alte Testament* (Tuebingen, 1934); Aage Bentzen, *Introduction to the Old Testament* (2 vols., 1949). For presentation of the early dating arguments see J. F. Steinmueller, *A Companion to Scripture Studies* (2 vols., 1942); E. J. Young, *An Introduction to the Old Testament* (1949 rev. ed., 1958); Merrill F. Unger, *Introductory Guide to the Old Testament* (2nd ed., 1956).

With the fall of the Chaldean Empire in 539 B.C., imperial sway passed out of the hands of the Semites. The Persian, Greek, and Roman empires of the interbiblical period were ruled by Indo-Europeans or Aryans. The vast Persian imperial power which dominated the ancient biblical world from 539 B.C. to 331 B.C. witnessed the consummation of the Old Testament period as well as the commencement and considerable development of the interbiblical period. Cyrus the Great conquered Babylon, which was being ruled by Nabonidus and the crown prince Belshazzar, in 539. Cambyses his son (530-522) conquered Egypt. Darius I (522-486) advanced against Greece, but was defeated at Marathon in 490. Xerxes I or Ahasuerus (486-465) likewise attempted to conquer the Greek states, but was effectually repulsed at Thermopylae and Salamis in 480.

Bronze coin minted in Palestine in the Persian period, inscribed "Judaea"

Persian gold daric (enlarged). King holds bow and spear as he kneels

With the reign of Artaxerxes I (465-424) the interbiblical period began and developed under Xerxes I (424-423), Darius II (423-404), Artaxerxes II (404-358), Artaxerxes III (358-338), Arses (338-336) and Darius III (336-331).

During this long period of Persian dominance, Judaea was a part of the empire, which was divided into provinces called satrapies, each administered by a Persian governor called a satrap. Palestine fell within the boundaries of the Fifth Persian satrapy, with capital located at Damascus or Samaria.[2]

I. ALEXANDER'S REMARKABLE CAREER OF CONQUEST

With the rise of Philip I of Macedon (359-336), the power of Greece began to be consolidated. The battle of Chaeronea (338) brought to an end the autonomy of the individual Greek city-states.

[2]J. McKee Adams, *Biblical Backgrounds* (Nashville, 1934), p. 287.

The death of Philip in 336 set the stage for the phenomenal rise to power of his son Alexander. Becoming king of Macedonia, Alexander commandeered the respect of all Greece by pitilessly destroying the Greek city of Thebes that dared to revolt against his authority.[3] Promptly the various city-states formed a league, appointed him as its leader and general, and dispatched soldiers to augment his army. Sagaciously Alexander assumed the role of champion against Asia and punisher of Persia for invading Greece in the days of Xerxes, a century and a half earlier.

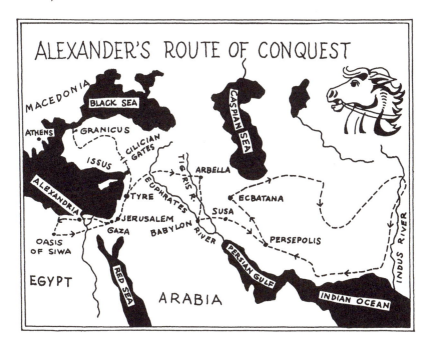

1. *Alexander's Lightning-like Triumphs*

In 334 B.C. Alexander invaded the East with a formidable army, accompanied by a distinguished retinue of philosophers, writers, and scientists. At the river Granicus, which flows into the Hellespont, he clashed with the Persian forces of the western satraps. Both militarily and psychologically a decisive victory was won. The Persian army was not only scattered, but the superiority of the Greek cavalry was demonstrated.

[3]James H. Breasted, *The Conquest of Civilization* (New York, 1926), p. 431. For a comprehensive study of Alexander's career, see C. A. Robinson, *Alexander the Great* (New York, 1947); W. W. Tarn, *Alexander the Great,* 2 vols. (Cambridge University Press, 1948).

The mighty Persian Empire began to split apart. City after city in Western Asia began to yield to Alexander without opposition.[4] Pushing on through the Cilician Gates, Alexander advanced on the Plains of Issus at the northeast corner of the Mediterranean. There in 333 B.C. he defeated the main Persian army under the personal command of Darius III (336-331), who barely escaped with his life.

In 1831 in the ruins of ancient Pompeii, a mosaic in colored glass was recovered depicting Alexander's spear piercing a nobleman who was protecting Darius as the routed Persians were desperately endeavoring to take Darius from the field of battle at Issus.[5] Little wonder this famous and decisive battle should be thus commemorated, for it changed the course of world history and opened Syria-Palestine, Egypt, and the East as far as India to Greek conquest and the influence of Greek culture.

2. Alexander in Phoenicia

From Issus Alexander marched south into Syria, Phoenicia, Palestine, and Egypt. Cities like Aradus, Byblus, and Sidon surrendered without resistance. Tyre, however, stoutly opposed on the

One of Alexander's "hele-poleis" (siege towers) — 20 stories high

---

[4] R. W. Rogers, *A History of Ancient Persia* (New York, 1929), pp. 272, 273.
[5] See Breasted, *op. cit.*, p. 432, figure 169.

grounds of neutrality in the Graeco-Persian conflict when Alexander demanded permission to enter the city and offer worship at the temple of the god Melkart. At this rebuff Alexander began the siege of the city that was to require an immense amount of work in building a mole out into the water to storm the walls of the island town, in addition to raising a navy of some 220 war ships from the kings of Aradus and Byblus and from the island of Cyprus. The mole or land bridge was constructed of cedar logs from Lebanon as piles and with the debris of the old land city of Tyre which previously had been destroyed by the army of Nebuchadnezzar (605-562 B.C.) in a thirteen-year siege (585-573). After seven months, the mole was brought up to the island, the walls were broken through and the city fell, strikingly fulfilling Ezekiel's prophecy that the stones, timber, and dust of Tyre would be laid "in the midst of the water" (Ezekiel 26:12).

3. Alexander in Palestine

The taking of Tyre was a feat, like his successes at Granicus and Issus, which immeasurably increased Alexander's prestige. The celebrated conqueror continued down the coast of Phoenicia and Palestine receiving the homage of city after city he encountered until he came to the redoubtable fortress city of Gaza in southern Palestine. Lying somewhat inland from the ancient coastal town whose harbor had silted up, the city of Alexander's day, constructed on a foundation more than sixty feet high with massive walls of defense, was beyond the reach of Greek siege machines and practically impregnable. Not to be frustrated, Alexander constructed a huge mound twelve hundred feet wide at the base and 200 feet high. From the man-made elevation his siege engines were able to break down the wall and take the city.

Silver tetradrachma coin inscribed with the name of Alexander the Great as king, and showing Zeus Aetophoros seated

Silver shekel of year 1 of the First Revolt (A.D. 66-67), showing three pomegranates and inscription "Jerusalem Holy"

The two-month siege yielded rich rewards in further increase in prestige, vast quantities of food and supplies, consolidation of his control of Palestine, and an open road of access to Egypt.

Josephus, the Jewish historian of the first century A.D., recounts a story, otherwise unsubstantiated except by the Jewish Talmud, to the effect that after the fall of Gaza, Alexander visited Jerusalem, received the high priest Jaddua in a friendly manner, read the prophecies of Daniel concerning himself, and offered sacrifice to God in the temple at Jerusalem.[6] While Josephus apparently appends melodramatic details, there is no ground for denying the historicity of Josephus' main statement. As Israel Abrams has pointed out, the visionary aspects of Alexander's alleged Jerusalem visit both in Josephus and the Talmud, although these sources disagree in detail, are eminently true to Alexander's character as a visionary.[7] Plutarch as well as Arrian give abundant evidence of the visionary nature of Alexander's temperament,[8] which would make his Jerusalem visit conform to type.

The old-line argument against the authenticity of Josephus' account that the Greek historians leave no loophole for a digression to Jerusalem has been shown to be untenable. The critical argument assumes that as soon as Gaza fell, Alexander proceeded by a seven-day forced march to Pelusium, leaving no room for an excursion into the Judaean hill country. A correct interpretation of Arrian, however, reveals that when Alexander removed his army from Gaza to Egypt, the march was rapid. But he did not leave Gaza immediately upon its fall. On the contrary, there was much to be done before he quitted the place. As Abrams says, " . . . there is nothing in Arrian or Curtius to imply that time failed for such an experience as Josephus decribes."[9]

4. Alexander in Egypt

With Syria, Phoenicia, and Palestine well under his control, Alexander pushed on into Egypt, arriving in Pelusium in the northeastern Delta. From there he went to Memphis in the southern Delta to worship at the shrine of the Apis-bull cult and win the goodwill of the Egyptians. In his advance to the northwestern part of the Delta, he selected a site for the city of Alexandria to be founded to perpetuate his fame. Little could he know the wisdom of his choice or visualize the vast growth and importance of this city and its prominent role in the development of both Judaism and Christianity.

[6]*Antiquities of the Jews,* translated by W. Whiston, Book XI, chapter VIII, 4, p. 282.
[7]Israel Abrams, *The Campaigns in Palestine from Alexander the Great, The Schweich Lectures,* 1922 (London, The British Academy, 1927), pp. 10-12.
[8]Abrams, *Ibidem.*
[9]*Ibidem.*

While army engineers were proceeding with plans for the new metropolis, Alexander visited the famous temple of the ancient and widely-venerated Egyptian moon god, Amon, located deep in the heart of the desert, now known as the Oasis of Siwa. As he came out of the desert sanctuary, he was styled by the high priest of the cult as the son of Zeus-Amon.[10] The whole episode was a part of Alexander's plan to attach the idea of deity to his person to emphasize his phenomenal career of conquest.

5. Alexander at Gaugamela

Alexander left Egypt in the spring of 331 B.C., retracing his course up the Palestinian and Phoenician coast to Tyre. From there he advanced up the Orontes Valley to Antioch and then north and eastward across the Euphrates and Tigris to clash with Darius on the plain of Gaugamela, 75 miles from Arbela on the great Persian royal road which connected Sardis in Asia Minor with Susa, one of the capitals of the Empire. As at Issus, Alexander's forces overwhelmed the obsolete Persian army. Once again Darius was put to ignominious flight, only to be stabbed to death a short while later by a treacherous attendant.

6. Alexander in India and His Death

The decisive battle at Gaugamela made Alexander complete master of Persia. Susa, Ecbatana, and Persepolis were at his mercy. At Persepolis he set fire to the palace of the Persian kings with his own hand. His ardor for conquest led him farther eastward to cross the Indus to the frontiers of India. Not until he descended the Indus and touched the waters of the Indian Ocean did he resume the severe journey homeward, arriving in Babylon in 323 B.C.

But the gruelling marches and immoderate drinking of the great conqueror extorted their toll. After a brief illness, Alexander died an untimely death at the age of thirty-three at Babylon in 323 B.C., at the zenith of his career.

II. The Results of Alexander's Conquests in the Hellenization of the Ancient World

The military successes of Alexander had remarkable and far-reaching effects on the political and cultural complexion of the ancient world that set the stage for the formation of the Graeco-Roman society

---

[10]Breasted, op. cit., p. 440. For a study of Alexander's conquests, see F. M. Abel, "Alexandre le Grand en Syrie et en Palestine" in Revue biblique 43 (1934), pp. 528-545; 44 (1935), pp. 42-61; T. Birt, Alexander der Grosse und das Weltgriechentum (1928); E. Schürer, Geschichte des jüdischen Volkes im Zeitalter Jesu Christi I, 4 (1901), pp. 31-111; 165-210; III, 4 (1909), 192-202; B. Niese, Geschicte der griechicshen und makedonischen Staaten (1893-1903).

of the first century A.D. and prepared the way for the eventual appearance of the New Testament revelation.

1. *Division of Alexander's Empire and Resulting Political Picture*

Alexander's sudden death precipitated a struggle for power among his generals. Seleucus, whose successors were known as the Seleucids with their center at Antioch, gained control of Mesopotamia and Syria, a sizeable slice of the territory that had comprised the Persian Empire. Ptolemy, whose line was known as the Ptolemies with its headquarters in Alexandria, came into possession of Egypt. These two Hellenistic empires which emerged from Alexander's empire took definite shape from the first and were most vitally and intimately to affect Jewish interbiblical history and the background of the New Testament era.

In the unsettled conditions that resulted upon Alexander's death, a third Hellenistic empire emerged by 277 B.C. This was Macedonia under Antigonus Gonatus (277-239 B.C.). This imperial line continued until Perseus (179-168 B.C.), when Macedonia came under Roman influence and was made a Roman province in 146 B.C. The Greek cities resisted Macedonian domination and made alliance with Rome until Rome gradually took over Greece and it became a province (27 B.C.).

Several smaller kingdoms emerged from Alexander's realm. Pergamum in Asia Minor continued under the Attalid dynasty until Attalus III (139-133), who willed his kingdom to Rome. Bithynia on the Black Sea in Asia Minor was founded by Ziboetes (327-c. 279 B.C.) and Nicomedes I (c. 279-c. 250 B.C.) and continued until Nicomedes III (94-74 B.C.), who, like Attalus III of Pergamum, willed his rule to Rome.

Other kingdoms of Asia Minor were Pontus on the Black Sea and Galatia on the Halys River, which was settled by Gauls about 278 B.C. and passed on to Rome in 25 B.C. at the decease of Amyntas. Pontus was ruled by the Mithridatids, commencing with Mithridates I (336-301 B.C.) and dominated by Rome by the middle of the first century B.C.

Another important political entity that ultimately emerged from Alexander's empire was Parthia. Traditionally, under Arsaces the rule of the Seleucids was cast off. From about 247 B.C. the Parthian era began with an expanding empire that gradually extended from the Euphrates River to the frontiers of India. By 53 B.C. the Parthians threatened to engulf Syria, Palestine, and Asia Minor after they defeated the Roman Crassus. In 40 B.C. they actually invaded Jerusalem, but in 38-39 B.C. Rome's might effectually repelled them, so that they were no longer a menace, although their kingdom continued with declining power until A.D. 224.

2. Alexander and the Dissemination of Hellenic Culture

It was not accidental that the golden age of Greek learning and philosophy immediately preceded the unification of the Greek states under Philip of Macedon and the world conquests of Alexander. Greek art and literature reached their peak of efflorescence before being spread far and wide to form the cultural background of the interbiblical period and the New Testament world. Pericles flourished (460-429 B.C.), Herodotus, "the father of history," traveled and wrote (c. 484-425 B.C.). The great philosophers and logicians, Socrates (c. 470-399), Plato (c. 428-348 B.C.) and Aristotle (384-322 B.C.) produced their great masterpieces that were to affect the intellectual and philosophical climate of the Graeco-Roman age and all subsequent generations as well.

In addition, the Greek language was to undergo a process of popularization and dissemination that was to prepare it to be a suitable vehicle for the writing of the New Testament as a universal revelation of truth intended for the whole world.[11] Alexander's army brought together recruits from the various city-states. Differences in dialect and orthography tended to vanish as soldiers from various parts of Greece and Macedonia, who had hitherto fought only in the isolated regiments of their own home states, now mingled freely and fought side by side in a common army. The resulting popularized language was carried rapidly into distant conquered lands to form eventually a *lingua franca* spoken throughout the Mediterranean world. This *lingua franca* was vitally to affect the Jews of the Diaspora and eventuate in the translation of the Old Testament Scriptures into the common Greek of the day. This Greek translation in turn was to become an important factor in the formation of the New Testament, as well as with it, the Bible of early Christianity.

Since Alexander's dream was to establish a world kingdom in which Greek and Oriental culture were to be wedded, Macedonian and Greek colonists followed in the footsteps of the victorious army.

Thus philosophically and artistically Greek thought and customs spread by Alexander were to be instrumental in fashioning the religous and intellectual thought of Judaism in the interbiblical period as well as in exerting a strong influence on Christian life and activity. The seeds of Hellenic culture scattered far and wide by Alexander's armies were to bear abundant harvest by the time of Jesus, Paul, and the other apostles. The process was one of many in preparing for "the

[11]See Chapter 18.

fulness of the time" when God sent forth His Son (Galatians 5:4). Alexander, the pagan, in a sense had as definite and far-reaching a purpose in preparing the way for Christianity as Paul, the Christian, did in preaching and propagating it.

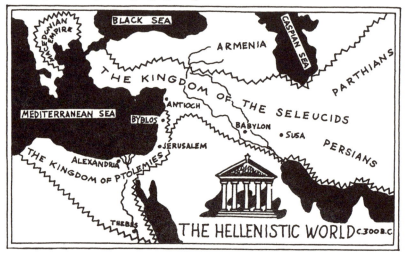

Everywhere the Apostle to the Gentiles went in the Graeco-Roman world, he found that Hellenic culture had gone before him to prepare the way for the reception of the Gospel of grace he proclaimed. He also discovered that the Judaism of the Diaspora and the far-flung synagogue in the Hellenic cities of Syria, Asia Minor, and Europe formed the bridge between the spiritual truths of Christianity and the heart of a godless paganism he was seeking to evangelize. In short, the message which had had its foundations in the revealed Hebrew Scriptures of an Oriental people, who were intensively exclusive and uncosmopolitan, was now broadened and liberated for an entire world outreach and ministry. And the world-transforming events which were to set the stage for this momentous event in the history of civilization required more than three and a half centuries from the time of Alexander the Great to Paul.

III. Hellenism and the Jews Under the Ptolemies

The New Testament in its formative background contains two fundamental elements—the Hebraic and the Greek—which in the course of pre-Christian centuries combined in its production as a document of universal human appeal. The Hebraic element is, of course, much the older of the two. It goes back to the earliest Old Testament times (since the New Testament is erected upon the foundation of the Old Testament), has its source and significance in the Old Testament, and is an unfolding of its meaning and a fulfilment of its prophecy. Hence the New Testament quotes from the Old Testament, employs Old Testament figures and symbols, uses Old Testament typology, claims fulfilment of Old Testament prophecy, and attests its unity with the Old Testament as the consummating revelation of the divine plan of redemption incipiently unfolded there.

But the New Testament, although written by Jews (in the main if not indeed in its entirety) is not Jewish, nor written in Hebrew, nor intended for Jews (as the Old Testament was) but is universal and slanted for all, imparting, since its appearance, a universality to the Old Testament which it never had until it became the indispensable introduction to the New Testament and its inseparable counterpart.

The element that was to bridge the gap between the isolationism of Judaism in the Old Testament to the universality of Christianity in the New was the Greek. The Greek language and Greek culture in the inter-biblical period were to interact with Hebrew theology and thought in four centuries of preparation not only for the coming Redeemer but for the written revelation that was to follow upon the consummation of His redemptive career. Only as it is perceived how Hellenism (the adoption of Greek language and customs) came in contact with and sometimes in collision with Judaism (for there was much in the former that was pagan and polluting as well as admirable and cultural) in the period between the Old Testament and the New can the background of the New Testament be understood and the nature of its message and the universality of its appeal be comprehended.

Ptolemy I, reproduced from a silver tetradrachma of the period (323-283 B.C.)

Silver tetradrachma coin of Ptolemy I (323-283 B.C.) showing eagle on thunderbolt

1. Ptolemy I Soter (323-283 B.C.)

Fortunately, upon Alexander's death Egypt and Palestine came under the rule of one of the most prudent and enlightened of Alexander's successors, Ptolemy I Soter. This able general founded a dynasty of Graeco-Egyptian kings which ruled Palestine until 198 B.C., and Egypt until its subjugation by Rome in 31 B.C. Though "Ptolemy" was the common, it was not the exclusive name of the kings of this line. They are better distinguished, therefore, by the surname Lagidae, from Ptolemaeus Lagus, Ptolemy's Greek name.

Ptolemy I adopted a liberal policy toward the Jewish people. He brought many thousands of them from Palestine to Alexandria, conferring full political and religious privileges upon them, and showed them other favors. He raised Alexandria to the highest rank of commercial prosperity and cultural progress. He himself had a reputation in letters and wrote an account of the campaigns of Alexander that was used as an authoritative source by Arrian, the celebrated Greek historian of the second century A.D.[12] Ptolemy was, in addition, a distinguished patron of literature, art, and science, and founded the famous library and museum of Alexandria. The special place this cosmopolitan metropolis took in philosophy, literature, and politics in subsequent times was in large measure due to the colony of Jews Ptolemy I founded in his capital city.

2. Ptolemy II Philadelphus (285-247 B.C.) and the Septuagint

Ptolemy II, called Philadelphus, continued the beneficent attitude of his father toward the Jews. Under his aggressive political and commercial policies, they prospered economically and socially. As a result of his munificent patronage of the arts and sciences, they enjoyed a cultural efflorescence. He spared no pains to fill the library of Alexandria with all the treasures of ancient literature. Under his auspices, tradition contends, the Old Testament Scriptures were translated into Greek as the wider cultural language of the time.

According to the letter of Aristeas,[13] some of the details of which are not critically above suspicion, Ptolemy's librarian suggested to his royal patron the importance of having a Greek rendering of the law of the Hebrews made for the library. The idea, it is said, pleased the king, who dispatched an embassage with rich gifts to the high priest at Jerusalem imploring him to send a copy of the Torah with scholars to translate it into the Greek tongue. The result was the *Septuaginta*,

---

[12]His *Anabasis* of Alexander the Great is still extant and has appeared in various editions.
[13]See H. T. Andrews in *Pseudepigrapha* (R. H. Charles, ed., Oxford, 1913), pp. 83-122. R. H. Pfeiffer, *History of New Testament Times* (New York, 1949), p. 224f.

or rendering of the "Seventy" Jewish scholars from the twelve tribes, now known as the Septuagint.

From this tradition it may safely be affirmed that the Law was first rendered about 260 B.C. or somewhat earlier, in the reign of Ptolemy II, to meet the liturgical needs of the Greek-speaking Jews at Alexandria and of the Diaspora in general, with the other Old Testament books following in the succeeding century. Moreover, the Septuagint was a vital influence in Alexandrian Judaism and philosophy for several centuries. Most significant of all, it released the great revealed truths of creation, redemption, sin, and salvation from the narrow isolationism of the Hebrew language and people and made them available to the world through the providentially prepared vehicle of the Greek *lingua franca* of the times. In performing this task, it bridged the chasm between Hebrew and the Greek-speaking peoples of the ancient world, spanning the gap between Oriental and Occidental cultures.[14]

In this significant way the Septuagint constituted a preparation for the advent of Christianity by releasing the Hebrew Old Testament in the same international tongue in which the New Testament was destined to appear. The far-reaching result of this in the history of redemption was that the completed divine revelation became available to all men in the *one* cosmopolitan tongue of the period. The Greek New Testament in course of time was to share with the Greek Old Testament the momentous ministry of presenting revealed truth to the peoples of that age. Before the New Testament appeared, the Greek Old Testament was the Bible of early Christianity. After the New Testament was written, it was added to the Septuagint to constitute the completed Scriptures of Christianity.

3. *Hellenism and the Jews from Ptolemy III Euergetes (247-222 B.C.)*
to the Wane of Egyptian Power Over Palestine

The Ptolemies of Egypt were able to control Palestine for upwards of a century. During this period the Jews were happy and prosperous. Judaism both in its native Palestine as well as in Alexandria, Egypt, its chief center outside Palestine, was able to develop its distinctive aspects and crystallize its tenets against the background of Hellenistic thought. At the same time in Palestine it had opportunity to fortify itself against what was to turn out to be a violent collision with Hellenizing forces.

In Alexandria it was impossible that Judaism could remain unaffected, at least in degree, by Hellenic thought and institutions. But the natural conflict between Judaism and Hellenism did not become

[14]Merrill F. Unger, *Introductory Guide to the Old Testament* (Grand Rapids, 2nd ed., 1956), p. 156.

acute. The Jews there, enjoying political autonomy, kept their religious and commercial life distinct. However, on Palestinian soil the situation was different. The temple at Jerusalem and the whole system of Jewish worship were so inextricably bound up with every phase of Jewish daily life and so inexorably regulated by rigid ecclesiastical traditionalism that adamant resistance to the cultural and social pressures of Hellenistic thought and customs was produced. It was inevitable that trouble would arise if ever the attempt was made, as was done under Seleucid rulers, who followed the Ptolemies, to use force to impose Hellenism upon the Jews of Palestine.[15]

4. Archaeology and the Ptolemaic Control of Palestine

Archaeology has furnished abundant evidence from coins and pottery that many of the excavated sites were occupied during the era the Ptolemies of Egypt ruled Palestine. But there is a notable poverty of architectural remains in Palestine and Syria from the whole Hellenistic period, as compared to a wealth of such monuments in Asia Minor and Egypt.

The most important monuments of this period are the remarkable painted tombs of Marisa, north of Beth Gubrin (Eleutheropolis) on the road to Gaza, dated from the second half of the third century B.C. Discovered about 1902, these caves had been excavated for the heads of a Sidonian colony established there and beautifully painted with accompanying inscriptions and graffiti in Greek. They are thus of considerable historical value, giving much information on the life and religion of the Edomite settlement in southern Judah. Later, in the Maccabaean Age, John Hyrcanus conquered and forcibly converted the Idumaeans to Judaism. Still later, Antipater, the father of Herod the Great, was governor of Idumaea. The paintings at Marisa are a welcome archaeological sidelight of this period when the Jews at Jerusalem in Palestine and Alexandria in Egypt enjoyed the beneficent rule of their Hellenistic Egyptian overlords.

IV. HELLENISM AND THE JEWS UNDER THE SELEUCIDS

The Seleucids of Syria had constantly desired Palestine. They had fought with Ptolemy Philadelphus and Ptolemy Euergetes, but unsuccessfully. Ptolemy IV Philopator (222-205 B.C.) had held Antiochus III in check, but his successor, Ptolemy V Epiphanes (205-182 B.C.), was unable to do so. Antiochus III (223-187 B.C.), now a renowned conqueror, in 198 B.C. succeeded in expelling the Egyptians and annexing Palestine to the Seleucid empire. By this turn of events the

---

[15]For a discussion of the broad aspects of this problem, see W. O. S. Oesterley, *The Jews and Judaism During the Greek Period — The Background of Christianity* (London, 1941).

Jews became losers and were soon to find themselves struggling for their religious institutions and the faith of their fathers in the violent attempt of their Seleucid overlords to enforce submission to pagan customs and the Hellenistic way of life.

1. Antiochus IV Epiphanes (175-164 B.C.) and Enforced Hellenization of the Jews

Inheriting the fierce desire of his grandfather, Antiochus III, to retaliate against the Romans for curbing his sphere of conquest, Antiochus Epiphanes ("The Illustrious") planned to organize a pan-Hellenic league uniting all Greek-speaking peoples of Asia and Africa

Antiochus III the Great (223-187 B.C.) drawn from a silver tetradrachma coin

Enlarged drawing of a coin of Antiochus III (223-187 B.C.). Apollo appears seated on omphalos

against Rome. Conceiving an intense dislike for the Jews of Judaea, he determined to destroy their ancestral religious faith and to completely Hellenize them (169-167 B.C.). His fearful atrocities drew out their dauntless courage and enabled them to write in blood and death one of the most glorious chapters of their history.

Antiochus sacked Jerusalem, murdered thousands of the inhabitants, settled many Greeks and renegade Jews in the city, profaned the sanctuary, and offered sacrifices to Olympian Zeus on the altar of burnt offering. This gross act of sacrilege proved to the Jews that Antiochus was bent on destroying Judaism and substituting pagan culture in its place.

2. The Rise of the Maccabees

The standard of revolt against Antiochus IV Epiphanes was raised by Mattathias, an aged priest, and his five heroic sons who were residing at Modin, a village some twenty miles northwest of Jerusalem at the extreme corner of Judea. They were of the family of Hasmon. When offered handsome rewards if he and his sons would comply with the commands of Antiochus, Mattathias not only refused but with a show of valor that precipitated a courageous war for independence, struck dead a neighbor who stepped forward to make a pagan sacrifice, as well as the commissioner of Antiochus.

Judas Maccabaeus, Mattathias' eldest son, organized a guerilla army of patriots and took to the mountains to fight the well-trained Syrian armies. He was often outnumbered six to one, but was aided by Hellenized Jewish spies. In a series of victories (167-165 B.C.) he routed the Syrian armies, cleansed and rededicated the temple, reestablishing the regular worship. This was marked by

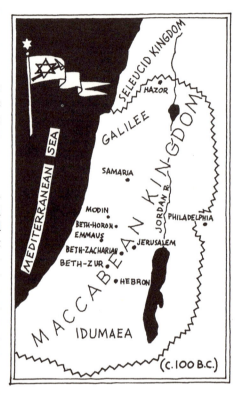

great rejoicing and the introduction of an annual festival known as the Feast of Lights or Dedication, still observed by the Jews.

3. *Archaeology and the Seleucids*

One of the most interesting monuments from this era is the mausoleum of the Tobiad family, discovered at Áraq el-Emir, not far from present-day Amman in central Transjordan. This ruling dynasty was founded by Tobiah, the Ammonite governor who allied himself with Sanballat, the governor of Samaria, in opposing Nehemiah's work in restoring the walls of Jerusalem (Nehemiah 2:10; 4:3, 7; 6:1-19). The mausoleum at Áraq el-Emir is inscribed in Aramaic of the third century B.C., bearing the name Tobiah, evidently the descendant of Nehemiah's foe and who, like his ancestor two centuries earlier, was governor of Amman. Not far from the tomb is an edifice whose architectural details done in vigorous Hellenistic style place it in the time of Hyrcanus, the last of the Tobiads, who was active on the eve of the Maccabaean age. The Tobiad family lost its prestige when the Seleucids overran Palestine and Antiochus Epiphanes launched his mad plan of forcible Hellenization of the inhabitants.[16]

The excavations of J. W. Crowfoot at Samaria in 1931-1933, continuing the earlier work of the Harvard expedition of 1908-1910, have brought to light Hellenistic tower fortifications, the oldest of which were built along the line of the casemated wall of Israelite times. These towers have been assigned an early Hellenistic date, and Albright assigns them to the period immediately following Alexander the Great's death, between 323-321 B.C., when Perdiccas, one of Alexander's generals, rebuilt Samaria, according to Eusebius. About a century and a half later, apparently during the Seleucid-Maccabaean Wars, a massive fortress with walls four meters thick was constructed at Samaria. [17] Numerous coins of Seleucid rulers have been recovered in various cities of Palestine-Syria, especially at Bethzur in southern Judaea on the borders of Idumaea. Some coins bear the names of Antiochus Epiphanes (175-164 B.C.) and his son Antiochus Eupator (164-162 B.C.).

V. Hellenism and the Jews Under the Hasmonaeans

Judas' great victories over the Syrian armies (167-165 B.C.), however, did not end the struggle with Hellenic paganism. The citadel at Jerusalem was still in Syrian hands, and Antiochus V Eupator sent a huge army to Jerusalem, defeated Judas and almost ended the Maccabean struggle, had not complications at the Syrian capital of Antioch made withdrawal necessary. But before retiring Antiochus V concluded a treaty with Judas allowing full religious liberty to the Jews, and appointed a pro-Hellenic high priest named Alcimus to office. This man, however, Judas refused to allow to function.

Meanwhile, Alcimus fled to Antioch to complain to the new king, Demetrius, who dispatched an army which was twice defeated and replaced by another. Finally Judas, whose ranks had thinned to 800 men, had to face more than 20,000 soldiers under Bacchides. In the fierce struggle the great Jewish patriot fell at Eleasa.

1. *Jonathan and Further Strides Toward Jewish Independence* *(161-143 B.C.)*

Judas' death left Alcimus and the Hellenizers in power, supported by Bacchides. Alcimus went so far as to order the barrier which separated the outer and inner courts of the temple to be removed so that there would be no difference between Jews and Gentiles. Such extreme concessions to Greek thought and customs caused the pendulum to swing the other way when Alcimus suddenly died in 160 B.C.

[16]See W. F. Albright, *The Archaeology of Palestine* (Pelican Books, 1949), p. 149f.
[17]Albright, *op. cit.*, p. 150.

Jonathan Maccabaeus, an adroit diplomat, was chosen as leader and was quick to take advantage of the current contest for the Syrian throne in 152 B.C. when Alexander Balas, a pretender, revolted against Demetrius I. By 150 B.C. Alexander Balas had secured full power and reigned from 150-145 B.C. Already under Demetrius, Jonathan had been permitted vassal rule over the Judaeans, kept in check, however, by Syrian garrisons in the citadel at Jerusalem and by fortresses built by Bacchides at Jericho, Emmaus, Bethhoron, Bethel, Bethzur and other strategic places. But under Balas, Jonathan's power soared, especially when he gained control of much of Philistia by fighting on Balas' side against a new throne-claimant, Demetrius II, who defeated Balas and ruled 145-140 B.C.

This favorable shift on the throne of Syria enabled Jonathan to lay siege to the citadel of Jerusalem. Although unable to take it, he built a great wall to seal it off, which led to its surrender under his successor, Simon. Simon fell a victim to treachery, but had made great strides toward regaining Jewish independence.

2. *Simon (143-135 B.C.) and the Inauguration of the Period of Jewish Independence (143-63 B.C.)*

Demetrius II (145-139 B.C.) desperately needed the loyalty of Simon in the uncertain struggle for power at Antioch, and accordingly recognized him as high priest, remitted payment of tribute and granted the Jews practically full independence (143 B.C.). Simon ruled well, expelled the Syrian garrison from Jerusalem, fortified the temple area, and conquered Gezer and Joppa. Antiochus Sidetes challenged these acts, but Simon's son, John Hyrcanus, thoroughly defeated the army of Antiochus, so that Simon was left at peace, recognized as civil, military, and religious head of Judaea, although he never styled himself king.

3. *John Hyrcanus (134-104 B.C.) and the Conflicting Parties in Judaism: The Pharisees, Sadducees, and Essenes*

John Hyrcanus succeeded to the Hasmonaean dynasty after his father Simon was assassinated. The reigning Syrian king, Antiochus VII (139-129 B.C.), seized the occasion as an opportunity to invade Judaea, conquer Jerusalem, and impose a heavy war tribute, but Antiochus' death five years later marked the virtual end of Seleucid power over Palestine, and John Hyrcanus and his successors were free to enlarge and strengthen their kingdom.

John Hyrcanus embarked on a career of conquest in Transjordan and then in Samaria where he destroyed the Temple on Mt. Gerizim, which for two centuries was a rival to the temple at Jerusalem, and thus intensified the hatred between Jew and Samaritan (cf. John

4:9, 20). Next he conquered the Edomites on his southern border and subjected them to forced conversion to Judaism or exile. Eventually he ruled over a small empire from Lower Galilee to the southern desert and from the Mediterranean to the borders of Nabataea.

Coin of John Hyrcanus I (134-104 B.C.) inscribed: "Johanan the high priest and the community of the Jews"

Bronze coin of Alexander Jannaeus (103-76 B.C.) showing an anchor

With the wealth and captives he took in war, he beautified and strengthened Jerusalem, erecting a new fortress and palace and apparently a high level aqueduct. The city was to bear permanent memorials of this period of Jewish conquest and political efflorescence.[18]

During the Maccabaean period, the two great parties of Judaism, the Pharisees and Sadducees, which figure so prominently in the time of Jesus,[19] came into existence. The Pharisees were apparently the successors of the Hasidim ("the Pious") who preferred death to violation of the Law and the traditions of the elders (oral law) when Antiochus IV Epiphanes proscribed Judaism in 168 B.C. (I Maccabees 2:29-38; 7:13; II Maccabees 14:6). Intensely devoted to the Law of Moses, they joined Judas Maccabaeus to gain the right to their religious convictions, but after the termination of religious persecution (164 B.C.), they were not eager to keep on fighting for political autonomy.

The name "Pharisee" apparently means "separated," but is explained variously.[20] The chief characteristic of the Pharisee was his

[18]The principal source of the reign of John Hyrcanus is Josephus *Antiquities* 13:8-10 and *Wars*. His history, alluded to in I Maccabees 16:23f., has not survived.
[19]Robert Pfeiffer, *History of New Testament Times* (New York, 1949), pp. 54-57.
[20]Cf. G. F. Moore, *Judaism* (Cambridge, 1927) Vol. I, pp. 60-62; R. Pfeiffer, *History of New Testament Times*, p. 54.

punctilious observance of the law, both oral and written.[21] The Pharisees are first mentioned in Jonathan's time (161-143 B.C.), somewhat irrelevantly, but actually appear in the flesh as opponents of John Hyrcanus in his assumption of the holy office of priest as well as civil ruler. They devoted themselves to interpreting and teaching the law,

Handwashing among the Jews was to a large extent ceremonial. In Jesus' day it had degenerated into an empty ritual and a cover for hypocrisy, for which reasons He denounced it (Mark 7:1-8)

that the nation might indeed be holy before God. Their watchwords were repentance, prayer, and charitable giving. They looked for the Messiah and the resurrection of the faithful at His advent. They had an admirable beginning in the fires of Maccabaean suffering, but gradually degenerated by Jesus' day into proud and empty religionists, devoid of faith or spiritual life.

[21]Josephus *War* 2:8,14; *Antiquities* 17:2,4; *Life* 38; Mark 7:3; Matthew 15:2; 23:1-25, etc.

The Sadducees,[22] probably "Zadokites," descendants or partisans of Solomon's priest Zadok (I Kings 2:35), were principally aristocratic, worldly-minded priests, obeying the literal commands of the law, but not stretching them, denying future resurrection and retribution, and skeptical of the supernatural. They naturally welcomed Hellenic culture and were willing to gain worldly advantage through adroit diplomacy or military strategy, etc. They were despised by the Pharisees who regarded them as being devoid of real piety. Such virulent animosity developed between these two parties that they eventually wrecked the Hasmonaean kingdom rather than settle their own differences.

Another group of Jewish society (a sect rather than a party) were the Essenes. Josephus, as well as Philo and Pliny, describe this ascetic group.[23] Until the discovery of the Dead Sea Scrolls since 1947, these were the only sources of information concerning this communal order. Now a great deal more is known of them from Khirbet Qumran, their center in the west side of the Dead Sea. The Qumran manuscripts are copies of Old Testament books and other treatises, including a book of rules of the order. These great archaeological discoveries make it highly probable that the Qumran Community consisted of a group of Essenes[24] or a very closely affiliated order, with actual headquarters located at this Dead Sea site, as the extent of the library found would indicate.

4. *Aristobulus* (*105-104* B.C.) *and Alexander Jannaeus* (*103-76* B.C.) *and Forebodings of the End of the Hasmonaean Dynasty*

Before Hyrcanus died, he tried to ease the opposition of the factions in his kingdom by appointing his eldest son high priest and his wife as his civil successor. But Aristobulus imprisoned his mother and seized the kingship. He died shortly after, however, and the third son of Hyrcanus, Alexander Jannaeus, assumed control and conducted himself in such a treacherous, vengeful, and unworthy manner that he completely alienated the Pharisees, estranging the loyalty of the finest Judaeans to the Hasmonaean dynasty. He also greatly intensified the mutual hatred and distrust of the Pharisees. Although he was a great conqueror, he sealed the eventual doom of the Hasmonaean house.

---

[22]See Josephus *Antiquities* 13:5, 5; 13:10, 6; 18:1, 4; 20:9, 1; *War* 2:8, 14; Mark 12:18-27; Matthew 3:7; 16:1-12; Luke 20:27-40; Acts 4:1; 5:17; 23:6-9.
[23]Josephus *Antiquities*, 13:5, 9; 15:10, 4-5; 18:1, 5; *War* 2:8, 2-13; Philo, *Every Good Man Is Free* 75-91, translated by F. H. Colson, *Loeb Classical Library* IX (1941), pp. 53-63; Pliny, *Natural History* 5:17.
[24]H. H. Rowley, *The Zadokite Fragments and the Dead Sea Scrolls* (1952), pp. 78f., *The Dead Sea Scrolls and their Significance* (1955), p. 20; *Theologische Zeitschrift* (1957), pp. 530-540; A. Dupont-Sommer, *The Jewish Sect of Qumran and the Essenes*. See also chapter IV.

5. *Alexandra (76-67 B.C.) and the "Golden Age" of Pharisaism*

Alexander Jannaeus' wife succeeded her husband and reversed her husband's policy by favoring the Pharisees, who abused their power and put many Sadducees to death. Elementary education by scribes instead of by parents was introduced in Alexandra's reign, and the Sanhedrin was organized with scribes admitted to its membership.

6. *Hyrcanus II's Struggle with Aristobulus II and the End of the Maccabaean Age*

Hyrcanus, the elder son of Alexandra, had been made high priest during his mother's reign. Aristobulus, another son of Alexandra, was ready to seize the throne at his mother's death and permit his brother Hyrcanus to remain as high priest. But Antipater, the governor of Idumaea, persuaded Hyrcanus to flee to Petra, to secure the aid of the Nabataean prince Aretas in winning the throne of Judaea. In the struggle that ensued, an appeal was sent to Rome to settle the quarrel. The Pharisaic party expressed its desire that Rome take over political control of Palestine, which Pompey agreed to do in 63 B.C., thus ending the Hasmonaean monarchy. Internal dissension of the Jewish parties thus was a factor in the loss of political liberty.

Pompey organized the Decapolis league in Transjordan, restoring local liberty to these Hellenistic cities to balance the power of the Jews, and reduced Judaea to its former smallness. Hyrcanus was left as nominal ruler for 23 years. But these were years full of turmoil which made Roman rule a necessity.

7. *Archaeology and the Maccabaean Period*

The cities of Bethzur, Gezer and Marisa, which figure prominently in Maccabaean history, exhibit interesting remains of this period. Gezer yielded a fortress of Simon Maccabaeus. Marisa yielded an entire Hellenistic city with characteristic arrangement of streets running at right angles and forming regular blocks much as in a modern town. It is significant also that at Bethzur, Gezer, and Marisa a series of Jewish coins comes to an end about 100 B.C., demonstrating that these three towns were abandoned soon after Alexander Jannaeus (103-76 B.C.), the most empire-minded king of the Maccabaean dynasty, had conquered all Palestine and it became unnecessary to maintain these points as strong outposts. Pottery found substantiates the witness of coins, as usual, in the matter of dating.

But the most rewarding site illustrating the Maccabaean period is Bethzur, strategically located on the Jerusalem-Hebron road on the Judaea-Idumaea border. Excavated by W. F. Albright and O. R. Sellers in 1931 with work resumed in 1957,[25] the site has yielded extensive Maccabaean remains, confirmed by coins of the period whose testimony dovetails with the notices in the First Book of Maccabees, where Bethzur prominently figures in the Maccabaean struggles with the Seleucid tyrants. Precisely the literary evidence indicates that Bethzur was relatively unimportant prior to the second campaign of Lysias in 163-162 B.C. after Judas had turned it into a fortress following his victory over Lysias in 165 B.C.[26]

Phase I of the Bethzur citadel is dated by Robert Funk in the Ptolemaic period. Phase II, which is oriental in plan, is not certainly dated (coins from Antiochus IV) but Phase III is now known to be the work of the Syrian Bacchides some time after 161 B.C.[27] The evidence from coins demonstrates that Bethzur was sparsely settled during the sixth to the fourth centuries, revived under the Ptolemies in the third, and prospered under the Seleucids and Maccabees in the second century. Coins and pottery recovered show that during the relatively tranquil periods of the second century (175-165 and 140-100 B.C.) the population overflowed the city wall. In this way archaeology is expanding the horizons of history and illuminating ancient literary references, and filling in details and gaps in the historian's knowledge.

Eagle drawn from a silver tetra-drachma from Ascalon, dated 29 B.C.

[25]O. R. Sellers, *The Citidel of Beth-zur* (1933), and in *The Biblical Archaeologist* 21 (1958), pp. 71-76; Robert W. Funk in *Bulletin of the American Schools of Oriental Research* 150 (April, 1958), p. 8-20.
[26]Robert W. Funk, *Bulletin of the American Schools* 150 (April, 1958), p. 16.
[27]Funk, *op. cit.*, p. 16.

CHAPTER 3

PALESTINE AND THE ROMAN WORLD
AT THE TIME OF CHRIST

Under Alexander Jannaeus (103-76) the Maccabaean kingdom reached the zenith of its power and greatness, being practically coterminous with the territories won and controlled by David nine centuries before. Coins recovered from this prosperous era of Jewish independence bear the proud title of "king" stamped in Hebrew and Greek as the designation of the reigning Hasmonaean. Although Jannaeus' widow, Alexandra, was to rule as queen for some nine years (76-67), the days of Jewish autonomy were numbered. The sons of Jannaeus, Hyrcanus II and Aristobulus II, in becoming rival claimants for the throne, both taking the fatal steps of calling upon Rome to intervene, sealed the fate of the Hasmonaean dynasty. Aristobulus II and his followers in their struggle for power were destined to suffer defeat under Roman intervention, while Hyrcanus' regime as high priest and ethnarch (63-40 B.C.) was merely a puppet rule under Roman domination.

Drawing of a bronze coin of Antigonus (40-37 B.C.) with his name and title of king inscribed about an ivy wreath

Coin of Alexander Jannaeus (103-76 B.C.) with anchor

50

I. HEROD THE GREAT, KING OF THE JEWS

The Herodian line of kings under which Christ lived and died and under which the Christian Church had its beginning was not of Jewish stock, despite the legend circulated by Herod the Great that his family had descended from a distinguished Babylonian Jew.[1] But Herod was always detested by the Jews as a half-foreigner and a cunning opportunist who cultivated friendship for Rome merely to further his own power. As an Edomite (Idumaean), Josephus dubbed him a "half-Jew."[2]

1. Herod the Great and His Rise to Power

The Herodian dynasty sprang from Antipater I, whom Alexander Jannaeus had appointed as governor of Idumaea[3] when the latter conquered the Idumaeans and forcibly "converted" them, subjecting them to circumcision about 125 B.C.[4] When Antipater I died (78 B.C.), his son and namesake, Antipater II, succeeded him. It was this astute politician who won great power and in turn set the stage for the rise of his son, Herod the Great. Herod's father, Antipater II, adroitly used two levers to force his way to power—the unconquerable might of Rome and the pitiable weakness of the decadent Hasmonaean dynasty. From about 55 B.C. to 43 B.C., Antipater II was virtual ruler of Palestine under Roman grant, Julius Caesar appointing him procurator of Judaea, Samaria, and Galilee about 47 B.C.

In 43 B.C. Antipater II was assassinated, leaving four sons, Phasael, Herod the Great, Joseph, and Pheroras. The second of these sons was destined to raise the Herodian dynasty to the acme of its power and prestige, commencing his notable career as governor of Galilee. He early won Roman favor by his success in raising tribute money for the imperial government and in ridding Galilee of roving bands of freebooters. These initial accomplishments won him rapid promotion, and Antony made him tetrarch of Judaea in 41 B.C.

The Parthian invasion in 40 B.C. and the resulting temporary demise of Roman authority in Palestine forced Herod temporarily to leave his domain, which was seized by Antigonus, sole surviving son of Aristobulus II, who became king and high priest of the Jews for

---

[1]Josephus, *Antiquities* XIV, 1, 3.
[2]*Ibid.*, 15, 2. What is known of Herod is mainly gathered from Josephus in his *Antiquities* and *Jewish War*, from Strabo and Dio Cassius among the classics, and from modern archaeological research.
[3]The Greek and Roman name of Edom (Mark 3:8). In the post-exilic period the Edomites were gradually driven northward by the Nabataeans and by 150 B.C. were settled in the southern half of Judaea in Hebron and as far north as Bethzur (I Maccabees 4:29; 5:65).
[4]*Antiquities* XIII, 9, 1.

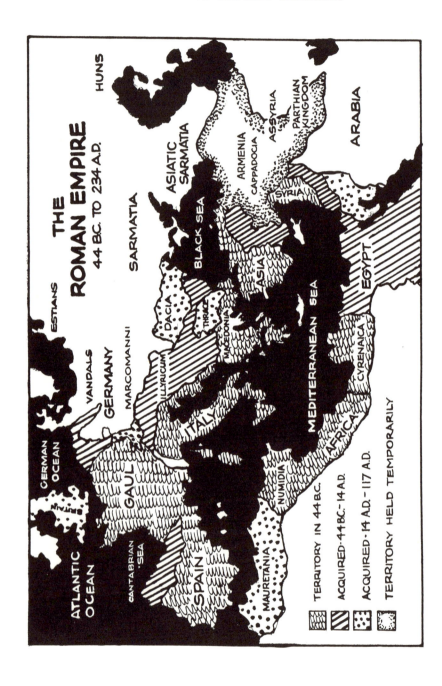

THE ROMAN EMPIRE
44 B.C. TO 234 A.D.

TERRITORY IN 44 B.C.

ACQUIRED · 44 B.C. - 14 A.D.

ACQUIRED · 14 A.D. - 117 A.D.

TERRITORY HELD TEMPORARILY

three years (40-37 B.C.),[5] the inscription on whose coins reads "Of king Antigonus," inscribed in Greek, and "Mattathias the high priest," inscribed in Hebrew.

But Antigonus' seizure of power was the final spasm of the dying Hasmonaean house. In the meantime Herod was at Rome seeking the crown of Judaea, which he obtained through the favor of Antony and Augustus in 37 B.C., and by the sword as soon as he arrived back in Palestine, putting to death Antigonus and forty-five of his principal supporters.

2. Herod, Client-King of Rome

Herod's advent on the stage of history toward the end of the period of Roman conspiracies and civil wars and the commencement of the imperial period was propitious. The second triumvirate (Antony, Octavian, and Lepidus) defeated the republican forces under Brutus and Cassius at Philippi (42 B.C.), and finally after the victory at Actium (31 B.C.), Octavian, under whom Herod was destined to rule so long as a client-king, emerged as sole ruler of the vast Roman world.

On January 16, 27 B.C. the Roman senate conferred on Octavian the title *Augustus* and recognized his supreme authority. The title, rendered *Sebastos* in Greek, connoting the generalized idea of "worshipful," did not imply that the bearer was to be an object of actual worship. Augustus always discouraged any ceremonial that might suggest he was a god, though his "father" Julius Caesar had been formally deified after his death. However, in the course of time Caesar-worship was to develop, especially in the east "where since time immemorial divinity had hedged a king, the cult of the emperors spread far and early."[6]

Such was the overlord and patron for whom Herod did everything his subtle political sagacity could conjure up to please. Augustus on his part realized Herod's outstanding capabilities to rule a region of such strategic importance as Palestine was to the Roman imperial scheme, Palestine being the bridge between the rich province of Syria, the granary of Egypt, and the lucrative trade routes via Petra and the west, as well as constituting an important buffer territory against the Parthian peril on the east.[7] But Herod's client-kingship in Judaea was no new institution in Rome's expanding government. It had already existed for two centuries, and client kingdoms at this period were found in Armenia, Cappadocia, Galatia, and Commagene, in each case Rome making even kings the instruments of servitude. Herod might

---

[5]Josephus describes the brief reign of Antigonus in *Antiquities* 14:14-16; *War* 1:14, 1-18, 3, who pledged the Parthians 1,000 talents and 500 Jewish women to secure the throne.
[6]Stewart Perowne, *The Life and Times of Herod the Great* (London, 1956), p. 88.
[7]Perowne, *op. cit.*, pp. 89-94.

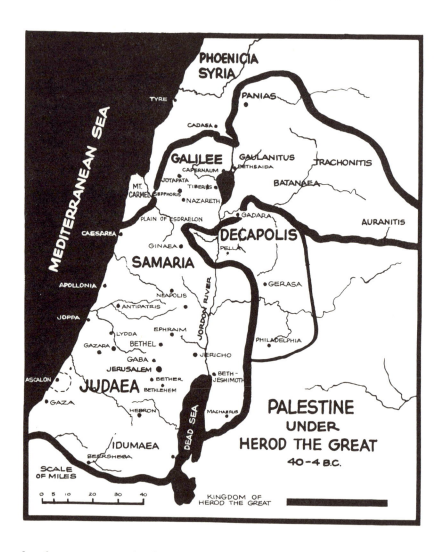

be the means to rule the difficult-to-manage Jews of Palestine, but it was really Rome that ruled, and always the client king held his kingdom on the basis of imperial favor. If this was offended, he could be dethroned at will. Rome considered its supreme calling to govern, and it mattered little who the instrument was — proconsul, procurator, legate, or king. Roman rule and Roman law were the important factors.

However, the client-king was entitled to the crown, the scepter and the purple, and was supreme in his kingdom in legislative, administrative, judicial, and fiscal matters. Moreover, he had enjoyed two important privileges—exemption from tribute for himself and his kingdom and from the garrisoning of Roman troops on his people at their

Artist's drawing of a relief from an altar commemorating the Peace of Augustus (13 B.C.). Pious Romans, in characteristic dress, form a religious procession honoring the emperor

expense. Exemption from taxation of client-kings was apparently, however, abolished by Augustus, according to Luke's account. "In those days a decree went out from Caesar Augustus that all the world should be enrolled" (Luke 2:1).[8] Although Herod was in high favor with Augustus, he came perilously near losing both his crown and his head when he sent Nicolaus of Damascus to Augustus for his defense concerning the charge of treason against Rome made by Syllaeus in the matter of the Nabataean uprising.[9] As sole ruler of the Empire, there is nothing unnatural in Augustus' decreeing a universal enrolment for all his subjects, although critics commonly deny it applied to Palestine.

[8]Sir William Ramsay presents evidence from Appian and Strabo that client kingdoms were as really under Roman rule as the provinces, both senatorial and imperial (*Was Christ Born at Bethlehem?* pp. 118-124).
[9]Cf. Josephus *Antiquities* XV, 10; A. T. Robertson, *Luke the Historian in the Light of Research* (New York, 1930), p. 121.

Artist's reproduction of the statue of the god Hadad from Khirbet et-Tannur, southeast of the Dead Sea in Nabataea. Dusares was the chief Nabataean deity, but the Syrian storm-god Hadad was revered at Tannur and identified with Zeus

A delicate fragment of Nabataean pottery displaying the art and industry of the remarkable Nabataean people who made the desert blossom on the fringes of Palestine-Syria in the New Testament era. Courtesy Nelson Glueck

3. Herod's Character and Matthew's Account of the Magi and the Slaughter of the Infants

The picture presented of Herod in Matthew's gospel in connection with events following the nativity of Christ is remarkably vivid and singularly in agreement with the personal character of Herod as known from extra-biblical sources. These events catalogued in Matthew 2:1-23 occurred in the last years of the king's reign when the twin demons of jealousy of power and maniacal suspicion had overpowered him, converting him into a Jewish Nero, who bathed his own house and kingdom in blood.

It is pathetic to see the aged monarch, soon to die, so agitated over the question of the Magi, "Where is he who has been born king of the Jews?" (Matthew 2:2). At the very mention of a rival claimant to his throne in an atmosphere of fervid Messianism, his deep-set jealousy for power set in motion the same craftiness and insane suspicion that had caused Herod to murder numerous members of his own family, including his favorite wife, Mariamne. Trials and executions of his own conspiring sons were conducted with the condonement of the Roman authorities, for Herod was crafty enough not to violate his position as a client-king of Rome. Yet so thoroughly were the intrigues, tragedies and mutual recriminations of Herod's court known at Rome that with the murder of Mariamne's sons, Augustus is said to have exclaimed: "I would rather be Herod's hog than his son."

It is precisely such a character that appears so graphically in the biblical reference to Herod. Completely perturbed at the rumor of a new king of the Jews being born, Herod, jealous of power, immediately sets in motion the machinery of inquisition, using in this

Myrrh, a gum resin used for perfume, for embalming, and as an ingredient in the holy anointing oil. It was one of the gifts of the Magi to the infant Jesus (Matt. 2:11)

Frankincense, which produced a white aromatic gum, was used in the holy anointing oil (Ex. 30:34) and as fragrant incense in the meal offering (Lev. 2:1), typifying Christ's sinless humanity. It was accordingly an appropriate gift of the Magi to the Babe of Bethlehem (Matt. 2:11)

instance scribes, Pharisees, and ancient Hebrew prophecies as his informants. When frustrated in his diabolical cunning by the wisdom and divine warning to the Magi, his uncontrollable rage so characteristic of the man when outwitted, manifests itself in the brutal massacre of the young children of the Bethlehem area. The whole episode portrays a man, although possessed of great talents and abilities, captivated and corrupted by his lower nature and appearing in the starkest contrast to the divine King of whom he was so irrationally suspicious.

Such a barbarous and superstitious act as Herod perpetrated upon the helpless children of Bethlehem was by no means unheard of in pagan antiquity where the life of a newborn babe was at the mercy of the father or of the state. A few months before the birth of Augustus, a prodigy presaging the nativity of a king for the Roman people, having taken place, the frightened Senate decreed that none of the children born that year were to be brought up.[10] At a later era, Nero was so upset by the appearance of a comet that he ordered the execution of leading Roman citizens, whose children were driven from the city and died of hunger and exposure.

4. Herod and the Herodium

Not long after his contact with the Magi and the ruthless murder of the infants of Bethlehem, Herod died at Jericho in the spring of 4 B.C., dropsical, gangrenous, and in the throes of loathsome disease. In the days preceding his death, horror and tragedy, which had often stalked his palace, reigned supreme. In the midst of his terrible sufferings, he attempted suicide with a paring knife, and soon afterward ordered the execution of his son Antipater only five days before his own death.

In full royal regalia the funeral procession of the deceased king left Jericho for its destination, southeast of Bethlehem, in the very country he had recently deluged in sorrow by an act of insane criminality. Herod's body lay on a golden, gem-encrusted bier, beneath a long purple pall. His diadem with golden crown was on his head and his scepter was placed in his right hand. Immediately behind his bier were his sons and all his family, followed by the Royal Guard, the Thracian Regiment, the German Regiment, the Galatian Regiment and Regiments of the Line, all in full battle order. This imposing procession was followed by 500 servants of Herod carrying spices. It moved up the steep road south of the Wadi Qelt beneath Cypros, the traditional Valley of the Shadow of Death, and across the barren downs of the Wilderness of Judaea to the Herodium, one of Herod's fortress castles which he had chosen as the site for his final resting place, and where his body was interred.

The Herodium was identified by the early Palestinian explorer-archaeologist Edward Robinson with the so-called Frank Mountain (Jebel el Fureidis) some half-dozen miles southeast of Bethlehem. The hill on which Herod's fortress-castle was built was raised until it resembled the shape of a woman's breast, according to Josephus. A polished-stone staircase of 200 steps gave access to the castle, which was fortified with four circular towers from which there was a magnificent view of the entire countryside dear to Herod because here he had won an important victory over the supporters of the last Maccabaean king. Within the Herodium itself were sumptuous apartments. Ruins of a surrounding wall still remain on the northeast base of the hill skirting the Bethlehem-to-Engedi road on either side of the

---

[10]Perowne, op. cit., p. 172.

former ascent stairway, and a present-day road to the summit skirts south off the Bethlehem road near the remains of the old city and gives access to the summit from a westerly direction. At the northern base of the hill are ancient ruins of buildings, cisterns, walls, and pools, and the surrounding plain was dotted with villas and estates of relatives and courtiers.

Bethlehem with ruins of the Herodium at left-center in the distance. Courtesy Mrs. Lowell Orth

The Herodium was another of Herod's brilliant building operations like the temple and other constructions in Jerusalem, and like his magnificent architectural accomplishments in Samaria (Sebaste), Strato's Tower (Caesarea), Antipatris, Jericho, Phaesalus, Askelon, Damascus, Tyre, Sidon, Tripoli, Antioch on the Orontes and even in Athens. The Herodium was Herod's bid for a unique mausoleum to perpetuate his memory, the idea for which he evidently got from a colleague client-king, Antiochus of Commagene in southeastern Asia Minor, north and northwest of Syria. King Antiochus planned a similar unique mausoleum on the Nemrud Dagh in the Taurus Mountains, having gravel piled over his tomb to a depth of a hundred feet, raising the elevation of the entire mountain. Ruins of the statue of the gods Ahuramazda, Mithras, Verethragna, Commagene and Antiochus can still be seen atop Nemrud Dagh. If Herod's and Antiochus' crypts are still intact, it is hoped future excavations may recover them.

In the Jewish-Roman War (A.D. 70) the Herodium was destroyed when Jewish rebels who held it were finally defeated. As a result of the destruction which took place at the time, the top of Frank Mountain assumed its present-day crater-like appearance.

5. *Herod and Archelaus, and the Flight of the Holy Family to Egypt*

Matthew's gospel not only introduces Herod into the Christmas story, but also the flight of the holy family into Egypt to escape the wrath of the aged tyrant. Egypt since 30 B.C. had been one of the most important provinces of Rome, a world in itself, and in a sense the bread basket of the Empire, ruled by a prefect. Fleeing there doubtless by way of Bethzur or Hebron to the coastal plain and via the old highroad to Pelusium, Joseph and Mary breathed more easily when once they were outside the jurisdiction of Herod. In Egypt they remained until the death of Herod in the spring of 4 B.C. (Matthew 2:15).

After his unsuccessful attempt at suicide and the execution of his son Antipater only five days before his death, Herod once again made a new will, his fourth and last, by which he appointed Archelaus, his son by the Samaritan Malthace, as king of Judaea. It was when Joseph was divinely warned that those who sought the child Jesus' life were dead, that he left Egypt, but he was afraid to go into Judaea "when he heard that Archelaus reigned over Judaea in the place of his father Herod" (Matthew 2:22).

Archelaus, realizing the client status of the Herodian kingdom, prudently refrained from ascending the throne until Herod's will was approved by Augustus, which the emperor did in its essential provisions, against both Jewish opposition and that of Archelaus' younger brother Herod Antipas, who appeared as a rival. But Archelaus received only the title of ethnarch, "ruler of the people," which was inferior to that of a king.[11] His rival Antipas, however, was given only a tetrarchy.

Archelaus, according to Josephus, was barbarously cruel both to Jews and Samaritans who had opposed his accession to power and had a quarrel with him. Both groups had dispatched embassies to Augustus to complain of his ruthlessness. The holy family had undoubtedly heard of his severe repression of a passover riot in B.C. 4, in which 3,000 people were killed, even before he was confirmed in power, and decided to keep clear of his domain. In the tenth year of his administration (A.D. 6) Augustus deposed him and banished him to Vienne in Gaul, and his wealth was put in the imperial treasury.[12]

---

[11]Josephus, *Antiquities* XVII, 8, 1; 9:7; 11:5.
[12]Josephus, *War* II, 7, 3.

6. *Herod and the Party of the Herodians*

In his ardent love of Hellenistic culture and his devotion to Caesar Augustus and the luxurious ways and habits of life of the Romans, Herod the Great continually offended his legally austere Jewish subjects by the introduction of Roman athletics, pagan architecture, heathen temples, and non-Jewish customs into his realm. As a brilliant and thorough-going Hellenizer, he often exhausted his talents as a shrewd diplomat and masterful tactician to placate and mollify the Jews. His most colossal attempt was his erection of the magnificent temple in Jerusalem, which was so transcendently beautiful that Josephus seems tireless in describing its splendors, and even Titus, out of regard for its magnificence, was anxious to spare it when the city fell in 70 A.D. But despite this and many other dispensations of charity in time of famine, and tactful yielding to Jewish prejudices whenever possible, his subjects saw in Herod only a usurper to the throne of David who maintained himself by the strong arm of the detested Roman oppressor, and who was always ready to rob his own people for self-aggrandizement and in order to give munificent gifts to the Romans.

Coin of Herod the Great with tripod (obverse)   Tiara with star and palms from a coin of Herod the Great (reverse)

Although Herod's Hellenizing activities were staunchly resisted by most Jews, his influence on the younger Jews was not without far-reaching effects. Slowly a distinct party arose, partly religious, partly political, partly cultural, which became known as the Herodian party, composed of those who were Jews in external religious forms, but devotees of easy-going, world-conforming Hellenism in matters of dress and general view of life. Members of this party were a bitter offense to the nation as a whole, but made common cause with mutual

Bethlehem today. Courtesy of Dr. John F. Walvoord

Shepherds Field outside Bethlehem (cf. Luke 2:8). Courtesy of Dr. John F. Walvoord

enemies, the Pharisees and Sadducees in their opposition to Christ (Matthew 22:16; Mark 3:6; 12:13).

II. ARCHAEOLOGY AND LUKE'S ACCOUNT OF JESUS' BIRTH

Interwoven prominently in the Christmas story as narrated by Luke in Chapter 2 of his gospel is a pivotal passage of immense historical importance (Luke 2:1-7) that has been furiously assailed until comparatively recent times as being almost completely unhistorical, a mere legend, at best a bundle of blunders.

1. *Luke the Historian and the First Taxation Enrolment*

In this important passage Luke asserts that (1) such a census (enrolment) first took place under Caesar Augustus during the reign of Herod, (2) that it involved the return of everyone to his ancestral home, (3) that it constituted part of an empire-wide enrolment ("all the world"), meaning the sphere of the Roman Empire, (4) and that it was held during Quirinius' first governorship of the province of Syria.

Although as a result of archaeological discoveries it is now widely admitted in critical circles, both by theological and historical scholars, that these four declarations of Luke may be authentic, such was emphatically not the case before Sir William Ramsay's researches on the subject of Luke's historical reliability in the first decade of the twentieth century.[13] Despite the fact that it is still rare to find the same critic admitting all four of Lukes' assertions,[14] scientific advance has done much to vindicate his historical reliability, though some problems still remain. No longer, however, can the arbitrary attitude of earlier critics be defended who assumed that Luke was bound to be wrong simply because he stood unsupported by other ancient authorities, forgetting that the genuine worth of a historian, when he stands alone is put to the acid test of whether he blindly follows tradition or has conducted original investigation for the facts (cf. Luke 1:1-4).

Supporting the possibility that the census may have taken place in Herod's reign is the assertion of Josephus that toward the end of his rule as a client-king Herod was dealt with by Augustus as a subject rather than a friend.[15] Also Luke's reliability in this aspect of the complicated issues involved in this crucial passage (Luke 2:1-3) is supported by the evidence that this procedure was normal with client

---

[13]*The Bearing of Recent Discovery on the Trustworthiness of the New Testament* (The James Sprunt Lectures for 1911, reprint Grand Rapids, 1953) pp. 238-300.
[14]For example, Lily Ross Taylor who grants the first three of Luke's assertions, but is not persuaded that Quirinius was Syrian legate at the time (*American Journal of Philology* LIV, 1933) pp. 120 ff.
[15]*Antiquities* XVI, 9,3; XVII, 2,4.

kingdoms, as Tacitus notes that such an enrolment was imposed on the vassal kingdom of Antiochus.[16]

Supporting also the now widely admitted possibility that Luke's census may have involved the return of everyone to his ancestral home is the evidence from periodic enrolments in Egypt which were conducted on a fourteen-year cycle and were by households.[17] The edict in question is that of G. Vibius Maximus, prefect of Egypt and dated 104 A.D. "Since the enrolment by households is approaching, it is necessary to command all who for any reason are out of their own district to return to their own home, in order to perform the usual business of the taxation . . ."[18]

In addition a letter from the late third century contains a request that the writer's sister endeavor to enroll for him but if that is not possible, to let him know that he may come and do it himself.

> To my sister, lady Dionysia, from Pathermouthis, greeting. As you sent me word on account of the enrolment about enrolling yourselves, since I cannot come, see whether you can enroll us. Do not then neglect to enroll us, me and Patas; but if you learn you cannot enroll us, reply to me and I will come. Find out also about the collection of the poll tax, and if they are hurrying on with the collection of the poll tax, pay it, and I will send you the money; and if you pay the poll tax get the receipt. Do not neglect this, my sister, and write to me about the enrolment, whether you have done it or not, and reply to me and I will come and enroll myself. I pray for your lasting health.[19]

Supporting also the now widely admitted possibility that Luke's census may have constituted part of an empire-wide enrolment is the evidence from the papyri of periodic enrolments from 11 and 8 B.C., the evidence for an Egyptian census in 10-9 B.C. being practically conclusive.[20] Discoveries among papyri from the sands of Egypt prove that a periodic fourteen-year census was taken in Egypt and doubtlessly throughout the empire. Definitely dated census returns come from the years A.D. 34, 48, 62 and numerous examples extending

---

[16]*Annals*, VI. 41.

[17]Cf. A. T. Robertson, *Luke the Historian in the Light of Historical Research* (New York, 1930), p. 125. The title is always *apographe kat' oikian* "enrolment according to a household," the same word for enrolment or census (*apographe*) as that used in Luke 2:2. Cf. also A. Deissmann, *Light from the Ancient East* (1910), pp. 268 ff.

[18]Frederic G. Kenyon and H. Idris Bell, *Greek Papyri in the British Museum* III (1907), no. 904.

[19]Adolf Deissmann, *Licht vom Osten, Das Neue Testament und die neuentdeckten Texte der hellenistisch-romischen Welt* (4th ed., 1923), p. 231. "Thus the situation presupposed in Luke 2:3 seems entirely plausible" (Jack Finegan, *Light from the Ancient Past*, rev. ed., 1959), p. 261.

[20]F. F. Bruce, "Census" in the *Twentieth Century Encyclopedia of Religious Knowledge* (1955), Vol. I., p. 222. cf. V. Wilcken, *Papyruskunde* I (1912), pp. 192 ff.

to A.D. 202, authenticating the fourteen-year cycle.[21] Returns whose dates are not extant apparently belong to A.D. 6, A.D. 20, and A.D. 34.[22]

Supporting the possibility that the census of Luke 2:1-4 may have been held during Quirinius' first governorship of Syria, the evidence is not as yet completely satisfactory as might be desired, and problems still remain to be cleared up by further archaeological research. The crux of the problem is that it is difficult to fit Quirinius' governorship of Syria into the years before 4 B.C., whereas it is rather known to have begun about A.D. 6 in connection with the commencement of Coponius' procuratorship of Judaea[23] and Josephus' dating of the taxings conducted by Quirinius in the thirty-seventh year of Caesar's victory over Antony at Actium, September 2, 31 B.C., so the date would be September 2, A.D. 6.[24] But an enrolment held in A.D. 6/7 is patently too late to be related to the birth of Jesus, although some critics argue that the birth of Christ did not occur until that late date.[25]

The solution to this vexing problem is that Quirinius apparently was twice associated with the government of the province of Syria. Sir William Ramsay accepted the inscriptional evidence contained in Titulus Tiburtinus, construing the words "iterum Syriam," i.e. "a second time Syria" to refer to Quirinius.[26]

Likewise the inscriptions of Aemilius Secundus (*Lapis Venetus*) mentions P. Sulpicius Quirinius in connection with the census (perhaps the first). But Ramsay has adduced additional inscriptional evidence that Quirinius commanded the Homanadensian campaign as legate of Syria between 12 and 6 B.C.[27] Ramsay's inscription, discovered at Antioch of Pisidia in 1912 and dated 10-7 B.C., refers to Gaius Coristanius Fronto as "prefect of P. Sulpicius Quirinius duumvir." Another inscription from the village of Hissardi close to Antioch discovered by Ramsay mentions the same man, Gaius Coristanius Fronto, as "prefect of P. Sulpicius Quirinius duumvir" and "prefect of M. Servilius."[28] "Thus Quirinius and Servilius were governing the two adjoining provinces, Syria-Cilicia and Galatia, around the year 8 B.C., when the First Census was made,"[29] says Ramsay.

[21]*The Oxyrhynchus Papyri* II, p. 207, cf. no. 255.
[22]*The Oxyrhynchus Papyri* II, nos. 254, 256.
[23]Josephus *Antiquities* XVIII, 1, 1.
[24]*Antiquities* XVIII, 2, 1.
[25]Cf. Kirsopp Lake, *The Expositor* (Nov., 1912), pp. 462f. Alfred Plummer maintains that in the matter of Quirinius, "We must be content to leave the difficulty unsolved" (*Commentary*, p. 50).
[26]*Was Christ Born at Bethlehem?* p. 109.
[27]*Bearing of Recent Discoveries on the Trustworthiness of the New Testament* (1915), pp. 223 ff., *Journal of Roman Studies* VII, 1917, pp. 271 ff.
[28]*Bearing of Recent Discovery*, p. 300.
[29]*Ibid.*

The fact that Tertullian[30] asserts that Jesus was born when Sententius Saturninus was governor of Syria (9-6 B.C.), represents his unwarranted attempt to correct Luke because the first periodic enrolment of Syria was made under Saturninus (8-7 B.C.). But Ramsay shows that the enrolment of Palestine was delayed until the late summer or fall of 6 B.C., when Varus was controlling the internal affairs of Syria and Quirinius was directing its armies and its foreign policy.

III. PALESTINE UNDER THE RULE OF THE CAESARS

In a passage remarkable for its historical comprehensiveness and accuracy, Luke pinpoints the commencement of the public ministry of John the Baptist and necessarily also that of Jesus. "In the fifteenth year of the reign of Tiberius Caesar, Pontius Pilate being governor of Judaea, and Herod being tetrarch of Galilee, and his brother Philip tetrarch of the region of Iturea and Trachonitis, and Lysanias tetrarch of Abilene, in the high priesthood of Annas and Caiaphas, the word of God come to John the son of Zachariah in the wilderness" (Luke 3:1, 2).

The Emperor Augustus (31 B.C - 14 A.D.), Roman ruler during the birth of Jesus at Bethlehem and His boyhood at Nazareth

The Emperor Tiberius (14-37 A.D.), Roman ruler during the public ministry and death of Jesus

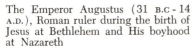

[30]*Against Marcion* IV, 19.

1. *Tiberius and the Procuratorial Government of Palestine*

Caesar Augustus, the first Roman Emperor, under whose reign Jesus was born and grew up to young manhood, died in A.D. 14 and was succeeded on the throne by Tiberius, his adopted son and son-in-law (he married the Emperor's daughter Julia). Tiberius, who reigned till A.D. 37, is mentioned specifically by name only in Luke 3:1, but is the person referred to as "Caesar" in the gospel accounts (except Luke 2:1).[31] Tiberius was of the Claudian family, and the son of an officer of Julius Caesar and Livia. As a result of his conspicuous service in the army, especially in campaigns along the Danube and the Rhine, he became "the first soldier of the Empire," establishing the imperial organization in Europe and becoming military governor of the Roman provinces in A.D. 12. As *Imperator* he was noted for rigid economy in the government of the Empire, leniency in the matter of taxation, justice in punishing unprovoked oppression, and interest in trade and communication.

Under Tiberius, Judaea was governed by procurators, who had exercised authority since the deposition of Herod's son Archelaus under Augustus. The first procurator of Judaea was Coponius (A.D. 6-9), followed by Marcus Ambivius (A.D. 9-12) and Annius Rufus (A.D. 12-15). In Tiberius Caesar's reign, procurators were Valerius Gratus (A.D. 15-26), Pontius Pilate (A.D. 26-36) and Marcellus (A.D. 36-37).

Procurators were governors of the equestrian order subject to the Emperor and who could summon assistance from the legate of Syria, if needed. They resided in Caesarea, but if special emergencies arose, they might take up temporary residence in Jerusalem. The procurators were a special class of imperial administrator be-

Silver denarius with head of Tiberius Caesar (obverse). Reverse—figure holds scepter. PONTIF(EX) MAXIM(US)

cause procurement of funds or financial management was their principal interest, and they were appointed where difficult or turbulent conditions existed, as in Palestine. This form of government proved to be unhappy among the Jews because Roman business men who were selected for these jobs were unable to understand an Oriental people

[31]Cf. Matthew 22:17; Mark 12:14; Luke 20:22; John 19:12.

bound by innumerable ceremonial laws and capable of much fanaticism in matters of their religion. As a result, the procurators made one mistake after another, and often allowed their patience to be exhausted in outbursts of cruelty in dealing with the intransigeant and often incomprehensibly stubborn Jews. The inefficiency of procuratorial government was one of the major causes of the Jewish-Roman War of 67-70.

Important archaeologically are the coins which date from the period of the Judaean procurators. Coins struck by the procurators from Coponius to Antonius Felix are extant. Of special interest are

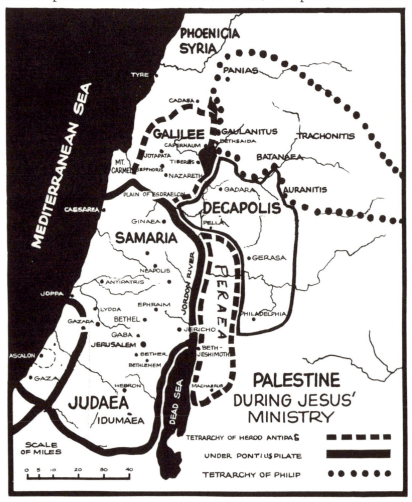

examples from the second to the sixth year of Pontius Pilate A.D. 27/28 to A.D. 31-32.[32]

2. Pontius Pilate the Most Famous Procurator of Judaea

Because of his dramatic connection with the trial and death of Jesus, Pontius Pilate (A.D. 26-36) is a household name to Bible readers. Philo describes Pilate in the severest terms of condemnation,[33] but various apocryphal writings from the third to the fifth centuries and later, present him in a favorable light together with his wife, who was said to be a Jewish proselyte at the time of Jesus' death and later with her husband to have become a Christian. Her name, along with Pilate's, is honored both in the Greek and Coptic Church.

Actually, however, Pilate was apparently ruthless, and being appointed through Tiberius' prime minister Sejanus, who hated the Jews, he antagonized his subjects and dealt cruelly with them when they resisted his measures. Luke incidentally records one of Pilate's acts of violence, otherwise unrecorded, how he mingled the blood of certain Galileans with that of their religious sacrifices (Luke 13:1).

History, however, records other atrocities. On one occasion he used the sacred temple treasure, called "corban," to finance an aqueduct to bring water into Jerusalem. When a crowd demonstrated against this violation of Jewish principle, he had the rioters beat down mercilessly.[34] On another occasion, his soldiers brought ensigns bearing the image of the emperor into Jerusalem, violating Jewish scruples. Crowds of excited Jews hurried to Caesarea to petition Pilate for their removal. For five days Pilate refused to hear them. On the sixth day he threatened them with instant death if they did not cease to bother him. Whereupon the entire crowd of petitioners bared their necks to die rather than compromise their convictions. Pilate, unwilling to execute so many, yielded the point and removed the ensigns.[35] A similar episode occurred over some gilt shields Pilate dedicated in Herod's palace in honor of the emperor. These contained no representation, but simply the name of the donor and of him in whose honor they were set up. When the Jews petitioned him to have them removed, he refused, but an appeal to Tiberius resulted in the removal of the disputed shields to Caesarea.

A final act of violence against a crowd of Samaritan religious enthusiasts led to Pilot's deposition. Misled by a pretender who promised that if the Samaritans assembled at Mt. Gerizim he would

---

[32]Cf. Florence A. Banks, *Coins of Bible Days* (1955); A. Kinder, *Israel Exploration Journal* 6 (1956), pp. 54-57.
[33]*Legatio and Caium* XXXVIII.
[34]Josephus, *Antiquities* III, 2; *Wars of the Jews* II.
[35]Josephus, *Antiquities* XVIII, 3, 2.

show them the sacred vessels which he alleged Moses had hidden there, Pilate's cavalry attacked the crowd of zealots and many of them were killed. Upon appeal to Vitellius, the legate of Syria, Pilate was displaced by Marcellus (A.D. 36-37) and was ordered to Rome to render an account to Tiberius.[36]

Tacitus, relating the atrocities Nero perpetrated on the Christians, mentions the fact that Christ, from whom the name "Christian" derived, was put to death under Tiberius by the procurator Pontius Pilate.[37] Little is known of Pilate except that which is derived from the new Testament and from the Jewish writers, Philo of

Two sides of the same bronze coin from the procuratorship of Pontius Pilate (year 17 of Tiberius Caesar, A.D. 30-31)

Alexandria and Josephus. The fact that he was able to rule the Jews for a decade in the light of the extreme difficulty of his task argues for some administrative talents. His role at the trial of Jesus, while weak and compromising, displays beneath his outward actions traces at least of the older Roman virtue of love for justice. Only when he discovered that the doing of justice imperiled his position did he reluctantly give in to the demands of the Jews, whose bigotry and hypocrisy he utterly despised. Although his cowardice caused him to act against his conscience and deeper moral sense, yet he still had compunction and a sense of moral rightness. He was guilty, but as a pagan Roman less so than the Jewish leaders to whom he yielded.

3. Herod, Tetrarch of Galilee

Together with the emperor Tiberius and the procurator Pontius Pilate, in presenting the political complexion of Palestine-Syria at the time of the beginning of the ministry of Jesus' forerunner, John, Luke mentions "Herod the tetrarch of Galilee" (Luke 3:1, 2). This is Herod Antipas, son of Herod the Great by Malthace, a Samaritan woman, and therefore not even a "half-Jew" like his father. He was tetrarch of Galilee and Peraea from 4 B.C. to A.D. 39. This is the Herod who ruled during Jesus' youth and public ministry, and hence is referred to

[36]*Antiquities* XVIII, 4, 1-2.
[37]*Annals* XV, 44.

more frequently in the New Testament than any other of the Herods who reigned.

He it was who outraged his Jewish subjects by incestuously marrying his niece, Herodias, former wife of his half-brother Philip, and revived the memory of the infamous cruelty of the house of Herod by murdering John the Baptist (Matthew 14:1-12). He it was who was "perplexed" about Jesus and expressed a desire "to see him" (Luke 9:7, 9). But Jesus was well aware of his crafty wickedness and sly treachery, calling him "that fox" (Luke 13:32) and characterizing his banefully evil influence as "the leaven of Herod" (Mark 8:15).

Herod Antipas is also the ruler to whom Pilate sent Jesus and who "set him at nought and mocked him, and arrayed him in a gorgeous robe, and sent him again to Pilate" (Luke 23:6-15). Because of their mutual dealings concerning Jesus, Pilate and Herod became fast friends (Luke 23:12). In Acts 4:27 Herod Antipas is again linked with Pontius Pilate, the Gentiles, and the people of Israel as being "gathered together" against God's "holy servant Jesus."

Herod's capital city was Sepphoris, located about four miles north of Nazareth. After Herod the Great's death in 4 B.C. zealots practically destroyed the site, which Herod Antipas restored. Galileans worked on Antipas' building operations there, which included an aqueduct and an amphitheater. Being so close to Nazareth, it is not impossible that Joseph the carpenter or even the lad Jesus might have worked there.

About A.D. 26, however, Herod Antipas built Tiberias, a new capital on the southwestern shore of the Lake of Galilee near the warm springs of Hamath and not far from Sennabris (present-day Sinn en Nabra) and less than a half-dozen miles from Beth Yerah at the outlet of the lake. On the southern end of modern Tiberias are old ruins, but later than Antipas' day. However, ruins of what may prove to be Herod's palace exist on the hill known as *Qasr bint el melek*, or "Castle of the King's Daughter." Tiberias was accordingly a newly-found city in Jesus' day, with few if any Jews in residence, since it was considered ceremonially unclean, because Herod Antipas had erected it on the site of an old burial ground. This may explain why Tiberias is not recorded as being the scene of any ministry of Jesus.

Some scholars[38] connect the imprisonment and death of John the Baptist with Tiberias to fit the details of the gospel accounts (Matthew 14:3-12; Mark 6:17-29; Luke 3:19, 20), while Josephus places these events at the remote fortress of Machaerus some five miles east of the Dead Sea in the extreme southern frontier of Peraea, in a barren and almost inaccessible location, "a very inconvenient

38Cf. Emil Kraeling, *Rand McNally Bible Atlas*, p. 385f.

place to which to bring the Galileans for a birthday party."[39] This formidably strong fortress (second only to Jerusalem in strength, in Pliny's opinion) originally built by Alexander Jannaeus (103-76 B.C.), was destroyed by Pompey's general Gabinius in 63 B.C., but was impressively rebuilt by Herod the Great. The German traveler Seetzen discovered the place in the early Nineteenth Century, but the site is as yet archaeologically unexplored. However, its ancient name is still preserved in the present-day designation, el-Mekawer. From the ancient fortress of Machaerus Herod's first wife escaped to her father Aretas, king of Nabataeans, who thereafter became the tetrarch's deadly enemy. Herod suffered banishment to Gaul around A.D. 39, and Herodias voluntarily accompanied him.

4. Philip, Tetrarch of the Region of Iturea and Trachonitis

This Herod, known as Herod Philip II, is generally styled Philip the Tetrarch. He was the son of Herod the Great by Cleopatra of Jerusalem, and according to the will the aged Herod rewrote a few days before his death in 4 B.C., Philip inherited Gaulonitis, Trachonitis, Batanaea and Paneas. Gaulonitis lay east of the Sea of Galilee and Galilee proper. Batanaea was situated east of Gaulonitis. Trachonitis lay northeast of Batanaea toward Damascus. Auranitis lay south of Trachonitis. Paneas was the district about the southern foothills of Mt. Hermon. Luke employs abbreviated geographical terminology to refer to Philip's kingdom, introducing the term Iturea, which was situated southeast of Mt. Hermon and was well-known as an independent kingdom in Maccabaean times.

Thus Philip ruled over a territory bounded on the north by Mt. Hermon, on the northwest by Phoenicia, on the southwest by Galilee, on the south by the Decapolis and in the southeast, east and northeast by the kingdom of the Nabataeans. Philip's subjects were principally Gentiles. He ruled with discretion and integrity for almost four decades (4 B.C.-A.D. 34), perhaps the best of Herod the Great's sons.

Among Philip's accomplishments was his rebuilding of the city of Panias (Paneas), renaming it Caesarea to honor the emperor. It came to be known as Caesarea Philippi (Matthew 16:13; Mark 8:27) to distinguish it from Herod's metropolis on coastal Palestine founded in 22 B.C. Philip also enlarged and rebuilt Bethsaida, just east of the place where the Jordan River enters the Lake of Galilee, calling it Bethsaida Julias.

There is no record that Jesus' ministry extended into Philip's kingdom, except in the western portions contiguous to Galilee and the Jordan River, in the north of Caesarea Philippi, and in the southwest

[39]Kraeling, in. loc.

on the eastern shores of the Lake. The larger part of the kingdom being Gentile, it was outside the pale of His earthly ministry (cf. Matthew 15:24).

5. *Lysanias, Tetrarch of Abilene*

This tetrarchy was named from its capital Abila, which was situated on the Barada River some nineteen miles northwest of Damascus, where the present-day village of es-Suk stands. Nearby is a gorge with a Roman road cut in the cliff, an ancient cemetery and the traditional tomb of Abel.[40] The territory of Abilene accordingly lay north of Philip's realm.

An inscription at Abila, dating from the reign of Tiberius, mentions Lysanias as tetrarch at that time,[41] thus confirming Luke's statement. Luke's accuracy in distinguishing Abilene from Philip's tetrarchy is also confirmed extrabiblically. Some years later the tetrarchies were still separate, for the Emperor Caligula (37-41 B.C.) gave the "tetrarchy of Philip," by that time deceased, and the "tetrarchy of Lysanias" to Herod Agrippa,[42] and Emperor Claudius confirmed to him "Abila of Lysanias."[43]

6. *The High Priesthood of Annas and Caiaphas*

Annas, the Greek form of the Hebrew Hannaniah ("The Lord is gracious"), is called Annas by Josephus. He was appointed to his high priestly office by Quirinius, the governor of Syria, about A.D. 7, and deposed by Valerius Gratus, the procurator about A.D. 16. Annas had five sons, all of whom became high priests. He himself was the father-in-law of the high priest Caiaphas.[44]

Annas figures prominently in the trial and arrest of Jesus, although at that time he was no longer actually officiating as high priest, but still bore the title and exercised great influence by virtue of his age and prestige. To him Jesus was first conducted (John 18:13) and after being examined by him was sent bound to Caiaphas. Later Annas was prominent among the Jewish dignitaries who examined Peter and John when they were arrested (Acts 4:6).

Joseph Caiaphas was appointed to the office of high priest by the procurator Valerius Gratus, the immediate predecessor of Pontius Pilate, and is prominent in the events that led to Jesus' condemnation, and death (John 11:49-53; 18:14). At his official residence the conference of chief priests, scribes, and elders assembled to devise means

---

[40]The tradition doubtless arose purely from the coincidental similarity of sound between Abila and Abel. Abila is apparently derived from Semitic *'abel*, "a meadow."

[41]John D. Davis, *A Dictionary of the Bible* (4th rev. ed., 1954), p. 5.

[42]Josephus *Antiquities* XVIII, 6, 10. This Herod was the Herod of Acts 12.

[43]*Antiquities* XIX, 5, 1.

[44]John 18:13; *Antiquities* XVIII, 2, 1 and 2.

to arrest Jesus (Matthew 26:3-5). Like his father-in-law, Annas, he was not only deeply culpable in the matter of condemning Jesus, but also in the trial of the apostles, Peter and John, who were brought before him (Acts 4:6). Vitellius, the legate of Syria, deposed Caiaphas in A.D. 36.[45]

[45]*Antiquities* XVIII, 4, 2.

Chapter 4

The Dead Sea Scrolls and the Ministry of John and Jesus

Much interest in Biblical archaeology has been aroused in the last decade and a half by remarkable and widely publicized manuscript discoveries in the Dead Sea area of Palestine. Since 1947, when the first batch of manuscripts came to the notice of the scholarly world, having been stumbled upon quite accidentally by a Bedouin shepherd who found them in an isolated cave in the limestone cliffs less than a mile north of Khirbet Qumran, the archaeological world has been set agog as a result of the historical, biblical, and philological importance of the new material, augmented by subsequent finds (1947-1953) at Qumran, Wadi Murrabb'at, and Khirbet Mird in the region northwest of the Dead Sea.

One reason contributing to the significance of the Scrolls for biblical studies, particularly in elucidating the backgrounds of the New Testament, is their date. Three lines of evidence converge to demonstrate that they have been correctly dated by W. F. Albright and other competent palaeographers well before A.D. 70.[1]

The first line of evidence is the *palaeographic.* The stylistic formation of the letters employed by the various scribes in the recovered scrolls represents a period of more than a century, the letters themselves being intermediate between the known script of the third century B.C. and the middle of the first century A.D. "All competent students of writing conversant with the available materials and with palaeographic method" date the Scrolls "in the 250 years before A.D. 70."[2]

The second line of proof supporting a date 200 B.C. to A.D. 70 is

---

[1]W. F. Albright, "The Bible After Twenty Years of Archaeology 1932-1952" in *Religion in Life* XXI, 4, 1952, p. 540.
[2]Albright, *op. cit.,* p. 540; cf. John C. Trever in *The Biblical Archaeologist* II (1948), pp. 46 f.; Albright in the *Bulletin of the American Schools of Oriental Research* 115 (Oct., 1949), pp. 10-19; Solomon A. Birnbaum, *Bulletin of the American Schools of Oriental Research* 115 (Oct., 1949), pp. 20-22 and in the Bulletin's *Supplementary Studies* 13-14 (1952); also Birnbaum's *The Hebrew Scripts* (1954). For a table of the letters of the Hebrew alphabet as written in the scrolls, cf. E. L. Sukenik, editor, *The Dead Sea Scrolls of the Hebrew University,* p. 40.

the evidence from the carbon 14 test, which dates the linen in which the scrolls were wrapped to the general era 175 B.C. to A.D. 225.[3]

The third line of evidence substantiating an early date for the scrolls is *archaeological*. The pottery from Cave 1, including two intact jars as well as a mass of potsherds, belongs to the end of the Hellenistic period (first century B.C.), while additional pieces were dated in the Roman period in the second or third centuries A.D.[4]

Scholars now posit three periods for the Qumran manuscripts. (1) An archaic period (c. 200-150 B.C.), (2) a Hasmonaean period (150 B.C.-30 B.C.), and (3) a Herodian period (c. 30 B.C. to A.D. 70).[5] The vast majority of the Qumran manuscripts are now adjudged to belong to the second and third periods, especially to the latter half of the second period and the latter part of the third period when activity at Khirbet Qumran was at its height.[6] Other finds from later caves date in part from the second century A.D.

The established early date of the Dead Sea manuscripts notably enhance their value. They come from a period of immense significance, which connects the New Testament with the Old, and which has contained serious gaps in matters of history, particularly with regard to interbiblical background and the era of John the Baptist and Jesus. These new discoveries add a flood of light and broaden the horizons of New Testament religious and cultural history.

I. THE CONTENTS OF THE DEAD SEA SCROLLS

The contents of the new manuscripts from the Dead Sea caves are partly biblical and partly intertestamental.

1. *The Contents of the Scrolls from Cave 1 at Qumran*

Perhaps the most important find from Qumran is the Isaiah Scroll (1QIs[a]).[7] This is a parchment twenty-four feet long and approxi-

---

[3]Cf. Ovid R. Sellers, "Radiocarbon Dating of Cloth from the 'Ain Feshka Cave" in the *Bulletin of the American Schools of Oriental Research* 123 (Oct. 1951), pp. 24 f. *Annual of the Department of Antiquities of Jordan* 1 (1951), p. 6.

[4]*The Dead Sea Scrolls of the Hebrew University*, E. L. Sukenik, editor, p. 20; R. de Vaux, "Fouilles au Khirbet Qumran" in *Revue Biblique* LXI, 1954, pp. 231-236.

[5]Frank M. Cross, Jr., "The Oldest Manuscripts from Qumran," *Journal of Biblical Literature* LXXIV, Sept. 1955, p. 164.

[6]Cross, *ibid.*; also "The Manuscripts of the Dead Sea Caves," in *The Biblical Archaeologist* XVII, 1 (Feb. 1954), p. 20.

[7]According to a system of abbreviations adopted internationally by scholars, the material on which the writing is found is indicated by "p" for papyrus, "cu" for cuprum, copper, "o" for ostracon, and no sign indicating leather. The place of discovery is shown, 1 Q meaning cave 1 at Qumran. The contents of the document are indicated by regular abbreviations for the canonical and apocryphal books. A commentary is shown by "p" (*pesher*). New works are designated by the letter of the first word as it occurs in Hebrew, e.g. "S" (*serek*) meaning "order" or "rule," refers to the Manual of Discipline (1 QS). "The War of the Sons of Light With the Sons of Darkness" (IQM, from *milhamah* meaning "War").

mately ten inches high, containing practically the entire book of Isaiah in a high state of preservation.[8] It comprises a text remarkably similar to the standard Masoretic Text of the Hebrew Bible which goes back to the early tenth century A.D. textual tradition.

Another important find from Qumran is the Habakkuk Commentary (1QpHab),[9] a roll about four and a half feet long and somewhat less than six inches wide, containing chapters 1 and 2 of Habakkuk's prophecy with accompanying comments.

A third document, now known as a Genesis Apocryphon (1QApoc),[10] is an Aramaic rendering of several chapters of the book of Genesis with a number of legendary stories interwoven into the lives of the patriarchs. The roll measures some nine feet in length and is twelve inches wide. It was unrolled with extreme difficulty because of the poor condition in which it was found.

The scroll named "The War of the Sons of Light with The Sons of Darkness" (IQM)[11] is more than nine feet in length and six inches in width and describes a victorious conflict engaged in by the Israelite tribes with their enemies called the Kittim.

Another work from the Qumran collection is the so-called "Manual of Discipline" or "Rule of the Community" (1QS).[12] This parchment roll, measuring more than six feet in length and about nine inches in height, contains the rules and regulations which guided the pre-Christian sect of Essenic Judaism which flourished at Qumran.

Another scroll from Qumran is composed of "Thanksgiving Psalm," called in Hebrew *Hodayot* (1QH),[13] very similar to the canonical Psalms. The extant scroll is fragmentary, preserved in three

[8]*The Dead Sea Scrolls of St. Mark's Monastery I, The Isaiah Manuscript and The Habakkuk Commentary*, ed., Millar Burrows (1950).
[9]*The Dead Sea Scrolls of St. Mark's Monastery I, The Isaiah Manuscript and The Habakkuk Commentary;* translated by Millar Burrows, *The Dead Sea Scrolls* (1955), pp. 365-370; Theodore Gaster, *The Dead Sea Scriptures in English Translation* (1956).
[10]Nahum Avignad and Yigael Yadin, *A Genesis Apocryphon, A Scroll from the Wilderness of Judaea, Description and Contents of the Scroll, Facsimiles, Transcription and Translation of* Columns II, XIX-XXII, translated by Millar Burrows, *More Light on the Dead Sea Scrolls* (1958), pp. 387-393.
[11]E. L. Sukenik, editor, *The Dead Sea Scrolls of the Hebrew University* (1955); translated by Theodore H. Gaster, *The Dead Sea Scrolls in English Translation* (1956), pp. 281-301.
[12]Millar Burrows, editor, *The Dead Sea Scrolls of St. Mark's Monastery II, Facsimile 2, Plates and Transcription of the Manual of Discipline* (1951); William H. Brownlee, *The Dead Sea Manual of Discipline, Bulletin of the American Schools of Oriental Research, Supplementary Studies* 10-12 (1951); P. Wernberg-Moeller, *The Manual of Discipline Translated and Annotated with an Introduction*, J. Van der Ploeg, editor, *Studies on the Texts of the Desert of Judah* 1 (1957).
[13]E. L. Sukenik, editor, *The Dead Sea Scrolls of the Hebrew University* (1955); Theodore H. Gaster, *The Dead Sea Scriptures in English Translation* (1956), pp. 123-202.

separate leather leaves and seventy separate pieces. It was originally a roll about six feet long and thirteen inches high.

In addition to the first Isaiah scroll (1QIs^a), a second copy of the book of Isaiah was also recovered at Qumran (1QIs^b).[14] Unlike the first scroll, this second scroll of Isaiah is not complete. It is in a much poorer state of preservation, with chapters 38-66 better preserved than chapters 1-37. However, like the first Isaiah Scroll, it is surprisingly similar to the Masoretic text of the Hebrew Bible dating a millennium later.

From Cave 1 at Qumran have also come portions of the book of Daniel on three small pieces of leather (1Q71, 72).[15] Also as the result of the excavation of cave 1 by R. de Vaux and G. Lankester Harding in 1949, numerous fragments of biblical texts in Hebrew and Aramaic have been recovered (including Genesis, Exodus, Leviticus, Deuteronomy, Judges, Samuel, Psalms, Micah and Zephaniah, besides several apocryphal books, etc.). Pottery finds were sufficient to reconstruct forty large jars twenty-four inches tall and ten inches in diameter, such as originally held the cache of scrolls.[16]

2. Contents of the Scrolls from Other Qumran Caves

In 1952 a series of other caves in the general area of Cave 1 at Qumran were discovered. Cave 2 (2Q) yielded fragments of Exodus, Leviticus, Numbers, Deuteronomy, Ruth, Psalms, Jeremiah, and Jubilees, and bits of numerous non-biblical books. Cave 3 yielded, besides fragments of a dozen manuscripts, an interesting document listing the hiding places of some sixty caches of treasure over Palestine. This enigmatic scroll was bound in copper, finally opened in 1956 in England, and returned to the Jordan Museum in Amman. Whether it is a compilation of folklore concerning the burial place of ancient treasure hordes or a directory of treasures hidden away by the Essene communities, has not been determined.[17]

Caves 4, 5 and 6 in the Qumran area were discovered later in 1952. Caves 5 and 6 contained comparatively few manuscript fragments, but Cave 4 (4Q) proved a sensational find, eclipsing even the remarkable discoveries of the original Cave 1, and yielding tens of thousands of fragments of manuscripts. From 1952-1956 painstaking work assembling and identifying these manuscripts was in progress, with the happy result that some 330 manuscripts have been identified, about 90 of which are biblical books. All the books of the Old Testa-

[14]Sukenik, op. cit.

[15]D. Barthélemy and J. T. Milik, Discoveries in the Judaean Desert, I, Qumran Cave 1 (1955), pp. 49-155.

[16]Barthélemy and Milik, op. cit., I, pp. 8-17.

[17]Cf. A. Dupont-Sommer, Revue de l'histoire des religions 151 (1957), pp. 22-36.

ment are represented with the sole exception of Esther. Of unusual significance is a copy of Samuel (4QSamᵃ), which is more than eighty percent complete. Its unusual feature is that it follows the Septuagint rather than the Hebrew Text, differing in this case from the Isaiah Scrolls from Qumran, which closely follow the Masoretic tradition.[18]

The Dead Sea from the Dead Sea Hotel. Courtesy Rev. Thomas Roth

Cave 4 at Qumran also yielded five manuscripts of books of the Pentateuch, ten of Psalms, twelve of Isaiah, and seven of the Book of the Twelve Prophets, besides fragments of the book of Ecclesiastes (4Q Qohᵃ), inscribed in a middle second century B.C. script, showing that at least by this date this critically disputed book was accepted by the Qumranites.[19] Numerous other works are represented in the rich find of fragments in Cave 4 at Qumran, and other caves in the region are adding new material to the incredible store already in the Palestine Archaeological Museum in Jerusalem and elsewhere.

[18]Cf. Frank M. Cross, Jr., in the *Bulletin of the American Schools of Oriental Research* 141 (Feb. 1956), pp. 9-13.
[19]Cf. James Muilenberg in the *Bulletin of the American Schools of Oriental Research* 135 (Oct. 1954), pp. 20-28.

3. The Contents of the Scrolls from the Caves of Wadi Murrabb'at and Khirbet Mird

Four large caves at Wadi Murrabb'at about a dozen miles south of Qumran, yielded a number of Aramaic and Greek business documents and several letters written in Hebrew on papyrus. They were excavated in 1952 by an expedition of the Jordan Department of Antiquities, the École Biblique in Jerusalem, and the Palestine Archaeological Museum. Two of these documents turned out to be written by the leader of the Second Revolt, Simeon ben Kosiba (Bar Kokhba). Fragments of biblical books include Genesis, Exodus, Deuteronomy, and Isaiah, containing a text practically identical with the Masoretic Text. Since some of the Qumran manuscripts differ from the Masoretic Hebrew, the new material has important bearings on the question of the transmission of the sacred text.

Farther south of Qumran, some four miles northeast of the Mar Saba Monastery in the Wadi en-Nar, is located the ancient ruin of Khirbet Mird, the site of the Hasmonaean fortress of Hyrcania, rebuilt by Herod the Great. In 1952 manuscripts were discovered in this region by the indefatigably active Bedouin, and an expedition of the University of Louvain in 1953 located the source at Khirbet Mird. This site yielded fragments of the Wisdom of Solomon in Greek uncials, fragments of Mark, John, and Acts dating from the fifth to the eighth centuries, as well as Christo-Palestinian Syriac fragments of Joshua, Matthew, Luke, Acts, and Colossians. The manuscript discoveries at Khirbet Mird are, therefore, much later than those at Qumran,[20] but highly important in their own right.

II. THE QUMRAN COMMUNITY AND THE ESSENES

Among important results of the manuscript finds and the excavations in the Dead Sea area have been the discovery not only of a substantial literature shedding light on the rules and practices of the Essenes, one of the most important sects of Judaism at the time next to the Pharisees and Sadducees, but also the discovery and exploration of the center of the sect on the western shore of the Dead Sea about seven miles south of Jericho, known as Khirbet Qumran. Within a few years this ruin (Khirbeh) of an ancient monastic community has become one of the most publicized sites in Palestine because of the phenomenal manuscript finds taking place in the cave-dotted cliffs around it since 1947.

[20]Charles T. Fritsch, The Qumran Community, Its History and Scrolls (1956), p. 51.

1. *Khirbet Qumran, Headquarters of the Essenes*

The recovery of the Manual of Discipline or Rule of the Community (1QS) among the initial discoveries in Cave 1 at Qumran sparked intense interest in the nearby ruin to ascertain whether it had connections with the hiding and preservation of the cave-deposited manuscripts, and more particularly whether the Manual of Discipline describes a sect of monastic Judaism of the time called Essenes, well-known in antiquity from the writings of Philo, Josephus, and Pliny, which may have had its headquarters there.

In 1949 when G. Lankester Harding, Director of the Jordan Government Department of Antiquities and R. de Vaux, Director of the École Biblique in Jerusalem, were exploring Cave 1 at Qumran, which had yielded the first sensational batch of manuscripts, their attention was directed to the ruins on the plateau about a mile farther south, which Clermont-Ganneau had examined in 1873-1874, and of which he had left the first authentic description of its pottery, walls, and adjacent cemetery.[21]

De Vaux and Harding's systematic excavations at the site of the Kirbeh from 1951-1956 have fully verified the place as the center of Essenic Judaism, and by the aid of recovered coins, pottery, and architectural remains, the story of Khirbet Qumran's occupation can now be told. Four periods in the later history of the site are traced. The first extends from its evident founding (c. 110 B.C.) under John Hyrcanus (135-104 B.C.), since numerous coins of this ruler were dug up as well as of other Hasmonaean rulers through Antigonus (40-37 B.C.), the last ruler of this line, to the seventh year of Herod (31 B.C.) when a severe earthquake apparently leveled the site.[22] During the main part of Herod's reign, indications are that the place was abandoned.

Period two at Qumran dates from its rebuilding and enlargement about the year A.D. 1,[23] to its destruction by the Roman Tenth legion in June A.D. 68. During this period in the lifetime of Jesus, John the Baptist, and the early Christian apostles, the Qumran Community flourished and had its influence upon them as upon Judaism and the early Christian Church in general. Many of the 750 coins recovered from Qumran date from the time of Archelaus (4 B.C.-A.D. 6) and the

---

[21]C. Clermont-Ganneau, *Archaeological Researches in Palestine During the Years 1873-1874*, II (1896), pp. 14, 15; cf. G. Dalman, "Chirbet Kumran" in *Palästinajahrbuch* X (1914), p. 10; XVI (1920), p. 40. Dalman perspicaciously reasoned that the ruins were a military outpost of Roman times.

[22]Cf. Josephus *Antiquities* XV, 5, 2; XIX, 3; cf. Charles T. Fritsch for a discussion of the evidence for non-occupation during Herod's reign in *Journal of Biblical Literature* 74 (1955), pp. 22-25. Only a single coin from Herod's reign was found; cf. also Fritsch, *The Qumran Community*, pp. 22-25.

[23]Fritsch, *The Qumran Community*, p. 14.

Roman procurators down to the second year of the First Jewish Revolt (A.D. 66-70). A few are from Caesarea and Dora (dated A.D. 67-68) under Nero, attesting that the Roman army which took Jericho in June A.D. 68, likewise took Qumran, as one coin marked with an X, belonging to the Tenth Legion, as well as iron arrowheads and a layer of burnt ash discovered in the excavations, demonstrate.

Some scholars suggest that the monastic community at Qumran at this time may have been allied with the Zealots who led the rebellion against Rome,[24] or actually are to be identified with this group.[25] At any rate, Qumran fell to Roman occupation and some of the coins inscribed *Judaea Capta* and dating from the reign of Titus (A.D. 79-81) mark period three as that of Roman occupation after Jerusalem's destruction in A.D. 70. In addition, evidence that the Qumran structures were converted into army barracks seems to indicate that a Roman garrison was stationed there from A.D. 68 to c. 100 A.D., when the site was again abandoned.

| Artist's drawing of Judaea guarded by a soldier under a palm tree, inscribed "Judaea Capta S. C." From a coin minted at Rome, A.D. 71 | Bronze coin from Second Revolt (123-135 A.D.) during Hadrian's reign when Jerusalem was rebuilt by Aelia Capitolina. Jupiter and two attendant deities |

Period four at Qumran is marked by the reoccupation of the site during the Second Jewish Revolt (A.D. 132-135). Thirteen coins dating from this period, found at the bottom of the tower where Jewish patriots made their last stand, indicate that the Jews employed this isolated place as a fortress in their final futile attempt to drive the Romans from their country. Thereafter Qumran knew Arab shepherds on their way to water their flocks at the waters of 'Ain Feshka, spo-

[24]Cf. H. H. Rowley in the *Bulletin of the John Rylands Library, Manchester* 40 (1957-1958), p. 144.
[25]Cecil Roth, *Commentary* 24 (1957), pp. 317-324.

radic temporary encampments in later times being indicated by a sprinkling of Byzantine and Arabic coins.[26]

2. Buildings and Other Installations of the Essenes at Qumran.

The main community structure was a building 100 feet by 120 feet, which formed the nucleus of a complex of rooms and cisterns.[27] The northwest corner of this central structure was occupied by a massive defense tower with three-feet thick walls reinforced by stone embankments. A cache of coins from the time of the Second Jewish Revolt found in one of the secret chambers attests to its use as a bastion to the end of Qumran's history.

A room with several fireplaces east of the tower evidently was the community's kitchen, while rooms to the southwest of the tower served as assembly halls or refectories, a low, carefully plastered bench along the four sides of one of them suggesting a meeting place of the sect.

Alongside this meeting room in the largest hall of the main building was the scriptorium, containing pieces which, when patiently assembled in the Palestine Museum in Jerusalem, turned out to be a long narrow table and a companion bench. Two inkwells of the Roman period, one of which actually contained some dried ink, indicate that here the manuscripts had been copied by the community's scribes. A little platform with cupped-out basins also found in the debris was doubtless employed for ritual washings by the scribes when copying the sacred texts.

To the south of the main building was a large room, twenty-two feet in length, probably a dining hall for the communal meal, since what was evidently a pantry adjoined it, in which were stacked against the wall more than a thousand bowls.

In the southwest part of the main building were two cisterns or artificial reservoirs, carefully constructed and plastered. One of these cisterns contains fourteen steps leading into the pool, railed off into four passages, as if to conduct people into it for baptisms and ablutions.[28] Yet of the approximately forty cisterns and reservoirs at Qumran, the bulk of them at least must have been used purely for storage in the hot arid climate where the very life of the community depended

[26]Charles Fritsch, The Qumran Community: Its History and Scrolls (1956), pp. 19-20.

[27]For an account of the excavations at Khirbet Qumran (1951-1956), see R. de Vaux in Revue Biblique 60 (1953), pp. 83-106; 61 (1954), pp. 206-236; Fritsch, op. cit., pp. 1-25; James L. Kelso in Journal of Biblical Literature 74 (1955), pp. 141-146.

[28]This is the interpretation of Fritsch, op. cit., pp. 5-8, who quotes from the Qumran literature to show that the Qumranites were a baptizing sect. But it is difficult to imagine that water in sufficient quantities could be stored purely for bodily immersions, especially when ritually clean water was stipulated.

on an adequate water supply. The spring at 'Ain Feshka, and the Jordan not prohibitively distant, provided abundant fresh water for these purposes. All the water, however, for the intricate system at Qumran was conducted across the plateau by a stone aqueduct, traces of which can still be discerned.

Ruins at Qumran. Courtesy of Dr. John F. Walvoord

The cemetery adjacent to the Qumran Community, containing approximately one thousand graves, was the burial ground of the sect. R. de Vaux excavated about a score of these tombs, which are notable for their lack of any jewelry or finery, as would be expected from the ascetic monastic sect, and for the orientation of the corpse north and south and not east and west, which the Clermont-Ganneau explorations (1873-74) had determined were at least non-Moslem burials.[29] Potsherds in the grave fill also point to the fact that the cemetery is coeval with the existence of the Qumran Essene Community. As far as excavations have been conducted, the main cemetery consists of adult male skeletal remains, but women and children are interred in adjacent similar burial areas.[30]

3. Khirbet Qumran and the Essenes

That the Jewish ascetic community at Qumran is to be identified with the important reformatory movement in first century Judaism

[29]Clermont-Ganneau, *op. cit.*, pp. 15, 16.
[30]Cf. R. deVaux in *Revue Biblique* 63 (1956), pp. 569-572.

known as the Essenes[31] is indicated by the similarity of location and of attested practice at the Qumran Community with what is known of this group from Josephus, Philo, and Pliny.[32] Pliny locates them in precisely the spot where Qumran is situated "on the west side of the Dead Sea." He also speaks of "the town of Engedi" as "lying below the Essenes," by which he obviously means south of them, with Masada next in order from north to south.[33]

Philo extols their moral virtues, their industry, their rejection of slavery and covetuous commerce, their communal life with a common treasury and common meal. He calls them "Essenes or holy ones."[34] In his "Apology for the Jews," fragmentarily preserved in Eusebius' *Praeparatio Evangelica*, Philo says of the Essenes, "The test of their freedom is their life. Not one of them can abide to be possessor of anything whatever as his own private property . . . but once for all they lay all down in the midst, and reap their harvest from the common prosperity of all."[35]

Josephus stresses the unselfish and industrious communality of the Essenes, their love for honest toil, their devotion, their being clothed in white, the probationary three-year period before admission to the sect, and their strict discipline when one of their number falls into serious sin.[36]

In *The Antiquities of the Jews* Josephus mentions their lustrations, their number (4,000), their celibacy, their piety, their belief in the immortality of the soul and the rewards of righteousness.[37]

When the descriptions of the Essenes given by Philo and Josephus are compared with the teachings and practices of the Qumran sect, many striking similarities are immediately obvious, which make it difficult to escape the conclusion that the Qumranites were Essenes, or at least a closely related group. For example, communal life was practiced by the two groups, both emphasizing community of goods and the common meal. Both sects abhorred slavery and practiced equality, each member in the Qumran Community being free to ex-

[31]Probably derived from the Aramaic *hese* "pure, holy." Philo connects the term with the Greek noun *hosiotēs* "holiness" and says the name Essene is given these people "because they have shown themselves especially devout in the service of God . . ." (*Every Good Man Is Free*, trans. F. H. Colson in *Loeb Classical Library* IX, 53-63); for twenty-five different entymologies of the word, cf. K. Cook, *The Fathers of Jesus* (2 vols., London, 1886), II, pp. 48-49.
[32]Cf. H. H. Rowley, *The Zadokite Fragments and the Dead Sea Scrolls* (1952), pp. 78f., and in *Theologische Zeitschrift* 13 (1957), pp. 530-540; A. Dupont-Sommer, *The Jewish Sect of Qumran and the Essenes*, tr. R. D. Barnett (1954).
[33]*Natural History* V, XV in the Loeb Classical Library, II, 277.
[34]Philo, *Every Good Man Is Free* IX, pp. 53-63.
[35]VIII, 11 translated by K. Cook, *The Fathers of Jesus* II, 5-8.
[36]*Jewish War* II, 8.
[37]XVIII, 1, 5.

press his opinion and vote in the common session (1QS, VI, 19). The manner of initiation into the sect is strikingly similar in Josephus and at Qumran (1QS, V, 1 to VI, 23). Disciplinary dealing with sin is much the same in both groups (1QS, VIII, 20 to IX, 2). A notable parallel is the ban against spitting, stated so plainly in Josephus and also in the Qumran Manual (VII, 13). The special interest of the Essenes in the Bible and in ancient literature, reflected in Philo and Josephus, is attested by the large library discovered at Qumran. Not only did they meticulously copy sacred literature but carefully preserved it. It may yet prove true that such extracanonical books as Enoch, Jubilees, The Assumption of Moses, and the Testaments of the Twelve Patriarchs are Essenic in origin, a theory held by certain scholars long before the Qumran literature was discovered.[38]

However, identification of the Qumran sect with the Essenes is not without some difficulties. Both Philo and Josephus relate a number of details concerning the Essenes which are not mentioned in the documents from Qumran — for example, the Essene custom of rising before dawn and praying toward the East, although morning and evening prayers are mentioned (I QS, X, 10). Josephus declares the Essene novitiate received a loin cloth (for bathing), a hatchet (to bury his excrement), and a white garment as wearing apparel. None of these is mentioned in the Qumran sectarian document dealing with the rules of admission to the community (1 QS, VI, 13-23). Philo strongly asserts the Essenes had nothing to do with arms or fighting, but this seems at variance with the militant sect of 1 QM describing the conflict between the children of light and the children of darkness. But Qumran's military handbook may belong to an earlier period of the sect (the Maccabaean struggles) or may have a spiritual and eschatological sense. The more pacifistic Essenes of Philo may have belonged to a later time, and the militaristically inclined members of the party no doubt left the Essenes and joined the Zealots who led the open revolt against Rome.

But an overall study of the similarities between the organization and doctrines of the Essenes and the Qumran Community far outweigh the differences, and these differences evidently can be attributed either to prejudiced and faulty reporting by Philo and Josephus or to present inadequate knowledge of the history and teachings of the Qumran sect. It is therefore to be concluded that the Qumran Community is to be identified with the Essenes as presented by Philo, Josephus, and Pliny.[39]

[38]Cf. A. Dupont-Sommer, *The Dead Sea Scrolls*, pp. 94, 95.
[39]Fritsch, *op. cit.*, pp. 107-110.

4. *The Qumran Manual of Discipline and the Zadokite Document*

Since the discovery of the Qumran Manual of Discipline in 1947, it has become increasingly clear that this document has very close affinity with an older work found in 1896 in the *genizah* or storeroom of a medieval synagogue in Cairo, Egypt, and known as The Cairo Document of the Damascus Covenanters (CD) or more briefly, the Zadokite Document.[40] The Zadokite Document tells of the "sons of Zadok," Jews who migrated to Damascus, and under the leadership of the "Star" organized the Party of the New Covenant or Covenanters of Damascus. This Zadokite work, consisting of two parts — (1) the origin and migration of the Covenanters (chaps. 1-9) and (2) the regulations of the sect (10-20) — describes a "teacher of righteousness" whom God raised up to lead the group in a solemn covenant they made to separate from evil of every sort. Alongside the "teacher of righteousness" is his antagonist, the wicked priest or "man of lies," terms which probably could be used to designate the representative of the true priesthood of the sect and the false priesthood of the Jewish Temple at any time between the Maccabaean struggle and the fall of the house of the Hasmonaeans.[41] It seems that both documents set forth the underlying struggle between the sect and the corrupt Jerusalem priesthood, but evidently apply to different phases of the conflict.

A comparison of the organization and teaching of the Qumran Community with the Community of the Covenant (Damascus Covenanters) closely relates the two groups, if not actually equates them as identical. However, because of certain differences[42] it appears that the Zadokite Document and the Qumran Manual of Discipline represent different stages in the development of the one sect. It is significant, therefore, that an actual fragment of the Zadokite Document (6QD) was found at Qumran.

[40]S. Schechter, ed., *Documents of Jewish Sectaries* (2 vols. New York, 1910) Vol. I *Fragments of a Zadokite Edited from Hebrew Manuscripts in the Cairo Genizah Collection now in Possession of the University Library, Cambridge, and Provided with an English Translation, Introduction and Notes* (1910); Chaim Rabin, *The Zadokite Documents* (1954).

[41]H. H. Rowley sets the scene under Antiochus Epiphanes and the Maccabaean revolt; *Bulletin of the John Rylands Library, Manchester* 40 (1957-1958), pp. 114-146; Frank M. Cross, Jr. places the allusions to the "teacher of righteousness" under Jonathan and Simon Maccabaeus (160-142 B.C.), *The Ancient Library of Qumran and Modern Biblical Studies* (1958), pp. 95-119. Cf. also W. H. Brownlee, "The Historical Allusions of the Dead Sea Habakkuk Midrash" *Bull. of the Am. Schs.* 125 (1952), pp. 10-20 for a list of the various views of the historical background of 1Qp Hab.

[42]For a full discussion of these see Fritsch, *op. cit.*, pp. 76-89.

III. THE DEAD SEA SCROLLS AND THE NEW TESTAMENT

Although the Dead Sea Scrolls have already proved of immense value in the area of Old Testament studies in dealing with the Hebrew text, Hebrew history, palaeography, literary criticism, etc., and in the intertestamental era in elucidating its life, history and literature, it is in the field of New Testament studies that the Qumranite and the Dead Sea literature are proving especially significant.[43]

1. The Qumran Community and John the Baptist

Luke gives a concise statement concerning the childhood and young manhood of John the Baptist which is now rich in suggestion in the light of the Essenic community at Qumran in the desert. "And the child grew and became strong in spirit, and he was in the wilderness till the day of his manifestation to Israel" (Luke 1:80). Since the home of John's parents was in "the hill country of Judaea" (Luke 1:39, 40, 65) and John is not said to have resided with them during this formative period, it is highly probable in the light of John's acquaintance with Essenic thought that he resided in the Qumran Community and received his theological education among them. He may actually have been adopted by them, in accordance with their custom of choosing out "other persons' children," while they were pliable, and fit for learning to train them in their doctrines and practices.[44] Whether this is true or not, he was at least cognizant of the group and influenced indirectly by them, as close parallels between his ministry and message and the Qumran Community attest.

Both John and the Qumranites feature Isaiah 40:3. "Now when these things come to pass in Israel to the Community, according to these rules, they will separate themselves from the midst of the session of perverse men to go to the wilderness to prepare there the way of HUHA (surrogate for Yahweh), as it is written: In the wilderness clear the way . . . make level in the desert a highway for our God" (QS, VIII, 12-14; Matthew 3:1-3; Mark 1:2, 3; Luke 3:4-6).

However, John evidently became convinced that the Essenes, although they were endeavoring to prepare themselves, were not preparing the nation for the advent of the Messiah, and so he must have broken with them, giving himself to an active ministry of preaching repentence and baptizing in the Jordan Valley. His message in featuring repentance (Matthew 3:2; Mark 1:4; Luke 3:3), moreover, struck also a vital note in the theology of the Qumranites who believed

[43]Cf. F. M. Cross, Jr. "The Scrolls and the New Testament" in *Christian Century* (Aug. 24, 1955).

[44]Cf. Josephus' statement of this custom among the Essenes (*Wars of the Jews* II, 8, 2); cf. also W. H. Brownlee, "John the Baptist in the New Light of Ancient Scrolls," in *Interpretation* IX (1955), pp. 71-90.

they belonged to a "covenant of repentance" (CDC, IX, 15b) and styled themselves "the penitents of Israel" (CDC, VI, 1; VIII, 8; IX, 24).

The baptism of repentance which John administered is also paralleled by the Qumranite sect among whom this rite was featured (1QS3:4-9; 5:13, 14). John's baptism was an outward indication of an inward spiritual repentance, enabling the recipients to recognize and receive the Messiah when He came. Qumranite baptism, however, was purely ritual and the recipients were enjoined to separate themselves rigidly from any who did not belong to their community.

The severe indictment of the Jewish nation, so salient a feature of John's rugged preaching (Matthew 3:7-9; Luke 3:7, 8), was also characteristic of the Qumran sect, who regarded all outside their community as "sons of darkness" belonging to the realm of Belial. Members of the sect were the true Israel living in accordance with the Torah, and they alone could be sanctified by purifying water, and for them alone the baptismal rite therefore could have any meaning (IQS, III, 8, 9).

Conspicuous also in John's message is the coming Messiah who would "baptize . . . with the Holy Spirit and with fire . . . " (Matthew 3:11), the baptism with fire being the judgment upon the unrepentant in an eschatological sense. Such a judgment of fire is graphically described in one of the Qumran hymns under the figure of a fiery river overflowing in wrath "on the outcasts" and in "the time of fury for all Belial."[45]

The baptism with the Holy Spirit, on the other hand, is prophesied by John to be the portion of those who would repent and receive the coming Messiah (John 1:33). In the Qumran literature not only does God "sprinkle upon him (the Messiah) the spirit of truth as purifying water so as to cleanse him from all abominations of falsehood and from being contaminated with the spirit of impurity" (1QS, IV, 22-32), but Messiah Himself sprinkles His people with His Holy Spirit, thus constituting them His anointed ones (CDC II, 9; 1QS, IX, 11).

But John differed from the Qumran Community not only in being intensely missionary and evangelistic in the proclamation of his Messianic message, whereas the Qumranites had no discernible program for adding new adherents, except adopting children to train in their ways, but also the Baptist stands in contrast to the Qumran sect in actually being vouchsafed the high honor of preparing the way for the true Messiah and being His forerunner. The members of the Qumran Community, in spite of their Messianic fervor and piety, never recog-

[45]For complete translation, see A. Dupont-Sommer, *op. cit.*, p. 73.

nized the Messiah when He came, insofar as is known. The ascetic, self-developing, unevangelistic movement they evolved in the desert became a dead-end street, for it never conducted them to the One whom John immediately recognized when He appeared as "the lamb of God, which taketh away the sin of the world" (John 1:29). But the piety and devoted loyalty of the group to God's laws were not fruitless, for one who was imbued with their teachings and expectation of the Messiah, and who may well have actually been a member of an Essenic group, was divinely privileged to prepare the way for the Lord's Anointed.

2. *The Qumran Community and Jesus the Messiah*

Although the Qumran Community had a well-defined Messianic doctrine like the Old Testament, yet they could not comprehend the combination of King and Priest in *one* Person (Psalm 110:1, 4; Zechariah 6:9-15) as their ancient Scriptures taught. Neither could they see in the union of the same one Person the additional office of Prophet, although they featured the prophecy of Deuteronomy 18:18, 19 in their literature. Their great priest was "Messiah of Aaron," their great military leader, the "Messiah of Israel." But the Prophet referred to in the Rule of the Community is set down alongside the "Messiahs of Aaron and Israel," apparently as a separate Messianic figure, emphasizing the fact that there is a radical difference in the Messianic concept as found in the Bible and that current among the members of the Qumran Community, although the latter's concept bears many striking similarities.[46]

In addition to the Messianic concepts at Qumran, there are many similarities between the organization and teachings of the Qumran group and the teachings of Jesus and the organization of the Christian Church.[47] For example, the passage in Matthew 18:15-17 concerning dealing with an erring brother has an interesting parallel in the Qumran literature, where there is also stipulated first a personal reproof, then a reproof before witnesses, and finally a reproof before the whole group or community (1QS, V, 25 to VI, 1). With the new material, the background of the gospel stories is much more richly illustrated. The Sermon on the Mount, the Last Supper, and numerous other aspects of the earthly life and ministry of Jesus are fitted into a larger framework of historical background material, and to that extent are better understood on the human side.

[46]Cf. L. H. Silberman, "The Two Messiahs of the Manual of Discipline" *Vetus Testamentum* V (1955), pp. 77-82.
[47]Cf. J. L. Teicher, "Jesus' Sayings in the Dead Sea Scrolls," *Journal of Jewish Studies* V (1954), p. 38. W. H. Brownlee, "The Cross of Christ in the Light of the Ancient Scrolls," *United Presbyterian* Nov. 30, Dec. 7, 14, 21 and 28, 1953; J. Daniélov, "Le Communauté de Qumran et l'organisation de l'Eglise ancienne," *Revue d'Histoire et de Philosophie Religieuse* XXXV (1955), 104-116.

3. The Dead Sea Scrolls and the Literary Criticism
of the New Testament

The phenomenal manuscript discoveries from the Dead Sea area have had a stabilizing effect upon the critical views of the date and authenticity of New Testament books. In the light of the new material, the New Testament appears as a Jewish book with a Christian theology with less Greek influence in its formation then Jewish, and there is reason to date the synotic gospels, beginning with Mark, between about A.D. 60 and 65.

The gospel of John is now shown to have been written about A.D. 80. The new Essene materials from the last century and a half preceding Jesus' ministry have decisively discredited the rationalistic criticism of the nineteenth century which customarily dated John's gospel about A.D. 150 or later, or the earlier twentieth century views that placed it between A.D. 90 and 130, thus effectually removing it from the authentic tradition of the apostolic age and treating it as essentially an apocryphal book.[48] That the fourth gospel reflects the genuine Jewish background of John the Baptist and Jesus and not that of a later second-century Gnostic milieu is clearly attested by the remarkably close parallels to the conceptual imagery of John's gospel in the Essenic literature from Qumran. Now on the basis of the new evidence, there is every sound reason to believe in the genuineness of John's gospel and "there is no reason to date the gospel after A.D. 90; it may be earlier."[49]

Another extremely significant archaeological find that adds its voice to the Dead Sea Scrolls in showing the unsoundness of making John's gospel a late production of a second century Gnostic environment is the recovery of thirteen codices containing some forty-nine Gnostic documents. In 1945 these were accidentally discovered in Upper Egypt at ancient Sheneset-Chenoboskion in the vicinity of Nag Hammadi thirty-two miles north of Luxor.[50] Written in Coptic, they date from the middle of the third century A.D. and apparently rest on Greek originals. These important documents include discussions of the nature of gospels, epistles, apocalypses and evidently belonged to a group of Gnostics initiated into the sects' doctrines. Among them is the Apocryphon, or Secret Book of John, purported to have been given by Jesus to John on Olivet[51] and containing typical Gnostic her-

---

[48]Cf. Lucetta Mowrey, "The Dead Sea Scrolls and the Background for the Gospel of John" in *The Biblical Archaeologist* XVII (Dec. 1954), pp. 78-97.
[49]W. F. Albright, "The Bible After Twenty Years of Archaeology," *Religion in Life* 21:4.
[50]Victor R. Gold in *The Biblical Archaeologist* 15 (1952), pp. 70-88.
[51]Three copies were recovered at Chenoboskion and another was already known in the Berlin Coptic Codex 8502 from the fifth century. See W. T. Till *Die gnostischen Schriften des koptischen Papyrus Berolinensis* 8502: *Texte und Untersuchungen zur Geschichte der altchristlichen Literatur* 60 (1955).

esy described by Irenaeus (A.D. c. 180) in his work, *Against Heresies.*[52] The new material from Sheneset-Chenoboskion, coupled with the evidence from Qumran, proves that Gnosticism is much later than the gospel of John, although the Gnostics based much of their teaching on the gospel.

Evidence is also available that helps to date the Pauline epistles from about 50 A.D. to the early 60's. Elders and bishops (overseers), once thought to be late, now must be considered early in the light of the Manual of Discipline from Qumran about 100 B.C., where leaders are mentioned, called overseers, and described in detail.

Both the catholic epistles (particularly Peter's second epistle) and the book of Hebrews may now be definitely dated before the destruction of Jerusalem in 70 A.D. The latter book apparently was penned to offset the Essenic idea of two anointed ones, one a prince and the other a priest, presenting the Christian and Old Testament doctrine (cf. Zechariah 6:9-15) that the Messiah would be king and priest in one person. Likewise, the book of the Revelation, although doubtless penned toward the end of the First Century, may now possibly be dated earlier (before A.D. 70) on the basis of its Hebraic background being illumined by evidence from the Dead Sea Scrolls.

4. *The Dead Sea Scrolls and the Gospel of Thomas*

It has been noted in the preceding section how the thirteen Coptic codices (containing forty-nine Gnostic treatises) from Nag Hammadi in Upper Egypt have had bearings on the literary criticism of the date and authenticity of the fourth gospel. But the significance of this phenomenal archaeological find extends far beyond this particular contribution to biblical studies and presents a discovery comparable in importance to the Dead Sea Scrolls (although not nearly so profusely publicized) and of even greater moment to students of the New Testament. Robert M. Grant says, "It may be that future historians of criticism will look on the fifties as the Dead Sea Age and the sixties as the age of Nag-Hammadi."[53]

Of all the documents from Nag-Hammadi, however, perhaps the most important is the Gospel of Thomas. Other apocryphal gospels of the second and third centuries are the Gospel of the Hebrews, the Gospel According to the Egyptians, the Gospel of Peter, the Gospel of

---

[52]A. Roberts and J. Donaldson, eds., *The Ante-Nicene Fathers, Translations of the Writings of the Fathers down to* A.D. 325, 10 vols., (1885-87) I., pp. 353f.

[53]Robert M. Grant, "Two Gnostic Gospels" in the *Journal of Biblical Literature* 79 (March 1960), pp. 1-11. The thirteen codices of the Nag-Hammadi library contain about 1,000 pages of which nearly 800 are complete (Cf. R. Grant, *op. cit.,* p. 1). The bulk of them have been acquired by the Coptic Museum in Cairo. Cf. R. McLachlan Wilson, "The Gnostic Library of Nag-Hammadi," *Scottish Journal of Theology* (June 1959), pp. 161-170.

Truth and the Gospel of the Twelve. The Gospel of Thomas is partic-ularly significant because it is the only complete early apocryphal gospel thus far uncovered.[54] In the Gospel of Thomas are 114 logia or sayings attributed to Jesus. But inasmuch as the Gospel of Thomas is limited to sayings, Quispel defines it "not at all a Gospel, but a collection of about 114 sayings attributed to Jesus and allegedly written by the Apostle Thomas."[55]

The Gospel of Thomas apparently reflects three sources. The first is the canonical gospels, one-half of the contents being in this category. The second is the apocryphal gospels, principally The Gospel According to the Egyptians and The Gospel According to the He-brews. The third is an unknown source of sayings unique to this Gospel.[56]

In its relationship to the canonical gospels of the New Testament, two possibilities exist. One is that this work has an origin independent of the canonical gospels and therefore may give authentic facts con-cerning the sayings of Jesus. The other is that the Gospel of Thomas is a Gnostic writing derived from the canonical gospels but intention-ally adding to or moulding the canonical gospels to propagandize the Gnostic system.

Representing the first view are those who contend that Thomas, or at least those sayings in it which resemble our canonical gospels, merits equal respectful treatment as the synoptic gospels since, it is contended, it stands about as close to the oral tradition as they do.[57]

Quispel suggests that Thomas reflects an Aramaic Jewish-Chris-tian gospel tradition independent of the sources of the canonical gos-pels, i.e., from the tradition referred to as "Q," but allows for the intro-duction of "elements which lead toward Gnostic conceptions."[58]

The other view is that the Gospel of Thomas is a Gnostic inven-tion in support of the claim of the Gnostics "that they themselves were the only ones who understood what Jesus really meant."[59] As Grant says, " . . . since the Gnostics found such gospels necessary they did

[54]Robert M. Grant, *The Secret Sayings of Jesus* (New York, 1960), p. 39. A Guil-laumont, Henry-Charles Puech, Gilles Quispel, Walter Till and Yassah abd Al Masih (trans.), *The Gospel According to Thomas* (New York, 1959), pp. 1-62; R. McLachlan Wilson, "The Gospel of Thomas," *Expository Times* 7 (Oct. 1958-Sept. 1959), pp. 324-325.
[55]G. Quispel, "Some Remarks on the Gospel of Thomas," *New Testament Studies* 5:276-290 (1958-59).
[56]Walter C. Till, "New Sayings of Jesus in the Recently Discovered Coptic 'Gospel of Thomas,'" *Bulletin of the John Rylands Library, Manchester* 41:446-458 (March, 1959).
[57]Cf. Robert M. Grant, "Two Gnostic Gospels" in *Journal of Biblical Literature* 79 (March, 1960), p. 2; *The Secret Sayings of Jesus*, p. 29.
[58]G. Quispel, "Some Remarks on the Gospel of Thomas" in *New Testament Studies* 5 (1958-59), pp. 277 ff., p. 287.
[59]Robert Grant, *The Secret Sayings of Jesus*, p. 65.

invent them — not out of nothing, but (in the case of Thomas) out of the oral traditions in circulation in the second century, out of the four canonical gospels, and out of the apocryphal gospels as well."[60]

This is doubtless the correct view of the relation of the Gospel of Thomas to the New Testament gospels, especially in the light of its significant and marked omissions, in striking contrast to the fulness found in the canonical gospels. Thomas is silent about sin, forgiveness, miracles, or the deeds of Jesus, demons, or exorcisms. So marked a phenomenon is this incompleteness that an inadequate and distorted representation of Jesus is the result, and doubtless why the work was deemed uncanonical by the church. Grant's summary statement is to the point: "With all its fascination, we should beware of valuing the new Gospel of Thomas too highly. It is important as a witness to the development of Gnostic Christology, not to the teachings of the historical Jesus."[61]

[60]Grant, "Two Gnostic Gospels" *Jour. of Biblical Literature* 79, p. 2.
[61]*Op. cit.,* p. 4.

CHAPTER 5

PLACES WHERE JESUS WALKED AND WORKED IN JUDAEA AND THE JORDAN VALLEY

Modern scientific archaeology is making substantial contributions toward a better understanding of the gospel narratives and the apostolic period, although the net result of research cannot be expected to be so astonishing as is the Old Testament field where over a millennia and a half of history is illuminated, as over against less than a century in the case of New Testament backgrounds, and where incomparably more was known of the latter from extra-biblical sources than of the former before the advent of archaeological inquiry. But the New Testament field, although comparatively short-spanned, represents a period of quintessential importance to the Christian student because of its connection with our Lord and the proclamation of the Christian Gospel which enhances the value of such discoveries as are made concerning it. These discoveries mainly concentrate in illuminating the complex political and cultural milieu in which the ministry of Jesus and the apostles took place, recovering long-lost knowledge of geographical and other details of the gospel accounts and occasionally authenticating the sacred narratives against higher critical attacks alleging historical inaccuracies.

In attempting to retrace the steps of Jesus and to re-envision the times in which He ministered, it is fortunate that the village and country life of Palestine until recent times has remained much the same as it was in the biblical era.[1] Local customs and daily life can be reconstructed. Moreover, many of the places mentioned in the gospel narratives and the New Testament as a whole have been known from earliest times. Others once doubtful are now certain. Some still remain to be identified with the progress of archaeological research. Those which are known are becoming better known as a result of systematic scientific excavations.

[1] Cf. Alfred Edersheim, *The Life and Times of Jesus the Messiah*, Vols. I, II (New York, 1940); A. C. Bouquet, *Everyday Life in New Testament Times* (New York, 1954); F. F. Bishop, *Jesus of Palestine: The Local Background of the Gospel Documents*, 1955; Jack Finegan, *Light from the Ancient Past*, 2nd ed. (New York, 1959), p. 297.

1. Jerusalem and the Temple, Focal Point of the Bible

Of all Palestinian sites, the city of Jerusalem is the most interesting to the Christian student. This is true not only because of the city's long and checkered history in Old Testament times, but also because of its intimate connection with the life, death, resurrection, and ascension of our Lord and the beginning of the Christian church. To Jew and Christian it is pre-eminently "the Holy City," and next to Mecca and Medina in Arabia is the most important sacred place in the Moslem world.

1. *Jerusalem and Its Topography*

The city is located on the central highland ridge 2550 feet above sea level. Fourteen miles to the east lies the Dead Sea, nestled in the deep depression of the Jordan Valley some 1300 feet below sea level. Thirty-three miles to the west lies the Mediterranean.

To the east of the city lies the Mount of Olives, rising several hundred feet higher than the city and separated from it by the Valley

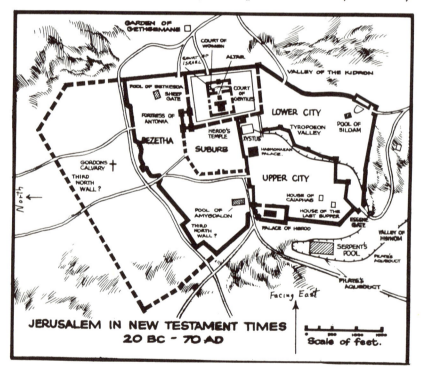

JERUSALEM IN NEW TESTAMENT TIMES
20 BC - 70 AD

Scale of feet.

of the Kidron (II Chronicles 32:4). To the south and west runs the deep Valley of Hinnom. The city was built on the plateau which rises above these two valleys and connects with the central ridge on the north. The plateau itself is divided into two parts by a smaller north-south valley, commonly called The Tyropoeon ("valley of the cheese-manufacturers"). The Western Hill, called the Upper City, was larger and higher than the Eastern Hill, but the latter because of the water supply (the Gihon spring in the Kidron Valley and En-rogel at the juncture of the Kidron and Hinnom Valleys) was the site of the earliest occupation and fortress city of Old Testament times. This important fact of the location of the ancient bastion of Jebus conquered by David about 998 B.C. on the Eastern Hill rather than on the more imposing Western Hill, is a significant contribution of modern archaeological exploration of the city.[2] Hasmonaean zealots, moreover, cut down the

A Jewish ossuary from a Jerusalem tomb. These stone boxes held the bones of the deceased when room was required in the tombs for new burials. Large numbers of these ossuaries date from the era of Jesus and the Apostles, with common names occurring in the gospels and Acts—such as Jesus, Judas, Annanias, Lazarus, even a Jeshua (Jesus) son of Joseph—carved on them in Hebrew, Aramaic, or Greek

top of the Eastern Hill in the second century B.C. so that it might not rival the Temple area in eminence and filled in the valley between the fortress they built on the site of the old Lower City and the temple to the north. The Tyropoean Valley too was partially obliterated by the debris of centuries, so that the topography of Jerusalem has undergone change.

2. The Herodian City

By the time of Jesus, the city of Jerusalem had been greatly enlarged, particularly as a result of the building activities of Herod the Great. It now spread to the north and west. The use of cisterns and

[2]Cf. Jack Finegan, op. cit., pp. 178-180; Merrill F. Unger, Archaeology and the Old Testament (4th ed., Grand Rapids, 1960), pp. 206-209; G. Ernest Wright, Biblical Archaeology (Philadelphia, 1957), pp. 125-130; G. Ernest Wright, Floyd V. Filson; W. F. Albright, The Westminster Historical Atlas to the Bible (rev. ed., Philadelphia, 1956), p. 105.

aqueducts made this possible. It is definitely known, for example, that Pontius Pilate, Roman procurator of Judaea A.D. 26-36, aroused the ire of the Jews by appropriating temple funds to build or repair (probably the latter) an aqueduct into the city. The result of these building operations was that the central section of the city was no longer on the lower hill south of the temple, which had been known as Ophel in earlier periods, but to the north and west of the temple area. This situation demanded a revamping of the city's fortifications.

The first and second north walls, which were already built when Herod became king, were elaborately strengthened by him with magnificent towers. One was named Hippicus in honor of a friend, one Phasael, after a brother, and one Mariamne after his favorite wife. The tower of Phasael stood where the Tower of David now stands, with Mariamne east of Phasael and Hippicus evidently to the southwest. Herod's hand can be detected in the characteristic heavy masonry, as at the Wailing Wall. The first north wall ran west from about the middle of the temple area. The second north wall has not been decisively outlined, but evidently ran from the Tower of Antonia to the Jaffa Gate.

The Wailing Wall, Old Jerusalem, Jordan. Courtesy Rev. Thomas Roth

South of the towers Hippicus, Phasael and Mariamne, Herod built his resplendent palace. North of the temple he rebuilt the Baris, a Maccabaean fortress, and called it Antonia in honor of Mark Antony. This redoubtable fortification was constructed on a high precipice and was strengthened with four towers, the one at the southeast corner some 105 feet high, dominating the entire temple area and exposing to view all that transpired in the temple courts. Besides, access was possible to the temple courts by stairs and bridges, so that with a Roman cohort garrisoned in the fortress of Antonia, control of the Jews was possible in the whole temple area.

Under Herod Jerusalem expanded considerably. On the north a suburb developed called Bezetha. To enclose this new area, Herod Agrippa, grandson of Herod the Great and the last "king of the Jews," began a third wall begun about A.D. 42 which, however, was not completed until A.D. 66, shortly before the destruction of the city by the Romans. All these fortifications were so formidable that they excited

Coin of Herod the Great inscribed around wreath (obverse). Tripod with palm (reverse)

even the wonder of the world-conquering Romans and are described by the Roman historian Tacitus in connection with his comments on the siege of the city by Titus in A.D. 70.[3]

In addition to these structures, Herod, as an ardent admirer of Greek culture, built many other edifices in Jerusalem, including a hippodrome, theatre, and amphitheatre. It was his aim to fill his realm with architectural splendors in the best western tradition, as he did not only in Jerusalem but in Sebaste (Samaria), Caesarea, and elsewhere. His reign witnessed the triumph of Hellenism over the traditionalistic conservatism of his predecessors, the Maccabees.

3. *The Herodian Temple*

Herod's most elaborate building project, however, directed at ingratiating himself into favor with his Jewish subjects, was the temple. This magnificent enterprise was begun in 20-19 B.C., and although the sanctuary proper was finished in a year and a half, the larger plan envisioned by the monarch was not completed until A.D. 64. In Jesus' day the Pharisees declared that the temple already had been in the process of construction for forty-six years (John 2:20).

Herod lavished huge sums on the great structure to make it worthy of its fame as a center of pilgrimage for Jews from all over the Graeco-Roman world. Although its general plan was handed down from the ancient tabernacle and the existing second temple, Herod could adorn it with splendid colonnaded courts and porticoes. One such column was discovered in modern times in front of the Russian

[3]*History*, Book V, paragraphs 11 and 12; cf. Wright, *Biblical Archaeology*, p. 222.

cathedral north of the old city. Being found defective, it had been abandoned in the quarry and never used for the purpose for which it had been made.

To give the temple the spaciousness required for his ambitious plans and to accommodate the great throngs that crowded it on the occasion of the annual festivals, Herod constructed a sprawling plat-

PROCEDURES OF SIEGE USED BY THE ROMANS

form extending over the southeastern area where the terrace dropped sharply. This area had to be supported by stout columns and cavernous vaults and a huge retaining wall, parts of which are still visible. One of Jerusalem's early explorers, Sir Charles Warren, excavated this wall between 1867-1870 and discovered it to have been sunk to bedrock in places fifty feet below the present surface of the ground. The ruins of this architectural complex, traditionally but erroneously called "Solomon's stables," are quite unconnected with King Solomon's chariot-horse stables. The remains of the superb wall Herod built around the great court in which the temple stood offer the finest example of extant Herodian architectural skill in Jerusalem.

With data furnished by Josephus and the Mishnah (Tractacte Middoth), scholars are able to reconstruct the plan of the various parts of Herod's temple.[4] The splendid edifice had at least eight gates, four on the west, two on the south, one on the north, and one on the east. Magnificent porticoes graced the outer court. Particularly splendid was the Royal Porch facing the south, which was more spacious

[4]Cf. L. H. Grollenberg *Atlas of the Bible* (New York, 1956), p. 115, map 33. Wright and Filson, *The Westminster Historical Atlas to the Bible*, p. 109, plate XVII; Wright, *Biblical Archaeology*, p. 224, figure 168.

than the others and more lavishly columned. Solomon's Porch, where Jesus taught (John 10:23) and where Peter and the apostles later taught and preached (Acts 3:11; 5:12), faced toward the east across the defile of the Kidron. In the northern extremity of this spacious portico was the Golden Gate, opening to a road that led to Gethsemane across the Kidron and branching toward the north to connect

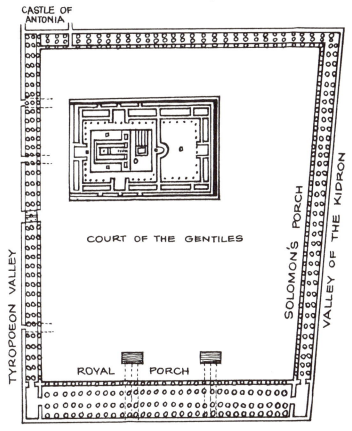

Ground plan of the splendid Herodian Temple. Herod made the Jerusalem temple an edifice of such magnificence that it was admired even by the Romans. The sumptuous colonnaded cloisters were not completed till A.D. 64, only six years before the entire complex was annihilated by the Romans

with the road to Jericho issuing from the Sheep Gate (John 5:2) near the pool of Bethesda, where Jesus healed the paralytic (John 5:1-14). The Beautiful Gate where the lame beggar was daily laid (Acts 3:2), evidently opening on to Solomon's Porch, was the Corinthian Gate. Here Peter performed the miracle of healing (Acts 3:2).

The Court of the Gentiles was entered on the south end and was adjacent to the Royal Porch. Beyond this was the wall of separation between Jews and Gentiles (Acts 21:28; Ephesians 2:14). Past this area, a non-Jew might not go. Notices in the Greek language at the gates to the inner courts warned Gentiles not to enter. It is interesting to note that the only two pieces of surviving stone which are known to have belonged to Herod's temple bear this very warning: "No alien may enter within the barrier and wall around the temple. Whoever is caught (violating this) is alone responsible for the death (-penalty) which follows." One of these stone pieces was recovered in a cemetery in 1935. Another turned up near St. Stephen's Gate in 1935. These discoveries not only illuminate Herod's temple but vividly recall Jesus' solemn prophecy from Olivet concerning its destruction. "Verily I say to you, There shall not be left here one stone upon another, that shall not be thrown down" (Matthew 24:2; Mark 13:2), which was literally fulfilled when the Roman legions of Titus destroyed the temple and the city.

Beyond the court of the Gentiles was the Court of the Women, beyond which no Jewish woman could go. In this area, contribution chests were placed. Here Jesus, sitting over against the treasury, saw the poor widow make a consecrated contribution which He immortalized by His words of commendation (Mark 12:41-44). Beyond the confines of the Court of the Women lay the Men's Court, entered by the Beautiful Gate on the east or by a stairway leading from the Court of the Women on the south. In this Court of Israel, situated before the actual place where the priests ministered, Israelite men could watch the sacrificial system in operation on the altar of burnt offering.

Steps leading up to an ornamental porch west of the altar of burnt offering opened up to the Holy Place, a chamber thirty feet by sixty feet, where priests officiated before the can-

Seven branched candlestick being borne as booty in the triumphal procession on the Arch of Titus at Rome (after the fall of Jerusalem, 70 A.D.)

dlestick, the altar of incense and the table of show bread. Beyond this, behind a veil, was the inner sanctuary or Holy of Holies, thirty feet by thirty feet, where the high priest alone entered to make expiation for the nation annually on the day of atonement (Leviticus 16).

Storerooms, treasuries, and priests' chambers were located in the temple area at convenient places. Just west of the temple area was a council chamber where the Sanhedrin met. Easy access to the temple courts and the Upper City was made possible by a viaduct across the Tyropoeon Valley.

The Temple was oriented toward the east "and its back" was "turned westward."[5] Its impressive appearance and wealth were recognized by the Romans[6]. Today the area lies within the holy precincts called by pious Muslims, who venerate this spot next to Mecca and Medina in Arabia, the Haram esh-Sherif, "the Noble Sanctuary." The edifice Qubbet es-Sakhra ("Dome of the Rock") built on the sacred site at the end of the seventh century A.D. encloses a rocky ledge which probably served as Araunah's threshing floor and the place where David erected an altar[7].

4. *Other Places in Jerusalem*

Herod's palace on the western side of the city was lavishly magnificent, according to Josephus. It had sumptuous bedrooms and dining halls and was surrounded on the south by pleasure gardens with fountains and watercourses. Entirely walled about to a height of forty-five feet, the walls on the west and north being identical with the city walls, the northwestern sector was graced by the gorgeous towers Hippicus, Phasael, with Mariamne on the north.

After Roman occupation (A.D. 6) the Roman procurators of Caesarea resided in the palace on visits to Jerusalem, and hence it became known as the praetorium. Pilate's praetorium (Mark 15:16) is, therefore, probably to be connected with the Herodian palace, although later tradition links the praetorium with the fortress of Antonia. If this tradition is true, Pilate was residing in the Castle of Antonia at the Passover season to be near the temple, when Jesus was arraigned before him, and the Pavement called Gabbatha (John 19:13) was possibly the very one excavated in the central court of the fortress of Antonia below the Ecce Homo arch of the Hadrianic era.

[5]Cf. *The Letter of Aristeas*, 88, translated by H. St. John Thackeray (1917), p. 41.
[6]Tacitus called it "a temple of immense wealth" (*History* V, 8), and Jesus' disciples reflect their impression of its magnificence (cf. Mark 13:1).
[7]Floyd Filson in *The Biblical Archaeologist* 7 (1944), p. 81; A. T. Olmstead, *Jesus in the Light of History* (1942), p. 85; F. J. Hollis *The Archaeology of Herod's Temple* (1934), pp. 84-86; Hans Schmidt, *Der Heilige Fels in Jerusalem* (1933), pp. 26, 55.

Excavations of the French Archaeologist H. Vincent of the Dominican Biblical School in Jerusalem have outlined the position and general plan of Herod's fortress of Antonia, and led this scientist to be-

The Ecce-Homo Arch, Jerusalem, traditional spot where Pilate cried to the mob, "Behold, the man!" (John 19: 5). The structure, however, has no connection with the life of Jesus, being part of a triple arch erected by the Emperor Hadrian (A.D. 117-138)

A street in old Jerusalem, Jordan. Courtesy Dr. Paul Bauman

lieve that this was the location of Jesus' interrogation and scourging before Pilate. In this event, the Via Dolorosa, or "Way of Sorrow," would run west from Antonia and then southwest to Golgotha (the mound called "skull," Latin "calvary") outside the wall of that day on the northwest corner of the city.[8] Near at hand was also the garden and the tomb of Joseph of Arimathaea (John 19:41). However, the Pavement (*Lithostroton*) may possibly have been situated in front of Herod's old palace in the Upper City. The question involved is not as yet finally resolved.

Another interesting building in Jerusalem was the palace of the Hasmonaeans. This was situated on the eastern side of the Upper

[8]Cf. Marie Aline de Sion, *La forteresse Antonia à Jerusalem et la question du Prétoire* (1956). Millar Burrows in *The Biblical Archaeologist* 1 (1938), pp. 17f.

Traditional site of Golgotha. Courtesy of Dr. John F. Walvoord

Traditional Garden Tomb, Jerusalem. Courtesy of Dr. John F. Walvoord

City and commanded an excellent view of the temple. It was possibly in this building Jesus was arraigned before Herod Antipas (Luke 23:7). Later in the reign of Nero, Herod Agrippa II clashed with the Jews over a wall the priests built to hinder his view into the temple.

The Tower of Antonia at Jerusalem, reconstructed (after Vincent). This formidable fortress at the northwest corner of the temple area was rebuilt from a Maccabean structure by Herod the Great and named in honor of Mark Antony

Between the palace of the Hasmonaeans and the Temple was an edifice called the Xystus, near a viaduct leading across the Tyropoean Valley and connecting the Upper City with the temple area. Robinson's Arch is a remnant of an ancient bridge near the southwestern corner of the temple area. Wilson's Arch is a similar ruin farther north.[9] Traces of Pilate's aqueduct run along the western side of the Hinnon Valley and then southeastward on the other side near the Gate of the Essenes in the southmost extremity of the city and northward east of the Tyropoean Valley to the temple area from the west. Ancient traditions place the house of Caiaphas south of the present walls of the Old City. The Upper Room of Pentecost (Acts 1:13) and the Last Supper are also traditionally placed in this southernmost section north of the Gate of the Essenes, which opened upon the Valley of Hinnon, where offal was dumped and burned, and which Jesus

[9]Charles W. Wilson and R. E. Warren, *The Recovery of Jerusalem* (1871), pp. 72-85.

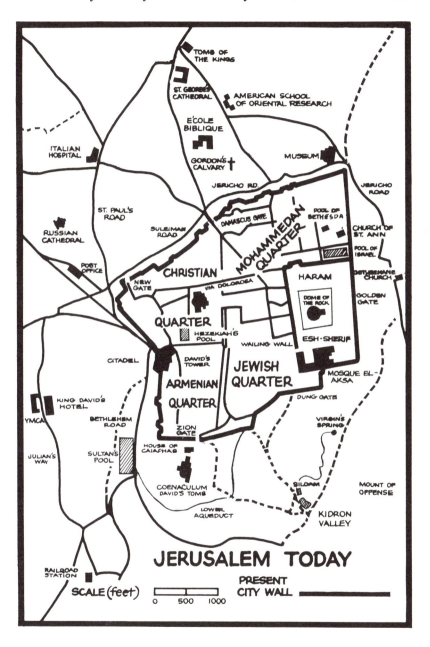

JERUSALEM TODAY

SCALE (feet) 0 500 1000

PRESENT
CITY WALL

used as a figurative term of eternal hell where the wicked would go (Mark 9:43, 45, 47).

The well-known Pool of Siloam where Jesus healed the man born blind (John 9:7) was located in the Lower City at the end of Hezekiah's underground conduit which brought water from the Gihon Spring, so vitally essential to the existence of Jebus and later to the city of David (I Kings 1:33). The Tower of Siloam which collapsed and killed eighteen people (Luke 13:4) also was in this general area of the most ancient part of Jerusalem. Akeldama ("the Field of Blood") referred to in Acts 1:19 has been located in the Valley of Hinnon below En-rogel since the fourth century A.D.

5. The Present-day City

In the course of centuries, Jerusalem has shifted northwestward. Flanked on the east and south by the deep gorges of the Kidron and Hinnon, the city naturally expanded in the direction where no valleys hindered its growth.

Until the beginning of the twentieth century, the inhabitants of Jerusalem were not numerous enough not to be accommodated within the sixteenth century walls erected by Sultan Sulaiman II the Magnificent. The modern city, capital of the Israeli State, sprawls far beyond the walls to the northwest and has a population of some

Arches by the Dome of the Rock (former site of the temple), Jerusalem, looking east to the Mt. of Olives. Courtesy Dr. John F. Walvoord

150,000 people, embracing also a much larger area than the old city in the territory of Jordan, which has about 70,000 souls squeezed in the 250 acres within its walls.

II. The Mount of Olives and Its Environs

Closely associated with Jerusalem in the ministry of Jesus is the Mount of Olives and the surrounding countryside and villages, notably Gethsemane, Bethphage, and Bethany. A present-day aerial view of this country reveals its outstanding features, the Mount of Olives east of the temple area and south of it the so-called Mount of Offence, at the foot of which lies the village of Silwan, whose name is reminiscent of the conduit of Shiloah and the Pool of Siloam just west of it on the east slope of Jerusalem. The name given to this southern hill by the early Christians ("The Mount of Offence") connects it with Solomon's apostasy and the worship of false gods (II Kings 23:13).

1. The Mount of Olives and Jesus

The Mount of Olives, a mile-long spur of limestone hills, was a favorite haunt of Jesus and His disciples and one of the most conspic-

A branch of olives. The olive, one of the finer trees of Palestine, has an almost sacred character for Christians because of its association with Jesus (Mark 13:3; 14:26; John 7:53)

Mustard plant, of which several species flourish in Palestine. All have tiny seeds (Matt. 17:20; Luke 17:6) and attain considerable size, as in Jesus' illustration (Matt. 13:31; Mark 4:32; Luke 13:19)

uous landmarks of Jerusalem, towering several hundred feet to the east above the plateau on which the city was built. The chain of hills of which the ridge is composed has several elevations, the northernmost contiguous to Mount Scopus near the Hebrew University and British War Cemetery is 2723 feet above sea level, and has been held by many as the place where Jesus ascended to heaven (Acts 1:11), being known as *Viri Galiloei*. However, the chief hill of Olivet is just south of that elevation and is actually called "The Ascension" (2641 feet) and here the Tower of the Ascension of the Russian Orthodox Church juts skyward and is visible for miles around the city. Islam's claim to the place of Christ's ascension is marked by a Moslem chapel. The next elevation is popularly known as "the Prophets," being erroneously connected with the tombs of Old Testament prophets by the credulous. The southernmost elevation, although sometimes considered separate, is the Mount of Offence, which is about the same elevation as the temple hill (2411 feet).

Old Testament references to the Mount of Olives are sparse. During Absalom's rebellion, David escaped barefoot over its brow (II Samuel 15:30) and worshiped on its summit, possibly in a shrine located there (II Samuel 15:32). Ezekiel envisioned the removal of the Shekinah glory from Jerusalem and saw it stand "upon the mountain which is on the east side of the city" (Ezekiel 11:23). Zechariah in eschatological vision prophesied the second advent of Messiah bodily to the "mount of Olives, which is before Jerusalem on the east" (Zechariah 14:4).

A Palestinian olive press, a familiar scene in the days of Jesus

Jesus frequented the Mount of Olives, especially in the evening hours (John 7:53; 8:1). Tradition names it (probably erroneously) as the place where He instructed His disciples in the model prayer (Luke 11:1-4), and this belief is memorialized in a chapel erected on the east slope where the model prayer may be read in thirty-five languages on the chapel walls. Over its roads Jesus came and went to Jericho and thence northward through Peraea to Galilee. Often He resorted to the familiar way that led over its slope to Bethany (John 11:1). From the town of Bethphage Jesus rode down Olivet's slopes and across the Kidron and entered Jerusalem (according to tradition) by the Golden Gate in the eastern wall in His Triumphal Entry (Matthew 21:1-12; Zechariah 9:9). Thither He resorted with His disciples after this public event (Mark 11:11).

The Garden of Gethsemane (one of the traditional locations). Courtesy Mrs. Lowell Orth

On Olivet's brow in full view of Herod's resplendent temple and just before the events that culminated in His arrest and death, Jesus prophesied the destruction of the temple as His disciples were admiring its sumptuous splendor (Matthew 24:1, 2; Mark 13:1-3). It is significant that from the strategic summit of the Mount the invincible legions of Rome under Titus poised for the siege of the city that was to bring its destruction and the utter ruin of the temple in fulfilment of Jesus' ominous words.

After the solemn Last Supper in the Upper Room in Jerusalem, Jesus and the eleven disciples went out to the Mount of Olives (Matthew 26:30), where among the ancient olive trees in Gethsemane He agonized in prayer, was betrayed by Judas, and arrested by the Romans (Matthew 26:47-56).

2. Gethsemane and Jesus' Agony

Above the present road from Jerusalem to Bethany four traditional locations of Gethsemane are to be found today. Ancient olive trees in the walled Franciscan Garden mark the site claimed by the Latin Church. But other sites (Armenian and Russian) are located on the lower slopes of the Mount, also containing ancient olive trees, and lay claim for the site of Jesus' agony in prayer. Not far away in the lower portions of the hill are numerous Jewish and Herodian tombs, popularly but unhistorically assigned to Absalom, King Jehoshaphat, St. James, and others.

Matthew (26:36) and Mark (14:26, 32) give the name Gethsemane, but John, although he does not mention the name, gives a distinctive note for the localization of the place. "When Jesus had spoken these words, he went forth with his disciples over the brook Kidron, where there was a garden, into which he and his disciples entered" (John 18:1). All that can be said is that Gethsemane was located in this general area across the Kidron, but how far up the olive-clad hill is unknown. In the fifth century up to the era of the Crusades, it was thought to be situated on the ground where the Church of the Tomb of the Virgin now stands and the spot of Jesus' prayer a little distance up the hill (Luke 22:41).

The meaning of the name Gethsemane is also not certainly known. Usually assumed to mean "press of oils," this is philologically dubious. Jerome connected it with Hebrew *ge'e shemanim*, "Valley of oils" or "Fat Valley" (cf. Isaiah 28:1), and may be correct in hinting that it was in a valley in which there were many olive trees.

3. Bethphage and Bethany

The exact location of Bethphage is unknown. However, Beth-Page is found in rabbinic writings in close connection with Jerusalem, suggesting its proximity.[10] Mentioned as the easternmost point in Jerusalem's territory,[11] the name has usually been derived from *pag*, "unripe, juiceless fig," and so would mean "house (or place) of unripe fig(s)." Dalman, however, suggests a possible derivation from Latin *pagus* ("a country district"), meaning "the place of the *pagi*" i.e., "the country district of Jerusalem, her suburb."[12] To this place somewhere on the Mount of Olives near Bethany Jesus sent disciples to fetch the

[10]Gustav Dalman, *Sacred Sites and Ways*, pp. 252, 253.
[11]Cf. Neubauer, *La Géographie du Talmud*, p. 149; T. K. Cheyne, *Encyclopaedia Biblica*, "Bethphage."
[12]Dalman, *op. cit.*, p. 253.

ass for use as His mount for the triumphal entry into Jerusalem (Matthew 21:1; Mark 11:1; Luke 19:29).

4. *Bethany, the Town of Mary and Martha*

That Bethany lay east of the Mount of Olives is clearly suggested by the notices in the gospel narratives.[13] It is to be found in the vicinity of the present-day small village *el-'Azariyeh,* "The Place of

An Oriental house, courtyard, and roof (cross section view), with well

Lazarus," in which the Arabic name preserves the tradition of the connection of Lazarus with Bethany. The exact location of the first century village is ascertained by considering the Lazarus tomb which was pointed out since about A.D. 300 and over which a church was erected before A.D. 380. The tomb is situated on the side of the hill called *Ras esh-Shiyah,* and above and near it is the present-day village. But the old village extended farther east where there are springs and ancient cisterns, and since Bethany is said to have been about fifteen furlongs (1¾ miles) from Jerusalem, it was not so near the tomb of Lazarus as the more recent western part of the present-day village. Archaeological finds have shown that the present village, in part, goes back to pre-Christian times, so that within its confines was located the house of Mary and Martha (John 11:1) and the house of Simon the leper (Matthew 26:6; Mark 14:3).[14]

[13]Dalman, *op. cit.,* pp. 249-251.
[14]Dalman, *op. cit.,* p. 249.

5. *Jesus Retires to Ephraim with His Disciples*

After the raising of Lazarus and the increased hostility of the Jewish leaders, John's gospel relates that "Jesus therefore no longer went about openly among the Jews but went from there (Bethany) to the country near the wilderness, to a town called Ephraim; and there he stayed with his disciples" (John 11:54, R.S.V.). This is undoubtedly the Ephraim near Bethel, captured by Vespasian in the Jewish-Roman War and identical with the Aphairema, capital of a district bordering on Samaria mentioned in I Maccabees 11:34.

Perhaps the Hebrew spelling was Ephron or Ephrain (cf. II Chronicles 13:19). The place is to be identified with *et Taiyibeh,* a secluded village close to the rocky gorges leading down to the Jordan Valley, four miles northeast of Bethel. Here Jesus and His disciples would be away from the beaten path and could relax in seclusion as the malignity of their enemies grew more intense.

A yoke of oxen, a common sight in Jesus' journeys about Palestine

An ancient Palestinian well, showing drawing and carrying water as in the days of Jesus (cf. John 4:6)

III. JERICHO AND THE JORDAN VALLEY

From Jericho to Jerusalem is a journey of 17 miles, with a steady ascent from over 1,000 feet below sea-level to almost 3,000 feet above sea-level. The desolate road through barren mountainous country was infested with robbers, a circumstance reflected in the parable of the Good Samaritan (Luke 10:30-37). Jesus often traversed this route from Jerusalem to Jericho, up the Jordan Valley through Perea to Scythopolis and thence to Galilee.

1. *New Testament Jericho*

The city of Jesus' day was Herod's winter capital. He and Archelaus elegantly beautified it with magnificent Hellenistic structures such as are reflected by the extant superb ruins at Graeco-Roman Gerasa (Jerash). These included a sumptuous winter palace, a theatre, a fortress, and a hippodrome. The palace in which Herod died was burned by a former slave of the king, but rebuilt by Archelaus on a sumptuous scale.

In the winter of 1950 the American School of Oriental Research and the Pittsburgh-Xenia Theological Seminary undertook the excavation of portions of the New Testament site known as Tulul Abu el-'Alayiq, one mile west of the modern city where the Wadi Qelt enters the Jordan Valley. James L. Kelso directed the operations.[15] The ancient ruins lie on both the north and south sides of the Wadi Qelt. On the south side under the ruins of an eighth or ninth century Arabic fortress lie portions of a civic center constructed perhaps by Archelaus and beneath that Herodian masonry with a still lower level of Hellenistic remains. Sounding on the north side of the Wadi shows fortresses and other structures there.

The architecture of New Testament Jericho is strikingly reminiscent of Rome, Pompeii, and other cities of the Graeco-Roman world. Unlike the older cramped Canaanite and Hebrew town, the Jericho of Jesus' day was elegantly lined with trees such as the sycamore, which grows only in the Jordan Valley and on the coast. Along one of the streets Zacchaeus sat in such a tree to see Jesus pass (Luke 19:2-10). Bits of wood used for bonding the wall of a tower at Jericho have been shown to be sycamore at the Yale School of Forestry.[16] Here along the roadside just outside the city blind Bartimaeus sat begging (Mark 10:46) as Jesus passed on the way up to Jerusalem, which skirted the south bank of the Wadi Qelt and continued up the "Ascent of Adummim" (present-day *Tal'at ed Damm*) to the "Inn of the Good Samaritan," where the first glimpse of the Mount of Olives (*et Tur*, "the Mount") is had.

2. *The Jordan Valley and Jesus' Route to Jerusalem*

In traveling from Galilee to Jerusalem, as Jesus often must have done from boyhood to attend the sacred feasts in Jerusalem, three roads were open — a middle route traversing the highlands of Samaria via Sychar, a western along the coast through the plain of Sharon, through Antipatris, Lydda, and Bethhoron, and an eastern road

---

[15]James L. Kelso and Dimitri C. Baramki, *Excavations at New Testament Jericho and Khirbet en-Nitla, Annual of the American Schools of Oriental Research* 29-30 (1955); James M. Pritchard, Sherman E. Johnson and George C. Miles, *The Excavation at Herodian Jericho* (1951), *Annual of the American Schools* 32-33 (1958). For preliminary reports, see James L. Kelso, *Bulletin of the American Schools of Oriental Research* 120 (Dec. 1950) and James B. Pritchard in *Bulletin* 123 (Oct. 1951), pp. 8-17.

[16]Emil Kraeling, *op. cit.,* p. 395.

through Peraea and the Jordan Valley (cf. Matthew 19:1; Mark 10:1). As this latter route was not the shortest, nor the quickest, there were undoubtedly special reasons for following it, such as avoiding Samaritan or Jewish enemies, or desire for solitude and retreat, or special ministry.[17]

The Jordan River as it leaves the Lake of Galilee. Courtesy Dr. John F. Walvoord

If Nazareth was the starting point, the road would have been followed via Endor and Scythopolis (ancient Bethshan at the eastern entrance of the Plain of Esdraelon), and thence by ford across the river and southwest in Transjordan past Pella, the city that remained loyal to Rome during the Jewish-Roman War (A.D. 66-70) to which Christians from Jerusalem fled for safety. Beyond Pella, Jesus was in Peraea, Josephus' name for the territory referred to biblically as "the coasts of Judaea beyond Jordan" (Matthew 19:1), "the farther side of Jordan" (Mark 10:1) and "beyond Jordan" (John 10:40). Peraea paralleled Samaria and Judaea and extended from Pella to Machaerus east of the northern half of the Salt Sea where an isolated fortress of the Hasmonaeans was imposingly reconstructed by Herod the Great,

[17]Cf. Dalman, *op. cit.*, pp. 233-239 for a discussion of the Peraean-Transjordanian route.

and where Josephus says John the Baptist was executed (Mark 6:14-29).

But Jesus' fruitful ministries in Peraea where "many believed on him" (John 10:42) and from which He was called to the sick bed of Lazarus (John 11:3), apparently did not extend southward beyond Bethany (Bethabarah) where John baptized (John 1:28), located somewhere east of the Jordan north of the Dead Sea, and an important ford not far from Jericho.

When Jesus journeyed and ministered in Peraea, Herod Antipas, son of Herod the Great, whom Jesus characterized as "that fox" (Luke 13:32), ruled it and Galilee as a tetrarch (B.C. 4-A.D. 39), and with a subtly evil influence Jesus' referred to as "the leaven of Herod" (Mark 8:15). But the country, consisting of picturesque and rugged highlands and dotted with fruitful valleys and prosperous cities, which included part of the Decapolis and such towns as Pella, Succoth, Penuel, Gadara, Gerasa (Jerash), Madeba and Amathus, and bordered by the progressive and remarkable Arab Nabataean kingdom on the east and south, was not the scene of any extended ministry of Jesus, at least not according to the gospel records, and then only as He ministered to Jews who resided there within the reach of His travels to and from Galilee. Yet Peraea was heavily populated with Jews and, with Galilee and Judaea, was reckoned by them as the three provinces, Samaria being denied such dignity.[18]

If Jesus had wished to travel from Capernaum to Jerusalem via Peraea, a route led through Tiberias along the western side of the Lake of Galilee to Scythopolis and thence southward through Aenon near Salim, where John had baptized (John 3:23). This road continued southward on the western side of the Jordan River, skirting east of Alexandrium, where Herod the Great had rebuilt a Hasmonaean fortress and used it as a depository for his wealth. This route then ran southward to Jericho and on to Jerusalem.

It was also possible for Jesus to have traveled a road east of the Lake of Galilee through Bethsaida, Hippos, and Gadara on to Pella and points south in Peraea.

[18]*Baba Bathra* III, 2; Michael L. Rodkinson, *New Edition of the Babylonian Talmud* 10 vols., (1903, 1916).

Chapter 6

Places Where Jesus Walked and Worked in Northern and Central Palestine

While the climactic and concluding events of Jesus' life and ministry occurred in Jerusalem and its environs, most of the recorded events in the career of Christ took place in Northern Palestine, particularly in Galilee and more especially in the populous cities that dotted the region contiguous to the northwestern shore of the Sea of Galilee. There in the city of Capernaum Jesus seemed to center His activities and may be said to have had His headquarters, insofar as He had any radiating point of operation. Matthew says that Jesus left Nazareth "and lived (*katōkēsen*), "took up residence" in Capernaum" (Matthew 4:13), therefore calling it "his (Jesus') own city" (Matthew 9:1) and declaring that many of Jesus' "mighty works" were performed in it (Matthew 11:23). From Capernaum Jesus' ministry extended to the Galilean countryside as well as to such towns as Nazareth, Chorazin, and Bethsaida.

I. Nazareth and Other Towns of Galilee

In the days of Jesus, Galilee, whose precise delimitations varied in different epochs, was a Roman province, consisting of two main parts — Upper and Lower Galilee. Upper Galilee comprised mountainous and plateau country from 2,000 to 4,000 feet in elevation. Into this region the eleven disciples were directed to go for a post-resurrection appearance of Jesus (Matthew 28:16, 17). Lower Galilee included parts of the Plain of Esdraelon, most of the western shore of the Lake of Galilee, and the western banks of the Jordan River to the upper tip of the Waters of Merom. On the west and northwest, Galilee was bordered by Phoenicia, extending some four miles south of Caesarea along the entire Mediterranean coast, while the Decapolis lay southeast, Gaulanitis on the east, and Ulatha on the north and northeast.

1. Nazareth and the Boyhood of Jesus

The village of Nazareth, secluded among surrounding hills, was not a significant place (cf. John 1:46) until it was immortalized in New Testament times as the boyhood home of Jesus. The site is not mentioned in the Old Testament (cf. Joshua 19:10f.), nor by the historian Josephus, although the latter enumerates forty-five Galilean towns. Nor is it referred to in the Talmud, which names sixty-three. In fact, the mention of the village as the residence of Joseph and Mary (Luke 1:26, 27) in connection with the childhood of Jesus (Matthew 2:23; Luke 2:4, 51) together with other allusions in the gospels, constitute the oldest-known literary references to the place.[1]

Nazareth was not only a little-known place, it was apparently not very old. There is no archaeological indication beyond potsherds of Iron II (600 B.C.) in the neighborhood.[2] The reason is evidently to be found in the fact that this territory had been controlled by Japhia (Japha) of the tribe of Zebulon (Joshua 19:12), a strong fortress city a mile and a half to the southwest,[3] or possibly by Chessuloth of the tribe of Issachar (Joshua 19:18), a mile and a quarter to the southeast. As an outpost of one of these strong fortress cities, Nazareth was just a small village of farmers and artisans, such as the carpenter Joseph.

Then, too, the village did not lie on any important trade route in Jesus' day. The commercial artery from Damascus to Egypt ran across the Plain of Esdraelon some half-dozen miles to the south of Nazareth, while a branch road to Accho (Ptolemais) ran about the same distance to the north of the town. South-bound travel, however, from Sepphoris would pass through Nazareth, so that, while Nazareth was not a bustling emporium, it was far from isolated from the busy Galilean cities and the stirring events of the time. It was, it may be supposed, an ideal place for Jesus to grow to manhood and to enjoy the solitude that was to precede His public ministry. When the time came for the latter, a teeming metropolis like Capernaum, with its welter of human need, was to form a more proper theatre for His activity.

Certainly the geographical situation of Nazareth was conducive to the contemplative life. The scenery was expansive, if not breath-taking. Although Nazareth itself lies on a sharp slope of the Galilean hills at an altitude somewhat more than 1150 feet, from the crest above the village a majestic panorama includes distant snow-capped Hermon on the north, nearby Mt. Tabor on the east, the extensive

---

[1] The only reference to Nazareth in Jewish literature is in the elegy of Kalir, a Jewish poem (ninth century A.D.), which contains very old material (second to third centuries). According to this poem a town written Nsrt in unvocalized Hebrew was the residence of the priestly order of Happizzez (A. V. Aphses in I Chronicles 24:15) in the second century A.D. (Emil Kraeling, Rand McNally Bible Atlas, p. 358).

[2] Catholic Biblical Quarterly 18 (1956), p. 42.

[3] Present-day Yafa, an ancient place listed among the Palestinian places subdued by the Egyptian empire-builder Thutmose III in the fifteenth century B.C.

Plain of Esdraelon like an enormous carpet on the south, and the headland of Mt. Carmel and the blue Mediterranean on the west. Although the gospel accounts are almost silent on these momentous character-forming years, Jesus is to be thought of as taking many long walks over the ridges of these noble hills in communion with God, His human nature developing in His theanthropic person and the vision of His life's work unfolding while He yielded Himself to the divine will, as His eye now met Tabor or distant Hermon, or caught the sunlit flash of the sea behind far-off Carmel.

The Valley of Megiddo (Plain of Esdraelon). Courtesy Dr. John F. Walvoord

Many of the illustrations from country life must have imbedded themselves in Jesus' consciousness from boyhood memories of the tiny agricultural town in which He was reared — the sower, the horticulturalist, the traveler on a long journey, the wine and the wineskin containers, the busy threshing floor, the olive and the fig tree, etc.

At Nazareth Jesus received the regular training of a Jewish lad in home and synagogue (Luke 2:21; 4:16). From the seclusion of the little village Jesus went to be baptized by John at Jordan (Mark 1:9) and returned to it after the temptation (Matthew 4:12, 13). After the violent opposition to Him in the Nazareth synagogue (Luke 4:16-30), there is no indication that Jesus ever came back to His boyhood haunts, although the name of Nazareth came to be applied to Him by both his friends and enemies (Matthew 21:11; Acts 2:22; 10:38).

Today, although Nazareth is a fair-sized town of about 22,000 and far larger than the modest village of Jesus' time, there is much in the city that recalls the ancient village. Carpenter and blacksmith shops front on the narrow, declivitous streets, and at Mary's Spring ('Ain Maryam) one can still see the women congregate to draw water with their pitchers picturesquely poised on their heads, just as the mother of Jesus did nineteen centuries ago. Actually, the source of the water is a spring behind the present-day Greek Church of the Annunciation, and the water is piped down the hill to Mary's Spring, so-called since the twelfth century.

"Lilies of the field" (Matt. 6:28-30). It was probably such a common species as this that grow among the grain and are regally colored that Jesus used to illustrate the Father's care of His children

Tares (darnel), a bothersome weed that grows among the wheat and can only be distinguished from it near harvest. Jesus employed it in a forceful illustration (Matt. 13:25-30)

The site of the synagogue in which Jesus spoke (Luke 4:16) has been traditionally marked by the Church of the United Greeks, but the Orthodox Greeks locate the place where the Church of the Forty Martyrs stood, and this location has been defended recently.[4] But the Nazareth synagogue of Jesus' day was, of course, destroyed, undoubtedly in the Roman-Jewish War of 66-70, and was replaced by a second century edifice. Ruins of these early synagogues no doubt underlie later Crusader and Byzantine constructions.

[4]Clemens Kopp in *Journal of the Palestine Oriental Society* 20 (1946), pp. 29-42.

Of particular interest is an inscription alleged to have come from Nazareth and brought to Paris in 1878, now in the Bibliotheque Nationale. Unfortunately numerous scholars deny the significance of the monument and some even doubt its authenticity. The "Nazareth inscription," captioned the "Ordinance of Caesar" has been for this reason or that assigned to practically every Roman emperor from Augustus to Hadrian. It concerns the crime of violation of tombs and carries with it the imperial decision that one found guilty be meted the death penalty. By those who assign the rescript to Tiberius, it has been construed as a witness to the resurrection of Jesus of Nazareth which came from the emperor at Rome in answer to a report from Pilate, which included reference to the rumor that the disciples of Jesus had stolen His body from the tomb (Matthew 28:13).[5] By those who connect the rescript with Emperor Claudius, the inscription is dated between 44-50 A.D., after the death of the puppet king Herod Agrippa, and is interpreted as "the first secular comment on the Easter story, and legal testimony to its central fact,"[6] issued when Claudius expelled the Jews from Rome (Acts 18:2) because of rioting in the ghetto "at the instigation of one Chrestos."[7]

Less than four miles northwest of the village of Nazareth lay Sepphoris, which Herod Antipas rebuilt splendidly, but which had

A Palestinian synagogue of the 1st and 2nd century restored. No 1st century edifice has remained, but the appearance was probably much like a 2nd or 3rd century building

[5]Cf. Jacques Zeiller in *Recherches de Science Religieuse* (1931), pp. 570-576; J. H. Oliver in *Classical Philology* 49 (1954), pp. 180-182; J. Carcopino in *Revue Historique* 167 (1931), pp. 34-35; E. Stauffer, *Jesus, Gestalt and Geschichte* (1957), p. 111.
[6]E. M. Blaiklock, *Out of the Earth* (*The Witness of Archaeology to the New Testament*) (1957), p. 39.
[7]Seutonius, *Claudius* 25:4. "Chrestos" is taken as a scribal error for *Christos,* and the cause of the Rome riotings, the Jewish opposition to the Christian proclamation of an empty tomb. Blaiklock, *op. cit.,* pp. 32-39.

been destroyed previously by the Romans assisted by the Nabataeans under King Aretas as a result of its having been seized and made a center of rebellion after the death of Herod the Great. It remained loyal to Rome in the Jewish War and was spared destruction. The University of Michigan conducted excavations there in 1931, uncovering a fort and a theatre, probably dating from the reign of Herod Antipas.[8] Undoubtedly Jesus had many times walked in the vicinity when the city was held by Judas or later among its ruins, or when it became a brilliant city under Herod Antipas and perhaps the Galilean capital until Tiberias was built.

2. Cana and Other Cities of Galilee

Another Galilean village made famous by the Presence of Jesus was Cana. There He began His miracle-working ministry (John 2:11) in converting the water into wine at the wedding celebration. There also He pronounced the word by which the son of the nobleman of Capernaum was healed (John 4:46-54). Nathanael was from Cana (John 21:2). The descriptive phrase "of Galilee" is appended to this Cana, apparently to distinguish it from another in Coelesyria mentioned by Josephus.[9] Josephus also alludes to Cana of Galilee.[10] The preferred site by most scholars is Khirbet Kana about eight and a half miles to the north of Nazareth,[11] from which the Plain of Achotis descends to the Sea of Galilee.

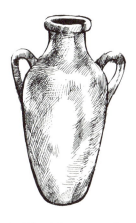

A Palestinian water jar. A large vessel of stone in which water was kept standing for ceremonial cleansing by Jews before and after meals (cf. John 2:6, 7). The "pitcher" of John 4:28 was an earthenware vessel for carrying water from the well

However, the traditional location of the village is Kefr Kenna, a site less than four miles northeast of Nazareth on the road to Tiberias. This latter place has been partially excavated and is amply watered and shaded by fig trees. As yet there is no archaeological evidence available to rule out Kefr Kenna, nor has Khirbet Kana been proved to be the site. Only additional research can settle the question of identity for certain.

[8]Leroy Waterman, *Preliminary Report of the University of Michigan Excavations at Sepphoris, Palestine*, in 1931, 1937, pp. 28f.
[9]*Antiquities* XV, 5, 1.
[10]*Life*, 16, 71.
[11]See Wright and Filson, *Westminster Historical Atlas to the Bible*, rev. ed. (1956), p. 123, Plate XII, A; XIV C. See also L. H. Grollenberg, *Atlas of the Bible* (1956), p. 146, and Kraeling, *op. cit.*, p. 254, Map V.

Another village of Galilee is Nain, where Jesus raised to life the only son of a widow (Luke 7:11-17). It is still called Nain (Nein) and is located five miles south-southeast of Nazareth in the northwest corner of Jebel Duhy (Little Hermon) and two miles west southwest

Grape harvest in Palestine, a common sight to Jesus and His disciples and a time of great rejoicing

Treading grapes in 1st century Palestine (cf. Isa. 63:2; Rev. 19:15)

of Endor. It is a tiny hamlet, almost a cluster of ruins, with ancient sepulchral caves on the east side of the village. Its elevation (1690 feet) gives the hamlet a superb view of the Plain of Jezreel (Esdraelon) on the south and southwest and of Mt. Tabor on the northwest.

II. The Sea of Galilee and its Cities

When Jesus left Nazareth and took up residence in Capernaum, He was moving out of His native highlands into a region along the lake shore 696 feet below sea level. But high plateaus surround the lake and frequently slope declivitously down into it, so that there were magnificent vistas of sky, land, and water. But Jesus was also moving into a region at the north and northwest sections of the Lake that was the center of a teeming population, where His ministry was desperately needed.

1. The Sea of Galilee

This beautiful body of fresh water enclosed by high hills is an integral part of the Jordan River which feeds it with water from snow-capped Hermon and the Labanons and then exists from its southern end to continue its serpentine journey southward to the Dead Sea. The lake is almost thirteen miles long and seven and a half miles wide at its broadest expanse opposite Magdala. Its greatest depth is 200 feet.

It lies in a depressed cup almost 700 feet below the Mediterranean Sea and enjoys a semi-tropical climate. Not far distant to the north are the perpetual snows of Lebanon. Sudden and violent storms, reflected in the gospel stories (cf. Matthew 8:23-27; Mark 4:35-41; Luke 8:22-25) often rush down from the mountain as the cold and warm air collide. The Lake abounds in fish, and fishing was an important industry, reflected so graphically in the vocation of Jesus' disciples (cf. Matthew 4:18-22; Mark 1:16-20; Luke 5:10, 11). There was also a fish preserving industry on the Lake, and Pliny mentions the city not referred to in the Bible named Tarichaea ("pickle town") where fish were salted and dried and shipped to distant points in the Graeco-Roman world.

The warm sunny climate, combined with health-giving sulphur springs in the environs of Tiberias along the Lake, have lured the sick and afflicted for centuries. Jesus' numerous physical healings were wrought in a region which in some sense was a health resort and which accordingly contained a larger number of sick people. This may be a fact in the prominence of the healing element in the Galilean ministry (Mark 1:32-34; 6:53-56).

In the northwest corner of the Lake, the rim of mountain wall flattens into the rich plain of Gennesaret and likewise the more severe heights on the east reaching 2,000 feet above the shore give way to the fertile district of El Batila in the northeast section where the rushing Jordan enters the Lake. But in the stony hills cultivation is arduous and the seed falling upon stony ground, growing up and soon withering, as Jesus records in the parable of the sower (Matthew 13:3-23; Mark 4:1-20; Luke 8:4-15), finds ready illustration.

The New Testament presents the Sea of Galilee as dotted with busy and populous towns in Jesus' day. These included Capernaum, Bethsaida, Chorazin, Magdala, and Tiberias.

2. Capernaum, Where Jesus Resided

This town lies on the northwestern shore of the Lake of Galilee in the territory of Zebulon and Naphtali (Matthew 4:13-16; Luke 4:31). It was a bustling fishing port, situated about two and a half miles southwest of the spot where the Jordan enters the Lake. The remains of the stone quays along the water front can still be seen. The site of Tell Hum where extensive ruins exist (cf. Jesus' prediction of the city's destruction, Matthew 11:23) is now generally recognized as the location of the ancient city rather than Khan Minyeh several miles south along the Galilean shore beyond 'Ain et-Tabgha ("Seven Springs"). On a pilgrimage in the sixth century A.D., Theodosius, in coming to Capernaum from Magdala, arrived at "Seven Springs" before he reached Capernaum, showing that Tell Hum rather than Khan Minyeh marks the ancient site.

The busy fishing emporium was also apparently a Roman military post. There the God-fearing Roman centurion sought Christ's healing touch for his ill slave (Matthew 8:5-13). Capernaum was also a toll-collecting station, to gather tax revenue from caravans passing along the great trade route from Damascus to the Mediterranean coast and Egypt. Here in the Capernaum toll house Jesus called to discipleship Matthew (Levi), a Jew in the employ of the Roman revenue bureau (Matthew 9:9). The tribute money which Peter found in the mouth of the fish and which at Jesus' direction he paid to the internal revenue officials at Capernaum (Matthew 17:24-27), illustrates the importance of the city in Rome's system of taxation.

Jesus conducted a far-reaching ministry of healing in His Capernaum headquarters (Matthew 9:1), including a paralytic (Mark 2:1-13); a demoniac (Mark 1:21-28, Luke 4:31-37); a nobleman's son (John 4:46-54); Peter's mother-in-law (Matthew 8:14-17; Mark 1:29-31), and many others (Matthew 8:16, 17; Mark 1:32-34; Luke 4:23, 40, 41). Despite His teaching and works, the citizens of Capernaum were unrepentant and Jesus prophesied the destruction of the city (Matthew 11:23, 24; Luke 10:15).

The great discourse on the bread of life (John 6:24-71), which

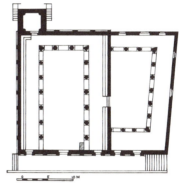

The Capernaum Synagogue, 3rd century. Top: Artist's sketch of restored structure. Center: floor plan. Bottom: modern ruins of the excavated structure. Courtesy Dr. John F. Walvoord.

followed the feeding of the five thousand, as well as many other discourses, was spoken in the Capernaum synagogue or elsewhere in the town (Mark 9:33-50).

Excavations in Capernaum have yielded ruins of one of the finest white limestone synagogues in Palestine. This structure has been restored by Franciscans.[12] According to prevailing custom, it was oriented toward Jerusalem. Rectangular in shape, the interior was seventy by fifty feet. It was colonnaded on three sides and had a balcony for women. Contrary to traditional Jewish dislike for any type of pictorial representation of living beings (cf. Exodus 20:4; Deuteronomy 5:8, which were construed as forbidding all such likenesses), the Capernaum synagogue in its decorative motif illustrates a more liberal policy, with centaurs, eagles, lions, palm trees, vines, and even boys carrying garlands exhibited in the ornamentation.[13]

Uncertainty has prevailed concerning the date of the Capernaum synagogue, some scholars dating it before the fall of Jerusalem in A.D. 70.[14] But in the light of the wholesale destruction of Jewish places of worship by the Romans in the Jewish-Roman War in the First Century and the second century rebellion of Bar Kokhba, the edifice is likely to be dated in the late second or third centuries, but no doubt similar in plan and perhaps built on the very spot where the synagogue in which Jesus taught stood. Other synagogues have been discovered at Chorazin, Bethsaida Julias, Meiron, Kefr, Bir'im, and at Beth Alpha in the Jezreel Valley. All date probably no earlier than the second century, that at Beth Alpha, famous for its mosaic work, being assigned to the sixth century.[15].

3. Chorazin, the Object of Jesus' Predicted Woe

Another town in the region of the Lake of Galilee, and like Capernaum the scene of many mighty works of Jesus, was Chorazin. Like its sister cities in the area, it remained largely unrepentant in spite of Jesus' ministry and received our Lord's stern warning of calamity (Matthew 11:21-23; Luke 10:13-15). The ancient site is to be located scarcely two miles to the north of Capernaum (Tell Hum) at Kerazeh, which was pointed out as the site by Rev. G. Williams in 1842. The Chorazin synagogue has been known for two hundred

---

[12]H. Kohl and C. Watzinger, *Antike Synagogen in Galiläa* (1916), pp. 4-41; E. L. Sukenik, *Ancient Synagogues in Palestine and Greece* (1934), pp. 7-21.

[13]Sukenik, *op. cit.*, pp. 61-64. The Jews violently opposed Herod's gold eagle decoration on the Jerusalem temple (*Wars* I, XXXIII, 2f.; *Antiquities* XVII, vi. 2), and clamored for the destruction of Herod Antipas' palace at Tiberias because it was decorated with animal pictures (Josephus, *Life*, 12).

[14]G. Oralfi, *Capharnaüm et ses Ruines* (1922), pp. 74-86; B. Meistermann, *Capharnaüm et Bethsaïde* (1921), p. 289.

[15]E. L. Sukenik, *The Ancient Synagogue at Beth Alpha* (1932).

years with its black basalt ruins and its "Moses' seat" where its distinguished teachers of the law sat (Matthew 23:2). Like the Capernaum synagogue, that at Chorazin was liberally ornamented with fruit motifs (grape-gathering and grape-pressing) and animal representations (centaurs in conflict with lions).[16] The extensive ruins of Chorazin are situated a little distant inland in a side valley branching off from another one which descends to the lake.

4. Bethsaida, the Home Town of Peter, Andrew, and Philip

The name Bethsaida suggests "houses, i.e., place of (fish) catching" and readily connects with the fact that Jesus' disciples Peter, Andrew, and possibly Philip were simple Galilean fishermen (Mark 1:16, 17) and natives of a lake town where this occupation was pursued by many of its inhabitants (John 1:44; 12:21).

Edward Robinson locates Bethsaida in close proximity to Capernaum, as also does Alfred Edersheim.[17] The latter infers that Bethsaida was the fishing quarter ("Fisherton") of Capernaum, thus explaining the fact that Mark names Bethsaida and John Capernaum as the original destination of Jesus' boat and also the circumstances of how Peter and Andrew, who according to John were of Bethsaida, are said by Mark as having their home in Capernaum.[18]

This explanation would posit two Bethsaidas, one on either side of the Jordan River

Carob pods, still often fed to swine and sometimes eaten by people, as in the case of the prodigal (Luke 15:16)

as it empties into the Sea of Galilee, as in the case of Kansas City, Missouri, and Kansas City, Kansas. Edward Robinson identified the western one with Tabgha, a fishing center with seven springs, located in Galilee proper.

Bethsaida Julias was the contiguous city on the east side of the Jordan in Gaulanitis. It was originally a small town, but Philip the tetrarch, who in addition to Gaulanitis ruled over Trachonitis, Batanaea, and Panias, regions north and east of the Sea of Galilee from 4

---

[16]E. L. Sukenik, *Ancient Synagogues*, pp. 21-24; Kohl and Watzinger, *Antike Synagogen*, pp. 41-58.
[17]*Life and Times of Jesus the Messiah* II, 3, 4.
[18]Edersheim, *loc. cit.*

B.C.-A.D. 34, rebuilt and greatly enlarged the place, raising it to the dignity of a city, renaming it Julia in honor of the daughter of Caesar Augustus. Since Julia was banished in 2 B.C., and Philip would scarcely have named a city for her after this unhappy event, the rebuilding of Bethsaida is to be reckoned as an activity of Philip at the very commencement of his reign (4-3 B.C.).[19]

Bethsaida Julias is commonly located at et Tell, a mound 800 feet by 400 feet and which rises to 100 feet almost a mile inland in the rich surrounding plain. Another site about 50 yards from the shore called Khirbet el Araj has been identified with Bethsaida the fishing village.[20] Archaeological research has not yet solved all the problems of exact location, but it is safe to assume that at least part of the village of Bethsaida was actually in Galilee, west of the Jordan in the vicinity where it empties into the Lake.

5. *Tiberias, Capital of Herod Antipas*

This city, built on the western shore of the Lake of Galilee by Herod Antipas as his new capital, was named in honor of the then-reigning emperor, Tiberius (14-37 A.D.)[21] The place still exists with some ancient ruins visible and is called Tabariya by the Arabs. It is about twelve miles from the northern end of the Lake and about three miles from its southern extremity. It is pleasantly located in a stretch of undulating plain rimmed in by steep mountain ridges. So important did it become as a capital city that its name began to be applied to the Lake, which became known as "the sea of Tiberias" (John 6:1; 21:1).

Uncertainty prevails as to the precise year the city was founded by Herod Antipas. On tenuous evidence from Josephus, the year A.D. 26 or thereabout is commonly suggested, merely because the Jewish historian alludes to Tiberias just after his taking note of the arrival of Pontius Pilate as procurator of Judaea (A.D. 26-36). But a better case archaeologically (coins and literary allusions) can be made for an earlier date (A.D. 18) on the occasion of the Emperor's sixtieth birthday and the twentieth anniversary of his holding the *tribunica potestas*.[22] This earlier date assuredly fits in better to the allusion to the city (6:23) and the Lake under this name (6:1; 21:1) in John's gospel.

The city was one of nine towns around the Lake which had more than 15,000 population, but initially had to be populated by foreigners

---

[19]Cf. Josephus *War* I, xxi, 1; *Antiquities* XV, xi.
[20]Emil Kraeling, *Rand McNally Bible Atlas*, pp. 388-389. For detailed discussion, see Dalman, *Sacred Sites and Ways*, pp. 161-183.
[21]Josephus *Antiquities* XVIII, 2, 3; *Wars* II, 9, 1. See Dalman, *op. cit.*, p. 176 f., 181f.
[22]Jack Finegan, *Light From the Ancient Past* rev. ed., (1959), p. 303, M. Avi-Yonah in *Israel Exploration Journal* 1 (1950-1951), pp. 160-169.

and indigents, Jews at first refusing to live in it because Herod Antipas had to remove many graves in order to make room for it. Jesus' is not recorded as having visited the city, probably because it had so few, if any, Jews in it, and having been so newly founded when His ministry was in progress. Early it became noted for its moral laxness as a hot bath resort visited by wealthy Greeks and Romans. Foreign customs prevailed, moreover, to such an extent as to give offense to Jews of stricter persuasion.

Tiberias and the Sea of Galilee. Courtesy Dr. John F. Walvoord

After the destruction of Jerusalem in A.D. 70, however, the situation changed, and Tiberias gradually became a virtual Jewish metropolis and a center of rabbinic learning. After the middle of the second century it became well-known as the seat of the Sanhedrin and the noted schools from which the Jerusalem Talmud (including the Mishnah and Gemara) came. From the sixth to the ninth centuries A.D., it became the center from which the Masoretic Hebrew Bible was edited, with "Tiberian" vowel pointings and traditional standardized text.

6. Magdala, the Home of Mary Magdalene

This village on the west side of the Lake of Galilee is probably to be identified with Mejdel, three miles northwest of Tiberias and situated between it and Capernaum at the southern end of the Plain of Ginnesar (Gennesaret). After feeding the 4,000 somewhere in the northeastern regions of the Lake, Jesus got into the boat and went to the region of Magdala (A.V.) — "Magadan" (R.S.V.). The parallel passage, Mark 8:10, has "the district of Dalmanutha." The latter place name is entirely unknown, as well as Magadan, and both names seem to be the result of textual corruption, and are probably to be traced back to Magdal (i.e. Magdala) and Magdal Nuna

(Nunaiya), i.e., "Magdal of fish" and identified as the same place.[23] Some would suggest the possibility that it be identified with the fish-drying and fish-packing town which Josephus designates by its Greek name Tarichaea.[24] At any rate, the important Palestinian Syriac gospel, a text which preserves native Palestinian tradition, has *Magdal* (Magdala). This is the apparent true reading, which became Magadan and then Dalmanutha by a series of scribal blunders in the hands of copyists to whom these names were foreign and meaningless.[25]

Magdala owes its chief interest to New Testament students as being the home of one of Jesus' most-devoted converts who ministered to Him of her substance (Luke 8:2) in gratitude for deliverance from "evil spirits and infirmities" (Luke 8:2; Mark 16:9). The epithet "Magdalene" or "Mary Magdalene" (Magdalene, a feminine substantive denotes, a "woman from Magdala") has this surname, in no sense to characterize her as a sinner, from which the current use of the word Magdalene has arisen, but merely to differentiate her from five other Marys mentioned in the New Testament — Mary, wife of Cleopas, Mary, the mother of Jesus, Mary of Bethany, Mary, the mother of Mark, and Mary of Rome (Romans 16:6).

Statue representation of Christ as the Good Shepherd, from 3rd century Rome. The figure also appears over a baptistry in a church at Dura on the Euphrates (also 3rd century)

Mary of Magdala was one of the faithful women at the cross (Matthew 27:56; Mark 15:40; John 19:25), observed the Lord's burial (Matthew 27:61), went to the sepulcher to anoint Jesus' body (Mark 16:1), found the stone rolled away, and told Peter and John that the body of Jesus had been taken away (John 20:1, 2). She was the first to whom the risen Christ appeared (Mark 16:9; John 20:11-17), and she reported His resurrection to the other disciples (John 20:18).

III. CAESAREA PHILIPPI AND THE DECAPOLIS

After healing the blind man in the vicinity of Bethsaida (Mark 8:22-26), Jesus and His disciples went northward "into the villages of Caesarea Philippi" (Mark 8:27). It was in this region where pagan Pan was revered that Jesus confronted His disciples with the momen-

---

[23]Cf. Jack Finegan, *op. cit.*, p. 303.
[24]*War* II, xxi, 4
[25]Kraeling, *Rand McNally Bible Atlas*, p. 388.

Pillars of Temple of Jupiter from
tunnel stables, Baalbek. Courtesy Dr.
John F. Walvoord

Altar rock for god at Baalbek.
Courtesy Dr. John F. Walvoord

tous question of His Messiahship and Person (Matthew 16:13-16; Mark 8:27-33; Luke 9:18-20).

1. Mt. Hermon and the Transfiguration

In coming into the region of Caesarea Philippi, Jesus and His disciples enjoyed the magnificently scenic region of Mt. Hermon, whose snowy majesty towered over them 9,101 feet above sea-level. Often they had seen its cool heights more than a hundred miles away through the shimmering heat of Jericho and the Jordan Valley or reflected in the waters of the Lake of Galilee.

Hermon was the "sacred mountain," sometimes called "Baal-Hermon" (Judges 3:3). It formed the northernmost boundary (Joshua 12:1) of the country beyond the Jordan (Joshua 11:17) which Israel was to conquer from the Amorites (Deuteronomy 3:8). It is called Mount *Sion*, i.e. high mountain, being by far the highest of all mountains in or near Palestine, and was sacred to the deities of the Canaanites and the religious center of primeval Syria. Its Baal sanctuaries gave it fame before the Exodus (Joshua 11:17). Pan worship flourished in the Graeco-Roman period, and Hermon became the center of the Druse religion in the tenth century A.D.

Significant in this paganistic environment was Peter's confession of Jesus' Messiahship. "Thou art the Christ, the Son of the living God" (Matthew 16:16). Was Jesus one of "gods many and lords many" of the pagans or was He the One living God manifested in humanity? Peter's confession takes on added significance in the background of Hermon and the region of Caesarea Philippi.

One of the solitary recesses of Hermon, rather than the summit of Mount Tabor, is believed by many to be the scene of the Transfiguration. Its nearness to Caesarea Philippi (Matthew 16:13) would argue for the case that the "high mountain" of Matthew 17:1, Mark 9:2, and Luke 9:28 is to be identified with this lofty peak, but proof for such a contention, of course, is lacking.

2. Caesarea Philippi and the Power of Ancient Paganism

The name Caesarea Philippi, that is the Caesarea of Philip, distinguishes this city in the Lebanon region from Caesarea in coastal Palestine. Both were named to honor a reigning Roman emperor. Caesarea Philippi is situated in the foothills of Hermon near the main source of the Jordan at the Paneion grotto, where abundant water issues from a cave (Mugharet Ras en-Neba) and where the pagan cult of Pan was centered.

Near this sacred spot Herod the Great built an exquisite temple of marble and dedicated it to Caesar Augustus. Philip, the son of Herod the Great, who ruled the region northwest of the Sea of Galilee

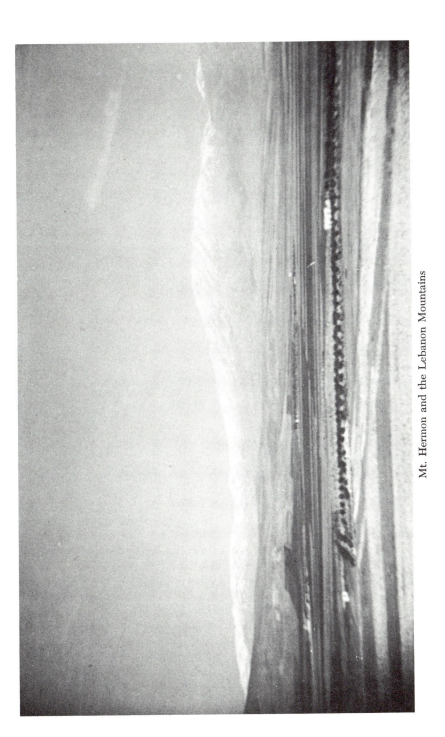

Mt. Hermon and the Lebanon Mountains

from 4 B.C. to A.D. 34, rebuilt and enlarged the town on this site and changed the name Panias, which had been given it in honor of the nature-cult god, Pan, to Caesarea in honor of the then-reigning Caesar, Tiberius. The epithet Philippi commemorated Philip the tetrarch's building the city. Later Agrippa II rechristened it "Neronias" in honor of Nero (54-68), but the old pagan name Panias has outlived both the names Philip and Agrippa II gave it, for it still clings to the present-day village in the form of Banias[26] and demonstrates the persistence and power paganism exerted over its devotees and over ancient culture and civilization.

Ancient Caesarea's acropolis is apparently buried under medieval towns and walls on the height above the present village. No trace remains even of the huge hippodrome where the victorious Titus compelled 2500 captive Jewish warriors to massacre each other as a spectacle for Agrippa II, Bernice, and himself. Only future archaeological research can locate the position of the magnificent Temple Herod the Great built to honor Augustus, which may lie beneath the Moslem shrine of Sheikh Khudr (St. George).

3. Baalbek and Its Famous Ruins in the Beqa

Farther north of Caesarea Philippi, deep in the mountainous belt of the Lebanon, the "white mountain," consisting of two ridges with the steep channel of the Beqa running between them, lies the awe-inspiring remains of Baalbek. This brilliant city of Syria with its magnificent ruins is a mute reminder of the present-day traveler of the splendor of ancient paganism. Situated in the scenic valley between Labanon and Antilebanon some forty miles north of Damascus, the ancient town was irregular in form and was surrounded by a wall two miles in circumference.

Baalbek was known as Heliopolis, "The City of the Sun," in the Graeco-Roman period, and its chief ruin is the Temple of the Sun (Baal-Jupiter), built in the era of Antonius Pius (A.D. 138-161) and Septimius Severus (A.D. 193-211). This massive edifice measured 310 by 175 feet, and some of the blocks employed in its construction are sixty feet long and thirteen feet thick. Its 54 Corinthian columns, of which six are still standing, were 68 feet high and 22 feet in circumference.

South of the Temple of the Sun is the exquisite Temple of Bacchus, one of the most magnificent examples of ancient architectural art in Syria. Although it is smaller than the Temple of the Sun, it is of colossal size (225 by 110 feet) and larger than the Parthenon at Athens. Nineteen of its 46 columns still stand. The quarries from which these great temples were hewn are in the immediate vicinity

[26]A simple substitution of the labial "p" for the labial "b."

of Baalbek and the small village that adjoins the ruins today. The art of Greece and the building genius of Rome were lavished on Baalbek from Augustus to Caracalla.

Although Jesus and His disciples never visited this ancient center of sun-worship, it was a cultic center such as they did visit at Caesarea Philippi on the border of Palestine and Syria. Under Julius Caesar, Baalbek became a Roman colony, and was garrisoned by Augustus. Under Constantine, its pagan temple became Christian churches, but sank into decay under pillaging by the Arabs in 748 and Tamerlane in 1401, with a violent earthquake completing its destruction in 1759. The Germans undertook important excavations in the early twentieth century, O. Puchstein publishing *Führer durch die Ruinen von Baalbek* in Berlin in 1905.

IV. PHOENICIA AND THE DECAPOLIS, FRINGE AREAS OF JESUS' MINISTRY

Galilee on the west and north was bounded by Phoenicia. Mark recounts that after ministry in the Capernaum region of Galilee (Mark 6:56; 7:17), Jesus made a journey to "the region of Tyre and Sidon" (Mark 7:24). This was a natural course of action since Phoenicia dipped down in close proximity to Upper Galilee, and in not more than a day's journey from Capernaum via Safed and Gischla (*ej Jish*) Jesus could be in Phoenician territory. No doubt Christ had good reason at this time to withdraw from the region of Herod Antipas' sway, inasmuch as that unscrupulous monarch had just ordered the execution of John the Baptist.

1. *The Region of Tyre and the Healing of the Syrophoenician Woman's Daughter*

This instance of non-Jews receiving the benefits of Christ's earthly ministry may have taken place in the border districts with partly Jewish and partly Gentile population, but more likely it occurred near Tyre itself, if not actually in the city (Mark 7:24-30; Matthew 15:21-28).

Tyre lay about 25 miles almost due west of Caesarea Philippi on the Mediterranean shore about 28 miles north of Ptolemais. It was much nearer Galilee than Sidon, which was 20 miles farther north on the coast. Mark also relates that when Jesus left the regions of Tyre and Sidon, "he came to the Sea of Galilee through the midst of the coasts of Decapolis" (Mark 7:31). This probably means that Jesus took the eastward road from Tyre to Caesarea Philippi and from there traveled south through Philip's kingdom of Gaulanitis to the Decapolis, which bordered on the Sea of Galilee along the entire south-eastern part of the Lake.

Nothing more is related of Jesus' Phoenician visit than deliverance of the demon-possessed girl. Inhabitants of these heathen cities, Jesus on occasion pointed out, were under much less responsibility than the places around the Sea of Galilee, which constantly witnessed His miracles and heard His preaching (Matthew 11:21, 22; Luke 10:13, 14).

The Gospel took hold at this historic town at a later date and the apostle Paul spent seven days at Tyre on his way to Jerusalem toward the end of his third missionary tour (Acts 21:3-6).

Sidon — harbor and Crusaders' Fort. Courtesy Dr. Paul Bauman

2. Sidon, Sister City of Tyre

How long Jesus sojourned in Phoenicia or whether He actually visited its two most ancient and historic seaports is uncertain. At any rate, Phoenicia is designated conspicuously in the gospel narratives as "the region of Tyre and Sidon" (Matthew 15:21; Mark 7:24).

Sidon was located on a promontory that slopes to the Mediterranean and re-emerges in a small island that was connected with the mainland by a bridge. About twenty miles north of the city lies modern Beirut (ancient Berytus). Oriented seaward, Sidon's long and checkered history is one of extensive commerce, wealth, and proficiency in arts and sciences. It is the oldest Phoenician emporium, famous and rich long before Tyre emerged into prominence. Modern Saida in the Republic of Lebanon marks its ancient location.

In the days of Herod Agrippa I (A.D. 41-44), the inhabitants of Tyre and Sidon for some reason displeased this monarch (Acts 12:20), although he adorned the city of Sidon architecturally and it enjoyed prestige under Roman rule. On his way to Rome, Paul was permitted to visit some friends of his at Sidon (Acts 27:3).

3. The Decapolis and the Outreach of Jesus' Ministry

Matthew states that "great multitudes of people ... from Decapolis" followed Jesus (Matthew 4:25). The demoniac of Gadara began to broadcast the fame of Jesus "in Decapolis" after his deliverance (Mark 5:20). Upon his return from the Phoenician country of Tyre and Sidon, Jesus "came to the sea of Galilee through the midst of the coasts of Decapolis" (Mark 7:31).

The Decapolis was a confederation of Hellenistic towns (originally ten in number) all except Scythopolis (ancient Bethshan, present Beisan, just west of the Jordan at the entrance to the Plain of Esdraelon) located in Transjordan southeast of Galilee, south of the tetrarch Philip's Gaulanitis, east of the northern half of Herod Antipas' Peraea, west and north of Aretas' sprawling desert kingdom of Nabataea. Pliny, a contemporary Roman historian, lists these cities as Damascus, Philadelphia (Amman), Raphana, Scythopolis, Gadara, Hippo, Dion, Pella, Galasa and Canatha.[27]

Interest for the New Testament student lies particularly in the town of Gadara, for Matthew (8:28, R.S.V.) notes that it was "in the country of the Gadarenes"[28] that the demoniac was healed.

In Mark and Luke's account, the deliverance of the demoniac and the episode of the swine rushing over a cliff into the sea are said to have occurred in "the country of the Gerasenes" (Mark 5:1; Luke 8:62 R.S.V.). Since in all these references other ancient authorities vary between "Gerasenes," "Gadarenes" or "Gergasenes," it is obvious the place name has been corrupted in transmission at the hands of scribes ignorant of Palestinian sacred sites and to whom the place name meant nothing geographically.[29]

Origen was of the opinion that the name Gadara was not the original name in these passages and adopted the reading Gergesenes.[30] If his contention is correct, then Gergesa would be a town of uncer-

---

[27]*Natural History* V, 16 *Loeb Classical Library* II, p. 277.
[28]Cf. Josephus, *Life* 42:44; Theodore Zahn, *Das Land der Gadarener, Gerasener, Gergesener Neue Kirschliche Zeitscrift* 13 (1902), pp. 923-945. G. Dalman, *Palestinajahrbuch* 7 (1911), pp. 20f.
[29]Just as Magdala was corrupted to Magadan and Dalmanutha (Mark 8:10, cf. Matthew 15:39).
[30]*Commentary on John* VI, 41. Jerome does not support his suggestion, however, by manuscript evidence.

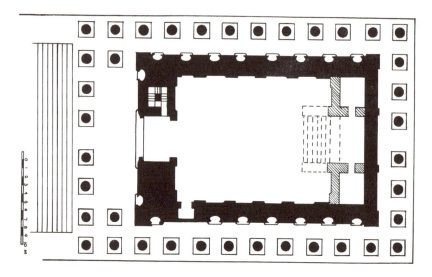

Floor plan of the Temple of Zeus at Gerasa (Jerash), erected about 163 A.D.

Ruins of the theatre at Jerash, including part of the stage and tiered seats at right. Courtesy Dr. John F. Walvoord

tain location on the eastern side of the Lake of Galilee.[31] It has been suggested that Gergesa is to be located at present-day Kersa, a tiny place on the eastern shore of the Lake of Galilee just below the Wadi es-Semak, where the topography of steep hills jutting into the Lake fits the story.[32]

Despite Origen's objection, the name Gadara may be correct. This Decapolis town included in Pliny's list (now Umm Qeis) is located five miles southeast of the southern tip of the Sea of Galilee beyond the Yarmuk River, and there is no reason to believe that the city's territory did not extend to the Lake shore. These progressive Hellenistic cities, enjoying a large degree of autonomy, grew rich and prosperous, with considerable landed interests and control around them.

Moreover, having been subjugated by Alexander Jannaeus (103-76 B.C.) before being liberated from Jewish authority by Pompey (64-63 B.C.), they contained a sizable Jewish population and considerable indoctrination in Jewish thought and customs, which no doubt was one reason why Jesus' ministry extended to them as fringe areas in His work (cf. Matthew 15:24).

After liberation by Pompey, these cities progressed in Greek thought and culture and developed economically, being merely subject to the legate of Syria, but being largely free to develop their cultural and material aspirations.

4. Gerasa (Jerash) and the Ministry of Jesus

One of the most splendid cities of the Decapolis, as revealed by modern archaeological excavations, is Jerash (Gerasa). The Revised Standard Version in Matthew 8:28 correctly connects the ministry of Christ to the demoniac with Gadara, but also anomalously and certainly incorrectly connects it with Gerasa (Jerash) in Mark 5:1 and Luke 8:26 ("the country of the Gerasenes"). The reading followed is obviously not the correct one, i.e., "Gadarenes" or "Gergasenes."

Gerasa (Jerash) is situated in an impossible location to be geographically connected with events which took place near the Galilean Lake. In fact, it lies fifty miles south of the Sea of Galilee on one of the tributaries of the Jabbok. Moreover, it is quite arbitrary to suppose another Gerasa near the Lake, so that there is no evidence that Jesus ever visited the city. However, Yale Univeristy and the British School of Archaeology in Jerusalem conducted excavations there in 1928-1930. In 1930-1931 and 1933-1934 Yale University and the

[31]See R. G. Clapp, *Journal Biblical Literature* 26 (1907), pp. 62-83; F. C. Burkitt, *ibidem*, pp. 128-133.
[32]Cf. Wright and Filson, *The Westminster Historical Atlas to the Bible*, plate XIV, p. 90. Jack Finegan, *Light From the Ancient Past* rev. ed., p. 309.

American Schools of Oriental Research continued archaeological work. As a result of these excavations, a brilliant city has been brought to light. Although most of the architectural remains date a trifle later than the New Testament era, the city was splendid in Jesus' day.

One of the interesting finds was a triumphal arch with an inscribed welcome to Emperor Hadrian on the occasion of his visit to the city in A.D. 130.[33] The excavated ruins display all the architectural refinements of a Hellenistic-Roman city with theatres, temples, forum, and spacious colonaded streets.

Head of Hadrian from a bronze coin of the period (117-138 A.D.)

V. SAMARIA AND THE WELL OF SYCHAR

Between Galilee and Judaea lay the religiously and politically inhospitable district of Samaria, through which ran the most direct route to Jerusalem. This road, requiring only three days of travel, was used by Galilean pilgrims in going up to the sacred feasts of Jerusalem, as is known from Josephus.[34] Such journeys through Samaritan territory appear prominently in the gospel accounts of Jesus' movements in Palestine (Luke 9:51-56; 17:11-19; John 4:1-43).

1. A City of Samaria Called Sychar

John's gospel reports that in traveling from Judaea to Galilee Jesus arrived at "a city of Samaria, which is called Sychar, near the portion of land that Jacob gave to his son Joseph" (John 4:5 cf. Genesis 33:19). This village in modern times has been customarily identified with Askar, a short distance southeast of Shechem in the Plain of Shechem on an important road to Scythopolis (Bethshan), and situated at the southeast foot of Mt. Ebal. Askar, however, is a mile northeast of the traditional Well of Jacob, which distance makes it improbable that it is the correct identification, since Jacob's Well was said to be at the city (John 4:6).

---

[33]Carl H. Kraeling, ed., *Gerasa, City of the Decapolis* (1938), p. 401, inscription no. 58.
[34]*Antiquities* XX, vi, 1.

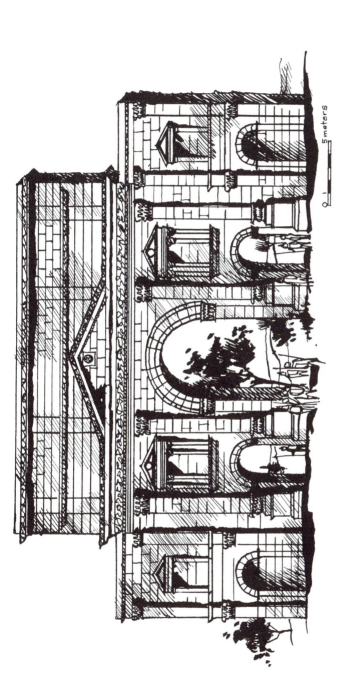

0 1 5 meters

The Triumphal Arch at Gerasa (modern Jerash)

This monument was built by Hadrian in 130 A.D. Gerasa was one of the brilliant cities of the Decapolis and was partly excavated (1925-1934). In Jesus' day Gerasa was a splendid Hellenistic city, but the heyday of its efflorescence was in the 2nd century A.D.

According to Jerome,[35] Sychar (Suchar) is a corrupted form of Suchem, i.e. Shechem. Recent excavations tend to demonstrate Jerome's correct conclusion, since Shechem was situated at *Balatah,* rather than at Nablus as used to be thought, the former site being nearer Jacob's well, and being occupied until A.D. 67, as Ernst Sellin's excavations between 1913 and 1934 have shown,[36] when it was destroyed by Vespasian, who built his new city Neapolis (Nablus) farther up the valley and left the old Shechem in ruins in A.D. 72. Today Nablus is inhabited by a remnant of the Samaritans.

Shechem was the metropolis and chief center of the Samaritans, located in the important pass between Mt. Ebal and Mt. Gerizim, thus controlling traffic north and south, and situated on the most direct route from Galilee to Jerusalem. It was the strategic stronghold of Samaritanism and an eminently fitting place for Jesus and His disciples

The grape vine in bloom. Grape growing was an important industry in Jesus' day and is featured in His illustrated teaching (cf. Matt. 21:33-44; John 15:1-10)

to stop and refresh themselves on their journey northward.

2. Jacob's Well and Jesus' Convert

Jacob's well at Sychar (old Shechem) was known since A.D. 333 and by A.D. 400 a church had been erected over it. It lies a half-mile east of Balatah (Sychar, old Shechem) on the highroad from Jerusalem to Galilee and the main road from Sebaste to Peraea. It is the first roadside well on the trip from Jerusalem to the north and a natural resting place for the traveler's midday meal.[37] Lying at the foot of Mt. Gerizim, the sacred mountain of the Samaritans, one can look up at the towering summit three thousand feet above and see the woman of Samaria pointing out the hill to Jesus as she said, "Our fathers worshipped in this mountain" (John 4:20). But she was to find the true object of worship in the Messiah who was talking to her and the true water of life, illustrated by the well, which although cluttered with debris, is still over seventy-five feet deep (cf. John 4:11).

[35]*Quaest. in Gen.* 66, 6; Epictetus (ed. H. Schenkl, 1894) 108, 13. Sychar is called "Shechem" in the old Syriac Gospels.

[36]See *Revue Biblique* 37 (1928), p. 619; Emil Kraeling, *Rand McNally Bible Atlas,* p. 391; W. F. Arndt and F. W. Gingrich, *A Greek-English Lexicon of the New Testament and Other Early Christian Literature* (1957), p. 803.

[37]Stephen Caiger, *Archaeology and the New Testament,* sec. ed. 1948, pp. 98f.

Mt. Gerizim seen from Jacob's Well (cf. John 4). Courtesy Mrs. Lowell Orth

CHAPTER 7

CHRISTIANITY IS BORN AND EXPANDS BEYOND JUDAEA

The Christian Church came into existence in Jerusalem as a result of the events of the day of Pentecost narrated in Acts 2. Gospel privilege based upon a crucified, risen, and ascended Messiah was introduced to Jews only, or at the most to proselytes of Judaism. The first seven chapters of the Acts give the history of this Jerusalem church, tracing its progress through persecution. Only indirect hints are given of the spread of the church to Judaea in general. But Luke assumes this wider outreach of the message in the announced scope of his historical sketch (Acts 1:8).

With Stephen's martyrdom, however, a decimating and climactic persecution flared up against the Jerusalem church. The evident direct target for the severe measures of repression taken by the persecutors was the Hellenists or Greek-speaking Jews in the church, of which group Stephen had been the leader. However, all the believers in the city were compelled to flee, "except the apostles." From this moment onward until the destruction of the city by the Romans in A.D. 70, the Jerusalem church seems to have consisted predominantly, if not almost entirely, of "Hebrews." After the Emperor Hadrian refounded the city as the Roman colony Aelia Capitolina in A.D. 135, the Jerusalem church then established there was a Gentile-Christian body and had no continuity with the Jewish-Christian church of the apostolic era.

The reason "all" the believers "were scattered abroad . . . except the apostles" (Acts 8:2) is evidently that the latter clung to their posts out of a rigid sense of duty and because the extreme hostility generated by Stephen's witness was not aimed so directly at them as at the leaders of the Hellenists in the church. The Diaspora, moreover, was providential. While the apostles remaining in the city assured the perpetuation of the witness there, the general scattering was the means of the expansion of Christianity "in all Judaea and Samaria . . ." (Acts 1:8) in accordance with our Lord's pre-ascension commission to His disciples. The words of an apocalyptic writer of the second half of the first century offer a parallel. "I will scatter this people among the Gentiles, that they may do good to the Gentiles" (II Baruch 1:4).

The principal leader in the violent Jerusalem persecution was Saul of Tarsus. Vested with authority from the Sanhedrin and imbued with an inveterate zeal for ancient Hebrew traditions, he saw the new faith as a dangerous threat to Judaism. He viewed the followers of the new sect not so much as misguided fanatics to be treated with a measure of pity but as deliberate impostors to be mercilessly eradicated. This he undertook to do on the basis that the protagonists of the new religion were foisting a blasphemous falsehood on their adherents in declaring that God had resurrected from the grave as Messiah and Lord "one whose manner of death was sufficient to show that the divine curse rested on him."[1]

I. THE INTRODUCTION OF THE GOSPEL TO SAMARIA

Two episodes comprise this section. The first involves Philip's preliminary ministry in Samaria (Acts 8:4-13) and the second Peter's opening of gospel opportunity to the Samaritans (verses 14-25). The latter episode cannot correctly be understood apart from the fact that the Samaritans were brought into the new spiritual era introduced to the Jews at Pentecost (Acts 2) and like them, through Peter's apostolic mediation, became recipients of the gift of the Spirit with all the blessings involved.[2]

1. *The District of Samaria*

After the division of the Kingdom of Israel subsequent to Solomon's death in the tenth century B.C., the so-called Northern Kingdom, comprising the Ten Tribes which seceded from Judah and Benjamin, became known as Samaria. The name is derived from the capital city which Omri founded in the second quarter of the ninth century B.C., calling it Shomron (Samaria) from the name of the strategic hill he bought on which to locate the town. The boundary of Samaria, which occupied central Palestine, extended from Galilee on the north to Judaea on the south, the southern limit marked by an uncertain line which ran through the weak buffer territory of Benjamin. The eastern boundary ran to the Jordan, and the western limit apparently did not reach the Mediterranean, for Accho belonged to Judaea.

Until the fall of the Northern Kingdom in 722-721 B.C., the history of Samaria was mainly that of the Ten Tribes. With the capture

[1]F. F. Bruce, *Commentary on the Book of the Acts* (Grand Rapids, 1954), p. 175.
[2]For a discussion of the theological aspects of Peter's ministry in Samaria, see Merrill F. Unger, *The Baptizing Work of the Holy Spirit* (Wheaton, Illinois, 1953), pp. 65-69.

of the city by the Assyrians, the independent history of the district began. The principal inhabitants were carried off by the Assyrians and numerous nationalities were imported and the population mongrelized. From this period began the intense animosity of the Jews toward the racially hodge-podge Samaritans, reflected so poignantly in the New Testament (John 4:9; Luke 9:52, 53).

The refusal of the Jews to accept the proffered aid of the Samaritans to rebuild the temple at Jerusalem under Sanballat, the Persian-supported governor of Samaria at the time of Zerubbabel, the governor of Jerusalem (Nehemiah 6), accentuated the hatred between Jew and Samaritan. The increased antipathy eventually led to the erection of a rival temple on Mt. Gerizim and the organization of a schismatic sect with headquarters in the vicinity of Shechem at Nablus. The Maccabean John Hyrcanus invaded Samaria about 128 B.C. and destroyed the temple on Gerizim. About a decade later, the capital city was razed by sons of Hyrcanus.

After the religious cleavage, the regime of Ezra and Nehemiah excluded the Samaritans from offering at the Jerusalem temple, and a rigid boycott of intercourse with them was enforced. This sad rift continued even in Jesus' day, so that centuries of virulent hostility had crystallized the enmity reflected in the declaration of the woman of Samaria, "The Jews have no dealings with the Samaritans" (John 4:9).

In 63 B.C. Samaria came under Roman domination and Pompey included it in the province of Syria. In 40 B.C., as a result of the Parthian threat to Jerusalem, the Romans gave most of Palestine to Herod, including Samaria, Herod ruling as a subservient king from 37-4 B.C. After Herod's death, Samaria, along with Judaea and Northern Idumaea, passed to Herod's son, Archelaus. Augustus, however, deposed him in A.D. 6 and put Samaria under the rule of a Roman procurator. This was the status of the country in the days of Jesus and the apostles.

2. The City of Samaria

According to Acts 6:5 (Codex Vaticanus), Philip in his evangelizing efforts "went down to *the* city of Samaria." The less attested reading is "*a* city of Samaria" (Codex Bezae). The meaning, despite critical objection,[3] is apparently found in the more difficult but better attested reading, "*the* city of Samaria" (meaning "the chief city of the country or district of Samaria"). The usage is confessedly unusual, but most certainly refers to Sebaste (modern Sebastiyeh), which in pre-Herodian times was known as Samaria, rather than to Gitta, Si-

[3]Cf. Kirsopp Lake and Henry J. Cadbury, *The Beginnings of Christianity* IV (London, 1933), p. 89; F. F. Bruce: *The Acts of the Apostles* (London, 1951), p. 183.

mon Magus' birthplace according to Justin Martyr, or to Neapolis (ancient Shechem, modern Nablus), the headquarters of orthodox Samaritanism.[4]   Kraeling suggests the reason for the vagueness of the writer of Acts in designating Sebaste "may be due to his reluctance to put the Apostles in this scene, where worship of the late emperor Augustus was the order of the day."[5]

The city of Samaria suffered greatly during the Maccabean wars, losing its fortifications and its strength. It was not until the Roman governorship of Gabinius from 57 to 55 B.C. that the walls were restored. In gratitude to its benefactor, the city was called Gabiniopolis and its loyalty to Rome was fostered. In 39 B.C. when Herod was fighting for the Romans against Antigonus, the Samaritans assisted him. In 30 B.C. the city was officially given to Herod by Caesar Augustus, and the wily client-king opportunely saw his chance both to strengthen his hold on the country and at the same time to advertise his gratitude and devotion to the emperor. Accordingly Herod began an ambitious program of beautifying and adorning the city in honor of Augustus, renaming it Sebaste (Augusta) and settling six thousand of his retiring war veterans there.

Herod also greatly enlarged the city, so that it stretched for two and a half Roman miles in circumference.

Excavations by the Harvard University expedition under the direction of George A. Reisner and Clarence Fisher (1908-1910) and resumed by the British archaeologist J. W. Crowfoot (1931-1935) have resurrected the Hellenistic-Roman city as well as the more ancient city of Old Testament times.[6] Herod erected a stout wall around this new city with defensive towers dotting it. The strategic location and centrality of the place were

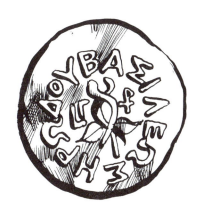

Drawing of bronze coin of Herod the Great with caduceus (serpent entwined wand surmounted with wings)

[4]Cf. Charles W. Carter and Ralph Earle, *Acts in The Evangelical Bible Commentary* (Grand Rapids, 1959, p. 112). Emil G. Kraeling, *Rand McNally Bible Atlas* (New York, 1956), p. 416.

[5]*Op. cit.*, p. 416.

[6]J. W. Crowfoot, Kathleen Kenyon, and E. L. Sukenik, *The Buildings at Samaria* (London, 1942), pp. 31-37. For a historical account, see Josephus, who devotes a whole chapter to Herod's buildings — *Wars* I, xxi, *Antiquities* XV, viii, 5 translated by H. St. Thackeray and Ralph Marcus (London 1926-1943).

not overlooked by the wily king as an ideal site for another of his fortress cities which were planned to rivet his rule on the country.

Perhaps the most ambitious undertaking of Herod was a grandiose temple erected to Emperor Augustus. This lavish structure was constructed on a podium so as to be conspicuous from afar, and was reached by an elegant flight of steps leading up from a large forecourt. The temple was rectangular in shape as well as the court in front of it. The remains of this edifice attest to its magnificence as a monument worthy of honoring the emperor of the world at that time.

Ruins of Herod's Summer Palace (Samaria - Sebaste). Courtesy Dr. John F. Walvoord

The forum, a characteristic feature of a Hellenistic city, was located east of the temple of Augustus and was apparently the work of Herod. But the finest ruin of the Herodian period is the spacious stadium, enclosed with a stone wall and a roof supported by Doric columns. It was regulation size, 638 feet long and 190 feet wide, comparable in size to the track used in the Olympic games in Greece. The stadium at Sebaste offers another attestation to Herod's devotion to Greek athletics, known also from his activities in this area at Jerusalem and Caesarea. In the latter city Herod supported the Olympic games and offered the handsomest rewards at the 192nd Olympiad.[7]

[7] G. Ernest Wright, *Biblical Archaeology* (Philadelphia, 1957), p. 219.

3. The Ministry of Philip and Peter

Philip's spiritual labors were attended with great success, especially in demon-expulsions and miracles of healing (Acts 8:5-8). However, there was opposition from a Satan-controlled occultist and demon-trafficker named Simon, who, however, professed conversion under Philip's preaching. Numerous legends have been handed down in early Christian writings concerning this person whose birthplace traditionally was said to be Gitta (modern Jett), some thirteen miles northwest of Sebaste (Samaria).

Simon belonged to a class, all too common in that era, consisting of Jews trading on the mysterious religious prestige of their race and imposing on the credulity of the heathen, boasting in the exercise of magical powers manifested in incantations, spells, and charms.[8] This instance of Simon of Samaria is paralleled by Bar-Jesus of Paphos in Cyprus (Acts 13:6-11) and offers another striking example in the Book of Acts of the clash of a young and virile Christianity with magic.[9]

Under Philip's preaching the Samaritans "received the word of God" (Acts 8:14), i.e., truths concerning "the kingdom of God and the name of Jesus Christ" (verse 12). Their baptism (verse 12) showed they believed in the death, burial, resurrection, and ascension of Jesus as the Messiah. One thing remained. They needed to be brought, as a mixed racial entity between Jew and Gentile, into the full spiritual privileges of the new age inaugurated in Acts 2. This was accomplished by the Jerusalem apostles dispatching "Peter and John" to pray for them that "they might receive the Holy Spirit" (Acts 8:14, 15). Peter was sent to be the apostolic intermediary, as in all the initial introductions of the full gospel privilege of the new age, to Jew (Acts 2:13), to Samaritan (Acts 8:14, 15) and to Gentile (Acts 10:44), according to the declaration of Jesus Himself (Matthew 16:18, 19). John was delegated by the Jerusalem church to be an apostolic witness of what was to transpire. It is noteworthy that this pivotal event in the outgoing of the Gospel providentially occurred in such a splendid, influential, and strategic city as Hellenistic Sebaste.

The city was a place eminently fitted for the far-reaching spiritual event which took place within its walls, just as the similarly significant city of Caesarea was to be divinely chosen as the scene of the introduction of gospel opportunity to the Gentiles (Acts 10). But in

[8]For an excellent characteristerization of Simon the Magician, see W. M. Ramsay, *The Bearing of Recent Discovery on the Trustworthiness of the New Testament* 4th ed., pp. 117-131.
[9]Cf. Ramsay, *op. cit.*, pp. 106-116.

both cases, the Christian Gospel thus introduced in a strategic center of population and culture within an ethnic group, soon spread to others outside in other centers of population within that group. "So then after giving their testimony and speaking the word of the Lord they (the apostles Peter and John) returned to Jerusalem and brought the good news *to many villages of the Samaritans*" (Acts 8:25, cf. 11:19-22).

II. THE CONVERSION OF THE ETHIOPIAN EUNUCH

The message of a crucified and risen Saviour with the consequent spiritual blessings of the new gospel age having been opened to the Jews (Acts 2) and the racially and religiously mixed Samaritans (Acts 8:1-25), an account of Philip's ministry follows closely in the incident of the conversion of the Ethiopian eunuch (Acts 8:26-40). The latter personage falls into the category of those who, like the Samaritans, either racially or religiously, or both, had affinities with the Jews and their religion, and who were not pure Gentiles.

This is why the conversion of the Ethiopian eunuch is catalogued *after* the official introduction of gospel privilege to the Samaritans and *in relation* to Philip's ministry, and *not* that of Peter and John. The incident furnishes an illustration of the norm of the salvation experience established for the new age. For this reason, in contrast to apostolic mediation by Peter witnessed by John, Philip's ministry and message alone are sufficient, and there is a conspicuous absence of apostolic imposition of hands and "receiving the Holy Spirit," or the giving of the Holy Spirit as a gift, as in the case of the official introduction of the Gospel to a people as an ethnic and religious group. In the case of the eunuch there was simple faith in Jesus the Messiah as the Son of God (Acts 8:37), followed by baptism as an outward attestation to the inward exercise of faith and the consequent salvation experience.

1. *The Road From Jerusalem to Gaza*

Philip was divinely directed to "rise and go southwards in the road which goes down from Jerusalem to Gaza" (Acts 8:26). Appended to the divine directive is the explanation, "This (either the road or the city being grammatically meant) is desert." The R.S.V. construes the latter, "This is a desert road." The A.V. chooses the former, "Gaza, which is desert," and would be a reference to the ruins of the older town destroyed by the Hasmonaean king, Alexander Jannaeus, in 93 B.C., and which became known as Old Gaza or Desert Gaza after the Roman Governor Gabinius, who in 57 B.C. erected the new city of Gaza nearer to the Mediterranean.

New Gaza, the Hellenistic town, according to Josephus,[10] was partially destroyed, but not until A.D. 66. It is distinguished by the ancient geographers from the older city,[11] and was located on the great caravan route connecting with Arabia, Egypt, Syria and Europe, being an important merchandise mart and the last town in Palestine on the way to Egypt.

Since there were several roads that lead south from Jerusalem to Gaza, one going by the way of Hebron and another farther to the west, and God knew well the road the Ethiopian eunuch would take to return to his native land, exact directions were necessary so that Philip might know the correct route to follow. One early tradition names the road south to Hebron, turning off at Bethzur southwestward to the plain. Here tradition, illustrated by the Madeba map, located the place where the eunuch was baptized. Another view held Philip turned off the Hebron road earlier at Bethter and traveled via Beit Jibrin, placing the baptism at a fountain near the former place.

Kraeling, understanding "go toward the south" in a broad general sense, places the route westward and slightly northwestward to Emmaus and then southwestward toward Azotus. Since water is not to be found south of Azotus, in the dreary rocky wastes through which the road winds, Kraeling suggests a spot for the baptism two miles north of Azotus, near the mound of the old Philistine city of Ashdod, where the highway reaches the source of the Nahr Sukrer, today the only water available on this part of the caravan route to Gaza.[12]

2. The Ethiopian Nobleman, Treasurer of Candace, Queen of the Ethiopians

As Philip obeyed the divine directive, he overtook "an Ethiopian man, a eunuch, minister of Candace, Queen of the Ethiopians, who had come on a pilgrimage to Jerusalem, and was returning, and was seated in his coach and reading the prophet Isaiah" (Acts 8:27, 28).

Although the word used for the vehicle in which the important Ethiopian official was traveling often means a war chariot or racing chariot (*harma*), it was probably more a wagon or carriage, yet certainly befitted the man of high station who rode in it, and was drawn by horses rather than being a mere "ox-wagon," as Lake and Cadbury suggest.[13] It cannot be imagined that the vehicle was not the finest and most comfortable the craftsmanship of the age could furnish, and

---

[10]*Antiquities* XIV, 4, 4.
[11]Diodorus Siculus XIX, 80, Arrian, Anabasis II, 26, 1, Strabo XVI, 2, 30. Cf. W. J. Pythian Adams, *Quarterly Statement of the Palestine Exploration Fund*, 1923, pp. 30f., George Adam Smith, *Historical Geography of the Holy Land*, pp. 186 ff.
[12]Kraeling, *op. cit.*, p. 418.
[13]*Op. cit.*, p. 96.

it need not be assumed the conveyance necessarily had to move slowly to facilitate reading. Probably, as a proselyte of Judaism, the Ethiopian was simply following the stipulations of the rabbis that the sacred Scriptures should be read on a journey, and that they (particularly the Law) should be read aloud.[14] Such an exercise suited him admirably as he endeavored to avoid the boredom of a long journey, especially through desolate country.

The Ethiopian to whom Philip ministered was a treasurer under Candace. This is a title, like the term "Pharaoh" among the Egyptians, and not a personal name. George Reisner has identified the pyramid tombs of reigning Candaces of Ethiopia at Meroe in the Anglo-Egyptian Sudan north of Khartoum, dating from the third century B.C. till the middle of the fourth century A.D.[15] Both Greek and Latin writers take note of a dynasty of Ethiopian queens bearing the title of Candace.

The theory behind the line of queens is that the king of Ethiopia was venerated as the child of the sun and regarded as too exalted to administrate the secular duties of royalty. These functions were carried out for him by the queen mother, bearing the dynastic title Candace.[16]

The ancient kingdom of Ethiopia which had the line of Candaces, or reigning queens, corresponds to present-day Nubia, and the Ethiopians were Nubians inhabiting the Nile district from Aswan at the first cataract of the Nile south to the vicinity of Khartoum, its two chief cities being Meroe and Napata.[17]

The Ethiopian treasurer is said to have been "a eunuch," that is, a castrated male. The inhuman practice of self-mutilation and the mutilation of others in this manner was rife throughout the ancient world. Men thus deformed were placed under serious religious disabilities by the Mosaic law, being excluded from public worship (Deuteronomy 23:1), in part because such mutilation was frequently practiced in heathenism in reverence to pagan gods, and in part be-

[14]Lake and Cadbury, op. cit., p. 96
[15]G. A. Reisner, "The Pyramids of Meroe and the Candaces of Ethiopia" in Sudan Notes and Records, 1922; F. L. Griffith, Meroe, the City of the Ethiopians, 1911. A. H. Sayce, "The Meroitic Hieroglyphic Inscriptions" in Proceedings of the Society of Biblical Archaeology, 1909.
[16]Bion of Soli, Aethiopica 1; cf. also Strabo Geography XVII, 1, 54; Dio Cassius, History LIV, 5, 4, Pliny, Natural History VI, 186; Eusebius, Ecclesiastical History II, 1, 13.
[17]The Ethiopians (Nubians) have been confused with the Abyssinians, who represent the ancient Axum in the mountains east of the Upper Nile. But ethnologically and geographically, Ethiopians (Semitic in language) and Abyssinians (Hamitic) are distinct (cf. L. Reinisch, Die Nuba-Sprache, 1879. F. Praetorius, "Ueber die hamitischen Sprachen-Ostafrika's" in Beitraege zur Assyriologie, II (1894), pp. 312 ff., E. A. Budge, The Egyptian Sudan, 1907.

cause a maimed creature of any description was considered unfit for the service of Yahweh (Leviticus 22:23-25).

It is, accordingly, providential that in this illustrative example of gospel privilege going out to those who were racially and religiously related to the Jews and their religion (like the Samaritans) or simply religiously related (like the eunuch), since he was apparently a non-Jew and a proselyte of the gate who had simply embraced Judaism, the grace now offered in Christ overleaped all barriers and disabilities imposed by the law of Moses, and granted full salvation to one who, although of noble position, had been excluded from the congregation of the Lord's people by a legal disability.

Eunuchs were commonly employed by the kings of Judah and Israel, aping their pagan neighbors, as guardians of the royal harem (II Kings 9:32; Jeremiah 41:16) and in military and other official posts (I Samuel 8:15; I Kings 22:9; II Kings 8:6; Jeremiah 29:2; 34:19; 38:7). The courts of the Herods were normally featured by the presence of eunuchs, as Josephus states.[18] With the Ethiopian court ruled by queens, it is little wonder to find an important official of the queen a eunuch.

III. Saul of Tarsus and His Conversion Near Damascus

The book of the Acts is an account of the expansion of Christianity through the witness of God-chosen human instruments from Jerusalem to "all Judaea and Samaria and to the end of the earth" (Acts 1:8). The first eight chapters present the radiation of the gospel message from Jerusalem to "all Judaea and Samaria." This involves the official introduction of gospel privilege to the Jews (Acts 2), with the history of the conversion of many Jews at Jerusalem (Acts 3-7), and to the Samaritans (Acts 8:1-25), with the illustration of the wider outreach to Jewish proselytes, such as the Ethiopian eunuch (Acts 8:26-40).

The rest of the book of the Acts is concerned with the official introduction of the Gospel to Gentiles (Acts 10:1-48), and with this introductory process completed and the norm of salvation established, the rest of the book is taken up essentially with the extension of the salvation message "to the end of the earth."

It is significant that the conversion of Saul of Tarsus, who was destined to be the great exponent of the Gospel "to the end of the earth," is introduced in chapter 9, *immediately after* the completed official opening of the Gospel to Jew, Samaritan, and Jewish proselyte, and *just before* the account of the introduction of gospel grace to pure Gentiles. He who was to become "the apostle to the Gentiles" is

[18]*Antiquities* XV, 7, 4.

seen already being prepared for his task while God was at the same time preparing the way for those who would hear the apostle's message.

1. *Tarsus, Birthplace of Saul*

After the conversion of "Saul of Tarsus" (Acts 9:11), his filling with the Spirit in Ananias' house, and his initial ministry in Damascus and Jerusalem, the Christian brothers conducted him to Caesarea to send him by ship "to Tarsus" that he might escape death at the hands of the Jews who were plotting to kill him (Acts 9:30). Saul was sent to Tarsus to escape danger evidently because it was his birthplace (Acts 22:3), and he enjoyed the citizenship of this free city (Acts 21:39). From Tarsus he was later fetched by Barnabas to assist in teaching the large number of Gentile converts in the church at Antioch (Acts 11:25, 26).

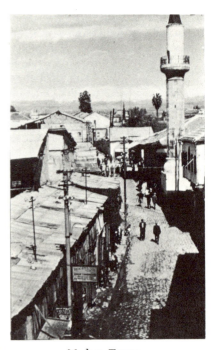
Modern Tarsus

Tarsus was located in the New Testament era in the Roman province of Cilicia in southeastern Asia Minor across the Gulf of Issos from Antioch's seaport, Seleucia. Cilicia was famous for its wool sheared from Taurus-ranging flocks and loomed into a textile called *cilium*. Although rimmed on the north and west by the Taurus Mountains, access from the west was through the renowned Cilician Gates which narrowly cut through the lofty mountains and gave entrance to the rich plain which formed the heart of the province and the setting for Tarsus, the most important metropolis of the country. Through the Cilician Gates moved the armies and the commercial caravans of antiquity. Paul himself passed through this artery of traffic as he went to found and establish the first Christian churches in Asia Minor and Europe, and his home town Tarsus in his day was a busy emporium swarming with traders, travelers, and military men. Today, remains of the old Roman road connecting Tarsus with the Cilician Gates can still be seen. It in turn

Coins from Tarsus. Above, l.: head of the city goddess (1st century). Above, r.: grain ship transporting "corn of Tarsus" from Egypt (Emperor Caracalla, 211-217 A.D.). Center: The crown of the chief priest of Cilicia in the imperial cult—a circlet of gold surmounted by busts of the emperors (Emperor Gordion, 235-238 A.D.). Below: Apollo atop a column, with Perseus and city god worshiping beside the altar, in front of which lies a bull (3rd century A.D.)

connected with the ancient trade road from the Euphrates, joining the road from Antioch and points south fifty miles east of Tarsus.

In addition to being strategically situated on this network of highways by land, Tarsus was ideally located on the sea lanes as well. Although an inland city built on the banks of the Cydnus River ten miles from the Mediterranean Sea, the swift-flowing stream branched out into a lake just below the city, forming a natural harbor, easily reached by Mediterranean sea trade and thoroughly safe for international shipping. As a result of this unique waterway, the city enjoyed a prosperous maritime commerce in addition to its land trade.

With such an ideal location, there is little wonder the site was very early inhabited and that the founding of the city is wrapped in legend. The town is mentioned on the Black Obelisk as a conquest of the Assyrian emperor Shalmaneser in the ninth century B.C. Persia ruled the city through satraps, and in Xenophon's day (fourth century B.C.) the city was renowned and thriving. Alexander the Great's advent in 334 B.C. left a permanent Hellenistic stamp on the place to temper its earlier Oriental character.

Under the Seleucids, Greek influences were fostered. Antiochus Epiphanes IV, about 170 B.C., constituted Tarsus an autonomous Greek town and settled a colony of Jews there to stimulate the economic growth of the city. To them he granted equal civil rights with Greeks.

When Roman power took over in 64 B.C., Tarsus became the seat of the governmental administration of the province of Cilicia. It was probably when Antony decreed full Roman citizenship on all the Tarsians (including the Jews) that Saul's family received this important benefit, which stood the apostle in good stead when later this fact changed the attitude of Roman governmental officialdom toward him and gave him right of appeal to Caesar (Acts 22:28-30). These privileges were confirmed by Augustus, so that Tarsus became a favored town and its citizens proud of its civic-mindedness and progress. Paul, with eminent justification, could say to the Roman tribune when he was arrested in Jerusalem, "I am a Jew, from Tarsus in Cilicia, a citizen of no mean city" (Acts 21:39).

The Greek culture and intellectual life of the city were also strong factors substantiating Paul's pride in his home town. Tarsus was the seat of a famous state-supported university and had a reputation for the keen interest of its native students for learning and philosophy, in this particular emulating even the more famous Athens in Greece and Alexandria in Egypt. Whereas the latter cities had a heavy influx of foreign students, native Cilicians crowded the halls of the Tarsian university.[19]

Famous philosophers of Tarsus included the Stoics Antipater, Archedemus, Nestor, Athenodorus surnamed Cordylion, friend and confidant of the younger Marcus Cato and his slightly later namesake who was the tutor of Augustus and the later reviser of the Tarsian constitution and restorer of its democratic processes. Another philosopher was Nestor, who tutored famous Romans. The grammarians Artemidorus and Diodorus and the tragic poet Dionysides are included in Strabo's list of distinguished Tarsians.

Precisely what effect Paul's boyhood in Tarsus had on the later ministry of the apostle or just how long he studied in his native town is impossible to say. At Tarsus he learned the trade of Cilician cloth manufacture which later he engaged in to support himself in his missionary endeavors throughout the Graeco-Roman world (Acts 18:3; 20:34; I Thessalonians 2:9; II Thessalonians 3:8). But certainly this was only one element that providentially fitted into his great future ministry. Tarsus with its world trade, its oriental traditions, its cosmopolitan learning, its Hellenic culture, its autonomous government, its Stoic and Cynic philosophers who graced its busy agora or sauntered along the Cyndus River in erudite discussion, was bound to have exerted a far-reaching effect on one of its citizens designed to be the most famous and useful of all the great men it produced. Uniting Jewish nationality with membership in a Greek state and Roman citizenship, with prodigious learning in Judaism, his conversion to Christianity and the divine revelation of its distinctive message were the climaxing events that made Saul of Tarsus the peculiarly equipped personality for the magnificent and colossal task divinely assigned him.

2. Damascus and the Beginning of Saul's Ministry

At the time of Saul's conversion and escape from the city, Damascus may have been temporarily under Nabataean rule, for "the governor of King Aretas was guarding the city of the Damascenes" (II Corinthians 11:32). However, as a free city and a member of the Decapolis, a chain of ten autonomous cities including Bethshan (Scythopolis) on the west side of Jordan, and Pella, Dion, Kanatha, Raphana, Hippos, Gadara, Philadelphia, Damascus, and Gerasa (Jerash) on the east side of the Jordon, Damascus like its free sister cities had the right to coin its own money. Moreover there are extant coins of the city from the reign of Augustus, Tiberius, and Nero, but none from the time of Caligula (37-41 A.D.) who may possibly have handed

[19]Cf. Sir William Ramsay, *The Cities of St. Paul* (reprint Grand Rapids, 1949), pp. 228-235.

over the city to her neighbors, since "such an act on the part of the paronoiac emperor is quite possible. . . ."[20]

On the other hand, the Romans would not likely have ceded so important a free city to Aretas IV (9 B.C.-40 A.D.), especially since they had planned a punitive expedition against him when he conducted a successful war against his son-in-law Herod in 36 A.D., because the latter had divorced his daughter in order to marry Herodias.[21] But the erratic Caligula may have sided with Aretas, for in 40 A.D. he ceded to Herod Agrippa I the tetrarchate that had belonged to Herod Antipas.

But since "the governor" was an "ethnarch," the ruler of an ethnic group in a city, numerous scholars adopt essentially the position of C. S. C. Williams that "rather than to suppose that Aretas was in possession of the city over which his representative was placed or that there were so many more Arabs than Jews there that Aretas appointed its governor, it is easier to assume that the ethnarch waiting for Paul was outside the city, perhaps a neighboring sheikh, hoping to catch Paul as he emerged."[22]

Straight Street in Damascus in modern times. Courtesy Dr. John F. Walvoord.

[20]Guiseppe Ricciotti, *Paul the Apostle* 1953, p. 30. John Davis, *A Dictionary of the Bible* (4th ed. rev., 1954), p. 52.

[21]Josephus, *Antiquities* XVIII 5, 1-3. Cf. Mark 6:17-29; G. E. Wright, *Biblical Archaeology* (Philadelphia, 1957), p. 226.

[22]*The Acts of the Apostles* in *Harper's New Testament Commentaries* (New York, 1957), p. 126. Cf. E. Kraeling, *Rand McNally Bible Atlas* (New York, 1956), p. 426. Lake and Cadbury, *Beginnings of Christianity* V, 193; H. J. Cadbury, *The Book of the Acts in History,* 1955, pp. 19-21.

The problem of Aretas' relationship to Damascus at the time of Paul's escape, however, cannot be solved fully, but from Galatians 1:17 it is known that Paul's stay in Damascus was punctuated by his trip to Arabia. It is also certain that his withdrawal to Arabia did not last beyond the third year of his conversion (Galatians 1:18), apparently in the year 39, before Aretas' death in 40 and after Caligula's accession. Under this theory, Paul fled the city when it no longer belonged to the Romans but to Aretas.

Paul's early associations with Damascus have highlighted this ancient city, so famous in the Old Testament period as well as in the New Testament era. But the poverty of the city's antiquities is remarkable, since it has been continuously occupied for millennia and therefore unexcavated. Some of its walls, however, are ancient, and several of the Roman gates are well preserved. The "Street Straight" still bisects the city from the eastern to the western gate. The Church of John the Baptist of the fourth century A.D. still preserves an important Christian inscription, although the edifice was turned into a mosque in the eighth century and has been burned several times. According to R. A. S. MacCalister, the inscription reads: "Thy kingdom, O Christ, is an everlasting kingdom, and thy dominion endureth throughout all generations."[23]

3. Saul's Sojourn in Arabia

Although the reference to the trip to Arabia is clear from Galatians 1:17, the geographical designation is far from precise. Did the apostle go to some spot in Aretas' sprawling kingdom of Nabataea, stretching northeast, east, and south of the Decapolis? At this era the Nabataean kingdom of Aretas was far from being a desert but was a prosperous, irrigated region of hundreds of thriving towns, beautiful temples and high places, established by the marvelously enterprising people known as the Nabataeans. Their kingdom lay astride the important trade routes between Arabia and Syria. Well-known high places include that at Petra, first discovered by George L. Robinson in 1900, and that at Jebel et-Tannur, situated southeast of the Dead Sea, excavated by Nelson Glueck in 1937.[24]

However, since Arabia from Old Testament geographical representations suggests an isolated desert region conducive to receiving spiritual revelations similar to those vouchsafed to Moses (Exodus 3:1), to the nation Israel at Sinai (Deuteronomy 4:10) and to the

---

[23]As quoted by Camden Cobern, *The New Archaeological Discoveries and Their Bearing Upon the New Testament* (New York, 1917), p. 545.
[24]For a survey of the Nabataeans and archaeological discoveries, see Nelson Glueck, *The Other Side of the Jordan* (New Haven, 1940), Chapter VI, "The Civilization of the Nabataeans," pp. 158-200. *Bulletin of the American Schools of Oriental Research* 131 (Oct., 1954), pp. 6-15.

prophet Elijah (I Kings 19:1-21), a locality in the more distant and vast peninsula of Arabia may be meant. This area, about one-third as large as the United States, is bounded on the west by the Red Sea, on the south by the Indian Ocean, on the north by the Fertile Crescent, the ancient rim of desert-skirted civilization, and on the east by the Persian Gulf. Somewhere in the depths of its illimitable solitudes, perhaps at Horeb, the very mount of God, the newly converted Saul of Tarsus was given the far-reaching spiritual truths to be taught and preached in the new age that was in the course of being opened to Jew (Acts 2), Samaritan and Jewish proselyte (Acts 8), and Gentile (Acts 10).

IV. Caesarea and the Pivotal Expansion of Christianity

Heretofore, the Gospel based upon the finished redemption of a crucified, risen, and ascended Saviour had been introduced to Jews (Acts 2) and the racially and religiously mixed Samaritans (Acts 8:5-25). One more instance of such official apostolic introduction to a distinct ethnic group remains (Acts 10:1-48). After this pivotal event in the extension of gospel privilege to the Gentiles and the spread of gospel witness "to the end of the earth" (cf. Acts 1:8), Luke represents the Holy Spirit as received with neither delay, apostolic mediation, imposition of hands, nor any other circumstance or condition other than simple faith in Christ.

1. Cornelius the Roman Centurion

"The range of the apostolic message has been steadily broadening, and now the time has come for it to cross the barrier which separated Jews from Gentiles and be presented unambiguously to Gentiles."[25] Cornelius was a very common Roman name since Publius Cornelius Sulla in 82 B.C. granted freedom to 10,000 slaves who were enrolled in the gens Cornelia to which he belonged, and whose family name these freedmen acquired. As a centurion (corresponding roughly to a "captain"), Cornelius was a man of considerable importance, commanding approximately a hundred men ("century"), which was one-sixtieth of a Roman legion of 6,000 men. Centurions like Cornelius and Julius (Acts 27:1) may have been separated from the legion to which they were properly assigned, in order to discharge special duties. Ordinary duties of a centurion included inspection and drilling and commanding men under him, but other duties, corresponding to a non-commissioned officer, were sometimes delegated to him.

Cornelius belonged to one of the auxiliary cohorts (Greek speira)

[25]F. F. Bruce, Commentary on the Book of Acts (Grand Rapids, 1954), p. 214.

in Judaea. Inscriptional evidence demonstrates the presence of such an auxiliary band in Syria about A.D. 69 entitled *Cohors II Italica civium Romanorum,* that is, "second Italian cohort of Roman citizens."[26] Commanders of this rank were required to be good, valorous, level-headed leaders, and formed the essential strength of the Roman army.

In addition Cornelius was one of those Gentiles known as "God-fearers." Like numerous other non-Jews, he was drawn to the simple monotheism of Judaism and the sound morality of the Jewish way of life, but shied away from proselytism involving circumcision and the keeping of the Jewish law, as well as baptism in the presence of witnesses. His fear of God was manifested in his regular prayers to the God of Israel and his charitable donations to the Jewish people.

That he as the first Gentile to be admitted to gospel privilege was a God-fearer is highly important. Such God-fearing Gentiles, who, however, commonly attended the synagogue, and who kept the Sabbath and abstained from certain foods, later form the first converts and the nucleus of the newly-formed churches in one community after another in Paul's great missionary tours.

2. Peter's Ministry in Lydda and His Preparation for Gentile Evangelism at Joppa

According to Acts 9:32-43, the apostle Peter conducted an important ministry in the coastal area of Palestine, apparently itinerating among the Christian assemblies already founded there. At Lydda he healed a paralytic named Aeneas who had been bedridden for eight years, and the knowledge of this miracle was the means of numerous converts in Lydda and all over the coastal plain of Sharon (Acts 9:32-35), which extended more than fifty miles north from Lydda and Joppa to Mount Carmel south of Haifa. This well-watered garden area of Palestine contained not only the cities of Lydda and Joppa, but Antipatris, Appolonia, Caesarea, and Dor as well. Over its coastal road and its expansive sandy beaches moved the caravan traffic from Arabia, Egypt and the Tigris-Euphrates world, and flowed religious and cultural influences into other parts of Palestine.

Lydda, about eleven miles southeast of Joppa, and lying on the Jerusalem to Joppa road, is found as Lod in Old Testament times (I Chronicles 8:12; Ezra 2:33; Nehemiah 7:37), and was famous in Crusader times as the traditional site of the martyrdom of St. George, who was adopted as the patron saint of England through Richard Coeur de Lion and venerated as the patron of Syrian Christianity.

The Seleucids ceded Lydda (Lod) to Jonathan Maccabaeus in

[26]Cf. H. Dessau, *Inscriptiones Latinae Selectae* (Berlin, 1892-1916), no. 9168.

145 B.C. Although Pompey stripped the city of its Jewish rights, Caesar restored them, and it became the capital of a Judaean district. The ancient name of the town survives in present-day Ludd, where a modern airport is located and the impressive ruins of the Crusader Church of St. George are the only reminder of the older phases of the city, whose remains apparently lie buried beneath the present settlement.

From Lydda Peter was called to come to Joppa where he miraculously restored the charitable and beloved widow Dorcas to life and where he resided for an extended period "with one Simon a tanner" (Acts 9:36-43), whose house was on a street skirting the Mediterranean Sea (Acts 10:6). In Old Testament times Jaffa was the port of Palestine, when it was the only harbor between Mt. Carmel and Egypt. But it was never really satisfactory, notably lacking a breakwater, so that Joppa longshoremen became famous for their dexterity in safely landing cargoes through rough surf. From its port the fleeing Jonah took ship for Tarshish (Jonah 1:3). The city is very ancient, appearing as Japho in the Old Testament (Joshua 19:46), in the lists of conquests of Thutmose III at Karnak, in the Amarna Letters as the chief center of Egyptian provincial government around 1400 B.C., and as *Yapu* in the Assyrian records. From the time of the Maccabees the city was possessed by the Jews and Rome confirmed this status. Under the Herodian regime it was included in Herod's realm, and it remained fanatically Jewish until the campaign of Vespasian in A.D. 68. In fact, the city stoutly resisted pagan contacts and persisted in Judaistic traditionalism and as a pharisaical center highly suitable for the place of the divine revelation of "clean" and "unclean" things vouchsafed to Simon Peter as an indispensable preparation for his ministry to the Gentiles in Caesarea (Acts 9:43-10:33).

At the time of Peter's residence there and his reception of the vision which broke down his Jewish and pharisaical prejudices, the city had lost much of its importance as a maritime emporium, for Caesarea had been developed by Herod the Great as the chief harbor and had become the virtual capital of Palestine. Today Joppa (Jaffa) exports the famous Jaffa oranges cultivated in the Plain of Sharon.

3. Caesarea and the Outreach of the Christian Gospel to the Gentiles

At the time of Peter's ministry to Cornelius' house and the opening of gospel opportunity to the first representative Gentiles, the city of Caesarea was one of the most cosmopolitan and important centers of Palestine, and as fitting a place for the vastly significant event that transpired there under Peter's preaching as Joppa had been for the revelation vouchsafed to Peter in preparation for that event. The brilliant city, built by Herod the Great between 25-13 B.C., became the

Ruins of an ancient aqueduct to Caesarea. Courtesy Dr. John F. Walvoord

Ruins of Caesarea, Palestine. Courtesy Dr. John F. Walvoord

seat of the Roman government in Judaea, and there were naturally many Roman officials and army contingents stationed in the city. It thus had a large proportion of pagans in its population, as well as a large segment of Jews. Having been made a fine seaport by Herod the Great, Caesarea had ready access to all parts of the Roman world and was an ideal city for the spread of the gospel witness to far-flung places by virtue of the continual flow of land and sea traffic, since it also lay astride the important road north and south connecting with Asia Minor, Mesopotamia, Egypt, and Arabia. The choice of this elegant Hellenistic city for the introduction of Christianity to pagans was indeed providential.

When Herod dedicated the city in 12 B.C. in honor of Caesar Augustus, he renamed it Caesarea, having built it on an earlier site called "Straton's Tower." Foremost among Herod's constructions was a huge sea mole, 200 feet wide and which stood in 120 feet of water, the remains of which are still visible.[27] The Link Expedition to Israel in the summer of 1960 sponsored by the American-Israel Society and Princeton Theological Seminary, with financial assistance also given by the American Philosophical Society and *Life* Magazine, began a chapter in underwater archaeology or "aqueology" in its preliminary explorations of the harbor and Herodian installations at Caesarea.[28] The circular breakwater which enclosed the harbor has been charted and the entrance on the northern side has been found and carefully explored by the divers. Among many objects found was a coin apparently depicting the ancient port of Caesarea and issued to commemorate "some important occasion at Caesarea in the first or second century A.D."[29] Upon the coin's face is the representation of the entrance to a port flanked by round stone towers surmounted by statues. Arches border the jetty on either side of the towers, and two sailing ships are on the point of entering the harbor. "Two letters, KA, may well be the abbreviation for the word Caesarea."[30]

The main part of Caesarea with its sumptuous public buildings was enclosed by a semicircular wall, and contained the temple to the divine Caesar which faced the harbor and could be seen far out to sea, a theatre, a forum, a stadium, and an amphitheatre. Israeli archaeologists located the amphitheatre by means of aerial photography. The arena, oval in shape, was somewhat larger even than the Colosseum in Rome itself, being more than 300 feet long and 200 feet wide and

---

[27]For a detailed account of the construction of Caesarea and its harbor, see Flavius Josephus, *Jewish Antiquities* XV, 9, 6 and *The Jewish War* I, 21, 5-8.
[28]Charles T. Fritsch and Immanuel Ben-Dor, "The Link Expedition to Israel, 1960" in *The Biblical Archaeologist* XXIV, 2, May 1961, pp. 50-59.
[29]Fritsch and Ben-Dor, *op. cit.*, p. 56.
[30]Fritsch and Ben-Dor, *loc. cit.*

was the scene of bloody gladiatorial contests in 10 B.C. when Herod publicly inaugurated the town. In 70 A.D. hundreds of Jewish prisoners were slaughtered in such combats staged by Titus in the same arena.

The Hellenic-Roman character of Caesarea is further accentuated by the stadium for athletic games and the theatre where Greek and Latin dramatic productions were given to a cosmopolitan population where the spirit and fashions of Rome were copied. Here, if anywhere, pagan culture and customs had been introduced and planted on the soil of Palestine. The introduction of the Christian Gospel in such a city is highly significant as it poised itself for extension "to the

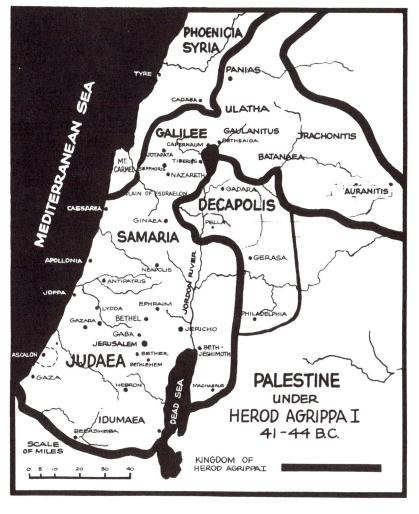

PALESTINE
UNDER
HEROD AGRIPPA I
41–44 B.C.

KINGDOM OF
HEROD AGRIPPA I

SCALE OF MILES
0 5 10   20   30   40

uttermost part of the earth" (Acts 1:8). It is because of this unique significance that Luke highlights the story of Peter's ministry in Caesarea (Acts 10:1-11:18).

V. HEROD AGRIPPA I AND THE DISPERSAL OF THE APOSTLES

In the persecution which erupted at the martyrdom of Stephen, "all" the believers were scattered "except the apostles" (Acts 8:1). In the events of chapter 12 of the Acts, the apostles themselves are violently dispersed by a new and fierce persecution against the church at Jerusalem.

1. *Herod Agrippa I, the Last King of the Jews*

"About that time Herod the king laid violent hands upon some who belonged to the church. He killed James the brother of John with the sword; and when he saw that it pleased the Jews, he proceeded to arrest Peter also" (Acts 12:1-3, R.S.V.).

This decisive persecution was doubtless of as great providential import as was that incident upon the death of Stephen. However, since Luke is featuring the extension of the Gospel to the west, he is silent concerning what happened to the other apostles (apart from Peter and James) as well as concerning the expansion of the church eastward and southward of Judaea (except the incident of the Ethiopian eunuch).

Drawing of a bronze coin of Herod Agrippa I (40-44 A.D.). Obverse—Umbrella. Reverse—three ears of grain

But the question arises, how did "King Herod" have the authority to imprison Peter and put James to death? Luke does not explain this circumstance but history and archaeology furnish an answer.

In 41 A.D. the Herodian dynasty enjoyed a return to power in Judaea and Samaria in the person of Herod Agrippa I, son of Aristobulus, and grandson of Herod the Great and Mariamne. Under Caligula he began his rise to power, being given authority over the northern tetrarchies which Herod Antipas, Philip, and Lysanias had ruled. Claudius placed Herod Agrippa also over Judaea and Samaria. From A.D. 41-44 he practically ruled the same domain as his grandfather, Herod the Great. It is he who is the "King Herod" of Acts 12:1, who had full authority to execute James, the son of Zebedee and brother of John, and to imprison Peter.

2. *The Death of Herod Agrippa I at Caesarea*

By divine intervention Peter escaped the clutches of Herod Agrippa I. What the fate of the other apostles was is not related, nor is the region to which they actually fled, if they actually fled, mentioned. Eusebius, the early church historian, was of the opinion that the Twelve Apostles were scattered throughout the world during this period after the martyrdom of James, but Luke narrates only Peter's departure (Acts 12:17), probably to Antioch, and it is quite conceivable the other apostles and Peter returned soon after Herod's death, since it is certain that the Jerusalem church was by no means obliterated or that its numerous members all fled, inasmuch as Herod's ire was apparently not directed particularly at them. This is certainly the truth, despite the fact that the history of the Jerusalem church is not further pursued in the Acts (which, if this had been the case, would have been contrary to the scope of the book announced in 1:8), and is only noted as it interacts with the Antiochene church or with the life and ministry of Paul. The Apostolic Council of Acts 15 is evidence enough of the strength and importance of the mother church at Jerusalem after Herod Agrippa's death.

After Peter's escape Herod Agrippa went to Caesarea. He evidently made the trip to participate in the quadrennial festival in honor of the Roman emperor, which would have taken place in 44 B.C. His short kingship over the Jews ended ignominiously with his decease in that year when he arrogated to himself divine honors (Acts 12:20-23) in addition to his crimes in persecuting Christians in order to ingratiate himself into Jewish favor.

CHAPTER 8

ANTIOCH, THE BIRTHPLACE OF CHRISTIAN MISSIONS

The city of Antioch on the Orontes (Acts 13:1-4) possesses remarkable importance in apostolic church history as the location of a strategic Gentile church which projected the first great missionary activity of Christianity. The church at Jerusalem, Jewish in its background and circumscribed in its vision, apparently had never initiated missionary movements beyond its immediate environment, except by dint of fierce persecution that scattered it after Stephen's martyrdom (Acts 8:1-4). Refugees from persecution-ridden Judaea fled to Phoenicia, Cyprus, and Antioch with the Christian evangel (Acts 11:19).

The crowning goal of the new missionary endeavor was the Syrian capital and metropolis, Antioch. At first the Gospel was preached to Jews only and with limited results. When some men of Cyprus and Cyrene undertook Gentile evangelism, there was instant and phenomenal success at Antioch. A large church soon came into existence in the city, and in contrast to the church at Jerusalem, the church at Antioch spontaneously assumed missionary responsibility that was to place it in the vanguard of evangelistic advance into areas unreached by the Gospel. Rightly it can be said that "this city could claim in a more real sense even than Jerusalem to be the mother of the churches of Asia Minor and Europe ... and the birthplace of foreign missions."[1]

Luke, the historian, specifically notes the gifted nature of the Antiochene church and its spiritual ministrations that envisioned it for missionary advance. Among the talented prophets and teachers enumerated are Barnabas, Simeon called Niger, Lucius of Cyrene, Manaean the foster brother of Herod the tetrarch, and Saul, whom Barnabas had fetched from Tarsus (Acts 11:25, 26; 13:1). Teaching, fasting, and prayer are listed as the featured activities of the assembly at Antioch that eventuated in the call of Barnabas and Saul for large-scale missionary undertaking (Acts 11:26; 13:2-4). The spiritual vi-

[1]Bruce M. Metzger, "Antioch-on-the-Orontes," in the *Biblical Archeologist* XI, 4, Dec. 1948, p. 70.

tality of this church, strategically located in the third city of the Empire, is indicated by the theological terminology employed by the sacred historian. "As they ministered to the Lord, and fasted, *the Holy Spirit said*, Separate to me Barnabas and Saul for the work unto which I have called them" (Acts 13:2 Greek). "So they *being sent forth* by *the Holy Spirit* left for Seleucia" (Acts 13:4) and from this, the seaport of Antioch, set sail on the first missionary journey, which was to prove so momentous for the Western world in all subsequent centuries.

I. ANTIOCH THE BEAUTIFUL

The splendid, sprawling city of Paul's day was third in size in the Roman Empire, being exceeded only by the capital on the Tiber and Alexandria in Egypt.[2] Even though the apostle was accustomed to the magnificence of Greek towns, he himself being a native of the brilliant town of Tarsus in Cilicia, which he proudly declares was "no mean city" (Acts 21:39), yet he and Barnabas, who also was used to Hellenistic cities, must have thrilled every time they climbed the last hill on their return to this city, and saw it stretched out majestically in a scenic valley on the banks of the Orontes River at the foot of Mt. Silpius. The whole countryside formed an unforgettable panorama. The noble Lebanon chain runs northward and the Taurus range skirts southward. At this point the Orontes bends and breaks through the mountains, about twenty-three miles from the Mediterranean, to form nature's fine setting for the city that was destined to be the focal point for the spread of Gentile Christianity, and the place where converts were numerous and distinctive enough to be first called "Christians."[3]

1. *The Early History of Antioch*

Antioch had over three centuries of history and development to prepare it providentially for its significant role in apostolic history

[2]Cf. Josephus *War* III, II, 4. The only other city in the Orient which could be compared to Antioch was Seleucia on the Tigris. Cf. Emil G. Kraeling, *Rand McNally Bible Atlas.* (New York, 1956), p. 427.

[3]Rather "got the name of Christian" (Acts 11:26), possibly as a derisive epithet, since the Antiochenes were notorious for scurrilous nicknaming. They dubbed Emperor Julian the Apostate "the Butcher" because of his sacrificial offerings at the shrine of his deities and "the goat" because he wore an unstylish long beard in imitation of his revered philosophers. However, "Christian" may have been an official name of Jesus' disciples given by Roman officials at Antioch (cf. Eric Peterson in *Miscellanea Giovanni Mercati,* Vol. I (1946) pp. 355-372; cf. *Pompeiani, Sullani* and other party names). Even *Herodiani* (Matthew 22:16) may be legitimately traced to Roman influence (C. J. Ellicott in *A New Testament Commentary,* Vol. II, New York, 1883, p. 75). Tradition also ascribes the origin of the term "Christianity" to Bishop Ignatius of Antioch (i. e. *Christianismos* as opposed to *Judaismos*) in expressing the whole system of faith and life of a Christian (Ellicott, *in. loc.*)

and Christian missions. Founded in 300 B.C. by Seleucus I Nicator (312-280 B.C.), its site was allegedly pointed out by an oracle of the god Zeus Kasios, and named after Seleucus I's father Antiochus.[4]

Seleucus I is famous as an ancient city-founder. His craze and prodigality in this activity resulted in his founding no fewer than thirty-seven towns, which he dubbed after his own name or those of his relatives.[5] According to the *Chronicle* of John Malalas, a Byzantine monk of Antioch in the sixth century A.D., Seleucus I Nicator named Antioch after his son Antiochus I Soter, rather than his father.[6] Since Seleucus I built fifteen other Asiatic cities named Antioch, Antioch-on-the-Orontes was often called "Antioch-by-Daphne," a famous suburb lying southwest of the city.

Under the reign of Antiochus I Soter (280-261 B.C.), Antioch became the Seleucid Empire's western capital and for two and a half centuries continued in the role of a center of imperial government. Antiochus I on the east added a second quarter to the original city. Seleucus II Collinicus (246-226 B.C.) constructed a third area on the island in the Orontes River. Antiochus IV Epiphanes (175-164 B.C.) built a fourth section on Mount Silpius. Strabo in his *Geography* described the city as "a Tetrapolis" since it consisted of "four parts" with "each of the four inhabited areas ... fortified both by a common wall and by a wall of its own."[7] Substantial portions of the city wall of Antioch, especially on Mount Silpius, encircling Ephiphaneia, the area constructed by Antiochus Epiphanes, have been recovered and are clearly discernible today.

Enjoying a strategic location commercially, by land with easy access for Eastern caravans and by sea through its seaport, Seleucia, Antioch grew under its Seleucid rulers as successive kings vied with each other to adorn it with numerous architectural monuments. In 83 B.C. the city came under the sway of Tigranes of Armenia for almost two decades till Rome took it over.

2. Antioch Under Roman Rule

In 64 B.C. Pompey came into control of the Syrian capital and initiated a new era in the development of the city. He exhibited great favor to the inhabitants and aided in repairing damage resulting from a recent earthquake. Julius Caesar in 47 B.C. was acclaimed by the metropolis on a visit and granted it internal autonomy. He donated the Caesarium, an important public building, and was after-

[4]Kraeling, *op. cit.*, p. 427.
[5]Cf. Victor Schultze, *Altchristliche Staedte und Landschaften* III, *Antiocheia* (Guetersloh, 1930) p. 5.
[6]Matthew Spinka, *Chronicle of John Malalas*, Books VIII-XVIII, *translated from the Church Slavonic* (1940) VIII, 1-2 (pp. 13 f.).
[7]XVI, II, 4.

wards held in revered memory by the citizenry. Augustus added further adornments and made his son-in-law, Agrippa, governor of the province of Syria, whose capitol was Antioch. Agrippa in turn erected the celebrated Agrippianon, a sumptuous public bath, and built a district which came to be known as the quarter of the Agrippites. Herod the Great embellished the town with a colonnaded street and a paved highway to the suburb of Daphne.[8] Emperor Tiberius likewise graced Antioch with a marble-paved thoroughfare running in an east-west direction through the southern section of the city. He notably reared a temple to Jupiter Capitolinus and built other shrines. But perhaps the most interesting feature of "Antioch the Beautiful" — "The Queen of the East" — was its distinction of being the only ancient city known to have possessed a regular system of street lighting. Jerome of the fourth century A.D. by a chance allusion to the lighting of the street lamps at Antioch makes this known to us.[9]

3. Antioch of Paul's Day

Paul and Barnabas were familiar with the Old City of Seleucus I Nicator in the western sector and often must have walked along its three-century-old streets and its ancient encircling walls, as well as the handsomely colonnaded avenue that ran through the city from east to west. Also well-known to them was Antiochus IV's beautiful quarter of Epiphaneia to the south with its stout outer walls skirting Mount Silpius and the Acropolis. Within Epiphaneia but near the wall separating it from the Old City was the busy Agora, where Paul, if he did what he did in Athens, reasoned with the crowds which resorted there.

The view from Mount Silpius with the Acropolis to the east, Caesar's baths to the west, and the large amphitheatre to the north must have been inspiring even to one who recognized his "citizenship" to be "in heaven" (Philippians 3:20). No doubt Paul, Barnabas and other leaders in the church carried on personal evangelism here or held open air meetings in the poorer and more populous sections of the old city, or taking the familiar street through the Daphne Gate on the west with the thronging crowds on a special holiday, preached the Gospel to the masses of pagan worshipers and pleasure seekers around the temples and gardens of the famous suburb.

Paul and Barnabas must have frequently crossed the bridge that spanned the Orontes and led to the sector known as the New City, where the Roman governor of the province of Syria resided in the splendid palaces built by Seleucid kings. They also traveled the road running northward from the Old City, turning in a northwesterly

[8]Josephus *Wars* I, XXI, 11; *Antiquities* XVI, V, 3.
[9]*Dialogue Against the Luciferians*, 1.

direction after it crossed the Orontes toward Antioch's seaport Seleucia.

4. Daphne and Antioch's Morals

The laxity of Antiochene morals became proverbial in the third city of the Empire. As a melting pot of Oriental and Occidental cultures and religions, the more undesirable features of both traditions were unhappily perpetuated. The material prosperity of the city and the motley complexion of its large population were features that tended to luxurious living and moral degeneracy.

Chrysostom says that Antioch had "a citizenry (*demos*) reaching the number of 200,000."[10] If the term *demos* did not embrace slaves, women and infants, as is possible, the population about A.D. 300 was about 500,000 and may have run as high as 800,000, if the population of the suburbs was not reckoned by Chrysostom.[11]

Such a concentration of diverse ethnic elements offered a superb challenge to the efficacy of the Christian Gospel to transform human life. This was especially true since the city was notorious in the ancient world for its laissez-faire living and vice. "In no city of antiquity," declares Mommsen, "was the enjoyment of life so much the main thing and its duties so incidental, as in 'Antioch-upon-Daphne,' as the city was significantly called."[12]

The pleasure gardens and parks of the suburb of Daphne became the symbol of Antioch's depravity. Situated on an elevated area southwest of the city proper, the playground of Antioch was superbly located on a plateau more than 300 feet above the average level of the metropolis. It was dotted with cypress groves, handsome villas, temples, and a theatre constructed in a natural bowl overlooking the Orontes valley.

Wealth, dissolute practices of effete Oriental cults, and lust for pleasure combined at Daphne to make it a hotbed of vice of every description. "Daphne morals" became a byword and a terse definition of human dissoluteness. The celebrated Roman satirist Juvenal could take no sharper thrust at his own degenerating city of Rome than to assert that the Orontes had flowed into the Tiber, inundating the imperial city with the depravity of the Orient.[13] Gibbon in his celebrated *Decline and Fall of the Roman Empire* depicts in lively fashion the beauty and debauchery of Antioch's dissolute suburb.[14]

[10]*Homily on St. Ignatius,* 4.
[11]Cf. Wm. F. Steinspring, *The Description of Antioch in Codex Vaticanus Arabicus 286* (unpublished dissertation Yale University 1932), pp. 2, 3 of commentary.
[12]Theodore Mommsen, *The Provinces of the Roman Empire from Caesar to Diocletian,* Eng. trans., 2nd ed., vol. II, 1909, p. 128.
[13]*Satire* III, 62.
[14] Chapter XXIV.

It was providential that the Gospel of grace should call out a large and spiritually vitalized church in such a sophisticated and morally corrupt city. Thereby was demonstrated the power of the Christian Gospel to transform multitudes, weary with the inanity and moral turpitude of pagan cults. Moreover, the strategic importance of the location of this great city is proved by the fact that it became the birthplace of foreign missions. The church founded in its polluted atmosphere was destined not only to become the mother of the churches of Asia Minor and Europe, but also in a sense the mother of the churches of the entire Western Hemisphere.

5. *Antioch and Its Jewish Population*

Although there was a substantial Jewish community in Antioch, having equal political privileges with Greeks with its rights engraved on bronze tablets, there is reason to believe its prestige diminished sharply as a strong Gentile church was established, since there was much less hindrance to the new faith from Jews in Antioch than was true elsewhere.

Modern Antioch on the Orontes

Besides Greek dislike of Jews because of their hatred of idolatry and annoying separatism, the Maccabean War on Hellenism in Palestine had furnished additional reasons for anti-Semitism. In addition, a Jewish uprising in Antioch in 39 A.D., when Paul was probably there, further reduced Jewish influence. A quarrel ensued between partisan groups in which the Jews were somehow involved. Many of them were killed and their synagogue was destroyed. A detachment of Jews under Phinehas of Tiberias invaded and terrorized the city.

The Emperor Caligula crushed the uprising and severely punished the Jews. As a result, their power in Antioch was seriously curtailed.

These events, unfortunate as they might be, were obviously providential. The mother church of Christian missions was in a measure freed from fierce Jewish persecution and, what was more important, was relieved of the peril of infiltration by legalism. The Gospel of grace was enabled to expand and be propagated in distant regions and remain safe on the home base.

II. EXCAVATIONS AT ANTIOCH

Present-day Antakiyeh is a mere village in comparison to the splendid metropolis of antiquity. Covering only a small portion of the ancient city's area, with only a fraction of its population (about 35,000), the modern site, however, offers exceptional advantages for archaeological research. Unlike many ancient sites encumbered by contemporary occupation, Antioch has been largely accessible to the archaeologist's spade.

1. *Pre-War II Excavations*

Work was begun at Antioch in 1932 by Princeton University in conjunction with the Baltimore Museum of Art, the Worcester Art Museum and the Musees Nationaux de France. The results of these researches were published in several volumes.[15]

These excavations uncovered the circus, one of the largest in the Roman Empire. The Acropolis was located and turned out to be on Mount Stauris instead of on Mount Silpius. The island city which had been lost to modern view under the accumulated silt of the Orontes was brought to light, as well as the wall of Justinian dating back from the sixth century A.D. Numerous baths, Roman villas, cemeteries, and a stadium of Byzantine times were also found.

2. *Floor Mosaics at Antioch*

Of all the wealth of material recovered at Antioch for the study of the art and culture of the Graeco-Roman world, the most striking are the gorgeous floor mosaics dating from apostolic days to the sixth century of the Christian era. Several of these have been interpreted as representing scenes of the cult of Isis, one of the popular mystery religions of the ancient Near East which spread to all parts of the Roman world. One of these is fragmentary and, according to Doro

---

[15]*Antioch-on-the-Orontes, Publications for the Committee for the Excavations of Antioch and Its Vicinity*. I, *The Excavations of 1932*, ed. by G. W. Elderkin, 1934. II, *The Excavations of 1933-1936*, ed. by Richard Stillwell, 1938. III, *The Excavations 1937-1939*, ed. by Richard Stillwell, 1941.

Levi, depicts the "Voluntary Death," the climax and essence of the sacred initiation into the mysteries of Isis, the Queen of Heaven.[16]

Another mutilated mosaic from the same house as the *Mors Voluntaria*, according to Doro Levi, also represents another solemn celebration belonging to the Isis cult.[17] This is the *Navigium Isidis* marking the resumption of Mediterranean sailing after the winter storms. The festival was held on March 5 when the image of the goddess was transported from her shrine to the seaside, where a new vessel was launched with priestly ceremonies and appropriate vows for the ship's protection by the goddess. The middle part of the mosaic portrays two ships against the background of the sea and other details suggesting connections with the cult of Isis, whose owner was evidently a devotee.

The Mosaic of the Phoenix, now in the Louvre, is an extraordinarily well preserved Mosaic, more than forty feet long and thirty-three feet wide. It consists of a border of rams' heads enclosing a huge mass of roses with a phoenix perched on a rock in the center with a halo about its head.[18] This striking piece of art recalls the popular ancient myth that this fabulous bird after living for five or six centuries would immolate itself on a funeral pyre and rise again to youthful vigor from its own ashes. Early Christians connected the fable of the phoenix with bodily resurrection and pagans used it as a general symbol of eternity or renovation, as does its representation on coins and medals of the Roman emperors.

A mosaic from the sixth century retrieved from a building north of St. Paul's Gate in Antioch bears resemblance to a phrase in I Kings 16:4 and is apparently the only biblical allusion in all the inscriptions which have been edited.

3. The Charonion

On a limestone cliff northeast of the city, the bust of Charon, the ferryman over the River Styx, was chiselled out in bold relief. Sixteen feet in height, this large carving was in plain view from many parts of the city. According to John Malalas, who reports a tradition of the sixth century A.D., the image was executed in the reign of Antiochus Epiphanes (175-163 B.C.) to ward off a dangerous plague that struck

[16]"Mors Voluntaria, Mystery Cults on Mosaics from Antioch," *Berytus*, Vol. II, 1942, pp 19-55; *Antioch Mosaic Pavements*, Vol. I, pp. 163-164; for the reproduction of the mosaic, see *Berytus*, Vol. VII, 1942, plate 1.
[17]Doro Levi, "Mors Voluntaria," *op. cit.*, pp. 32-34 and *Antioch Mosaic Pavements*, Vol. I, pp. 164-165.
[18]See *Antioch-on-the-Orontes*, Vol. I, p. 84; Jean Lassus, *La mosaique du phenix, provenant des fouilles d'Antioche* (Paris, 1938, Presses Universitaires de France, plate 5, p. 42.

the city.[19] The figure is now badly weather-worn, but in the days of the founding of the Antiochene church was a striking landmark of the queen city of the East, familiar to Paul and Barnabas and other members of the Antiochene assembly.[20]

4. The Goddess Tyche of Antioch

The memory of this patron deity of Antioch is preserved in the fine marble replica now in the Vatican. The original statue dates from the founding of the city in 300 B.C., and portrays the graceful goddess sitting relaxedly on a rock with a youth (the Orontes) swimming at her feet. According to Pausanias,[21] the original was done by Eutychides, a pupil of Lysippus. Antioch's goddess of fortune was appropriated by other towns of the East. At Dura on the Euphrates she is practically identical with the goddess at Antioch, except that the Euphrates is represented by the swimming youth under her feet.

5. Christian Churches in Antioch

Christianity left an indelible impress upon Antioch architecturally. More than a score of Christian edifices have been identified. At Kaoussie, one of the city's suburban areas, a cross-shaped edifice of the fourth century was cleared. Epigraphic evidence dates the original building in A.D. 387.[22] Another famous church was the great octagonal edifice of Constantine, after which several other churches of this region were apparently designed. It had a great gilded dome.[23]

6. The Chalice of Antioch

This sensation-creating silver cup was found by some workmen digging a well at Antioch in 1910.[24] Gustavus A. Eisen in 1916 gave a report of it in the *American Journal of Archaeology*[25] which precipitated widespread interest and discussion. He made the sensational claim that its engraved figures represented the earliest portraits of Christ and the apostles and that the outer chalice belonged to the latter part of the first century.[26] It was only a step from this bold

[19]Bruce Metzgar, "Antioch-on-the-Orontes," in *Biblical Archaeologist*, XI, Dec. 1948, 4, p. 75.
[20]See Schultze, *op. cit.*, p. 21.
[21]VI, 2, 7.
[22]Jean Lassus in *Antioch-on-the-Orontes*. II, *The Excavations* 1933-1936, pp. 5-44. Jack Finegan, *Light From the Ancient Past* (Princeton, 1946), pp. 446-448. *Biblical Archaeologist* XI, 1948, 4, p. 69, fig. 1.
[23]Howard Crosley Butler, *Early Churches in Syria, Fourth to Seventh Centuries* (Princeton, 1929), pp. 192-193.
[24]H. Harvard Arnason, "This History of the Chalice of Antioch" in *Biblical Archaeologist*, IV (1941), pp. 49-64, Vol. V (1942) pp. 10-16.
[25]Vol. XX, pp. 426-427.
[26]Floyd V. Filson, "Who Are the Figures on the Chalice of Antioch?" *Biblical Archaeologist* V (1942), pp. 1-10.

conclusion to imagine that the inner cup was the original communion cup of Christ.

It was natural that such exciting claims should call forth a voluminous literature. Other scholars and experts on Christian art denied Eisen's extravagant conclusions, assigning the chalice anywhere from the second to the sixth centuries. It is scarcely a forgery, as a few have contended, but represents a product of early Christian art.

III. SELEUCIA PIERIA SEAPORT OF ANTIOCH

In the account in Acts the mention of Seleucia in connection with Paul and Barnabas' first missionary trip is prominent. Having been commissioned by the church at Antioch, "they . . . departed unto Seleucia; and from thence they sailed to Cyprus" (Acts 13:4).

The Chalice at Antioch (artist's sketch)

1. *Location of Seleucia Pieria*

In Paul's day Antioch's seaport, which was situated five miles up the Orontes from the Mediterranean, was an important city. It was built largely on a long rolling spur of a mountain called Musa Dagh, which dominates the mouth of the Orontes and towers over the sea south of the Gulf of Alexandretta. It formed an impressive fort and not only served as the gateway to Antioch and the seaport of the Syrian capital, but guarded the metropolis from invasion from the Mediterranean.

The city's walls extended downward to enclose the harbor, which is now largely a swamp. Two giant moles jutting out into the sea constitute the remains of the ancient important harbor.

2. *Founding of the City*

John Malalas in his *Chronicle* places Seleucia in the list of the numerous towns built by Seleucus I Nicator. According to this sixth century tradition, Seleucus constructed a city at the trading post of Pieria on the Mediterranean. He called the city Seleucia after himself and then proceeded to found the city of Antioch itself.[27]

[27]Matthew Spinka, *Chronicle of John Malalas, Books VIII-XVIII translated from the Church Slavonic* (1940) VIII, I-II (pp. 13-15).

3. *Seleucia Pieria and Archaeology*

From 1937-1939 archaeological work at greater Antioch was extended to include Seleucia Pieria. During these campaigns of the Princeton University expedition, numerous private dwellings were studied, the market gate, a Hellenistic temple, and notably a Christian "Martyrion" or Memorial Church dating from the fifth century A.D.[28]

The edifice showed three periods of construction, the earliest belonging to the original structure which seems to have been wrecked in the great earthquake of 526. This edifice had an inner quatrefoil surrounded by an ambulatory with a now-famous animal mosaic. Various animals and birds adorn this distinctive work of art with a scene of peace, with hyena and lamb walking together and the ibex and the lioness at peace, recalling in measure the millennial scene in Isaiah 11:6-9. The church was important since it was prominently located near a main colonnaded street and is of imposing size.

Through the Antioch Gate and up the north side of the Orontes, the highway led to the capital. As one stands before the ruined remains of this Gate, "one must think of how often Paul must have passed through here, not only on his arrival with Barnabas, but in the course of his later goings and comings."[29]

---

[28]W. A. Campbell, "The Martyrion at Seleucia Pieria," *Antioch-on-the-Orontes* III, pp. 35-54.
[29]E. Kraeling, *op. cit.*, p. 427.

CHAPTER 9

THE CITIES OF ST. PAUL'S FIRST MISSIONARY TOUR

Paul and Barnabas set sail for Cyprus from Antioch's port, Seleucia Pieria, in the year 45 A.D. It is highly probable that the two pioneer missionaries started at the commencement of the navigation season (the first week in March) since their destination was the 130-mile trip southwest to Salamis on the east coast of the island. Had they set out later, the westerly winds which blow throughout spring and summer would have compelled them to resort to a circuitous course skirting the Cilician coast and then, with the aid of land breezes and ocean currents, to head south to the north coast of the island.

Cyprus, the third largest island in the Mediterranean, about 148 miles long and from 15 to 40 miles wide, was the fatherland of Barnabas. Its principal physical features are a mountain range along a large part of the northern coast and a parallel range occupying a considerable portion of the south, with a broad tract of plain, known as the Mesaoria, between, extending on either end to the sea. As a native, Barnabas knew the island well, and doubtless his love for his homeland was one of the factors in deciding to head in that direction. He was still the leader and desired his native country and his relatives and friends there to hear the Gospel.

I. CYPRUS AND ITS CITIES

In choosing Cyprus as the starting point of their missionary endeavors, Paul and Barnabas (with John Mark, the author of Mark's gospel, as helper) were entering a country with a long pagan cultural history. The island first appears in history in the fifteenth century B.C. when it was listed among the conquests of the great Thutmose III of Egypt.[1] By the twelfth century B.C. Phoenician colonists had established themselves in the land, introducing their art and their religion in the form of Astarte. When Greek colonists followed, the licentious cult passed into the worship of Aphrodite, who specialized in sex and war, and whose temples were places of legalized vice in the form of sacred prostitution.

[1] James Henry Breasted, *Ancient Records of Egypt* (1906-07), sections 493, 511 (*Isy* is Cyprus).

181

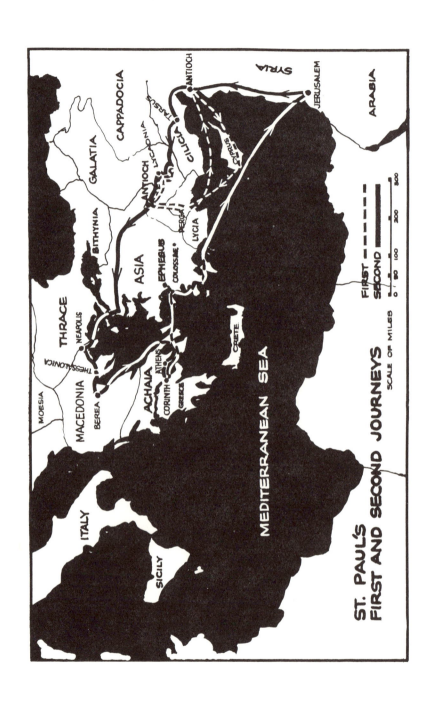

ST. PAUL'S
FIRST AND SECOND JOURNEYS

FIRST ------
SECOND ━━━━━

SCALE OF MILES
0 50 100   200   300

MEDITERRANEAN SEA

ITALY

SICILY

MOESIA

MACEDONIA

THRACE

NEAPOLIS

THESSALONICA

BEREA

ACHAIA

ATHENS

CORINTH

GREECE

CRETE

ASIA

EPHESUS

COLOSSAE

BITHYNIA

ANTIOCH

GALATIA

CAPPADOCIA

LYCAONIA

TARSUS

CILICIA

LYCIA

PERGA

CYPRUS

ANTIOCH

SYRIA

JERUSALEM

ARABIA

In the heyday of Assyrian power, Cyprus was under the rule of "the giant of the Semites," as Assyria was called. In 550 B.C. it once more reverted to Egypt, then came under Cambyses II in 525 B.C. and annexed to the Persian Empire. Under Ptolemy Soter it again reverted to Egypt as a dependency toward the end of the fourth century B.C. In this condition it remained till it was constituted a Roman province in 57 B.C.[2]

1. Christianity Comes to Salamis

The missionaries landed in the fine harbor of the largest city on the island at that period. Salamis was situated on the fringe of the fertile plain, the Mesaoria, opening up to the interior and giving access to the western part of the country. The city was some three miles distant from present-day Famagusta, but today its harbor has become filled with silt. Of its ancient remains, a large acqueduct is extant, sufficient to supply a city of 100,000 people. At the southern end of the spacious limestone forum was a Temple of Olympian Zeus.

Large numbers of Jews resided in Salamis, as well as in all the cities of Cyprus, especially after Herod the Great leased the copper mines from Augustus.[3] This situation is reflected in Luke's brief no-

[2]*Encyclopaedia Americana*, Vol. 8, (1951), pp. 369-370.
[3]Flavius Josephus, *Antiquities of the Jews*, XVI, 129. "The name Cyprus is derived from *cuprum*, Latin for copper," Olaf Moe, *The Apostle Paul*, translated by L. A. Vigness (Minneapolis, 1950), p. 196.

tation of Paul and Barnabas' ministry in Salamis, "And when they were at Salamis, they proclaimed the Word of God in the synagogues of the Jews ..." (Acts 15:5). So numerous was the Jewish population that a number of synagogues existed in the city.

The success of the gospel witness in Salamis is not indicated by Luke. Christianity, however, took hold in the island. Barnabas is traditionally claimed to have suffered martyrdom at Salamis, and a church memorializing this event was built there. At the Council of Nicaea in 325 A.D., three bishops were representatives from Cyprus, demonstrating that a strong church was established on the island.

2. Gospel Progress at the Pagan Center of Paphos

Quitting Salamis, the missionaries are said to have "gone through the whole island unto Paphos ..." (Acts 13:6). Since Paphos was located on the western coast, the journey involved traversing the entire island. Three routes were open. The northern route by a road along the coast, a southern route through the cities of Citium and Amathus, or the central route through the east-west plain (the Mesaoria) to Soli on the northwestern coast, where American engineers have rediscovered and reopened ancient copper mines that made Cyprus famous in antiquity[4]. From Soli the coast road led southwest to Paphos.

Although the Cyprus campaign began in Salamis, the largest city, it was soon shifted to Paphos (present-day Baffo) near modern Ktima on the western shore of the island, a much more famous town in antiquity for political and religious reasons. Favored by Rome, undoubtedly because of its fame as a cultic center, it became the governmental capital of the Roman province of Cyprus and the residence of the proconsul, who had the rank of a praetor.[5]

Augustus rebuilt the city a short distance from its original site after it had been levelled by an earthquake. This was New Paphos, officially designated Sebaste.[6] It appears in a third-century inscription under the appellation *Sebaste Claudia Flavia Paphos*, a holy city and mecca of the Cyprian states. By Jerome's time, it lay in ruins.[7]

Among the earthquake-ridden ruins of Old Paphos, less than seven miles to the southeast, was the ancient temple of Aphrodite dating to pre-Hellenic times. It was still highly renowned when Paul and Barnabas came to New Paphos with the purifying message of God's grace. Pagans from all over Cyprus, as well as from outside the island, flocked to this cultic mecca to honor the goddess of love and

---

[4]Edgar J. Goodspeed, *Paul* (Philadelphia, 1947), p. 40. Cyprus does not appear to have been densely populated. Pliny lists only fifteen centers of population (oppida) (*Natural History* V 35, cf. 31).
[5]Dion Cassius LIII, 12, 7;13:3; 15. LIV, 4, 1, sect. 324.
[6]Dion Cassius LIV, 23, 7.
[7]*Vita Sancti Hilarionis*, 17 in Migne, *Patres Latinii* 23, 52.

reproduction with sensuous and immoral rites. Tacitus recounts the visit of Titus to this temple during the Jewish war and comments particularly on the image of the goddess housed there.[8]

Providentially the Gospel was to win a notable trophy in pagan Paphos, but not without first running head-on into the demon-energized religious forces entrenched there. Sergius Paulus, the proconsul, like many officials in the ancient world — Babylonian, Assyrian, Chaldean, Persian, Greek and Roman — had a magician or diviner attached to his establishment.[9] In this instance, he was not a pagan but a Jewish occultist, who had two names — Bar-Jesus, his Jewish patronymic, and "Elymas," an appellative name or title, specifying his pretensions to wisdom and supernatural powers. Luke interprets the appellative as meaning "the magician" (*ho magos*) in Acts 13:8. It is derived either, as is commonly thought, from the Arabic *'alimun* ("wise," "learned"), or, according to a more plausible form, the Aramaic *'alima'*, "powerful."[10]

The sinister character of Elymas is disclosed when he "withstood" the missionaries, "endeavoring to turn aside the proconsol from the faith" (Acts 13:8), as well as Paul's scathing denunciation of him and his work (Acts 13:9-11). Whereas the fate of Elymas is not narrated, except the temporary blindness that befell him, the proconsul was apparently genuinely converted to Christianity. His position as a patrician and a high official of the Roman Empire were not impediments to embracing the faith, as it was not at this time (c. A. D. 45) material whether a provincial magistrate became Christian, was initiated into the mysteries of Isis, or espoused a Pythagorean sect. Christianity had not yet become a *religio illicita*.

3. Paphos and the Question of the Proconsulship

The author of the book of Acts indicates that the official designation of Sergius Paulus was that of "proconsul" (Acts 13:7). It was once claimed that Luke blundered in employing this term (*anthupaton*) instead of "propraetor" on the ground that Cyprus was an imperial province.[11] So it was, but in 22 B.C. it had become a senatorial province. At Soli, a city on the northwestern coast of Cyprus, a Greek inscription was found which contains the phrase, "under Paulus the

---

[8]*Historiae*, II, 2, 3.

[9]For a discussion of the demonic forces inspiring such professional occultists see Merrill F. Unger, *Biblical Demonology* (3rd edition, Wheaton, Ill., 1955) pp. 107-142.

[10]Franz Delitzsch, *Zeitschrift fuer die Lutheranische Theologie*, p. 7. Others connect with the Semitic root *'alam* "to bind" referring to magical powers over the occult (Guiseppe Ricciotti, *Paul the Apostle*, trans. by A. I. Zizzamia [Milwaukee, 1953], p. 254, n. 6).

[11]Cf. A. T. Robertson, *Luke the Historian in the Light of Research* (New York, 1930), p. 182. Ricciotti, *op. cit.*, p. 252, n. 2.

proconsul." The inscription is dated in the thirteenth year of Claudius (A.D. 52-53) and without any reasonable doubt refers to the Sergius Paulus whom Paul introduced to Christianity.[12]

The Proconsul is also presented by Luke as a "man of understanding" (Acts 13:7). Pliny the Elder makes mention of a Sergius Paulus, possibly the same person, who is cited among the authors used by him in the writing of his history, and well agrees with the representation in Acts.[13] As a patrician of culture and intellectual acumen, Sergius Paulus had leisure to gather around himself at the governor's mansion in quiet Paphos a coterie of magicians, astrologers and occultists of the day. His inquiring mind made these learned men of the day welcome, since they enjoyed much prestige in that age, as numerous Roman authors attest. The same spirit of open-mindedness made Paul, Barnabas, and young John Mark welcome to his circle. However, the Gospel which the proconsul was to hear from their lips was a harbinger of the fact that although "not many wise after the flesh, not many mighty, not many noble are called" (I Corinthians 1:26), yet *some are*. Sergius Paulus was among the first, and to mark this signal attestation of his call and harbinger of success among the Gentiles, the apostle abandoned his purely Jewish name Saul for his un-Jewish name Paul, and thenceforth becomes the leader. No longer is the designation "Barnabas and Saul" (Acts 13:2), but "Paul and his company" (Acts 13:13).

II. Pisidian Antioch and Gospel Penetration of the Greek World

When Paul and his party set sail from Paphos, they headed for Asia Minor. Crossing the 180 miles of water, they landed on the shores of the Pamphylian Sea, apparently not at Attalia, from which, however, they embarked on their return trip to Antioch (Acts 14:25). On the west of them was Lycia, on the east Cilicia, to the north the mountainous opening to the heart of Asia Minor, the gateway to Europe and the Western world.

For a millennium after Alexander the Great's conquests, Asia Minor, the land bridge between Oriental and Occidental cultures, was a strategic part of the Greek world. Hellenistic civilization had absorbed its older non-Greek population. Hittites, Celts, Armenians, Carians, Lydians and others were prepared by Greek culture for the

[12]This important monument was discovered and published by the American consul on Cyprus, L. Palma di Cesnola. Cf. *Cyprus, Its Ancient Cities, Tombs and Temples* (London, 1877), p. 425. D. H. Hogarth, *Devia Cypria*, pp. 114, 115. For Luke's accuracy in the intricate detail involved in distinguishing Roman provinces in general, see A. T. Robertson, *op. cit.*, pp. 180-182.
[13]*Natural History* II, 113 and beginning of Book XVIII. A Latin inscription (C. I. L. vol. VI, no. 31545) mentions a Sergius Paulus, who may be the Cyprian proconsul. Cf. Edgar Goodspeed, *op. cit.*, p. 228.

coming of Christianity through the intrepid missionaries of the cross, Paul and Barnabas.

1. *Perga, Stepping-Stone to Pisidian Antioch*

Paul and Barnabas' first objective was Perga, which was not directly on the sea, but some nine miles from the coastal city of Attalia at the mouth of the Cestros River. It was the chief city of Pamphylia and had its own port on the right bank of the Cestros River, where the missionaries landed. It was in the fever-infested coastal region and the center of the worship of the Asiatic nature goddess Artemis, "the queen of Perga." Frequently this deity, corresponding to Diana (Artemis) of the Ephesians (Acts 19:27), is represented on the coins of Perga[14] as a huntress, with bow in hand and stags at her side.

Asia Minor (Phrygia)

These coins, attesting the independence and importance of the city, were minted from the second century B.C. until the third century A.D., and refer to Perga as a metropolis.

The ruins of Perga, now called Murtana, are distinguished for their completeness. Scarcely any other city Paul visited has been better preserved, looking like a place inhabited or recently abandoned. The walls, tower-flanked, show the city to have been quadrangular-shaped. Broad streets intersecting each other divided the town into quarters. From the southern gate a street flanked with porticoes led up to the center of the citadel.

At a higher elevation was the acropolis. Here the earliest city was constructed and "for a length of almost a thousand yards and a depth of six hundred and fifty, battlemented walls stand perfect, with turrets seventy paces square, in many cases as high as when first built."[15] In later times the city extended to the south of the acropolis where most of the ruins exist.

---

[14]Goodspeed, *op. cit.*, p. 42.
[15]Goodspeed, *loc. cit.* For a report on the 1957 excavation, see Turk Arkeoloji Dergisi (1958), pp. 14-16.

At the foot of the acropolis are the remains of a spacious theatre, seating more than ten thousand, as well as a large stadium. The agora and numbers of baths are visible, as well as many tombs outside the walls. The city probably did not present an essentially different aspect when Paul, Barnabas, and John Mark made some momentous decisions there in one of the first century inns or caravanseries of the metropolis.

Paul and Barnabas' decision was to leave the low-lying coastlands for the highlands to the north and to press on into the heart of Asia Minor. The reason may have been particularly dictated by circumstances of health, since malaria prevailed along the coast, and Paul may have become ill (cf. Galatians 4:13), but whatever human factors lay behind the move, it was clearly superintended by divine leading. The Gospel was being carried to its predestined goal into Western Asia and thence on into Europe.

On the other hand, John Mark's decision to quit the tour at Perga and to return home evidently had some inexcusable factors in it, at least in Paul's mind (Acts 15:38). It may well be that the dangerous country to the north between Perga and Pisidian Antioch discouraged the younger missionary. The 100-mile trip was through a rugged stretch of country which was notoriously infested with robbers. This is supported by numerous ancient literary sources[16] and by modern archaeological evidence as well. Sir William Ramsay has adduced a number of inscriptions from the Pisidian area referring to the banditry and lawlessness of this region, as well as the armed soldiery that was necessary to guard the peace of the country.[17]

In addition to "perils by robbers," the hazardous journey to Pisidian Antioch and beyond presented "perils of waters" (cf. II Corinthians 11:26). No district in Asia Minor is more singularly subject to flash floods than the streams of the mountainous tract of Pisidia, particularly the Eurymedon and the Cestris, and the missionaries' journey to Pisidian Antioch was never very far from either.[18] Whether or not John Mark was daunted by these dangers is problematical. That such perils did not appall Paul and Barnabas is certain. Their future history-making successes lay beyond these severe testings and were divinely appointed prerequisites to them.

[16]Strabo XII, 6, 7; Xenophon *Anabasis* I, 1, 11; 9:11; III, 2, 14. Arrian I, 27, 28. Polybius V:72-77. Cf. W. J. Conybeare and J. S. Howson, *The Life and Letters of St. Paul,* Vol. I. New York, 1877, pp. 162-164.
[17]*The Church in the Roman Empire,* pp. 23-24; *Journal of Roman Studies,* 1912, pp. 82, 83.
[18]Conybeare and Howson, *op. cit.,* I, pp. 163-164.

Coins from Antioch of Pisidia

Roman standards with eagles perched over the flags. The coinage of the colony was modeled after that of imperial Rome itself

Genius of Antioch emptying a cornucopia over an altar, with scepter in her left hand (Emperor Verus, A.D. 161-166)

Peace hurrying through the city with olive branch and scepter (Emperor Decius, c. 250 A.D.)

2. Pisidian Antioch, Important Strategical Center of Asia Minor

No safe, well-paved and well-traveled Roman road led north from Perga to Antioch. But once the rigors of the steep and narrow mountain trails were behind them, and Antioch lay visible in the fertile tableland, affectionately called the "olive-clad Anthian plain" by the inhabitants, the missionaries at last found themselves in a center of radiating influence, through which a great east-west traffic artery ran across the highlands of Asia Minor. Westward it connected with Apamaea, Colossae, Laodicea, Magnesia, Ephesus, and the Greek world on the Aegean. Eastward it gave access to Lystra, Derbe, and through the Cilician Gates led on to Tarsus, Issus, and Antioch-on-the-Orontes. In bringing the Gospel to Pisidian Antioch, Paul and Barnabas were planting Christianity in the communication nerve center and heart of Asia Minor. The perils and hardship incurred to attain this were to prove strategically worthwhile.

Pisidian Antioch was one of the sixteen cities which Seleucus Nicator (312-280 B.C.) had founded, and like its more famous sister-metropolis on the Orontes in Syria, named in honor of his father Antiochus. It is now commonly referred to as "Pisidian" Antioch because subsequently in the late third century, during the reign of Diocletian, it was made the capital of a newly-created province named Pisidia. When Christianity was introduced to Antioch, however, it was a part of the Roman province of Galatia, in the district called Phrygia (as distinguished from other ethnical divisions of the province such as Lycaonia).[19] The recovery of Phrygian inscriptions from the area unmistakably points to its Phrygian occupation.

The Antioch sector of Phrygia was incorporated into the province of Galatia for military reasons. Any plan that envisioned controlling the wild tribes of the Pisidian mountains could not omit this important strategical city on the northwest. Seleucus realized this when he founded the town, as did Mark Antony when he bequeathed the city to Amyntas, the last king of Galatia. Amyntas himself realized the same thing, when in 39 B.C. he was entrusted with the task of quelling the turbulent highlanders of the area, with the result that he incorporated the Antioch sector into his kingdom of Galatia.

The Romans took over Antioch when Galatia became a province in 25 B.C. Augustus, too, realized the strategic significance of the city when he constituted it the chief of his military colonies in the region, with the official name *Colonia Caesarea Antiochia*. Greek authors correctly call it "Antioch toward Pisidia" or "Pisidian Antioch," as in

[19]Cf. Ramsay, *The Cities of St. Paul* (London, 1907), p. 254; *The Church in the Roman Empire*, p. 26f.

Acts 13:14,[20] linking it by a military highway called the Royal Road with the sister colony of Lystra, 120 miles to the southeast. According to legend preserved in *Paul and Thekla*, Paul and Barnabas traversed this road on their way from Antioch to Iconium (Acts 13:51).[21]

3. Pisidian Antioch in Paul's Day

From its foundation as a Roman colony, Latin became the official language of Antioch. It was well Romanized by the time of Paul's visit and continued to be until the Greek spirit revived in the third century. The apostle, however, doubtless had a Greek-speaking audience in the synagogue when he spoke on two successive Saturdays to large congregations.

Jews were an important element of the population, and they figure prominently in the narrative in Acts (Acts 13:14, 50). The missionaries' success in reaching the proselytes aroused the animosity of the Jewish leaders, who saw their influence being undermined. Trouble was bound to result as these proud Jews, many of whom could undoubtedly trace their lineage back three and a half centuries to the original Jewish colonists settled there by the Seleucids, found their prestige threatened by a new faith they were not prepared to receive.

An inscription of Apollonia, a neighboring city, dating probably from the first or early second century A.D., adds archaeological proof that there were Jews in Antioch. This is a funeral monument to a Jewess named Deborah whose ancestors held numerous offices in Antioch, and who married a Gentile official named Pamphylus. The public proclamation of this intermarriage "proves both the prominence of Deborah's family and the breaking down of Jewish exclusiveness."[22]

Besides the Jews in the synagogue at Antioch there were numerous proselytes of Judaism (Acts 13:17, 26, 43), doubtlessly composed principally of Greeks, but also containing a native Phrygian as well as a Roman element. The Roman stratum, while related to the military administration of the city, consonant with its position as a Roman colony, was not numerous but was influential in the synagogue.[23] To

[20]Strabo, XII, 6, 4. Luke customarily, as here, writes as a Greek rather than a Roman. cf. Robertson, *op. cit.*, pp. 180-182.
[21]Cf. Ramsay, *The Church in the Roman Empire*, pp. 27-36. Emil Kraeling, *Rand McNally Bible Atlas* (New York, 1952), p. 433.
[22]Camden M. Cobern, *The New Archaeological Discoveries and Their Bearing Upon the New Testament* (4th ed., New York, 1920), p. 532. Ramsay, *Cities of St. Paul*, p. 256.
[23]Cf. A. T. Robertson, "The Roman Colonies were small editions of Rome itself . . . military outposts to hold in subjection the surrounding country" *op. cit.*, p. 184. Cf. Souter "Colony," Hasting's *Dictionary of the Apostolic Church*.

this class of governing *coloni* evidently belonged "the devout women of honorable estate," and "the chief men" (Acts 13:50). These latter apparently were the husbands or relatives of the women who, while not converts to Judaism themselves, could readily be induced by the Jews to expel Paul and Barnabas from the area when the message of the Gospel was rejected. As a political and social aristocracy, the *coloni* were not so much affected by missionary influence as the humbler classes were, but as the principal burgher group, the Jews would naturally go to them for help, especially when they had synagogue connections.

4. Pisidian Antioch and Evangelism of the Gentiles

Paul's experience at Pisidian Antioch marked a decisive step in his evangelistic methods. Hitherto in Cyprus and apparently in Syrian Antioch[24] Gentiles had been addressed indirectly in the synagogue through the Jews. Now, however, the apostle turns from the gospel-rejecting Jews and preaches the Gospel to the Gentiles directly outside the synagogue. Paul had preluded this important advance by addressing Jews and Greeks as equal in his first Galatian sermon (Acts 13:38). Luke emphasizes the significance of this forward movement by the attention which he gives to this detailed discourse that was to result in the opening of the door of gospel opportunity to the Gentiles immediately and not mediately through the Jews.

The climactic events at Pisidian Antioch were expedited by the freer relations that existed between Jews and Gentiles in the Seleucid colonies of Phrygia where Hellenic education adapted itself to Oriental peoples. Each city was an experiment in the amalgamation of the Oriental and the Occidental. Only such a spirit of sympathy and cordiality as existed in Antioch between Jew and Gentile rendered it possible that almost the whole citizenry crowded together to hear a Jewish stranger speak (Acts 13:44) and that Gentiles in large numbers believed the message proclaimed (Acts 13:48).

5. Pisidian Antioch and Archaeology

The site of Antioch was discovered in 1833 by the British chaplain at Smyrna, Francis V. J. Arundell. It is situated on the right bank of the River Anthios on the lower slopes of a scenic mountain now called Sultan Dagh. The present-day ruins are not far from the Turkish town of Yalovach and lie in complete desolation on a plateau which ranges from fifty to two hundred feet above the fronting plain skirted by the River Anthios.

---

[24]Cf. Ramsay, *The Cities of St. Paul*, pp. 308-309. Had the door of gospel opportunity stood open in Syrian Antioch already, it would have been unnecessary and incorrect for Paul and Barnabas to declare that God had opened such a door on the first missionary tour. Cf. Acts 13:27.

Remains of an ancient aqueduct at Pisidian Antioch

On coins the river-god Anthios is pictured as sitting down, resting his left arm on an urn from which the water flows.[25] Above the river the ancient city's ruins show that it was stoutly fortified to withstand the war-like Pisidian mountain tribes. Remains of an aqueduct from Roman times, which brought water from the Sultan Dagh, are to be seen, although even in time of siege, water could be fetched from the Anthios, since the river flows not far from the city walls.

From 1910-1913 Sir William Ramsay excavated the sanctuary of Antioch's chief deity, Men. The sacred area measured 241 by 136 feet and was enclosed by a five-foot-thick wall. The huge altar within the sacred precinct measured sixty-six by forty-one feet. Many engraved tablets were found and emblems of Men with horned bull's head.[26] The soil under the sanctuary was found to be replete with bones and teeth of sacrificial animals. In one part of the sanctuary the throne of the deity was located, who was paired with Artemis (Diana), a Hellenized form of Cybele.

The discovery of this sanctuary is important because the Phrygian mysteries celebrated here were well-known to early Christians (Colossians 2:18)[27] and exerted a far-reaching influence upon the religious life of the Graeco-Roman world.

Among the more significant inscriptions found at Antioch is that which is engraved, "To Lucius Sergius Paullus, the younger," an important official at Antioch, whom Ramsay contends was the son of the proconsul at Cyprus.[28]

[25]Ramsay, *op. cit.*, pp. 248-249; fig. 27, p. 316.
[26]*Journal of Hellenistic Studies*, 1921, p. 111f. For a discussion of the god Men, cf. H. R. Hall, *Ancient History of the Near East* (1913), pp. 330-331. A. B. Cook, *Zeus. A Study in Ancient Religion*, Vol. I, index under *Men* (1914).
[27]Cf. Cobern, *op. cit.*, pp. 537, 538. Sir William Ramsay, *Annual of the British School at Athens* (1911-12); pp. 37-71.
[28]Cobern, *op. cit.*, pp. 538-540; Ramsay, *The Bearing of the Recent Discoveries on the Trustworthiness of the New Testament* (2nd ed., 1915), pp. 150-172.

Coin from Pisidian Antioch showing enthroned Cybele with tympanum in hand and lions at her feet—the Graecized form of the Phrygian goddess (3rd century A.D.)

The god of Antioch, Men, supporting Victory on his left hand with scepter in his right hand and his left foot on a bull's head with a cock beside it

Later excavations at Pisidian Antioch by the University of Michigan[29] have led to the uncovering of remains of the Roman city established by Augustus. Two splendid squares built on different levels are identified, the Square of Augustus and the Square of Tiberius, connected by a flight of steps adorned with three archways of the propylaea built in honor of Augustus. Lavishly adorned with sculptured reliefs of captive Pisidians, the archways depict Augustus' triumphs on land, while the frieze of Tritons, Poseidon, dolphins and other marine symbols, with which they are also decorated, represent the imperial triumphs at sea.

A temple of the Roman age, ornamented with a superb representation of bulls' heads garlanded with leaves and fruit, symbolizing Men, the local god who granted bounty, graced the Augustan Square in honor of the emperor. Architecturally and artistically these buildings and sculptures rank very high in Graeco-Roman art.[30]

Other discoveries include numerous terracotta pipes for distribution of the water brought by the aqueduct, gaming boards with which idle Romans amused themselves, an edict from Domitian's time, a triple gateway from the third century A.D. and a huge Christian basilica from the fourth century.[31]

III. ICONIUM, A CITY OF GALATIA

Driven out of Pisidian Antioch by mob violence instigated by un-

[29]David M. Robinson, *American Journal of Archaeology* (1924), pp. 435-444.
[30]Cf. David Robinson, *The Art Bulletin* 9 (Sept. 1926-June 1927).
[31]Jack Finegan, *Light From the Ancient Past* (Princeton, 1946), p. 262.

believing Jews, the missionaries took to the Royal Road toward Lystra, but turned aside to visit Iconium first (present-day Konia). This was a journey of somewhat more than one hundred miles, but not nearly so rigorous as the ardent trip from Perga to Pisidian Antioch had been.

The city to which Paul and Barnabas took the Gospel was a garden spot, situated in the midst of orchards and farms, but surrounded by deserts. Very similar in elevation, topography, and beauty to Syrian Damascus, Iconium must have looked inviting to the travel-worn soldiers of the cross after traversing the desolate tablelands along their route.

1. *Location of Iconium and the Accuracy of Luke*

Until the work of Sir William Ramsay in the first decade and a half of the twentieth century, the historical reliability of the Acts as a bona fide work of Luke was widely denied. An important detail of this critical suspicion existed in the matter of Luke's clear implication in Acts 14:6 that Iconium was in Phrygia, as distinguished from Derbe and Lystra which are said to be "cities of Lycaonia." Despite the fact that Xenophon[32] and Pliny[33] agree with Luke in listing it among Phrygian cities, the fact that Cicero[34] and Strabo[35] assign it to Lycaonia, caused criticism to side against the genuineness of Lukan authorship and accuracy.

In 1910 Ramsay recovered the now well-known inscribed monument which demonstrated that Iconium was such a thoroughly

Hellenized native hero drawn from a stele discovered at Iconium c. 1880. The monument from which the drawing was made was destroyed by a workman, despite efforts to save it

[32]*Anabasis* I, 2, 19.
[33]*Natural History* V, 41 al. 32.
[34]*Ad familiares* XV, 2.
[35]XII, 6, 1.

Phrygian city that the Phrygian tongue was still employed in dedicatory notices as late as the middle of the third century A.D.[36] Numbers of other inscriptions from Iconium and its environs substantiate the fact that racially the city could be described as Phrygian and administratively as Galatian. When Paul visited the city, it was one of the important centers of population in the southern part of the Roman province of Galatia.

Emperor Claudius conferred on the city the title of Claudiconium, which appears on its coins, but not until the time of Hadrian was it raised to the rank of a colony. In Paul's time it was still Hellenic-Phrygian in its complexion.

2. *Paul's Ministry at Iconium*

There was an important Jewish element in Iconium as at Pisidian Antioch, attracted there by its commercial prosperity. The fields of highland flax and the flocks of sheep and goats on the Taurus ranges furnished abundant raw materials to sustain the weaving shops of the city. Here Paul had little difficulty, it may be imagined, in finding work in one of the weaver's shops operated by a fellow Jew, thus earning his livelihood by his craft, as was his custom.

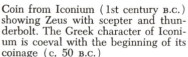

Coin from Iconium (1st century B.C.) showing Zeus with scepter and thunderbolt. The Greek character of Iconium is coeval with the beginning of its coinage (c. 50 B.C.)

Coin from Iconium (under Gallienus) showing Athena Polias, goddess of the city, holding a serpent-entwined spear in her left hand as protector and healer

Iconium, too, owed its bustling business activity to its location on the main trade route connecting Ephesus with Syria and the Mesopotamian world, as well as its orchard industries and farm produce. The city doubtless had a large and influential synagogue. There Paul began his spiritual labors, which were so successful "that a great mul-

[36]Ramsay, *The Bearing of Recent Discovery on the Trustworthiness of the New Testament* (2nd ed. 1915), pp. 45-47; (4th ed. 1920), pp. 53-63.

titude both of the Jews and of Greeks (Jewish proselytes) believed" (Acts 14:1), and the missionaries' ministry, encouraged by success, was continued a "long time" (Acts 14:3).

Aroused by jealousy of the great success of the Gospel, a group of those who rejected the new message united to stone Paul. Paul and Barnabas were compelled to escape to Lystra in Lycaonia. Once they crossed the boundary into Lycaonia, they were safe. The inscriptions show that Iconium's magistrates were supreme during their term of office and could whip and expel without trial any suspected criminals, if the people who gave them their office desired it or at least did not object to it. The missionaries' only recourse was to flee for their lives.

IV. LYSTRA AND DERBE IN LYCAONIA

Already two important cities of the Roman province of Galatia—Antioch and Iconium—had witnessed the stirring impact of the Christian message. Two more towns of the same province yet remained to experience Paul's powerful evangelism—Lystra and Derbe. Later when the apostle addressed his well-known letter to "the churches of Galatia" (Galatians 1:2), he is claimed by many scholars to have referred to them (and if so, correctly so), since they were all in the same Roman province of Galatia.[37] The Roman province was named from the smaller northern district of Galatia which it included, which in turn took its name from the Gallic tribes which settled it in the first quarter of the third century B.C. When Rome took over the extensive domains at the death of the last Galatian king, the territory was made a Roman province. When Paul wrote, many scholars contend he had the churches of Antioch, Iconium, Lystra, and Derbe in mind, rather than some other unknown churches in Galatia proper, as others contend.[38]

1. Archaeology and the Location of Lystra

The site of Lystra was uncertain until 1885 when J. R. Sitlington Sterrett, under the Wolfe Expedition to Asia Minor, identified its ruins near the modern town of Katyn Serai, some twenty-one miles southwest of Iconium, thus confirming the earlier conjecture of Leake (1820), who had placed its location there. The identification was certified by an inscribed Roman altar, still standing erect in its original position. The stone, three and a half feet high and a foot thick, bore

[37]Edgar J. Goodspeed, *The Story of the New Testament* (1916), p. 9. W. Ramsay, *A Historical Commentary on St. Paul's Epistle to the Galatians;* Hasting's *Dictionary of the Bible* II, pp. 81-89. Today this so-called "South Galatian" theory is popular. (*The New Schaff-Herzog Ency.*, 1955, pp. 854,855).

[38]James Moffatt, *An Introduction to the Literature of the New Testament* (3rd ed., 1918, pp. 90-101). Today in France and in Germany the "North Galatian" theory is popular (*The New Schaff-Herzog Ency.*, 1955, pp. 854, 855).

the Latin spelling of the city's name *Lustra,* with a notice that it had become a Roman colony under Augustus.[39]

The development of Lystra was attributable to its selection as the seat of a Roman colony, which required the construction of a Roman road to connect it with the other *coloniae,* such as Antioch and Derbe. This road had been constructed primarily for military reasons, but running near the real commercial center Iconium, it was however never more than a secondary road commercially, as Lystra was not an important trading or manufacturing center. There were few if any Jews resident there, and no synagogue is mentioned, as at Antioch and Iconium.

2. Paul's Ministry at Lystra

As a result of Paul's healing the life-long cripple, the native Lycaonians (Acts 14), not Greeks or Romans, regarded Paul and Barnabas as pagan gods visiting them in the semblance of men. According to their native cult (here appearing under a thin Greek guise), they called Barnabas "Zeus" and Paul "Hermes." Ovid's well-known tale, located in near-by Phrygia, names the same two divinities as appearing to Baucis and Philemon.

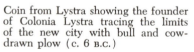

Coin from Lystra showing the founder of Colonia Lystra tracing the limits of the new city with bull and cow-drawn plow (c. 6 B.C.)

The city god of Lystra, crowned with crescent and sitting on rocks with personified river at her feet and corn ears in her hand, signifying prosperity

The accuracy of detail of this part of the Acts narrative, however, is not only demonstrated from literary sources, but from epigraphic evidence as well. One inscription recovered in the vicinity of Lystra in 1909 lists by name several "priests of Zeus." Another relates how two devotees of the local cult "having made in accordance with a vow

[39]J. R. Sitlington Sterrett, *An Epigraphical Journey in Asia Minor,* 1888.

at their own expense (a statue of) Hermes Most Great together with a sun-dial, dedicated it to Zeus the sun-god."[40]

The appearance of persecuting Jews from Antioch and Iconium and the brutal stoning of Paul by the populace further illustrates the uneducated and superstitious nature of the Lycaonians, and that they and their religious and social institutions are accurately set forth to be saliently distinguished from the educated Greek and Roman society of the colony.

3. Paul at Derbe

From his near-death experience in Lystra, Paul pushed on with Barnabas to Derbe, the last city in distinctively Roman territory on the road leading from Southern Galatia to the East. Here commerce flowing westward into the province had to pay customs. Hence Strabo

Coin from Derbe showing Winged-Victory writing on a shield which she balances on her raised left knee. Coins from Derbe are rare. This one dates much later than Paul's time and was struck under the Empress Lucilla

Coin from Derbe presenting good fortune of the city in Roman style. Coin of the Empress Foustina the Younger

calls Derbe a "custom station."[41] This city owes its visit from Paul to its strategic importance and position on the great Roman road connecting east and west. Roman milestones have been found along the line of its route. The Emperor Claudius honored the city, and its coins have been found bearing the legend "Claudio-Derbe."

The location of Derbe was approximately identified by J. R. Sitlington Sterrett, and more accurately placed at Gudelisin, a large mound with late Roman remains, by Sir William M. Ramsay. As yet,

---

[40]For the inscriptions from Lystra, see J. R. Sitlington Sterrett, *The Wolfe Expedition to Asia Minor,* and Cronin, *Journal of Hellenistic Studies* (1904).
[41]XXX, 569. For a complete account of Derbe, see Ramsay's *The Cities of St. Paul,* pp. 385-404; G. Ricciotti, *Paul the Apostle* (Milwaukee, 1953), pp. 24; 270-271.

however, no absolute evidence has been forthcoming, and only further excavations can verify the present identification.[42]

At Derbe Paul "preached the gospel . . . and made many disciples" (Acts 14:21). But he and Barnabas did not extend their endeavors beyond this significant boundary into the kingdom of Commagene, under Antiochus, who, although a Roman vassal, was independent. Paul's labors were confined to the centers of Graeco-Roman culture, and his strategy did not comprehend a dubious field where kings "were protectors of certain cults and by virtue of their powers could act drastically."[43] The cult of Mithras prevailed in Commagene and the statue of this deity on the top of Nemrud Dagh in the Taurus has been recovered.[44] Paul manifested careful planning and concentration of effort in his missionary work in Asia Minor and was guided by principles that pointed his endeavors toward an immediate as well as long-range realization of success. That Paul was successful at Derbe is indicated in the Lukan narrative, as well as by the fact that he does not mention Derbe among the towns where he had suffered persecution (II Timothy 3:11).

4. The Return Trip to Syrian Antioch

Paul and Barnabas retraced their steps through Asia Minor, revisiting, organizing, and confirming the churches established. The only new evangelistic activity mentioned is their preaching the Word in Perga (Acts 14:25), which they evidently did to make up for not doing so on their outgoing journey. Thence they went to Attalia,[45] a seaport founded by Attalus II Philadelphus (159-138 B.C.), and possessing a wealth of archaeological remains, including ancient city walls, towers, and a Hadrianic gateway and aqueduct.

At Attalia the missionaries apparently found a ship waiting to sail, which left them no time for preaching. Weary but rewarded with assurance of success in their momentous tour, Paul and Barnabas welcomed the sight of Syrian Antioch and the fellowship of the mother church there.

---

[42]Ramsay, The Cities of St. Paul, p. 452, n. 18. Emil G. Kraeling, Rand McNally Bible Atlas (1956), p. 434.
[43]Kraeling, op. cit., p. 435.
[44]Cf. Kraeling, op. cit., pp. 364, 435. For inscriptions of the late Roman period from Derbe, see J. R. S. Sterrett, Wolfe Expedition to Asia Minor, nos. 18-52.
[45]Satalia of the Middle Ages, present-day Adalia.

CHAPTER 10

CHRISTIANITY PREPARED FOR WORLD-WIDE PROCLAMATION

Paul's phenomenal success in preaching the Christian Gospel among the Gentiles of Galatia on his first missionary journey furnished him and Barnabas with ample material for a glowing report to the church at Antioch upon their return from their evangelistic labors. Luke, the historian, specifically stresses the fact that when they arrived home "and had gathered the church together, they rehearsed all things that God had done with them, and that he had *opened a door of faith unto the Gentiles*" (Acts 14:27). The "door of faith" opened to the Gentiles was not merely a typical Pauline metaphor[1] describing the far-reaching impression the testimony the returned missionaries made on the Antiochene Christians. It was an announcement that the Christian message, apart from the ceremonies of Judaism and the legalism of the Mosaic system, had been divinely authenticated as the medium of salvation to the nations. It was a summary declaration that in the practical arena of life, Christianity had been demonstrated to be an international religion, completely severed from the legal requirements as well as the narrow isolationism of the Hebrew faith, and reaching out to the numberless multitudes and boundless regions of the vast pagan world extending to "the uttermost part of the earth" (Acts 1:8).

Although Paul had seen the divine authentication of Christianity's regenerating efficacy apart from the legalism of Judaistic religion, as he and Barnabas settled down again to their work of evangelization among the vast non-Jewish population of Antioch itself (Acts 14:28), they were shortly to witness a subtle and dangerous attack on the autonomy of the new faith they had proclaimed with such singular success. The very city that had first witnessed the disciples called "Christians" (Acts 11:26) was to witness the struggle of Christianity with Judaism (Acts 15:1, 2).

[1]I Corinthians 16:1; II Corinthians 2:12; Colossians 4:3; Galatians 2:9; also John in Revelation 3:8.

201

I. THE NEW FAITH LIBERATED FROM LEGALISM

"Certain men" (Acts 15:1) recognizable in the large number of priests in Jerusalem who "were obedient to the faith" (Acts 6:7) and converted Pharisees (Acts 15:5) came down from Judaea to Antioch with the avowed purpose of destroying the autonomy of Christianity and making it dependent upon Judaism.

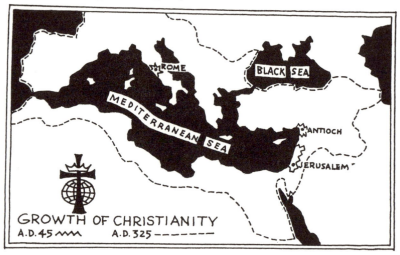

GROWTH OF CHRISTIANITY
A.D.45 〰〰 A.D.325 -------

1. The Problem of a Judaized Christianity

The Jewish visitors from Judaea taught specifically that Gentiles could not be saved unless they were "circumcised after the custom of Moses" (Acts 15:1). The teaching was tantamount to saying that Gentiles virtually had to become Jews to be saved and was diametrically opposed to the message Paul and Barnabas had proclaimed to their Greek converts in Syrian Antioch, Cyprus, and Galatia. "If it was permitted to go unchallenged, all their work would be undone, and their converts left in confusion and dismay."[2] In addition, the whole divine authentication of the Christian message on the first missionary tour would be set aside, unless this error, specious as it was from a purely Jewish standpoint, was answered.

Palestinian Jews were willing to open the door to the Gentiles, but only halfway. They would admit only those who, in addition to faith in the Messiah, submitted to Jewish rites, particularly circumcision. With them the question of religion and race were merged. As descendants of Abraham, they worshiped the one true God, Yahweh. Did not this fact retain all its ancient meaning? But those who were

[2]Edgar J. Goodspeed, *Paul* (Philadelphia, 1947), p. 54.

not Abraham's descendants could compensate with a substitute. Let them in addition to faith in the Messiah receive circumcision as the sign of the Abrahamic Covenant. Let them also submit to other legal rites, since Jesus Himself, they argued, faithfully observed the Mosaic Law and asserted that He had not come to set aside but to fulfill it (Matthew 5:17).[3]

Against this plausible line of reasoning stood the case of the opening of the Gospel of faith to the Gentile Cornelius and his family (Acts 10). But the Palestinian Jews dismissed this obvious instance of the conversion of uncircumcised pagans as an exception, which was clearly by special divine command, in which Peter had to justify his part in the incident before a general Jewish meeting (Acts 11:1-18).[4]

On the ground of special divine revelation corroborated in his personal experience and public ministry, Paul opposed the Judaistic thesis with all his resources. He and Barnabas "had no small dissension and debate" with the legalists (Acts 15:2 R.S.V.) He was willing to grant that the Christian Church, although in a sense Spirit-begotten in the womb of orthodox Judaism, and for a certain length of time identified with it in faith and practice, nevertheless from the start possessed its own life and individuality, was distinct from it, and clearly directed toward complete independence.

It was Peter who saw the infant Church, begotten at Pentecost (Acts 2), reach its full prenatal development (to continue the figure) and come to the birth with the admission of Gentiles at Caesarea (Acts 10), at Antioch (Acts 11:21, 22), and in vast numbers on Paul's first missionary tour (Acts 13:1-14:28). It was Paul, however, who dared to cut the last tie binding the Christian Church to Judaism— the umbilical cord of Mosaic rites and ceremonies. In this sense he may be said to have "delivered" the Church, making possible its own autonomous life. Thus with incalculable consequences for the history of the human race, the apostle set Christianity on its own course as a universal, international, world-engirdling spiritual movement, transcending all racial, social, economic, religious, and political barriers, and offering spiritual regeneration to everyone who believes.

2. The Council at Jerusalem

Although the apostle at Antioch took his momentous stand for Christianity versus Judaism, the battle had barely begun. Others besides Paul and the leaders and members of the Antiochene church had to see the all-importance of the issue at stake. Since neither side

[3]Cf. Clarence Tucker Craig, *The Beginning of Christianity* (New York, 1943), pp. 171-172.
[4]Craig, *op. cit.*, p. 173.

would yield, it was essential to get a decision from the highest authorities of the whole Church, which were the "apostles and presbyters" of the mother church at Jerusalem.[5]

At a congregational meeting, the church at Antioch commissioned Paul as one of a number to attend the council, but this corresponded to a revelation he himself had had in the matter (Galatians 2:1, 2). The group of delegates to the first Church Council of history traveled by land through Phoenicia and Samaria "declaring the conversion of the Gentiles," thus causing "great joy to all the brethren" (Acts 15:3). This was likely at the end of the year 49 or the beginning of the year 50.

The church at Jerusalem to which the Antiochene delegation reported was composed of three groups. The highest in authority were apostles, consisting of James, the brother of the Lord, Cephas (Peter), and John, the future evangelist. Paul calls these "pillars" (Galatians 2:9). The presbyters, who worked with the apostles, were next in authority, with the general congregation of believers composing the rest.

Peter was the first to give his views, which were practical and realistic. He decided in favor of the liberation of Christianity in three points. First, the evangelization of the Gentiles, apart from admixture of Mosaic legalism, which had initially begun under his own hand (Acts 10). Second, these earlier pagan conversions were on the same charismatic plane as that of the converted Jews, though they did not observe the Mosaic system (Acts 11:17). And finally, Peter described the law as an intolerable yoke, which no Jew had borne in its entirety, and against it he set the grace of the Messiah, which alone was efficacious to bring salvation to both Jew and Gentile (Acts 15:7-11).

The legalists found scarcely more comfort in the decision of James, their hoped-for champion, who enjoyed great prestige among pious Jews because of the singular austerity of his life. Although his speech revealed his deep devotion to Judaism, it essentially agreed with Peter and disappointed the hopes of the Judaizers. His discourse and that of Peter formed the basis of a "decree" directed toward the solution of the pressing problem of the relation of Judaism to Christianity as proclaimed and practiced by the believers of Gentile origin in Antioch, Syria, and Cilicia (Acts 15:23-29).

The decree specified that converts from paganism were not to be required to submit to circumcision or other precepts of the Mosaic law. This epoch-making document denying the claims of the Judaizing element was dispatched to Antioch with "Judas called Barsab-

[5]Guiseppe Ricciotti, *Paul, the Apostle,* trans. by Alba I. Zizzamia (Milwaukee, 1952), p. 276.

bas, and Silas" who were chief men among the Jerusalem believers (Acts 15:22), the latter being chosen as Paul's companion on his second missionary tour.

3. *Christianity Freed From Mosaic Legalism*

The church at Antioch greeted the returned messengers and the Jerusalem decree with much rejoicing. Gentile believers recognized it as a signal victory for the Christian faith, and although it did contain some concessions to Christian converts from Judaism, these were seen to be of a transitory nature and based on the principle of mutual love and deference to their Jewish brethren. These included abstinence from "meats offered to idols, and from blood, and from things strangled, and from fornication" (Acts 15:29).

The flesh of animals sacrificed in pagan ritual was abhorred because the Jew believed that one eating it partook of the idolatrous sacrifice in which it had been offered. Since idolatry was practically universal outside Jewish circles, it was often extremely difficult to avoid such meats, sold in the markets as they were with other foods, inasmuch as pagan buyers attached no significance whatever to their source, providing the commodity was fresh. Pagan converts on the basis of Christian charity (Romans 14:1-23; I Corinthians 10:23-33) and out of respect for Jewish believers were to avoid these foods in the *agapes* in a Christian community, so as not to cause offense to their weaker brother. When the occasion of stumbling was removed, so also was the precept.[6]

The use of blood of animals in culinary recipes or the eating of animals strangled and not previously bled[7] was abominated because Semitic peoples had the belief from dim antiquity (cf. Genesis 9:3, 4), which is reflected in the Mosaic injunctions (Leviticus 17:10-14), that the blood was the life, the seat of the soul. In eating the blood "one absorbed the soul of the animal with all its brutish qualities."[8]

The first three prohibitions of the Jerusalem decree deal with customs offensive to a Jew and are not *per se* illicit to a Gentile believer. The fourth, however, is directed against fornication, and is in its very nature immoral and prohibitory to any Christian believer — Jew

---

[6]Ricciotti, *op. cit.,* p. 279. These injunctions, however, have persisted in the Church. The martyrs at Lyons in the year 177 declared they could not eat blood (Eusebius, *Ecclesiastical History* V. I, 26). Echoes of the belief extend to the Middle Ages.

[7]Cf. Craig, *op. cit.,* p. 173. As distinguished from "things strangled" from the preceding rule, "this forbade the separate use of blood . . . as an article of food. Dishes so prepared were common in the *cuisine* both of Greeks and Romans . . ." (E. H. Plumptre in *The Acts of the Apostles,* ed. by C. J. Ellicott, New York, n. d., pp. 214, 248-249).

[8]Ricciotti, *op. cit.,* p. 279. According to rabbinic law, these first three injunctions were included in the seven precepts of Noah's sons and were binding upon non-Israelites residing in Israelite territory (*Sanhedrin,* 56b.).

or Gentile. It is mentioned in the decree because of its extremely widespread practice and corrupting influence in ancient polytheistic society where it was often associated with pagan worship, and not only looked upon as natural and permissible[9] but even abetted in the name of religion, for example, in the case of the harlot-priestesses of Aphrodite at Corinth and Paphos. In such instances of sinful indulgence, the man not only committed social immorality but also identified himself with the cult of the woman who was its avowed devotee, and thus was guilty of an aggravated inquity in the eyes of every Jew.[10]

Numerous scholars have held that the decree, despite its emphatic condemnation of the Judaizers, was "a compromise."[11] Sir William Ramsay declares that "it seems impossible that Paul could have accepted a decree which declared mere points of ritual to be compulsory."[12] Yet it seems difficult to see how this could be true when Paul and Silas on the second missionary tour delivered the very decisions of this decree to the churches of Galatia "for observance" (Acts 16:4), when he himself consistently taught the principle of love in the matter of things permissible in themselves, but which might cause another believer to stumble (Romans 14:1-23; I Corinthians 10:23-33) and when this aspect of his conduct was especially true in dealing with Jews in order to win them to Christ. When a matter of principle was concerned, as with Titus, Paul was unbending and would not have him circumcised (Galatians 2:3), while in the case of Timothy where the law of love in the interests of unity and peace came into play, the action was reversed (Acts 16:3).

In a real sense the Jerusalem decisions expressed the apostle's dealing with his own kinsmen according to the flesh during his entire ministry, while in his working with Gentiles, the decree was to him the magna charta of Christian liberty and marked the complete emancipation of Christianity from Judaism. But the apostle was realistic in his dealings with his Hebrew brothers, knowing the ritual and ceremonial chasm separating them from unadulterated Christianity. Having been a Jew himself and knowing his own dilemma, which was resolved only by a special revelation of Christian truth, he was able

---

[9]Cicero defended the practice explicitly (*Pro M. Coelio*, 20). Other ancient writers either attest its prevalence or speak of it lightly, such as Terence, *Adelphi*, 101; Seneca, *Controv.*, 2.4(12); Horace, *Satires*, 1, 3, 31; Petronius Arbiter in the entire *Satyricon*.

[10]Plumptre, *op. cit.*, pp. 243-244. Ricciotti, *op. cit.*, p. 280; Craig, *op. cit.*, pp. 173; 302, 307; Olaf Moe, *The Apostle Paul*, trans. by L. A. Vigness (Minneapolis, 1950), p. 236.

[11]See Sir William Ramsay, *St. Paul the Traveller and the Roman Citizen* (New York, 1896), p. 172, following Lightfoot and others.

[12]*Ibid*.

to sympathize with his countrymen and make some concessions to them in the spirit of the Jerusalem decree.[13] According to Schlatter, "the chief result of the agreement between St. Paul and the Jerusalem Church was that in the church the Jews and the Gentiles were not assimilated, but each kept their own traditions unimpaired by any attempt at uniformity."[14]

II. THE NEW FAITH TESTED BY DEFECTION

The decisions of the Jerusalem Council were electric in their effect on the spiritual life and missionary zeal of the great Gentile church at Antioch. Not only was there rejoicing (Acts 15:31) that the confusion precipitated by the intrusion of legalism had been dissipated and the whole question of Gentile salvation settled by apostolic agreement, but a powerful incentive was given the church to continue Gentile evangelism into new regions. Accordingly, Paul presently proposes another missionary trip to confirm converts already made and to reach out after others.

1. *The Beginning of Paul's Second Missionary Tour*

This evangelistic effort, which was to be history-making in its import and which was to witness the planting of the Christian faith in Europe, began in sharp dissension. Barnabas, who had worked with Paul on his first journey through Cyprus and Asia Minor, now separated from his colleague over his (Barnabas') cousin John Mark, whom Paul refused to take on the second journey because of his failure on the first journey. Accordingly Barnabas sailed for his homeland, Cyprus, with Mark, while Paul chose Silas (Silvanus), a member of the mother church at Jerusalem, to assist him. They set out for Asia Minor — this time by land, through north Syria, crossing Mt. Amanus at the "Syrian Gates" into Cilicia. Along the route the party stopped at the communities in this region where Paul had ministered before he was fetched to Antioch by Barnabas previous to the first missionary tour, and "strengthened the churches" (Acts 15:41).

Quitting Cilicia, undoubtedly from Paul's hometown of Tarsus, Paul and Silas traversed the formidable Taurus Mountains through the famed "Cilician Gates" (modern Gülek Bogaz, 3575 feet above sea level), where they braved a beast-infested and robber-haunted wilderness, as they pressed on over the road (often blocked with landslides and impassable with snow in winter)[15] which connected Antioch and Tarsus with Derbe across the Taurus.

[13]Cf. Adolf Schlatter, *The Church in the New Testament*, trans. by Paul L. Levertoff (London, 1955), pp. 130-138.
[14]*Ibid.* p. 137.
[15]So Cicero informs us in one of his letters (*Ad Atticum*, V, 21, 14).

From the heights of the Taurus, the missionaries could see the broad plain of Lycaonia, green with vegetation in spring when the trip was made, and soft with oozy mud. About ten days of slow progress, in which travelers unfamiliar with the route might find themselves bogged down in the marshy soil, brought the group to Derbe, a frontier Roman town on the border of the province of Galatia and the kingdom of Commagene.[16] While nothing is told of this present stopover at Derbe, a warm welcome was undoubtedly accorded the apostle by the church founded there on his first tour.

From Derbe the missionaries went to the Roman colony of Lystra.[17] Here the apostle invited the young man Timothy, who had been converted during Paul's previous visit to the city, together with his godly Jewish mother and grandmother (II Timothy 1:5), to join the evangelistic party. The young convert had meanwhile distinguished himself by the propagation of the Christian message, so that he was highly esteemed "by the brethren that were at Lystra and Iconium" (Acts 16:2).

Paul circumcised Timothy "because of the Jews" who were in this region (Acts 16:3). This act was performed for practical reasons of charity and peace, and was in no manner a denial of the position Paul had espoused at the Apostolic Council. In this case of Timothy the action involved only that which was permissible to a believer purely for traditional reasons, not as in the case of Titus, dealing with that which was claimed to be obligatory for salvation.

Scholars who reject this notation of Luke as unhistorical in the specious contention that Paul, who unflinchingly refused to circumcise Titus, could not now circumcise Timothy, not only transgress in composing history contrary to the documents, but fail to see that Paul subsequently on the same principle of charity (and not at all on the principle of doctrinal necessity) submitted to the Jewish ritualistic practices (Acts 18:18; 21:26) in accordance with I Corinthians 9:20— "And to the Jews I became as a Jew, that I might gain Jews; to them that are under the law as under the law, not being myself under the law, that I might gain them that are under the law."

Leaving Lystra Paul and Silas, now joined by Timothy, who was ordained (II Timothy 1:6) to become Paul's secretary and assistant, visited the churches established on the previous tour, including Iconium and Pisidian Antioch. Their main activity was instructing the new believers and communicating the decisions of the Jerusalem Council on the momentous issue of the relation of Christianity to Judaism.

[16]See Chapter IX.
[17]See Chapter IX. Cf. Souter "Colony" in Hasting's *Dictionary of the Apostolic Church*; A. T. Robertson, *Luke, the Historian in the Light of Historic Research* (New York, 1920), pp. 183-185.

"So the churches were strengthened in the faith and increased in number daily" (Acts 16:5).

2. The Epistle to the Galatians and the North Galatian Theory

With the task of visiting the fields of former labors finished, the problem arose what new regions were to be opened up and pressed to the fore. Having preached in the south of Asia Minor, Paul "obviously now intended to tackle the west coast, the region of the big Greek towns of Ephesus, Smyrna, and Pergamus.[18] But divine intervention restrained him from the populous cities and Jewish colonies of proconsular Asia. Instead the apostle was directed to Phrygia and the Galatian region (*Galatikē Chōra*) (Acts 16:6), that is, following the North Galatian thesis, he was led to the districts of central Asia Minor, and, supplementing the intentionally abridged account given in Acts, "now preached there in towns of mixed Phrygian and Galatian population, such as Amorium, Pessinus, Orcistus, and Nacolta . . ."[19]

According to this theory, the author of *Acts,* anxious to present Paul's activity in Europe, skims over this sojourn in Asia Minor in a few words,[20] which however, must have occupied several months at least, through the remainder of the year 50 and perhaps the beginning of 51. During this period Paul's serious illness is placed, which is differentiated from the "sting of the flesh" (Galatians 4:13-15). This sickness is made the occasion for his enforced stop among the "real" Galatians and his evangelization of this people residing in the northern part of the Roman province of Galatia.[21]

It was to these real Galatians, it is contended, Paul's Galatian epistle was addressed, and not to the Christians of Pisidian Antioch, Iconium, Lystra, and Derbe in the southern section of the Roman province of Galatia. These latter, according to the North Galatian hypothesis, could never be called "Galatians, because they were, and were called, Pisidians or Lycaonians, just as they spoke a Lycaonian dialect" (Acts 14:11). The inscriptions, moreover, are cited to prove that the administrative incorporation of Galatia, Pisidia, Lycaonia,

---

[18]Martin Dibelius, *Paul,* ed. and completed by Werner Georg Kümmel, trans. by Frank Clarke (Philadelphia, 1953), p. 75.
[19]Dibelius, *ibid.* For the Northern Galatian Theory, see James Moffatt, *An Introduction to the Literature of the New Testament* (3rd ed., 1918, pp. 90-101 and in *Encyclopaedia Biblica* IX, p. 972; Paul W. Schmiedel, *Encyclopaedia Biblica* (1899-1903), cols. 1592-1616.
[20]Ricciotti, *op. cit.,* p. 292.
[21]Ricciotti, *op. cit.,* pp. 21-23. The population of Galatia proper consisted of Celtic (Gallic) invaders mixed with the earlier Phrygians and Greeks and a few Romans. Hence the name *Gallogrecia* (Strabo, XII, 5, 1), Graecogallia (Livy, XXXVIII, 17). The Galatians were only superficially hellenized as they spoke a Gaelic dialect like that in Trier in Gaul as late as Jerome's era in the early fifth century. (*In Epistulam ad Galatos,* lib. II, *Praefatio* in Migne, *Patr. Lat.,* 26, 382).

etc. into the larger organization of the Roman province did not cancel out their separate nations.[22]

Further documentary evidence is cited by the North Galatian protagonists that at least in the second century A.D. the various regions which made up the Roman province had an assembly or *koinon* of its own. The *koinon* of Lycaonia and that of Galatia, for example, convened in Ancyra (modern Ankara) or Pessinus.

It is further pointed out that the early interpretations which prevailed to the latter part of the nineteenth century maintained the epistle of Paul was written to the actual Galatians in the northern part of the province. In agreement with this it is held that Luke asserts that the Pauline party passed through the "Galatian region," meaning the region of the Galatian tribes and not the province as a whole, since the missionaries were journeying from Lycaonia and Pisidia, which were part of the province of Galatia, and accordingly were already inside the province. Arguments advanced against these solid reasons underlying the older interpretation are held to be specious and learned quibbles.

3. The Epistle to the Galatians and the South Galatian Theory

The findings of modern archaeology, notably the researches of Sir William Ramsay in Asia Minor before World War I, have given impetus to the view that Paul wrote the epistle to the Galatians either solely to the inhabitants of Southern Galatia without having visited Northern Galatia at all, or that he did visit northern Galatia,[23] but "that the Epistle to the Galatians is primarily addressed to the Churches in South Galatia."[24] Archaeological discoveries have shown that it was entirely correct for Paul to address the believers in Antioch, Iconium, Lystra and Derbe as "Churches of Galatia," meaning the Roman province by that designation[25] and entirely right for him to refer to these people as "Galatians" (Galatians 3:1). Luke and Paul are both cited as designating the inhabitants of a city or district without making ethnographical distinctions, as between Romans, Greeks, Jews, etc. Illustrations cited are Pontians (Acts 18:2), Alexandrians (Acts 18:24), Asians (Acts 20:4), Corinthians (II Corinthians 6:11), Macedonians (Acts 19:29; II Corinthians 9:2, 4), Philippians

---

[22]Accordingly, the Emperor Augustus' legate to the province is not stated simply "Legate to Galatia," but accurately if tediously "The Legate of Augustus as praetor of the province of Galatia, Pisidia, Phrygia, Lycaonia, Isauria, Paphlagonia, etc." (*Corpus Inscrip. Lat.*, III, 291, supplement 6618.)

[23]Henry Clarence Thiessen, *Introduction to the New Testament*, 3rd ed., (Grand Rapids, 1946), p. 216.

[24]*Ibid.*

[25]Cf. Ramsay, *A Historical Commentary on St. Paul's Epistle to the Galatians;* Frederic Rendall in *The Expositor's Greek Testament* III, p. 128; E. J. Goodspeed, *The Story of the New Testament* (1916), p. 9.

(Philippians 4:15). The question arises, Why should Galatians 3:1 be an exception?

Protagonists of the North Galatian theory are undoubtedly correct in insisting that Paul entered North Galatia on his second tour. However, not all advocates of the South Galatian theory agree with this fact apparently indicated by Acts 16:6 (cf. 18:23). In these two sole instances where Luke employs the term, "Galatian region," he does so in the original territorial sense.

When, however, Paul employs the noun "Galatia," he uses it as the name of the Roman province, never as the territorial designation, except the two happen to be identical. Examples of his minute accuracy in the matter of Roman provinces are found in his use of the terms Asia, Achaia, Macedonia, Illyricum, Dalmatia, Judaea, and Arabia.[26] It seems unlikely that he would use the term "Galatia" (I Corinthians 16:1; Galatians 1:2; II Timothy 4:10) in any other sense.

Moreover, it would be singular indeed for Luke to recount so fully the founding of the churches of South Galatia by Paul (Acts 13:14-14:23) and for Paul himself to say practically nothing about them, or, on the other hand, to write so pivotal an epistle as the Galatian letter to churches which are scarcely mentioned in the Acts.

The reference to Paul's illness (Galatians 4:13), it is held by the advocates of the North Galatian view, is impossible to fit into the record of the apostle's ministry in South Galatia. But it apparently is unmentioned by Luke because it was not serious enough to interfere with Paul's preaching.

On the basis of these various considerations it is perhaps best to assume that although Paul undeniably visited North Galatia on his second tour and made disciples there (Acts 16:6), his epistle to the Galatians is addressed, primarily at least, to the churches in South Galatia.

4. The Lapse of the Galatians and the Galatian Epistle

Sometime after the apostle's visit to Galatia on his second tour, the Christian Gospel underwent a period of serious testing. Liberated from legalism by the decisions of the Council of Jerusalem and by the apostle's own uncompromising stand both in the practice and proclamation of the message of grace, the new faith was to endure the trial of defection. This experience that seemed for the moment to presage tragedy was, however, divinely overruled to further the triumph of the Christian evangel in calling forth the epistle to the Galatians, which was to be the magna charta of Christian liberty.

[26]Thiessen, *op. cit.*, p. 215. A. T. Robertson, *Luke the Historian in the Light of Research* (1920), pp. 181-182. Cf. Theodore Mommsen, *The Provinces of the Roman Empire* (Eng. trans. 1909).

More than the decisions of the Jerusalem Council, the fiery and eloquent Galatian letter was to prove itself the Church's great emancipation proclamation of the freedom of Christianity from the slavery of Jewish legalism, becoming the battle cry for Christian liberty not only in the Church's infancy but later at the time of the Protestant Reformation in the sixteenth century as well as time and time again.

It is impossible to ascertain how soon the legalistic teachers came to Galatia after Paul had visited them, nor how long it took for the apostle to learn of the lapse of these churches. Theodor Zahn, considering it Paul's earliest epistle, is of the opinion that Paul wrote Galatians from Corinth on his second tour.[27] If this is true, the defection began soon after Paul's departure, and may have been instigated by Jewish believers from Judaea or those resident in Antioch, Iconium, Lystra and Derbe, where legalistic adherents had been singularly malicious.

The common opinion is that Paul wrote the epistle on his third tour and that it belongs to the stylistic and doctrinal pattern of his other great epistles (I and II Corinthians and Romans) being first and dating from Paul's stay in Ephesus (54-57)[28] or written after I and II Corinthians from Macedonia or Greece (57 or 58).[29]

The legalists denied Paul's apostolic authority and the validity of his teaching of free grace. Hence Paul opens his letter by a vindication of his apostleship, his divinely received message, and his personal conduct (1:1-2:21). The heart of the letter is the defense of his doctrine of salvation by grace through faith by an exposition of Abraham's example and the purpose of the law in the light of the work of Christ (3:1-4:31). The remainder of the epistle is devoted to practical application (5:1-6:10), showing the proper use of Christian freedom in godly living. The whole letter constitutes a powerful refutation of the arguments of the legalistic teachers who sought to make Christianity a mere sect within Judaism.

III. THE NEW FAITH AND THE MACEDONIAN VISION

Traversing Phrygia and the "Galatian country" (Acts 16:6), that is North Galatia, since they were not permitted by divine direction to go directly westward into proconsular Asia, the missionaries no doubt visited Pessinus and Ancyra (present-day Ankara, capital of Turkey). Ancyra was the chief city of North Galatia and the capital of the entire province. There Paul undoubtedly saw the white marble temple which the council of the three Galatian tribes had built in

[27]*Introduction to the New Testament* Vol. I, p. 196.
[28]W. Sanday, "Galatians" in N. T. *Commentary for English Readers* II, ed. by C. J. Ellicott, p. 424.
[29]Cf. Sanday, *ibid;* Thiessen *op. cit.*, p. 218.

honor of Augustus and called the Augusteum. It may be that the apostle actually gazed upon the lengthy Latin inscription on its walls describing the life and public work of the Emperor, as he may have done at Pisidian Antioch and Appolonia, where fragments of other copies of the text have been recovered.[30]

1. *Divine Direction Westward*

Hindered from a direct westward course into proconsular Asia, ostensibly to bring Northern Galatia under the Christian Gospel, the missionaries are now just as clearly led westward by the Holy Spirit as they had previously been restrained from doing so. The passages which narrate the strategic course of the Gospel toward Europe are remarkable for their stress upon supernatural guidance and restraint — "Forbidden by the Holy Spirit to speak the word in Asia . . ." (Acts 14:6). "On reaching Mysia they tried to enter Bithynia but the Spirit of Jesus did not permit them . . ." (v. 7). "During the night a vision appeared to Paul" (v. 9) at Troas, calling him to Europe.

Asia Minor (Bethynia and Pontus)

Bithynia, which the missionaries attempted to enter, lay north and northwest of Galatia. But their urgent task lay west and so they had to leave the evangelization of this fertile and attractive district to others (cf. I Peter 1:1) and to turn away from its inviting cities of Nicaea, Nicomedia and Chalcedon, two of which (Nicaea and Chalcedon) were to become famous in later church history.

"Going alongside Mysia," Luke records, the missionaries were directed to Troas (Luke 16:8). Mysia formed the northwestern part of the Roman province of Asia since 190 B.C. It was closest to Europe and only the Propontis, the Hellespont, and the Aegean Sea separated it from that continent. In its borders lay ancient Troy (Ilion), Troas, Assos, and Adramyttium.

2. *Troas and the Splendor of Ancient Troy*

Troas, to which Paul and his party were directed, lay on the Aegean Sea. It was an old seaport town, which before 300 B.C. bore the name of its founder Antigonus, and was called Antigona Troas.

---

[30]The unextant original composed by August himself was executed in A. D. 14. Cf. *Res Gestae Divi Augusti.*, tr. F. W. Shipley, *The Leob Classical Library* (1924).

Afterwards the town became known as Alexandria Troas in honor of Alexander the Great, and for a time was the residence of the Seleucid kings. Later the city became free and struck its own coins, of which large collections have been found.

In 133 B.C. Troas came into the possession of Rome. The city received every kind of privilege from the *gens Julia* because of the Homeric memories associated with the origins of the family. Julius Caesar planned in his time to make it no less than the capital of the Roman Empire.[31] Augustus made it a Roman *colonia* and a free city independent of the provincial Roman governor of Asia, with its citizenry exempt from poll and land tax.

The ruins of the ancient seaport (known today as Ekistanbul) are extensive, giving mute evidence of the size and importance of the ancient city. But the site has long been used as a quarry and much of the architectural remains have been taken to Constantinople to construct a mosque and other buildings. Structures excavated are characteristic of the Roman period and include gymnasiums, baths, temple, theatre and an imposing aqueduct from the time of Trajan. The port from which Paul sailed for Europe was built by means of a mole with an inner and outer basin.

Northeast of Troas Alexandria lie the ruins of Troy-Illium of Homer's *Iliad* and *Odyssey*. The place is now called Hissarlik and is situated a few miles from the southwestern entrance to the Dardanelles. In 1870 Dr. Heinrich Schliemann began excavations there to confirm his identification of it as Troy-Illium. His adventuresome and successful diggings, continuing with interruptions until 1890, not only demonstrated that the site was Troy-Illium but that it had been occupied by at least seven cities.[32] Later excavations by the University of Cincinnati have traced the sequence of successive civilizations on the same site from the most remote era down to Roman times and have revised some of Schliemann's conclusions. At least nine cities are now traced, the Homeric town being fourth from the top.

3. The Call to Europe

At Troas Paul and his friends waited for divine direction. There they met Luke, a Greek physician, a member of that noble profession which Hippocrates, the father of medicine, from the Aegean island of Cos south of Miletus, had founded four centuries before. Goodspeed suggests that "perhaps Paul, now down on the seacoast after his journey over the uplands of Asia Minor, was stricken with malaria

[31]Seutonius, *Divus Julius*, 79.
[32]Cf. Schuchardt, *Schliemann's Excavations and Archaeological and Historical Studies* (London, 1891) also his *Schliemann's Ausgrabungen.* Schmidt, *Schliemann's Sammlung trojanischer Altertümer.*

again and had to call a doctor."[33] Whatever the circumstances, the new addition to Paul's party was to be of much-needed help in numerous ways.

At Troas Paul made one of the most momentous decisions of his career. Perhaps Luke, who seems to have been a native of Macedonia, had something to do with it, but the main reason for going to Europe was Paul's vision at night in which he saw a Macedonian "standing beseeching him, and saying, Come over into Macedonia and help us" (Acts 16:9).

Unusual guidance was given for an extraordinarily significant step. Christianity was to be taken beyond Asia, where it had been born, into Europe, where it was to make such an incalculable contribution. Severely tried and tested by Judaistic attack, it had survived to be a regenerative force for all mankind, instead of a mere sect within Judaism. It was liberated for a vast ministry and the door was being opened as Paul, Silvanus, and Timothy, now joined by Luke, set sail for Europe to take the Gospel of grace into a wholly new spiritual climate with results that could scarcely have been dreamed of by the small band of heralds of the cross.

[33]Edgar Goodspeed, *Paul* (Philadelphia, 1947) p. 71.

CHAPTER 11

THE CHURCHES OF MACEDONIA

On the journey to European Macedonia Paul's ship, Luke records, touched at Samothrace, an Aegean island. Here was the place where Demetrius Poliorcetes, "the taker of cities" in the fourth century B.C., set up the statue of the Winged Victory, which was discovered there in 1863, and has since adorned the Louvre in Paris as one of its most superb pieces. It may be that Paul saw this splendid monument of Greek art and religion. But if he did, "it meant to him only another evidence of the triumphant idolatry he was working to overthrow."[1]

The 175-mile trip between Troas and Neapolis (modern Kavalla) on the Macedonian mainland, was made without incident and required two days, including the stopover at Samothrace, about midway across. At Neapolis, the port of Philippi and the terminus of the great Egnatian Road, Paul and his group landed. Situated on a promontory with the Aegean on two sides, its position was important as a connecting link by sea with Asia Minor and by land with Europe. The latter connection was made by the Egnatian Way, which ran through nearby Philippi and thence across Macedonia to Dyrrachium (Durazzo) opposite Brundisium in Italy (across the Adriatic), where the Appian Way connected with Rome. In Neapolis a typical motley array of races and languages, characteristic of port towns, reigned. This was to be expected in a town that was the first point of contact for traffic that flowed between two continents.

I. GOSPEL PENETRATION OF EUROPE AND THE CHURCH AT PHILIPPI

From Neapolis the ten-mile journey inland to Philippi was made. Sir William Ramsay has advanced the attractive hypothesis that Luke himself was a Philippian,[2] which, if true, would explain the emphasis laid on the importance of the city (Acts 16:12) and the vivid detail of the narrative of Acts 16:11-40.

1. History and Importance of Philippi

The city took its name from Alexander's father, Philip II of Macedon, who was attracted there by the gold of nearby Mount

[1]Edgar Goodspeed, *Paul* (Philadelphia, 1947), p. 73.
[2]*St. Paul the Traveller and Roman Citizen*, pp. 200f.

Pangaeus, and transformed the ancient village of Krenides into a thriving fortress city. From this military base Alexander in 334 B.C. set out on his phenomenal career of world conquest.

In 42 B.C. on the surrounding plains along the Gangites River the battle took place between the murderers of Julius Caesar and his avengers. In commemoration of the hard-won victory there, Octavius constituted the city a Roman colony, which made it "a miniature Rome in the Middle East."[3] The Roman colonies were small replicas,

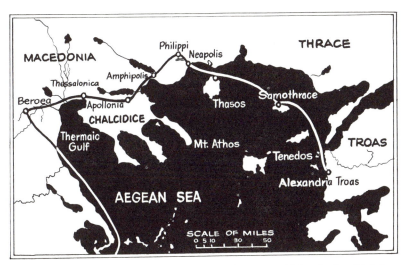

Map of Paul's journey into Europe showing the cities of Macedonia which he visited

in a sense, of Rome itself. Usually three hundred Roman citizens emigrated to found such a colony as an advance guard of the mother city to hold in subjection the surrounding country. Military roads were constructed to bind together the various colonies with themselves and with the mother city.[4]

To be constituted a Roman colony was a reward and an honor. It was a token that a city possessed special importance and was esteemed by the Emperor, and was deemed worthy to be the residence of Roman citizen-soldiers, who constituted the military and social aristocracy of the provincial town where they lived.

[3]M. S. and J. Lane Miller, *Harper's Bible Dictionary* (New York, 1952), p. 549. "From both coins and inscriptions it is well proved" that Philippi "was a Roman colony," Camben M. Cobern, *The New Archaeological Discoveries* (New York, 4th ed. 1920), p. 545.
[4]A. T. Robertson, *Luke, the Historian in the Light of Research* (New York, 1930), p. 183-185; A. Souter, "Colony" in Hastings' *Dictionary of the Apostolic Church*.

It is interesting that Philippi alone is termed a colony by Luke (Acts 16:12),[5] possibly because of his residence there and natural interest and pride in the city.[6] This was natural, since the colonies held themselves above the other cities. At any rate, his "pride in the city, his familiarity with its geography, and his vivid first-person narrative (16:10-17), all show that Luke had some personal connection with Philippi."[7]

Moreover the city was granted the *jus italicum,* which gave it tax exemptions and numerous privileges. As a colony it was a free city, but other towns, which were not colonies, were frequently given the status of "free cities," as they were called, and had self-government within the Roman province where they were located. It was not Roman policy, however, to grant a provincial constitution and a free status to a community which did not possess a certain degree of culture and ability for autonomous government. In any case, "the free cities and the colonies were points of power," and Paul went to them "as centres of influence."[8]

2. Archaeology and Luke's Reference to Philippi's Importance

Concerning this city, Luke remarks that it was *prōtē tēs meridos,* i.e. "first in that part" of Macedonia (Acts 16:12), meaning thereby either the first in political importance and rank or first which the apostle reached. If Luke means the first in political importance and rank, a difficulty results which has led some scholars to impugn Luke's accuracy either on the ground of an obvious blunder or an overstatement dictated by his civic pride. But it is highly improbable that Luke would blunder through ignorance in a passage distinguished for its vivid detail and evidences of minute accuracy. Would it not be inconceivable to imagine he did not know that Thessalonica was the capital of the province, or if he referred to the easternmost of the four districts into which Macedonia had been divided by the Romans in 168 B.C., that he was unaware that Amphipolis was its capital and, at least, this rival city would contest such a declaration?[9] The simple

---

[5]Numerous other cities, however, are referred to by Luke that were colonies at the time, such as Troas (since 20 B.C.), Lystra (since 12 B.C.), Syracuse (since 21 B.C.), Puteoli (since 194 B.C.), Ptolemais (since before A.D. 47), Pisidian Antioch (since before 27 B.C.) and Corinth (since 27 B.C.) — total eight, including Philippi.
[6]Robertson, *op. cit.,* p. 184.
[7]M. S. and J. Lane Miller, p. 549.
[8]Robertson, *op. cit.,* p. 185. Luke mentions Athens, Tarsus, Ephesus, and Thessalonica, which are known to be in the class of "free cities."
[9]Some scholars suggest a corrupt text (and the codices vary, see R. J. Knowling "Acts" in *The Expositor's Greek Testament* ed. by W. Robertson Nicoll, note on Acts 16:12). Scholars offer the following emendations: (a) for *prōtē tēs* read *prōtēs* "which belongs to the first region of Macedonia" (b) delete *meridos* as a gloss and read "which is a city of Macedonia of first rank" (though not necessarily *the* first city) (c) for *meridos* read *Pieridos* and read with Hort "a chief city of Pierian Macedonia."

explanation is that Luke being a native of Philippi would understandably claim for his own city the precedence over the rival town of Amphipolis "which his own townsmen were doubtless claiming then, and which claim was acknowledged a little later universally."[10]

Furthermore, as far as its dignity as a Roman colony was concerned, its rich historical associations with the Empire, and particularly its strategic geographical location as the Aegean doorway to Europe and through the Egnatian and Appian Ways to Rome and the West, certainly Philippi from Luke's point of view had some claim to be "the first city in the district of Macedonia."[11]

But another difficulty has long encumbered Luke's enthusiastic description of Philippi (Acts 16:12) in his allegedly impossible use of the well-known Greek word *meris* in a geographical sense to mean a "region" or "district." Even F. J. A. Hort, the famous New Testament textual authority, was convinced that Luke blundered in this usage.[12] Hort was correct insofar as archaeological light at that time could elucidate this word.

However, archaeological evidence has appeared to show that Luke was more intimately acquainted with Macedonian geographical terms than present-day experts. Excavations in the papyri-rich sands of the Fayum in Egypt have demonstrated that the resident colonists there, many of whom had emigrated from Macedonia where Philippi was located, idiomatically employed this very word *meris* to denote the divisions of a district. Now all scholars own that this word *meris* was used correctly by Luke, and evidence is furnished by archaeology to correct modern critics and once again to vindicate Luke.[13]

3. The First Converts in Europe

At Philippi the Jewish element was so inconsequential that there was no building for a synagogue. On the Sabbath what Jews or Jewish proselytes there were (evidently only women) gathered in an "oratory" (*proseuchē*) in the open air near a stream, where water was supplied for legal and ceremonial ablutions. The "river" may well have been the Gangites which flows less than two miles west of the city, but on the other hand it may have been one of the numerous springs or wells from which the ancient well-watered village of Krenides ("Fountains") took its name.

[10]Cobern, *op. cit.*, p. 546.
[11]Or did Luke use the adjective "first" in the sense of an honorary epithet, meaning merely "outstanding" or "noteworthy"? Cf. Guiseppe Ricciotti, *Paul the Apostle* (Milwaukee, 1953), p. 297.
[12]See the Appendix to Westcott and Hort, *Greek Testament*, Vol. II, Appendix, p. 96. Cf. D. G. Hogarth, *Authority and Archaeology*, p. 96.
[13]Cobern, *op. cit.*, pp. 545-546; J. P. Free, *Archaeology and Bible History* (Wheaton, Ill., 1950), p. 320.

The result of the meeting the first Sabbath was the conversion of a business woman named Lydia (i.e., "the woman from Lydia"), a dealer in purple dye and a native of the city of Thyatira in the extreme southern part of Mysia on the frontier of Lydia, and often considered part of Lydia. For this reason Lydia's name was apparently more of a surname. Thyatira was a colony of Macedonians and a prosperous market for purple. This fact explains the woman's presence in Macedonia as well as her occupation.

After Lydia and her household believed the Gospel and were baptized, she insisted that the whole missionary party make her house their headquarters. It was undoubtedly a large dwelling, befitting a successful career woman, and commodious enough to entertain four guests in addition to her own household. It may be supposed that the front entrance led to an atrium, ornamented with flowers and shrubbery and open to the sky. Beyond this would be a peristyle court surrounded by sleeping apartments on the second floor, which were made accessible through a gallery that circled the court above the columns of the peristyle.[14]

As new converts were added to form the church in Philippi, Lydia's home became the first private house in Europe to serve as the meeting place of Christians. On the first day of the week the church may be thought of as assembling in the atrium or peristyle of the house to sing psalms, read the Old Testament in Greek, pray and hear an exposition by Paul, Silas, or Timothy. The private houses of wealthier members were to serve as places of Christian assembly for two centuries and more before Christians would have buildings of their own constructed solely for worship.

4. The Place of Women in the Church

The beginning of the gospel movement in Europe auspiciously pointed to the different place women were to have in Christianity, especially in contrast to heathenism and Judaism. Woman's enslavement and debasement in numerous cults of Oriental paganism are notorious. In contrast, woman's liberation by Christianity is both characteristic and striking.

Even in reference to Judaism the change is striking. The low opinion of women in Judaism is reflected in Jewish liturgy, in which Israelite men fervently thank God they were not born women. Women were excluded from participation in the synagogue service and could witness the service only from galleries or behind curtains.

---

[14]Pansa's house in fashionable Pompeii, contemporary with Lydia's smaller dwelling, had this general plan, but contained no less than sixty rooms, though half of them facing the street were rented as stores and shops. Cf. E. J. Goodspeed, *Paul* (Philadelphia, 1947), p. 75.

They were granted only an extremely restricted access to the Temple, and suffered numerous severities under the Mosaic Law and the pharisaical traditions growing out of it.

The Church, on the other hand, from the beginning welcomed women, commended them, liberated them socially and spiritually, and granted them privileges of service and ministry they had never enjoyed before, although in matters of ruling and teaching in the house of God, they were never to usurp authority over a man, and thus introduce anarchy and confusion.[15]

5. Christianity Clashes With Heathenism

The Gospel of divine grace had progressed well in Philippi, in fact, had been quite successful. One thing must have caused the missionaries to wonder — the lack of opposition and persecution. This could be partly explained by the absence of a synagogue in Philippi and experiences of virulent synagogue animosity as in Galatia. But the question still remained unanswered. How could Christianity thus advance against the strongholds of paganism and remain unchallenged by the demonism which the apostle recognized from the Old Testament was the dynamic of idolatry (Deuteronomy 32:7; Psalm 96:5; 106:37, 38) and of heathen worship in general (I Corinthians 10:20, 21)?

The answer was soon to come and was to mark the end of the missionaries' stay in Philippi. One day as the group was going to the place of prayer, they were accosted by a young woman "having a spirit of divination" who brought her promoters a tidy income by her predictions (Acts 16:16). The maid was a spiritistic medium who had actual powers of oracular utterance[16] and was under direct demonic influence and control. This is the reason she harassed the missionaries, the evil spirit energizing her, subtly opposing and discrediting Paul's ministry by giving the appearance of commending it. With penetrating discernment, which was not to be imposed upon by Satanic cunning, the apostle after patiently enduring the veiled attack for many days, and realizing the real enemy was not the girl but the evil spirit indwelling her, turned and addressed not the maid but "the spirit" (Acts 16:18), expelling the demon, as both Jesus and the apostles regularly did in their ministry of deliverance.

To represent this girl as a mere "hysteria type," of "none too strong mentality," whose "confused utterances were taken as coming

---

[15]Cf. I Corinthians 11:5, 13; 14:34, 35; I Timothy 2:11, 12; I Peter 3:1.
[16]James M. Gray, *Spiritism and the Fallen Angels* (New York, 1920), p. 97. Edward Langton, *Essentials of Demonology* (London, 1949), p. 177.

from some supernatural power," as some critics[17] do, is to betray ignorance of the essential facts of demonological phenomena, as well as rejection of the explicit statements of the historian.[18]

This episode at Philippi was in reality a head-on collision of gospel light with pagan darkness, of the power of truth with error. It is valuable in illustrating the intimate connection between divination and demonism.[19] The maid is said to have possessed *pneuma Puthona*, that is, "a Pythian spirit." In Greek mythology Python was the name of a legendary dragon that haunted the region of Pytho at the foot of Mt. Parnassus in Phocis. It was claimed to guard Delphi, the most renowned of all ancient oracular shrines, and to have been slain by Apollo. Pytho is accordingly the older name of Delphi. Consequently, "the Pythian spirit," as Hesychius defines it, meant a "divining demon" (*daimonion mantikon*).[20]

In the course of time, the expression "Pythian spirit," came to be the generic title of the alleged source of the inspiration of diviners in general, including the slave girl, whom Satan employed as a tool at Philippi to oppose the progress of the Gospel into Europe.

The spiritistic maid at Philippi is interesting, too, in illustrating the fact that "the vehicles of manifestation resembling possession in the ancient world are almost exclusively women . . . Among the possessed prophetesses of historic times the most eminent is the Pythoness."[21] The Delphic seeress was originally a maid from the surrounding countryside. She was reputed to be filled with the god Apollo himself and his spirit. The god, as was believed, entered into the physical body, and the priestess' soul, loosed from her body, apprehended the divine revelations. What she uttered was spoken through her by the god (demon).[22]

6. Archaeology and the Philippian Persecution

When the promoters of the spiritistic medium (perhaps a group of pagan priests versed in occultism) saw that their dupe was exorcised and the means of their profit gone, lethargic paganism became aroused when its pocketbook was touched. As a result, a violent persecution was precipitated. Those affected financially dragged

[17]Burton Scott Easton, "Python," *Int. Stand. Bible Encyclopaedia*, IV, 2511.
[18]Acts 16:16-18.
[19]Cf. Merrill F. Unger, *Biblical Demonology* (Wheaton, Ill., 4th ed., 1958), pp. 119-142; Auguste Bouché-Leclerq, *Historie de la Divination dans l'Antiquité* (4 vols. Paris 1879-1882).
[20]Hesychius of Alexandria, The Lexicographer, as quoted by J. A. Thayer, *Greek English Lexicon of the N. T.*, p. 557.
[21]T. K. Oesterreich, *Possession, Demoniacal and Other Among Primitive Races in Antiquity, the Middle Ages and Modern Times* (New York, 1930), p. 311; cf. his description of the Delphic Oracle, *op. cit.*, pp. 311-331.
[22]E. Rhode, *Psyche, the Cult of Souls and Belief in Immortality Among the Greeks* (2nd ed. Freiburg, 1898) II, 60-61.

the missionaries into the market place before the rulers, and during the hearing so great was the anger of the populace that all formalities of trial, witnesses, pleas, etc. were dispensed with and the missionaries punished and jailed.

Singularly prominent, as would be expected in a Roman colony, is the Roman element in the narrative. The market place or forum (Greek *agora*), where the rulers presided, was in the center of the city. The general term "magistrates" (*archontes*) in verse 19, is exchanged for the specific title of *praetors* (*strategoi*) in verse 20.[23] These officials are attended by lictors (*rhabdouchoi*) (vs. 35, 38) who carry the fasces or bundle of rods having among them an ax with blade projecting and which was borne before Roman magistrates as a badge of their authority. With these rods the lictors ("scourgers") soundly beat Paul and Silas. Two lictors attended each praetor, protected him and executed his orders.

The charge, craftily diverted from the real issue of money, was fabricated to concern the public order ("they are making a disturbance"), anti-Semitism ("they are Jews"), and fidelity to Roman customs ("set forth customs which it is not lawful for us to receive, or to observe being Romans").

The historical difficulty in the narrative concerns the title of *praetor* which Luke assigns to these Roman officials. The highest officials in a Roman colony, two in number, were styled *duoviri* or *duumviri*. That this title was in use at Philippi is proved by the inscriptions.[24] Why then did Luke use the term "praetor" here? Did he blunder or did he have reason to use the terminology he employs?

Archaeology again has shown that Luke did not blunder. Inscriptions reveal that the term *praetor* was employed as a "courtesy title" for the chief magistrate of a Roman colony. It was an office of great dignity (next below a consul) and showed respect for the *duumviri*.[25] Luke is accurate, as usual, moving on the plane of idiomatic educated conversation in such matters, and not on the plane of rigid technical conformity.[26]

7. The Philippian Jailing and Paul's Citizenship

Although Paul's imprisonment was divinely overruled for good in the conversion of the jailer and extension of the gospel witness, his unjust condemnation without a fair trial, his brutal flogging and incarceration were violations of Roman law, which protected him as a

[23]Cf. vs. 22, 35, 36, 38.
[24]Heuzey and Daumet, *Mission Archéologique de Macédoine* 15, 127, Orelli No. 3746.
[25]Hogarth, *op. cit.*, pp. 351, 352. Ramsay, *St. Paul the Traveller*, p. 218. Cicero, *De lege agraria*, II, 34: Horace *Sat.* I, 5, 34; Orelli No. 3785.
[26]Cobern, *op. cit.*, pp. 546-547. Free, *op. cit.*, p. 321.

Roman citizen. But objection has been raised that Paul did not take advantage of his citizenship to prevent his scourging. However, the mob apparently raised such an uproar that the apostle had no opportunity to defend himself.

The next morning, when the magistrates had been persuaded by someone (perhaps Lydia) that they had acted hastily and ill-advisedly and had sent word for Paul and Silas to be released, Paul had his opportunity: "They have beaten us publicly, uncondemned men that are Romans, and have cast us into prison and do they now cast us out privily? nay, verily, but let them come themselves and bring us out" (Acts 16:37).

Paul's insistence on this mark of consideration was not dictated by personal pique at his mistreatment, but for the sake of the cause he represented and the people to whom he ministered. An honorable discharge from custody was a debt he owed his converts and which the future success of the work at Philippi required.

Ruins of Philippi

Paul's words had their desired effect, for the *strategoi* "feared when they heard that they were Romans" (v. 38). And rightly so! The *lex Valeria* of 509 B.C. had prohibited the striking of a Roman citizen without a previous popular decision. The *lex Porcia* of 248 B.C. had prohibited scourging a Roman citizen for any cause whatsoever. The magistrates had directly violated both these laws, and in addition condemned two Roman citizens (Silas was apparently a Roman citizen, too) without a regular trial and defense, which procedure was emphatically contrary to Roman law. No wonder the magistrates were filled with alarm and came themselves to offer apology and release the prisoners.

This is a clear instance in which Paul made use of his prerogatives as a Roman citizen to carry on his ministry of evangelization, and which gave him such an advantage in his office as Apostle to the Gentiles. "It was no doubt this citizenship ... which inspired him with the great plan of utilizing the civilization of the Roman state to spread the gospel along the lines of communication."[27] But the apostle did not selfishly use this privilege. He employed it for the good of others and was willing to leave Philippi after his clash with the Roman authorities.

8. Modern Archaeological Excavations at Philippi

Today Felibedjik ("Little Philippi") marks the site of the many-acred ruins of the ancient Roman colony. The École Francaise d'Athènes between 1914 and 1938 excavated Philippi, and the city is now much better known.[28]

The existing ruins of Philippi were found by French archaeologists to date for the most part to a period subsequent to Paul. These include the Roman baths, the theatre (rebuilt in the second century A.D.) and Christian churches (much later). The forum has been brought to light, being rectangular in shape and measuring 300 feet by 150 feet. Five porticoes adorned it, and it was surrounded by public buildings and temples. Here a rectangular podium with steps leading up to it was discovered. It evidently was a tribunal similar to that before which Paul and Silas suffered at the hands of the Roman authorities, and although dating from the second century when it was rebuilt, was not radically dissimilar to that of Paul's day.

One structure which is believed to date from Paul's period and even to be mentioned in the Acts account is the colonial archway to the west of the city. This archway may have designated the line of the pomerium within which foreign gods were not allowed. As the Via Egnatia left Philippi and headed west, it ran beneath this arch and then traversed the Gangites, a mile or so from the city. It seems natural to deduce, therefore, that the "gate" mentioned in Acts 16:13 "was this very archway, and that the Jews met beyond it because it was required by law, and that the 'river side' where Paul spoke to the assembled women was on the bank of the Gangites."[29]

[27]Maclean, "Paul" in One Volume Hastings' Dictionary of the Bible.
[28]Paul Collart, Philippes ville de Macédoine depuis ses origines jusqu'à la fin de l'époque romaine, 2 vols. 1937. Cf. also Bulletin de correspondance hellénique 44 (1920) to 60 (1936). Cf. W. A. McDonald, "Archaeology and St. Paul's Journeys in Greek Lands," Biblical Archaeologist III 2 (May, 1940), pp. 20-22.
[29]Jack Finegan, Light From the Ancient Past (Princeton, 1946), p. 271. Collart, op. cit., pp. 319-322; 458-460.

II. FURTHER VINDICATION OF LUKE'S ACCURACY AND THE CHURCH AT THESSALONICA

From Philippi Paul traversed the seventy miles to Thessalonica on the Via Egnatia. On his way he passed through Amphipolis and Apollonia, apparently without ministering there. Although Amphipolis was a free city, according to Pliny,[30] and capital of eastern Macedonia later in the time of Diocletian, yet at this period it possessed no great importance, being eclipsed by the growing influence of Philippi and Thessalonica. Christianity early took hold at Amphipolis, however, possibly through Paul's converts from Philippi and Thessalonica, as is evidenced by remains of an early Christian basilica excavated in 1920.

Apollonia, like Amphipolis, was unimportant. Neither city seemed to possess a Jewish population to present an opening for the Gospel, so Paul passed on to Thessalonica.

1. Thessalonica the City

Paul's far-sighted policy of introducing Christianity into the strategic commercial and political centers of the Roman Empire is well illustrated in Thessalonica. Under the Romans this was a city of first-rate importance. Situated on the site of ancient Therma ("Hot Springs"), whose name survived in the Thermaic Gulf (now the Gulf of Salonika), the location was so felicitous, because of its fine harbor with full access to sea lanes and its link with Macedonian cities and markets via the Egnatian Way, that it early attained commercial and military dominance which it has retained to this day.

Its growth dates especially from its rebuilding by Cassander in the late fourth century B.C. This general of Alexander the Great bestowed upon it the name of his wife Thessalonica, who was a sister of Alexander. It was a strong naval base during the period of civil wars, and was rewarded with the status of a free city (granted autonomy in its internal affairs) because of its loyalty to Octavius and Antony in their conflict with Brutus and Cassius. The poet Antipater, a Thessalonian, called the city "mother of all Macedon"[31] and Strabo the Greek geographer of the Augustan Age, described it as Macedonia's most populous town and the provincial metropolis.[32]

Today the city is called Salonika and is a bustling metropolis of more than 200,000 population, with Jews representing about one-half the total. Its ancient strategic position is illustrated in modern times by the important role the city played in World War I and II, as a key Balkan port.

[30]Natural History IV, 17.
[31]Jacobs, Anthol. Graec. II, p. 98, No. 14.
[32]VII, 323, 330. Cf. Harold R. Willoughby, "Archaeology and Christian Beginnings," Biblical Archaeologist II, 3 (Sept., 1939), pp. 32, 33.

2. Paul's Labors in Thessalonica

Upon his arrival, Paul at once set himself to his double activity of soul-winning and earning a livelihood. He found a friend in a certain Jason, who apparently was a Jew originally named Jesus.[33] Paul found a home with Jason and as soon as he could become located at his trade went to work once again weaving tent cloth, for later in his letters to the Thessalonians he reminded them that he had worked "night and day that we might not burden" any of them (I Thessalonians 2:9). He repeats the same statement in his second epistle (II Thessalonians 3:8).

Paul's spiritual labors began as usual through the entree furnished by the synagogue. That this medium secured the Gospel a large hearing on three consecutive sabbaths is indicated by the fact that a large number of Jews were resident in the city, realizing its commercial advantages. The commodious synagogue here is in contrast to the absence of one in Philippi. This is further evidenced by the large number of Greek proselytes and God-seekers, as well as women of distinction and position, who frequented the Jewish meetings. The prestige, wealth, and prominence of the synagogue members are further attested by their success in influencing the populace in the ensuing persecution.

Paul's synagogue preaching, together with his and Silas' personal work, resulted in the establishment of a strong church in the city. Much emphasis was placed upon prophecy both fulfilled in the Messiah at His first advent but especially unfulfilled in connection with His Second Advent. This appears strikingly in the first Thessalonian epistle, written evidently from Corinth not long after the founding of the Thessalonian church and also in the second epistle shortly after the first, probably while still at Corinth.[34] The eschatological emphasis fitted into the general period of Paul's life (A.D. 51) when there were vague adumbrations of impending judgment and doom

---

[33]Use of double names among Jews in both Palestine and the Diaspora was common in the Graeco-Roman period. Since Graeco-Romans invariably distorted the pronunciation of Semitic names, it was convenient to select a foreign name which had a rough assonance with the Hebrew name. Examples: The Maccabaean high priests Jesus (Jason) and Eliaqim (Alkimos, Alkim). Cf. also Saul (Paul). The second name, however, might be different: Alexander Jannaeus (Jonathan); John Mark, Jesus Justus (Colossians 4:11). The catacomb inscriptions attest the same custom in earliest Judaism in Rome (J. B. Frey, *Corpus Inscriptionum Judiacarum*, I, Vatican City, 1936, pp. LXVI-LXVIII). Most of these names (one-half) have a Latin name or cognomen, some (almost two-fifths) have a Greek name and very few (only a seventh) have a Hebrew or Aramaic name alone, according to Frey's research.

[34]Theod. Zahn, *Introduction to the New Testament* I, pp. 232-33. G. Milligan, *St. Paul's Epistle to the Thessalonians*, p. xxxix. Cf. I. Thessalonians 4:13-5:12; II Thessalonians 1:5-2:12.

attended by prodigies and expectations of some great event bringing rebirth pervading the pagan world.[35]

3. Jewish Persecutors and Subrostrani

Paul and Silas' notable success in gospel witness was not to go unchallenged at Thessalonica any more than it had gone uncontested at Philippi. "But the Jews, moved with jealousy, took certain base loafers and forming a mob, set the city in an uproar. They attacked Jason's house and sought to bring them out to the people; but not finding them, they dragged Jason and certain brethren before the magistrates of the city, shouting, 'These men who are setting the world in an uproar have come here too, and Jason has taken them in; and they are all acting contrary to the decrees of Caesar, saying that there is another king, Jesus'" (Acts 17:5-7 Greek).

Loungers of the type employed here by the Jews to attack Paul and Silas were common in the agora or forum of Graeco-Roman cities. They invariably assembled around the rostrum where an orator was speaking, and applauded or heckled according to who paid them, in this case being hired by the disaffected Jews in Thessalonica. Cicero gave them the apt designation of *subrostrani* ("those-under-rostrum"). These worthless fellows were always ready for the excitement of a riot, especially if paid to produce it. It mattered little to them that Paul and Silas were not in Jason's house at the time they assaulted it. They enjoyed dragging Jason before the magistrates, and their trumped-up charges were that these men were violating Caesar's edicts by setting up another ruler, "king" Jesus, in opposition to the Emperor. The accusation was based undoubtedly on some incidental remark of Paul concerning the kingdom of God and the reference to Jesus' kingdom in the sense Jesus Himself had used the term before Pilate (John 18:36). The charge was as fantastic as it was severe, involving high treason.

But the Thessalonian magistrates were much more discreet and unimpulsive then those at Philippi. They realized the insincerity and mercenary role of the *subrostrani*. They had the rioters to pacify, however, as well as their conscience to appease. So they "accepted bail from Jason and the rest and let them go" (Acts 17:9).

4. Archaeology and Luke's Politarchs

Numerous details in Luke's account of the Thessalonian mission are significant in illustrating its strict accuracy. At Philippi in a Roman colony, military rather than commercial, there were accordingly few Jews and no synagogue. The magistrates were praetors, attended

---

[35]Guiseppe Ricciotti, *Paul the Apostle* (Milwaukee, 1952), pp. 308-311; cf. Tacitus, *Annals* XII, 43, 64; Seutonius *Claudius* 46, Dion Cassius, LX, 35.

by lictors. Paul and Silas were accused of introducing customs contrary to those Romans might observe. They were beaten by lictors' rods and appealed to their Roman citizenship.

At Thessalonica there is striking contrast. Here the city is a great commercial emporium with many Jews and a large synagogue. It is a "free city" with a *dēmos*, or "people's assembly," headed by five or six *politarchs* (Acts 17:5-9). The charge against Paul is that of trying to supersede Caesar by another king, and the rioters wish to hail him before the *dēmos* or popular assembly.

Luke's use of the term "politarchs" used to be seriously questioned, since the title occurred nowhere else in Greek literature. But Luke's accuracy has been completely vindicated[36] by the appearance of the expression in at least seventeen inscriptions of this period which have come to light in Thessalonica and its vicinity. The most famous of these was inscribed on the arch of the Vardar Gate, which until the year 1876 stood at the western end of Salonica's main street and spanned the Via Egnatia. When the gate was removed, the inscription was acquired by the British Museum.

The word translated "turn upside down," *anastatoō* (Acts 17:6 A.V.), employed in connection with the charge made by the Jews and the *subrostrani* against Paul and Silas, is illustrated by an ancient letter recovered from Egypt, penned by a petulant boy to his father who had gone to Alexandria.[37] In the letter the boy relates how his mother is seriously disturbed. He writes: "And she said, 'He quite upsets me. Off with him!'" The same expression for "upset" (*anastatoō*) is used as in Acts 17:6. The word picture suggested is that just as a spirited boy "upset" his mother, so Paul and the missionaries were upsetting the complacency of the unbelievers in Thessalonica.[38]

III. SCRIPTURE SEARCHING AND THE CHURCH AT BEREA

The rabble-rousers at Thessalonica earned their pay, for even after the action of the politarchs the populace did not calm down. To avoid further incidents, "the brethren straightway sent Paul and Silas away by night to Berea." Paul's work was completed in Thessalonica. Moreover, he had grown accustomed to discern divine orders, sometimes through strange events and always through experiences of persecutions. He was getting to know when to move to other needy fields. When one door was closed, another was opened.

[36]Ernest DeWitt Burton in *The American Journal* of Theology 2 (1898), pp. 598-632.
[37]James Hope Moulton, *From Egyptian Rubbish Heaps*, pp. 37-39.
[38]J. P. Free, *Archaeology and Bible History*, (1950), pp. 321-322.

1. Paul's Brief Rest at Berea

Traveling the Via Egnatia toward the southwest, Paul and Silas came to Berea after about three days of travel. The time was evidently in the early part of the year 51. The town lay a distance from the coast. Cicero described it as an "out-of-the-way city."[39] But it had a restful atmosphere with the snowy splendor of Mt. Olympus to grace the horizon a little to the south and a broad plain lined with aqueducts and canals tranquilly stretching before it.

The location of the city not only breathed an air of serenity; Paul's reception in the local synagogue was also to prove peaceful. No doubt the apostle fervently hoped that sometime, somewhere, he would contact a spiritual Judaism so far removed from the bigotry of Jerusalem that it would welcome the Christian message as a fulfilment of Jewish hopes and Messianic prophecies. In Berea this expectation seemed realized. These Jews, it is declared, "were more noble than those at Thessalonica, in that they received the word with all readiness of mind, and searched the Scriptures daily, whether these things were so" (Acts 17:11).

The historian employs the word "well-born" to describe the Berean Jews, by which he means they possessed the generous, loyal disposition which was ideally supposed to characterize those of noble origin. This quality, which led them to examine the Old Testament prophecies open-mindedly and honestly, was that which Luke and the apostle Paul admired in the Bereans.

2. The Establishment of the Berean Church

Because of the admirably sincere reaction to Paul's expositions, many of the synagogue believed. Luke dwells with satisfaction on the fact that many Gentile converts were also made. The absence of narrow-mindedness and prejudice had enabled the Berean synagogue to reach many of the thoughtful and sensitive Greeks of the community. Especially significant are the women of the upper class who were won, as at Thessalonica (Acts 17:12; cf. 17:4). While not winning these God-seekers to the Jewish faith, it interested them in the broader values of Judaism and furnished them with the ideal introduction to the gospel revelation. "It was from this outer circle of the synagogue that Paul and his fellow workers drew their most significant converts, and to this extent his missionary work rested upon that of zealous Jews who had gone before him."[40]

Interference of the Jews from Thessalonica forced the apostle to retire to other fields. But as usual Paul's retreats before local de-

[39]*In Pisonem*, 36.
[40]Goodspeed, *op. cit.*, p. 85.

moniacally irrational pressures "became simply the basis for new advances."[41] Silas and Timothy were left to take care of the arrangements for the continuance of the work in Berea while Paul was free to look for new spiritual worlds to conquer.

[41]Goodsped, *op. cit.*, p. 86

CHAPTER 12

THE GOSPEL AND THE GLORY OF ANCIENT GREECE

When Paul left Berea because of the trouble-making Jews who came down from Thessalonica, he undoubtedly headed toward Pydna, twenty-five miles distant on the coast, and there took ship for Athens. Had he made the journey by land, he would have passed through Dion, Larissa, Pharsalus, and Thebes. Since no town is mentioned in what was a long land journey, he must have gone by sea around Cape Sunium on the southern tip of Attica and then northward to Athen's busy seaport of Piraeus, five miles from the metropolis.

Despite the fact that Corinth had forged ahead of Athens both politically and commercially at the time of the apostle's visit, and despite remaining evidences of destruction wrought by Sulla and his Roman army in 86 B.C., Piraeus was still a busy emporium and the gateway by sea to Athens. As early as the fifth century B.C. two long parallel walls had been constructed to connect with the city proper and to protect its life-line in time of siege. Piraeus itself was stoutly fortified since the days it had been established as a powerful naval base, which enabled Athens to be mistress of the Eastern Mediterranean world in the heyday of her political hegemony.[1]

The route the apostle used in entering the city, whether directly within the walls connecting it with Piraeus or through the Diplon Gate from the northwest, as Pausanias the famous traveler did about a century later,[2] or some other way, is unknown. If he followed Pausanias' itinerary, having passed through the Diplon he entered a long avenue of large buildings leading eastward to the Agora or marketplace — the heart of the city.

I. PAUL AT ATHENS, THE CULTURAL CENTER OF ANTIQUITY

At Athens Paul knew he was in a world-renowned center of philosophy, architecture, and art. But it would be a serious blunder to imagine he was esthetically exhilarated as he walked through the famous city. There are cogent reasons to conclude that the case was quite the opposite.

[1]W. A. McDonald, "Archaeology and St. Paul's Journeys in Greek Lands," Part II, "Athens" in *Biblical Archaeologist* IV, 1 (Feb., 1941), pp. 1, 2.
[2]McDonald, *loc. cit.*, p. 2.

1. *Athens, the City of Idol Worship*

Paul's state of mind at Athens is set forth by Luke with incisive psychological accuracy. "Now while Paul was waiting for them (Silas and Timothy) ... he was exasperated (*parotzuneto,* provoked) to see how the city was wholly given to idolatry" (Acts 17:16). The whole soul of the apostle, steeled in Judaism against the folly of polytheism and likewise as a convert to Christianity, revolted against the mixture of human learning and spiritual ignorance, of worldly philosophy and idolatrous blindness as he saw the streets of Athens filled with temples and statues of multitudinous deities.[3] To Paul the splendid beauty of Athenian temples, statues, and works of art was tarnished by being steeped in the darkness of paganism and idolatrous superstition.

Today, on the other hand, the Christian tourist cannot help being esthetically delighted at some of the most artistic objects and splendid temples man's hand has ever fashioned, even though these now are but a scant relic of the magnificent beauty that graced the city in Paul's day. But twenty centuries of Christianity have obliterated idolatry as such, and the objects admired appear as noble creations of art rather than as idolatrous representations and vehicles of pagan worship.

To Paul, however, the whole grand display was blasphemous, not only as an affront against the one true God, but as an open denial of all the apostle believed and preached. His message, however, in giving God and His salvation proper place in human conduct and experience, also at the same time gave proper place to art, architecture, and philosophy. All of these were to be refined and enriched in Christianity and accorded their highest expression in the use of God-given talents devoted to honoring God. Later the barbarian nations, which rejected Christianity, destroyed these very monuments, while whatever remains of such works of art is due to a large degree to the Christianity Paul proclaimed.

2. *Paul's Ministry in the Agora*

As elsewhere where it was possible, Paul began his ministry at Athens in the synagogue. However, the Jewish community here seems to have been small and little impression was apparently made on the Jews or Greek proselytes who worshiped together. The apostle, therefore, sought another opening for his message. Luke says, "He had discussions in the agora (market-place) every day with those who were there" (Acts 17:17).

[3]Various ancient authors describe Athen's idolatry (e.g. Livy XLV, 27). Petronius Arbiter's statement shows how widespread idolatry was in all of Greece: "Our country is so full of divinities that in it you may more easily find a god than a man" (*Satyricon,* 17).

The agora of a Greek city was the hub of its commercial life, and at Athens, as a center of philosophy and art, the heart of its intellectual life. Here was the mecca of traders, shop keepers, politicians, philosophers, rhetoricians, demagogues, and religious innovators. It was not the best place to preach the Gospel, but it offered an opening.

Athenian citizens frequented the agora daily. They spent their leisure in looking at the sights and listening to the harangues and discussions that took place there. They were idle and inquisitive, not so much for the truth, but to hear something new or exciting. Luke succinctly epitomizes the character of the crowd in the market place in words which agree with various pagan writers from the days of Demosthenes and Thucydides to the days of Pausanias: "Now all the Athenians and foreign visitors who were there spent their leisure in nothing else but to tell or to hear something new" (Acts 17:21).

The center of interest now was a foreign juggler or a street musician with a performing monkey; now an exotically-dressed Oriental pilgrim proclaiming some new cult, or some far-Eastern merchant arriving with strange wares captured the attention of a group; now some rhetorician harangued a crowd on politics or religion, or some clever clown parodied the mannerisms of some well-known figure.

This vain and to some extent insincere intellectual climate was scarcely good soil for Paul's solemn and destiny-determining message, and he apparently had little if any success among the market place idlers. But he was undiscouraged and determined to redeem the time at Athens while waiting for Silas and Timothy to join him. The apostle certainly was not disillusioned. From the start he does not appear to have regarded Athens as a promising place for his labors. In his youth he came in full contact with the Greek philosophical spirit at Tarsus, and he knew what to expect at Athens.

Paul's persistence in his street preaching, however, elicited some interest from the philosophical dilettantes who frequented Athens and its schools of learning. "Then some of the Epicurean and Stoic philosophers debated with him; and some said, 'What is this babbler[4] trying to say?' But others, 'He seems to be a proclaimer of foreign deities,' because he proclaimed to them Jesus and the resurrection" (Acts 17:18).

[4]That is "seed-gatherer" (*spermologos*), an epithet originally employed of birds (the magpie and the crow). In time it was applied to indigents who gathered up kernels of grain accidently spilled in the market. Its resultant meaning became applicable to a loquacious person, with a ready "gift of gab" (as our slang expression goes), but with not much logic or reason. Paul's message of sin and salvation, involving Christ's death and resurrection, well fitted into this expression from the pagan point of view.

This was a natural reaction of Athenian philosophers, for Greek and Roman paganism had invented a god to preside over every function and interest of human life. If Victory, Modesty, and Compassion, etc. had shrines erected to them, why may not this foreign visitor be setting forth a goddess named Resurrection as the consort of a god named Jesus, to add another couple to the already bulging Athenian pantheon?[5]

The Epicureans were adherents of the philosophy of Epicurus (B.C. 342-271). They gave up the search for pure truth by reason as hopeless, and gave themselves to pleasure through experience. In encountering Paul, it is significant that they came in contact for once with one who had found pure truth in the Gospel of grace he preached, not, however, on the basis of reason alone but of faith.

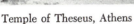
Temple of Theseus, Athens

A view of the interior of the Parthenon, Athens. Courtesy Mrs. Lowell Orth

The Stoics were followers of the philosophers Zeno (B.C. 280) and Chrysippus (B.C. 240). Their thinking was based on the premise of human self-sufficiency, the unity of God, and stern self-repression. In encountering Paul, it is noteworthy that this philosophic group came in contact for once with one who knew the fallacy of self-sufficiency, who preached the futility of mere self-repression, and who proclaimed the one true God revealed redemptively in Christ.

3. Archaeology and the Athenian Agora

This site offers some of the finest examples of systematic archaeological study in the world. Since 1930 the American School of Classical Studies under the direction of T. Leslie Shear has completely excavated the Greek agora, which is also being restored at a cost of

[5]Mohammed similarly misunderstood the Christian Trinity, construing the Spirit (*ruh,* a feminine word in Arabic) as a woman, the wife of the Father and mother of the Son, whom he then equated with the Virgin Mary (*Koran,* Surah 5, 116; also 5:77 and 4:169); cf. Arabic commentators.

a million dollars.[6] The Panathenaeum Road ran across the agora diagonally from the northwest to the southwest in antiquity. The Odeion or Music Hall, where musical and oratorical contests were conducted, projected into the open space of the agora from the south. The Stoa of Attalos on the east side was the first structure to be uncovered. This was unearthed by the Greek Archaeological Society prior to the excavations of the American School of Classical Studies.

In the southern section of the agora two long parallel Stoa (colonnaded porches) were found which skirted an area devoted to commerce. On the west side of the agora from north to south was the Stoa of Zeus Eleutherios (Deliverer) because he was believed to have saved the Athenians from the Persian invaders in the fifth century B.C. Next followed the Temple of Apollos Patroos (the Father) and the Shrine of the Mother of the Gods, the Bouleterion (the assembly room of the Athenian council of Five Hundred) and the circular Tholos, where were located the executive offices and dining room of the Boule or City Council.[7] "A fountain at the west edge of the area has cool running water to quench the thirst of the lawmakers."[8]

A little toward the center of the open space constituting the agora was the Temple of Ares (Roman Mars), the god of war. Located elsewhere in the earlier history of the city, it was taken down at the time of Augustus when many new buildings were constructed in Athens, and re-erected in the center of the ancient agora.[9] The famous Stoa Poikile where celebrated historical paintings were displayed and where Zeno, the philosopher and father of stoicism, lectured, is likely located in the extreme northern part of the Greek agora. Here archaeological digging has been hindred by present-day buildings and public utilities.

On the west side of the agora rises the hill known as Kolonos Agoraios. Here are located the ruins of the Hephaisteion, a temple devoted to Hephaistos, the god of fire and metal craft. A number of metal working shops around the temple have been excavated, making its identity certain.

Lying to the east of the ancient Greek agora is the Roman market place (forum), consisting of arcades and shops along the open rectangular area. It is likely the work of Julius Caesar and Augustus who

[6]George Ernest Wright, *Biblical Archaeology* (Philadelphia, 1957), p. 258. Cf. Oscar Broneer "Athens, City of Idol Worship" in *Biblical Archaeologist* XXI, 1958, 1, pp. 16-25. Cf. T. Leslie Shear in *Hesperia* 2 (1933), pp. 96-109, 451-474; 4 (1935), pp. 311-370; 5 (1936), pp. 1-42; 6 (1937), pp. 333-381; 7 (1938), pp. 311-362; 8 (1939), pp. 201-246; 9 (1940), pp. 261-307; 10 (1941), pp. 1-8.
[7]Broneer, *op. cit.*, p. 17. Jack Finegan, *Light From the Ancient Past* (Princeton, 1946), p. 274.
[8]Broneer, *op. cit.*, pp. 17, 18.
[9]Broneer, *op. cit.*, pp. 20-21.

financed the large undertaking as an extension of the Greek agora. Just beyond the Roman agora is the Horologium (Tower of the Winds), an octagonal marble structure with sundials on the exterior and likely a water clock in the interior. This was the Athenian public clock and was constructed in the second half of the first century B.C.[10]

4. Paul's Address to the Areopagus

Unusual interest attaches to the Areopagus because of Paul's courageous and tactful speech made there, or at least before the Athenian court that customarily met there. The meeting-place of the court was the 377-foot high hill a little northwest of the Acropolis. It was called the Areopagus, i.e. the Hill of Ares, god of war.[11] Steps hewn out of the rock lead to the summit of the hill where benches cut out of the rock forming three sides of a square are still discernible. This ancient court room, predating Athens' golden age in the fifth century B.C., was the assembly room of a council composed of the city fathers and had supreme authority in political as well as religious matters.

In Periclean times the court dealt largely with criminal matters, but in Roman times its functions reverted again to cultural, educational, and religious issues. New religious lecturers in the city were supposed to appear before this body, "which had among its police powers the duty of passing upon their competence to speak."[12] Hence Paul's philosophical auditors took him to this body for a hearing. Since both the hill and the court were called the Areopagus, it is not certain which is referred to in Acts 17:19, 22. However, since the hill was the usual place of meeting, it seems more likely Paul's address was delivered there. If this is not the case,[13] the scene of the apostle's masterly speech was the Royal Stoa, identified by some scholars with the Stoa of Zeus Eleutherios,[14] by others with the temple of Apollo Patroos[15] and unidentified by others as being a structure as yet unearthed in the unexcavated northern limits of the agora.

Paul's sermon itself is a masterpiece of sagacious adaptability to his audience. In this case he became a Greek to the Greeks, as he had become a Jew to the Jews, to win them to Christ (cf. I Corinthians 9:20-23). Employing the language of a Greek philosopher and ap-

[10]Henry S. Robinson in *American Journal of Archaeology* 47 (1943), p. 291-305.
[11]Cf. Broneer, *op. cit.*, p. 4.
[12]Edgar J. Goodspeed, *Paul* (Philadelphia, 1947), p. 76
[13]Walter Judeich, *Topographie von Athen* (in W. Otto, ed. *Handbuch der Altertumswissenschaft* III, II, 2, 2nd ed. 1931), p. 299. This conclusion is also supported by the text itself, for it says they took Paul "on" the Areopagus *epi ton Areion pagon* (Acts 17:19).
[14]Homer A. Thompson in *Hesperia* 6 (1937), pp. 5-77.
[15]Wilhelm Dorpfeld (*Alt Athen und seine Agora* (Heft 2, 1939), pp. 146-167.

proaching the mentality of the Greek mind, he makes no reference to the Hebrew Scriptures, but quotes instead one of their poets Aratus, a Stoic of the third century B.C.

> Zeus fills the streets, the marts,
> Zeus fills the seas, the shores, the rivers!
> Everywhere our need is Zeus!
> We also are his offspring.[16]

The apostle, moreover, does not allude to the revelation of the Old Testament, but discourses instead of knowing God through human reason, as various Greek philosophers had done, including Socrates who, almost in the same place, testified with his death. And using the splendid shrines and magnificent trappings of Athenian religiosity as a lively background, Paul declares "God that made the world and all things therein ... dwelleth not in temples made with hands ... neither is worshipped with men's hands ... we ought not to think the Godhead is like unto gold, silver, or stone, graven by art and man's device. And the times of this ignorance God winked at, but now commandeth all men everywhere to repent" (Acts 17:24-30).

At this point Paul left the domain of natural reason and entered the sphere of divine revelation. But the idea of repentance and divine judgment through a man resurrected from the dead was unacceptable, and Paul's listeners politely terminated their audience. The supernatural element, with its notion of resurrection, to these worldly-wise philosophers was neither serious nor dignified, and merited no discussion.

Paul's quotation of the inscription, "To an (or the) unknown god" (the absence of the article, common in inscriptions, makes both translations possible) offers a problem. No such an inscription has yet turned up at Athens. One found at Pergamum in 1909, however, is inscribed "to unknown gods."[17] Another found on an altar on Rome's Palatine Hill and dating from the late first century B.C. reads *Sei deo sei deivae sac(rum)*, "Sacred to a god or goddess."[18] Pausanias, the widely traveled geographer, visited Athens about 150 A.D., and devoted thirty chapters of his *Description of Greece* to a meticulous and accurate account of the city in that era. He declares that on the road from Phaleron Bay, Athens' old port, to the city he saw "altars of the gods named Unknown."[19] He also declares that at Olympia he sig-

---

[16]*Phaenomena*, 5. A similar line is found in an earlier Greek poet, Cleanthes, in his *Hymn to Zeus* 4 (c. 300 B.C.).

[17]Adolf Deissmann, *Paul*, tr. by W. F. Wilson (2nd ed. 1926), pp. 288-291. Cf. P. Bruin, P. Giegel, *Welteroberer Paulus, Auf den Spuren des Völkerapostels*, 1959, pp. 1-208.

[18]Guiseppe Ricciotti, *Paul the Apostle*. Trans. A. Zizzamia (Milwaukee, 1953), pp. 321-322.

[19]*Bomoi de theōn te onomazomenōn agnostōn* (I, I, 4)

The Parthenon, Athens

The Erechtheum, Athens. Courtesy Mrs. Lowell Orth

A view of the Acropolis, Athens. Courtesy Dr. John F. Walvoord

nalled out "an altar of Unknown Gods."[20] Apollonius of Tyana, a philosopher-traveler contemporary with Paul, visited Athens not far from the time of Paul's visit. In his biography written by Philostratus (after 217 A.D.), Apollonius is cited as saying that it is the part of sagacity "to speak well of all gods, especially at Athens, where altars are set up in honor even of unknown gods."[21]

Jerome asserts that the inscription Paul had seen at Athens was not in the singular but the plural, but that the apostle quoted it in the singular for the sake of his own argument.[22] But Jerome gives no basis for his assertion, and in the light of the evidence of dedicatory inscriptions to one god, who for some reason had not been identified, "there is really nothing strange about the reference which Paul makes."[23]

5. Archaeology and Other Sites in Athens

Nothing is said by Luke concerning the Acropolis, but Paul certainly visited this extraordinary hill, rising 512 feet above the surrounding city, and viewed its majestic architecture, mostly dating from the golden age of Pericles in the fifth century B.C. The most striking sight that met the apostle's eyes here was the Parthenon, then in the prime of its splendor. This famous temple housed the statue of the city's patron goddess, Athena, superbly carved of ivory and gold by Pericles' renowned sculptor Phidias (c. 438 B.C.). Later the entrance, the Prophylaea, and the celebrated temples, the Erechtheum and the shrine of Athena Nike were completed.

Perhaps most striking of all was the colossal bronze statue of Athena that towered above the Acropolis. Forged from the spoils of Marathon by Phidias' craftsmen, this monument of Athena Promachus, the goddess who fights in the front, so dominated the countryside that Pausanias says seamen rounding the perilous cape of Sunium could see the flashing sunlight reflected from the goddess' spear and helmet.[24]

At the base of the Acropolis toward the southeast was the Odeion of Pericles, where music concerts and contests were held, and also the Theatre of Dionysos. Farther to the southeast toward the Ilissos River was the Olympieion or Temple of Olympian Zeus, 354 feet long, 135

[20]*Agnōstōn theōn bōmōs* (V, XIV, 8.).
[21]*Agnōstōn daimōnon brōmoi.* Philostratus, *The Life of Apollonius of Tyana* VI, 3. Trans. F. C. Conybeare, *The Loeb Classical Library* (1912), II, p. 13.
[22]*in Titum* I, 12.
[23]Wright, *op. cit.*, p. 258.
[24]*Description of Greece* I, XXVIII, 2 in *The Loeb Classical Library* (1918-1935) I, p. 147.

The modern canal across the Isthmus of Corinth. Courtesy Dr. John F. Walvoord

Ruins of the Lechaeum Road, Corinth

feet wide and 90 feet tall, the largest temple in Greece and one of the largest in antiquity. Begun by Pisistratus in the sixth century B.C., it was not completed in detail until by the Emperor Hadrian in the second century A.D. At the southern base of the Acropolis was the colonnaded porches of Asclepius, the god of healing.

It was only natural after Athens' star had declined in subsequent centuries of the Christian era, and her temples had been destroyed or mutilated, for the modern world early to display interest in the archaeology and topography of the ancient city. As early as the seventeenth century such studies were begun by two French consuls and by the Capuchin monks. In 1678 Jacques Spons, a French physician, published *Voyage d'Italie, de Dalmatie, de Grèce et du Levant*. In 1682 Sir George Wheeler, an Englishman, published his *Journey Into Greece*.

In the eighteenth century appeared *The Antiquities of Athens* by James Stuart and Nicholas Revett, who did careful survey research in the city for several years. Their work consists of four large volumes (3rd edition, 1885). In the nineteenth century W. M. Leake published *The Topography of Athens* (2nd ed. 1841), and these preliminary studies laid the foundation for the modern era of scientific discovery in which the Greek Archaeological Society, the German Archaeological Institute, as well as others, but particularly the American School of Classical Studies, have amassed a great corpus of scientific information regarding one of antiquity's most cultured cities.

II. PAUL AT CORINTH, THE COMMERCIAL EMPORIUM OF THE AEGEAN

From Athens Paul went to Corinth. From the account of the historian, it cannot be gathered whether he made the trip by land or sea. If by foot, nothing is stated in the narrative of the cities Eleusis and Megora, through which the apostle must have passed. The presumption is therefore that the trip was made by water, and that after a pleasant day's sailing, Paul's ship landed at Cenchraea, Corinth's seaport on the Aegean.

It was with sadness the Apostle must have reflected on his experiences in the great intellectual and artistic center of Greece. Just a handful of converts — Dionysius, the Areopagate, and a woman named Damaris, "and others with them" (Acts 17:34). It was a poor showing. But what would be the story at Corinth, as the apostle moved to the most wealthy, dissolute, and thriving city of Greece?

1. Corinth of Paul's Day

The city lay just a mile and a-half south of the narrow isthmus joining central Greece with the Peloponnesus, and had two ports, one on the east side called Cenchraea and one on the west side named

Lechaeum. The former was the gateway to the West for ships from Egypt, Asia Minor, and the Aegean world. The latter was the gateway to the East for ships from Italy and the Western Mediterranean.

The strategic ten-mile strip of land connecting Corinth's two ports was the source of the city's commercial wealth. The cargoes of large freighters were hauled over by land and reloaded on waiting ships at the other side, while smaller vessels were hoisted out of the water and pulled bodily across on a sliding device. Marines had learned that this expense was well worth being spared the stormy 200-mile jaunt around Cape Malea at the southern extremity of Achaia.

In Paul's day there was, of course, no canal dug through, although Nero in A.D. 66 attempted such a venture and turned the first soil with a golden spade. Not until 1881-1893 was such a project completed, cutting a four-mile swathe across the isthmus at its narrowest point.

As the land bridge between the flow of East and Western sea traffic, Corinth was destined for commercial prosperity. The site was so strategic that from Neolithic times it had been occupied and its history interweaves with the oldest legends of Greece. In the eighth and seventh centuries B.C. it attained great power and planted numerous colonies. In 146 B.C. Corinth was strong enough to resist Rome, but was completely destroyed in the encounter. For exactly one century the city lay in ruins, until rebuilt by Julius Caesar, who made it a Roman colony.[25]

Two vices plagued the town — greed for material gain and lust. Corinth's bustling wharves and docks and its busy shops and factories fostered the one. The cult of Aphrodite, the goddess of love, entrenched here from time immemorial, fostered the other. The goddess' temple aloft the Acrocorinth was served by more than a thousand religious prostitutes, who lodged in luxurious quarters surrounding the shrine. But in a sense, the whole city was Aphrodite's shrine, indicated by the goddess' ephithet — Aphrodite *Pandemos* — "Aphrodite of all the people" — and by the widespread practice of the voluptuous and vicious forms of the goddess' worship, making the city a notorious seat of immorality.

Such terms "to corinthianize," meaning to enter into the immoral practices of the city; "Corinthian girl," to denote the type of life engaged in there; and even "Corinthian sickness," to indicate the inevitable physiological and psychological results of such a life, made their impress upon the Greek language itself.

Here was a testing ground for the efficacy of the Christian Gos-

[25]Strabo, *Geography* XVIII, IV, 8.

pel. If the heart of the message of grace was salvation for sinners, surely Corinth was a field ripe for reaping. If the self-satisfied intellectual and philosophical connoisseurs of Athens spurned the Gospel, would it not meet the need of such who began to feel the weight and the crushing wrong of pagan license, even though its hideous features were covered over with the halo of religious respectability?

2. Paul's Ministry in Corinth

The apostle entered the city in loneliness, uncertainty, and indigence. No word had yet come from Silas or Timothy concerning the churches in Macedonia. Was his work proving permanent or were his converts scattering? Then, too, he had to earn a living, and this pressing need was providentially met by his finding a Jew named Aquila and his wife Priscilla, with whom Paul found not only lodging but work, since his new-found friends were also tent-cloth weavers, as he was. The banishment of Jews from Rome by the Emperor Claudius[26] thus resulted in Aquila becoming Paul's employer.

A prosperous city like Corinth, of course, attracted numbers of Jews. At the foot of the Prophylaea, modern diggers found a stone inscribed "(Sy)nagogue of the Hebre(ws)." Although from a building perhaps later than Paul's time, it is interesting that the term "Hebrew" rather than Jew is employed, as is also done by Paul himself (cf. II Corinthians 11:22, Phil. 3:5).[27]

Paul presented gospel opportunity first to the Jew as usual, and conducted a ministry in the synagogue every Sabbath. Response was meager until, emboldened by the arrival of Silas and Timothy, he declared the messiahship of Jesus more emphatically. The result was rejection of the message, so Paul turned to the pagans.

The conversion of Justus who owned a house next to the synagogue was a signal victory. The house became Paul's headquarters. This was also accompanied by the conversion of Crispus, the chief ruler of the synagogue, and large numbers of the Corinthians. All uncertainty was dispelled by a vision similar to that at Troas, in which Paul was assured of divine success and large numbers of converts in the city (Acts 18:5-10).

Paul remained eighteen months in Corinth teaching and preaching, writing his two epistles to the Thessalonians during his stay.

3. Archaeology and Gallio's Proconsulship

Corinth had not only been a Roman colony since it had been

[26]Seutonius *Claudius*, 25. Orosius (5th century) VII, 6, 15 also states this fact, assigning it to the Emperor's ninth year, probably A.D. 49, which fits in well with Acts 18:2, "recently come from Italy," since Paul arrived at Corinth in A.D. 50.
[27]Cf. Emil G. Kraeling, *Bible Atlas* (New York, 1950), p. 445.

founded by Julius Caesar in 46 B.C., but in Paul's day was the capital of Achaia under senatorial administration and a proconsul. The proconsul began his term in April and was expected to be at his post by July.

In the summer of 51 A.D. the new annual proconsul who arrived in Corinth to commence his official duties was Gallio, the brother of the Stoic philosopher Seneca. This fact is evident from an important inscription from Delphi, the seat of the famed shrine of Apollo across the Corinthian gulf from Corinth. This monument makes it possible to date the arrival of Gallio in Corinth quite accurately. The inscription is in the form of a letter from the Emperor Claudius and contains a reference to Gallio "as Lucius Junius Gallio, my friend, and the proconsul of Achaia..."

The Emperor styles himself "Tiberius Claudius Caesar Augustus Germanicus, Pontifex Maximus of Tribunican authority for the twelfth time, imperator the twenty-sixth time, father of the country, consul for the fifth time..." The reference to the twelfth Tribunican year and the twenty-sixth imperatorship of Claudius dates this imperial communication between January and August A.D. 52, and Gallio must have arrived earlier in A.D. 51, since he had obviously been in office long enough to have given the Emperor information of consequence concerning the people of Delphi.

4. Paul's Appearance Before Gallio

It is possible in the light of these facts to date Paul's coming to Corinth in A.D. 50, since the apostle was apparently hailed before the proconsul by the Jews shortly after Gallio's assumption of official duties at Corinth, and had already been in the city a year and a-half (Acts 18:11).

The Jews' charge was that "this man is persuading men to worship God contrary to the law" (Acts 18:13). The question was of a new manner of worship, that is, in reality the preaching of a new religion, the propagation of which was forbidden by Roman law.

The hearing was apparently conducted in the agora on the platform (bema) with the accused and his accusers on a lower level before the proconsul, although it might have been held in the Julian Basilica, situated behind the south stoa, where excavators have recovered some fine statuary of the Augustan family.

The proconsul was the kind of man needed to deal with the Jews. Gallio decreed that the altercation involved minutiae of Jewish practice and did not properly belong to a Roman court concerned only with Roman law. The decision was a judicious one that enraged the Jews bent on doing Paul as much mischief as possible.

Ruins of the Temple of Apollo, Corinth. Courtesy Rev. Thomas Roth

Corinth—remains of an arch, with the Temple of Apollo in the background. Courtesy Dr. John F. Walvoord

A riot resulted. The "ruler of the synagogue" Sosthenes was beaten in an anti-Semitic outburst, which was being manifested elsewhere in the Empire at this period. Gallio's disdain of the Jews enabled Paul to continue his work.

5. *Modern Excavation Work at Corinth*

The American School of Classical Studies at Athens began diggings at the ancient city of Corinth in 1896 which have extended over a long period.[28] As in other Greek cities, the agora was the center of the town's life, and was surrounded by colonnades, buildings, shops, and monuments. The road from Lechaeum entered the agora from the north side through an ornate propylaea or gateway. The fountain of Pierene[29] was situated just east of this, and the road to Cenchraea ran from the eastern end of the marketplace.

North of the agora was the Temple of Apollo with its fine Doric columns. This structure dates from the sixth century B.C., and was a characteristic landmark locating the ancient ruins previous to modern diggings.

One of the features of the agora was the elevated platform or *bema* (Latin *rostra*), undoubtedly marking the very spot where Paul faced his Jewish accusers in the presence of Gallio (Acts 18:12-17). Another interesting discovery in the agora were shops used for vend-

[28]Cf. various vols. on *Corinth, Results of Excavations Conducted by the American School of Classical Studies at Athens, e.g.* I, 1 Harold N. Fowler and R. Stillwell, *Introduction, Topography, Architecture,* 1932; R. Stillwell, R. Scranton, and S. Freeman *Architecture,* 1941; *Am. Journ. Archaeology* 34 (1930), pp. 403-454; 37 (1933), pp. 554-572; 39 (1935), pp. 53-75; 40 (1936), pp. 21-45; 43 (1939), pp. 155-267. See also *Corinth, Results of Excavations Conducted by the American School of Classical Studies at Athens* Vol. XV, Part 1 (1948), Part 2 *The Potter's Quarters* by Agnes Newhall Stillwell (Princeton, 1952).
[29]Celebrated five centuries before Paul. Pindar called it "Pierene City." C. M. Cobern, *The New Archaeological Discoveries* (4th ed. New York, 1920), p. 497.

ing meats and other perishable foodstuffs. These were equipped with an underground channel connecting to a well. An inscription from the Augustan Age, or a little later, calls one of these vending places a "market," using the Latin term "macellum" which Paul used in the Greek "makkellon" in I Corinthians 10:25.

The name Erastus is found on another inscription dug up at Corinth. He could be the Erastus "the chamberlain of the city" mentioned in Romans 16:23, but this is not certain.[30] The piece of pavement in which his name occurs show that he was Commissioner of Public Works (aedilis) and an important official.[31]

[30]Cf. also II Timothy 4:20; Acts 19:22. H. J. Cadbury in *Journal of Biblical Literature* 50 (1931), pp. 42-58. Wright, *op. cit.*, p. 262.

[31]Numerous articles on Corinth and excavation reports are found in the *American Journal of Archaeology* and in *Hesperia*. For a survey discussion, see Oscar Broneer, "Corinth, Center of St. Paul's Missionary Work in Greece" in *The Biblical Archaeologist* XIV, 4 (Dec., 1951), pp. 78-96.

Chapter 13

Tribulations and Triumphs in Ephesus

After leaving Corinth via its seaport Cenchraea on the Aegean Sea in late summer or early autumn in A.D. 51, Paul sailed for Syria. Accompanying him were his new-found friends and fellow craftsmen in the tent-weaving industry, Priscilla and Aquila. The party disembarked at Ephesus, where Priscilla and Aquila remained, probably to establish a branch of their business there in the metropolis of the province of Asia. Paul himself, however, after a brief ministry in the Ephesian synagogue pressed on in his journey, setting sail for Palestine. Luke mentions Paul's landing at Caesarea, the port of Palestine, and a visit to Jerusalem to greet the church and testify of the remarkable triumphs of the Gospel in the West.

From his apparently brief jaunt to Jerusalem, the apostle returned to his home base at Antioch, thus completing the second missionary tour (Acts 18:22). Almost three years had elapsed since he had been in Antioch. In the meantime Paul had achieved a phenomenal advance in missionary outreach. He was eager to report to his original sponsors of his gratifying success in planting the Gospel in Europe and in the very heart of Greece itself. The Antiochene assembly would have ample cause for rejoicing, and Paul was careful that both Antioch and Jerusalem should hear the thrilling report firsthand, for he was well aware that the headquarters of the world-wide missionary movement were still in Syria and Palestine.

Luke does not feature the ending of the second missionary tour and the beginning of the third except to note briefly that "after spending some time" at Antioch Paul "departed and went from place to place through the region of Galatia and Phrygia, strengthening all the disciples" (Acts 18:23 R.S.V.). This was the apostle's third and last visit to the Phrygian and Galatian region, which he evidently made by land over the route through Tarsus and the Cilician Gates as on his second journey, rather than by sea to Perga and north to Pisidian Antioch as on the first tour.

Moreover, the visit was doubtlessly short. The apostle was eager to press on once the believers were fortified in the Gospel of grace against the claims of the legalists. The new missionary goal was the strategic and populous city of Ephesus where incipient work had already been begun when Paul had stopped there briefly on his way to Antioch at the conclusion of the second missionary journey.

I. Ephesus, Metropolis of Asia

When Paul headed for Ephesus, he was selecting a most strategic center for missionary labor. The city at the time was the metropolis of the Roman Province of Asia, vying in greatness with Antioch-on-the-Orontes and Egyptian Alexandria, being included in the top three great cities of the eastern Mediterranean world.

Located near the mouth of the Cayster River, three miles from the Aegean Sea, opposite the island of Samos, the artificial harbor rivalled that of near-by Miletus when, in the heyday of Ephesus' splendor, it was systematically dredged of the Cayster's encroaching silt to accommodate the largest sea-going vessels.

1. *Early History of Ephesus*

Connected with busy sea lanes by its harbor and situated at the entrance to a fertile valley that stretched far into the interior of Asia Minor which opened by easy passes to other valleys inland and which in turn were joined by a network of highways with the chief cities of the province, Ephesus was the most easily accessible city in Asia. Its strategic position early gave it prominence as a commercial, religious, and political center of unusual importance.

The early history of the city is wrapped in legend. Mythology names the Amazons as the builders of the earliest town and temple near the site where the mother goddess of the earth was reputedly born. This legendary Amazonian town is said to have prospered until the early Greek period when Androclus, prince of Athens, seized it and made it a Greek city. Other traditions connect Androclus' name with the founding of the city in the eleventh century B.C.

Under Greek administration Greek language and civilization gradually supplanted the earlier Oriental culture. The Asiatic goddess of the ancient temple assumed more and more the nature of the Greek Artemis. The city became a notable mixture of Oriental and Occidental religion and culture, and in the early historical period belonged to the league of twelve Ionian cities. For four centuries the Ionian city was situated on Mount Koressos, about a mile south of the ancient Temple and cultic center.

In 560 B.C. Ephesus fell into the hands of King Croesus of Lydia and three years later was captured by the Persians. Alexander the Great in the fourth century came into possession of it. At his death it passed to one of his generals, Lysimachos, who renamed it Arsinoe after his second wife.

In 133 B.C. Ephesus passed under liberal Roman rule when Attalus III (Philadelphus), king of Pergamum, at his death bequeathed the city to the Roman Empire, and it was a part of the Roman province of Asia. Thereafter Ephesus vied with Pergamum as the chief city of Asia and gradually outstripped it, becoming a racial melting pot and the cosmopolitan commercial emporium of the Eastern Mediterranean.

2. The Wealth of Ephesus in Paul's Day

When Paul came to Ephesus from Corinth, he sailed into the harbor (Acts 18:18, 19), which was a beehive of activity in his day. Since much of the enormous wealth of the metropolis was the result of its brisk harbor traffic, as is known from various literary records and inscriptions, wealthy Ephesian citizens were ready to donate large sums of money and initiate constant projects to keep the silt of the Cayster River dredged out.[1]

Land trade supplemented sea trade in augmenting the prosperity of the city. Besides easy access to the interior of Asia by interlacing highways and to the East by the great road running through Laodicea, Colossae, Apamaea, Pisidian Antioch, Tarsus and Syrian Antioch, Ephesus owned extensive districts in its environs, notably the coastal regions southward, including the cities of Phygela and Marathesium. The lower Cayster Valley, including the city of Larissa, also was a part of the large landed interests of the city that helped to swell its income and increase its reputation as a populous and opulent commercial center. Strabo designated it as the principal emporium in Asia Minor,[2] and its population has been estimated to have exceeded a quarter of a million.[3] Merchandise of every description from the East and West poured into its spacious warehouses stretching along the river and up the sides of Mount Coressos.

3. Ephesus and the Worship of Artemis

The most distinctive source of the prestige and revenue of Ephesus was the cult of the goddess Artemis or Diana. The city boasted such a roomy and magnificent temple to this deity, that the structure was known in antiquity as one of the seven wonders of the world. The Artemision, as it was called, was situated between the two hills Ayasoluk,[4] or Seljuk as the Turks now refer to it, and twin-peaked

---

[1]Floyd V. Filson, "Ephesus and the New Testament," in *The Biblical Archaeologist* VIII (Sept. 1945), No. 3, p. 74.
[2]*Geography* XIV, 1, 24.
[3]See T. R. S. Broughton in "Roman Asia Minor," in *An Economic Survey of Ancient Rome* edited by Tenney Frank, Vol. IV, 1938, p. 813.
[4]A Turkish corruption of the Greek *Hagios Theologus*, "The Holy Divine," referring to St. John the Revelator, in whose memory a church was constructed there in later times. Cf. Emil G. Kraeling, *Rand McNally Bible Atlas* (New York, 1956), p. 447. Cf. also Procopius (6th century A.D.) *Buildings*, V. 1, 4-6 trans. by H. B. Dewing, *Loeb Classical Library* VII (1940), pp. 317-319.

Pion, and was one of the largest buildings in the ancient world, covering about two-thirds of the area of St. Peter's Basilica in Rome.

The origins of the Artemision are lost in legend, but undoubtedly go back to the eighth century B.C. to a simple shrine to house the goddess. In subsequent centuries the edifice was rebuilt at least twice. In 559 B.C. when Croesus captured Ephesus, he not only spared the city because of its sacred character, but remodelled and embellished its then famous temple.[5] The splendid structure of Croesus' time was enlarged in building operations that continued for almost a century and a quarter. This magnificent sanctuary was destroyed by fire in 356 B.C., but a new and more splendid building was to arise on its ruin.

The new Hellenistic temple erected was planned by the famous Alexandrian architect Dinocrates around 350 B.C.. Work was still proceeding on it when Alexander the Great came to the city in 334 B.C. and offered to pay the cost of its completion.

This sumptuous temple 340 feet long, more than 160 feet wide, and decorated with 100 columns more than 55 feet tall adorned the city until destroyed in the Gothic invasion in A.D. 262. The Artemision was richly furbished by the art of the most famous sculptors and painters of antiquity and was a project to which all Asia contributed.

The goddess worshiped in this magnificent palace was a fertility deity similar in character to Cybele of the Phrygians and Astarte of the Phoencians. Through Greek colonists she became identified with their own

Reconstruction of the fabulous temple of Artemis (Diana) at ancient Ephesus of Paul's day

divinity Artemis, and to the Romans was known as Diana. Represented as many breasted, she belonged to a group of nature divinities, a

[5]Herodotus I, 26, 92. A. S. Murray in *The Journal of Hellenic Studies* 10 (1889), p. 9.

Magna Mater, whose function was to produce and preserve life. As patroness of birth, she presided at delivery and was believed to have been superintending at the birth of Alexander the Great the night her temple burned to the ground in 356 B.C.

In Persian times the worship of the goddess was presided over by a eunuch high priest called the *Megabyzos*. By the time of the Christian era, however, this function was entrusted to virgin priestesses.[6] Large numbers of officers both male and female formed the priestly organization and the temple personnel, and the inscriptions record many officers who were connected with the great festival of Artemis.[7]

A notable feature of the Ephesian temple was its prominence in financial matters. Not only was it the depository of the wealth of Artemis, but it was a bank, receiving funds for safe keeping, and lending money as well. In addition it was an asylum for fugitives and in some cases for runaway slaves. Under Tiberius a delegation of Ephesians went to Rome to defend their temple's "right of asylum" when, because of abuse, there was pressure upon the Senate to abolish this privilege.[8]

The chief festival honoring Artemis was in the spring in the month which the Ephesians named Artemisium, because Artemis was thought to have been born in it. A great procession in which the cult objects of the goddess were carried was a feature as well as various games and musical contests. This festival drew devotees from all over Asia and the Roman world.

4. *Archaeology and the Discovery of the Artemision*

The discovery of the most famous temple of antiquity next to Solomon's involves a fascinating story of dogged persistence in scientific research.

On May 2, 1863 the English architect J. T. Wood began the first systematic exploration of Ephesus with the avowed purpose of finding the long-lost and buried temple of Artemis. Until May 2, 1869, despite laborious researches, no signs of the temple were found except a few inscriptions. But on one of these inscriptions, dating a half-century after Paul's time, was found the clue to the location of the Artemision in the form of a description of one of the temple processions. It was stated that in carrying the sacred images of the goddess from the theatre to the temple, the processional passed through the Magnesian Gate. This magnificent gateway and its three exits, two for vehicles

[6]Guiseppe Ricciotti, *Paul the Apostle*, Milwaukee, 1953, pp. 15, 16; Lily Ross Taylor in *The Beginnings of Christianity* Part I, *The Acts of the Apostles*, Vol. V ed. by Foakes Jackson and Kirsopp Lake (London, 1933), pp. 253, 254.
[7]Lily Ross Taylor, *op. cit.*, p. 254.
[8]Tacitus *Annals* III, 60-61.

and one for pedestrians, as well as the thirty-five-foot marble roadway leading to the temple were soon found.

On December 31, 1869, at a depth of twenty feet, the white marble pavement of the temple itself within the sacred *temenos* was found more than a mile northeast of the city proper. During the next half decade the beautiful capitals, sculptured columns, and massive blocks in white, blue, yellow and red marble, which now adorn the Ephesian Gallery in the British Museum, were excavated, as well as exquisitely sculptured drums from ancient columns, splendid statues such as Hercules struggling with the Queen of the Amazons, and hundreds of temple inscriptions detailing the temple cult and its ritual.[9]

Thirty years after Wood's foundational work, David G. Hogarth under the auspices of the British Museum conducted further excavations at Ephesus (1904-1905).[10] The history of the Artemision was further clarified, and an amazing treasure-trove of rich deposits to the goddess was found under the pedestal which held the image of the deity.[11]

Many statuettes of the goddess were also brought to light as she was represented in the eighth century B.C., or somewhat later, not as the later multi-breasted idol, but as a beautiful woman or a mummy.[12]

5. *Archaeology and Other Discoveries at Ephesus*

Other important excavations at Ephesus were those conducted by the Austrian Archaeological Institute from 1896-1912. These researches were comprehensive and thorough, and distinguished scholars such as O. H. Benndorf and Rudolf Heberdey gave special attention to matters of topography as well as excavation and identification of many ruins. The results of these researches and subsequent work are set forth in a series of important publications.[13]

Continuous archaeological exploration has revealed the location of the various sites of the city. The early Greek town founded about 1044 B.C., composed of Greek and native elements, occupied a tract

[9]E. L. Hicks, *Ancient Greek Inscriptions in the British Museum,* part III, section II, 1890. J. T. Wood, *Discoveries at Ephesus* 1877; *Modern Discoveries on the Site of Ancient Ephesus,* 1890.

[10]D. G. Hogarth, *Excavations at Ephesus, the Archaic Artemisia,* 1908; *Encyclopaedia Britannica* VIII (1929), pp. 641-644.

[11]Camden Cobern, *The New Archaeological Discoveries and Their Bearing Upon the New Testament,* 4th ed. (New York, 1920), pp. 468-470.

[12]Cf. D. G. Hogarth, *Accidents of an Antiquary's Life,* 1910. *Excavations at Ephesus* (London, British Museum, 1908); *Journal of Hellenistic Studies* XXIX, p. 192.

[13]*Forschungen in Ephesos, veröffenlict vom Oesterreichischen archaeologischen Institute,* 4 vols., 1906-1937. Since World War II the Austrian expedition has conducted admirable work in a series of campaigns at Ephesus (*Türk Arkeoloji Dergesi* 8.1 (1958), pp. 12-25; *AnzWien* 93 (1956), pp. 43-52; 92 (1957), 13-25; (1958) 79-89; cf. *American Journal of Archaeology* 63 (1959), 84-85; 64 (1960), 66, 67.

along the Koressos Mountains about a mile to the north of the Artemision. A new era began about 560 B.C. when Ephesus, conquered by Croesus and a little later by Cyrus the Persian, was moved from the higher ground to a low-lying situation beside the Temple. This was the location of the city from 560 B.C.-287 B.C. In the time of rain a large amount of water poured through the city. Lysimachos determined to move the city to higher ground in a better location between Mt. Pion on the east and the hill of Astyages on the west. He deliberately stopped up the drains so that the city was flooded and the people were willing to move to the new site. The new city was the one Paul visited[14] and was so well located that it lasted for more than a

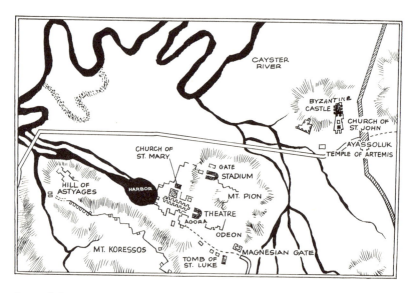

Map of the metropolis of Ephesus, chief city of Proconsular Asia and center of one of Paul's most successful evangelistic and teaching campaigns (Acts 19:1-41)

millennium. It was shaped like a bent bow, the two ends being Pion and the Hill of Astyages.[15]

The Great Theatre where the populace rioted against Paul was situated on the hollow slope of Mt. Pion. This spacious structure was about 495 feet in diameter and could accommodate about 24,500 spectators. It overlooked the city and had an imposing facade

[14]Strabo, *Geography* XIV, 1, 21. Merrill M. Parvis, "Archaeology and St. Paul's Journeys in Greek Lands" (Part IV, Ephesus) in *The Biblical Archaeologist* VIII (Sept., 1945), no. 3, p. 65.
[15]Parvis, *loc. cit.*

adorned with fine statuary. The extant ruins represent a reconstruction after Paul's day, but the plan of the structure was essentially the same as that in which Paul had such a thrilling experience.

Ruins of the Amphitheatre, Ephesus

The Arkadiane at Ephesus as it existed in Paul's day. The most beautiful thoroughfare in Ephesus, marble paved and monumented, it connected with the harbor and was gorgeously colonnaded and lined with shops

A beautiful marble-paved thoroughfare thirty-six feet wide called the "Arkadiane" and about a third of a mile long extended from the

theatre to the Harbor. It was magnificently colonnaded with buildings and stores behind it. The eastern end of the Arkadiane was
terminated opposite the square before the theatre by a double-arched
gate. At the western end it was entered by the beautiful Harbor Gate.

The Greek agora south and southwest of the theatre is another
important ruin. It was a rectangular area, adorned with colonnades,
ornate gateways and surrounded with public and commercial buildings. A magnificent marble library stood nearby, constructed with
imposing columns and its walls recessed with niches for bookcases.[16]
Close by toward the west was the Serapion.

The larger Roman agora was situated north of the Arkadiane and
contained many splendid structures. North of the theatre was a spacious gymnasium and farther toward the northeast near the Koressos
Gate was a huge stadium near the Sacred Way that continued on to
the Artemision.

In the southeastern part of the city was the Magnesian Gate
north of which are the ruins of another Gymnasium. The Sacred Way
which ran northeastward from the Magnesian Gate skirts tombs along
Mt. Pion. Not far to the north on the slope of Mt. Pion and southeastward of the Artemision is the so-called Cave of the Seven Sleepers.

Under the Christian persecutions during the reign of Decius,
249-251 A.D. or Diocletian 283-304 A.D., according to legend, seven
young men took refuge in this cave, fell asleep, and did not awaken
until the reign of the Christian Emperor Theodosius II (408-450 A.D.).
Conscious of having slept only one night, they were amazed to find a
new generation in the city with everyone become Christian. The
youths all died naturally on the day of their awakening, the tradition
says, and the Emperor had them buried in their cave, erecting a
church on the spot.[17]

Northwest of the Magnesian Gate was the Odeum, or lyric
theatre, corresponding to our music hall.[18] Southeast of the Odeum
and near the street leading to the Magnesian Gate is the so-called
Tomb of St. Luke. Wood mistakenly identified this circular structure
some fifty feet in diameter as the tomb of the beloved physician.
Later researches have proved it to be a Greek polyandrion or tomb of
a number of men of a particular family or who died in a common
cause or war.

On the extreme west of the city, with a superb view of the ancient harbor which then spread out directly east of it, is situated a
fort which tradition has anciently connected with the prison in which

[16]Camden Coburn, op. cit., p. 462. Jack Finegan, Light From the Ancient Past
(Princeton, 1946), p. 268.
[17]Parvis, op. cit., p. 70.
[18]Cobern, op. cit., p. 473.

Paul was confined. From its 450-foot elevation atop the Hill of Astyages it commands a dominating view of all Ephesus. The structure, however, is scarcely associated with the apostle's imprisonment, being much later than his time.

6. Archaeology and Christian Churches at Ephesus

Later archaeological remains at Ephesus which attest the effectiveness with which Christianity took hold of this pagan city include the ruins of Justinian's Church of St. John, situated south of the Byzantine Castle just northeast of the temple of Artemis on the holy hill of Ayassoluk.

Even more interesting is the double Church of the Virgin Mary, called also the Church of the Council, since an important Church Council in A.D. 431 convened here. Located northeast of the Roman agora, this famous edifice was constructed shortly before A.D. 350 on the ruins of the once-great Museum. The Christian architect who designed it skillfully brought the new structure into artistic relation and intelligent calculation with the extant remains of the Museum. The huge edifice was nearly 481 feet in length, and consisted of a three-nave, columnar basilica, with apse flanked by two side rooms, a narthex, consisting of an outer court with a columnar entrance, and a baptistry.[19]

II. CONTACT AND CLASH OF CHRISTIANITY WITH JUDAISM AND PAGANISM AT EPHESUS

In coming to proconsular Asia with its great metropolis and capital the apostle was fully aware that he was planting the Gospel in a radiating center of unusual significance. As a far-seeing spiritual strategist, Paul knew that a cosmopolitan area like Ephesus would be a focal point for disseminating the Gospel to the principal cities of the province such as Pergamum at the mouth of the Caicus River, Smyrna at the mouth of the Hermus, and Miletus at the mouth of the Meander. Moreover, St. Paul was also fully cognizant that the vast metropolis would be a missionary broadcasting station to the numerous other cities of the province numbering apparently 500, as recorded in Josephus and Philostratus.[20] It is understandable, in the light of these facts, that Paul would spend two years in such an important mission field, with the result that "all they who dwelt in Asia heard the word of the Lord Jesus, both Jews and Greeks" (Acts 19:10).

[19]For a discussion of this church, see Parvis, op. cit., pp. 70-73. Also Forschungen in Ephesos 4 vols. 1906-1937.
[20]This is the number of cities Josephus attributes to King Agrippa II when the latter attempted to dissuade the Jerusalem Jews from going to war against Rome, Wars of the Jews II, 366; cf. Philostratus, Lives of the Sophists II, 1, 4.

1. Christianity Versus a Hybrid Type of Judaism in Ephesus

Paul's ministry in Ephesus was introduced by contact with a strange type of religious experience that was evidently a mongrel between Judaism and Christianity. It was more than Judaism, since it accepted Jesus as the Messiah, but less than Christianity in that it knew only John's baptism, which was merely introductory and preparatory to the Christian Gospel and the Holy Spirit's baptism, following upon Christ's death, resurrection, ascension, and the consequent giving of the gift of the Holy Spirit. The dozen or so disciples the apostle met when he came to the city, insofar as their knowledge and their experience were concerned, were living in the pre-Pentecostal period, and apparently were ignorant of the coming of the Spirit and the ministries He performs in every believer during this age (Acts 19:1-7).

The reason for this subnormal spiritual experience of these Ephesians was that they were followers of the Alexandrian Jew, Apollos, who knew no other baptism but John's (Acts 18:25), and nothing at all of the coming of the Spirit at Pentecost (Acts 1:5; 2:4), and the work He performs in every believer in baptizing Him into Christ (Romans 6:3, 4) and into Christ's Body, the Church (I Corinthians 12:13).[21]

Apollos (the Hellenist name of Apollonius or Apollodorus), being from the great Jewish center of Egypt, was probably a pupil of Philo and undoubtedly followed the allegorical method of the latter, attempting to reconcile Moses with Plato, and at the same time expounding the Old Testament prophecies that pointed out Jesus as the Messiah. But Apollos lacked knowledge of the advent of the Spirit and the Christian Gospel of grace, which ignorance was reflected in his disciples (Acts 19:2). When the apostle asked them, "Did you receive the Holy Spirit when you believed?" their reply, "We have not heard that the Holy Spirit is," shows they knew nothing of the advent of the Spirit at Pentecost and the message and blessing of the Christian age.[22]

When the Ephesian disciples were instructed in the Christian Gospel and submitted to Christian baptism, they were introduced into the normal ministry of the Holy Spirit under Christianity by the imposition of the apostle's hands. This incident is obviously representa-

---

[21]For a theological discussion of this incident, see Merrill F. Unger, *The Baptizing Work of the Holy Spirit* (Wheaton, Ill., 1953), pp. 72-76.

[22]Cf. John's use of the same idiom in reference to Jesus' prophecy of the coming of the Spirit at Pentecost in John 7:39: "The Holy Spirit *was* not yet." After Pentecost it can be said, "The Holy Spirit *is*." It was of this coming and ministry of the Spirit in the Christian Church of which the defective disciples of Apollos were ignorant.

tive of many others that brought Jewish believers in the Messiah, who had not yet come in contact with the Gospel of grace, into the full spiritual blessings of Christianity. At Ephesus these subnormal disciples became normal Christians.

2. Paul in the Synagogue and the School at Tyrannus

At Ephesus there was a flourishing synagogue and, according to his custom, the apostle used this entree to evangelize the Jews and Greek proselytes. He was able to do this for three months before opposition forced him out. He went on with his missionary work in "the school of Tyrannus" (Acts 19:9).[23]

Tyrannus was in all likelihood a Greek rhetorician (as his name suggests) whose school was a rented room, which he sublet to Paul when he finished his lessons around eleven in the morning. The "Western text" specifies the hours Paul occupied the room as "from the fifth to the tenth hour" of sunlight, or from about eleven in the morning till four in the afternoon. The ancients got up early and the day's business (negotia) began at dawn and continued till nearly noon. Afternoons were devoted to leisure (otia), so that Paul had use of the room after about 11:00 A.M.

The apostle had been busy at his loom from dawn till he went to the lecture hall. For him there were no hours of negotia and otia. All his time — work as well as leisure—was dedicated to Christ, and the scholé of the Greeks (Latin schola), which was a place for conducting intellectual pursuits and imparting instruction, reached no higher use than when the apostle taught the unsearchable treasures of wisdom and knowledge of God revealed in Christ in the school of Tyrannus.

3. Christianity and the Collision With Demonism in Ephesus

Paul's powerful Spirit-indited ministry in Ephesus, resulting in charismatic and supernatural manifestations, notably numerous demon expulsions (Acts 19:11, 12), not only effectively advertised the Gospel among "all who resided in Asia" (Acts 19:10), but dynamically challenged the demon powers energizing the city's pagan idolatry,[24] as well as its paganistically contaminated Judaism.

Certain professional traveling Jewish exorcists, impressed by the apostle's success in expelling demons at Ephesus, attempted to do the

[23]Although the synagogue at Ephesus has not been found nor the Jewish quarters, the existence of Jews there is put beyond doubt by Josephus (Antiquities XIV, 10, 23), Luke, and other ancient evidence; cf. Filson, op. cit., pp. 77-78.
[24]Scripture clearly records demonism as the dynamic of idolatry (I Corinthians 10:19-22; Revelation 9:20, 21). The subtle allurement of idolatry and the fanatical zeal of its devotees are explainable on the Scriptural basis that "behind the idol are terrible spiritual presences—demons," Edward Langton, Essentials of Demonology (London, 1949), p. 185; pp. 183-186; Merrill F. Unger, Biblical Demonology (4th ed. 1958), p. 170; cf. pp. 36, 58, 81, 194.

same by the exorcistic use of the name of Jesus in conjurations, incantations, and religious or magical ceremonies, which were adapted from heathen ritual and practice, and in salient contrast to the Christian method of expulsion followed by Christ and His disciples. The result was a glaring exposé of the methods of these Jewish exorcists.[25]

The demons recognized Christ as Lord of the spirit realm and Paul as a servant of Christ. But an attempted magical and superstitious use of the name of Jesus, so far from effecting any control over the evil spirits, instead exposed the exorcists to their punitive fury to impress upon all the error of mixing Christianity with magic, and the truth of the Gospel with pagan superstition.

It is also highly significant that the demonstration of the power of the Christian message over the demon forces operative in contaminated Judaism and idolatrous paganism resulted in great gains for the Gospel, eventuating in many who "practiced magical arts" burning their "books" (Acts 19:19).

These books or scrolls are the *Ephesia grammata*. Since Ephesus was noted as a center of magical practice, "these Ephesian writings" were a familiar term in the Graeco-Roman world for magical texts,[26] and involved a custom associated with the Temple of Diana. These magical formulas were combinations of the letters of the alphabet or words which were believed to possess magical efficacy in cases of sickness, love, domestic problems and the like. These sayings in all likelihood arose as imitations of the mutterings of temple soothsayers. Gradually there emerged an industry of these small scrolls or leaflets, which were worn as a sort of amulet on the body. Clement of Alexandria alludes to them[27] and numbers of them have turned up from the sands of Egypt. Paul found the industry flourishing when he was in Ephesus, and many recent converts were still enamored of the local custom until liberated by the power of the Christian message (Acts 19:19).

The great public bonfire of magic writings constitutes a bit of local color that indubitably proves Luke's accuracy as well as Paul's remarkable success at Ephesus. The fifty thousand drachmas of silver (equivalent to about 9200 gold dollars) was an impressive and, indeed, an enormous sum for those times.

4. Christianity and the Cult of Diana

In the Lukan account of Paul's ministry in Ephesus, the contact of Christianity with the cult of Diana looms large. The apostle's suc-

---

[25]The formula, "I adjure you by Jesus" (Acts 19:13), is well illustrated by exorcistic formula in the magical papyri. Cf. Filson, *op. cit.*, p. 79.
[26]E. G. Kraeling, *op. cit.*, p. 448.
[27]*Stromata* V, 8, 45, 2 (ed. Stahlin, Vol. II., p. 356).

cess in the metropolis is described as so great that the mighty temple of Artemis and its devotees were seriously affected.[28] The prosperity of the local craftsmen, who made votive images for sale to pilgrims desiring to make a donation to Artemis in particular, was endangered. Many of these images and other objects donated to Diana have been found — those of terra cotta being used by the poorer worshipers and those of silver and gold by the more wealthy. Many references to images of the goddess also occur in the inscriptions, especially in the important Salutaris inscription.[29]

Demetrius who stirred up the riot was possibly the head of the silversmith group, or certainly an important member. Such guilds (*sunergasiai*) are alluded to in several inscriptions and exerted a dominant influence in the economic and social complexion of Greek cities.[30]

Demetrius' workshop manufactured hundreds of small shrines (naiskoi, *aediculae*) which were miniatures of the temple and enclosed a small statue of the goddess.[31] It was not the last time a labor union led in an uprising, and it was entirely natural for the rioters to rush into the theatre, since the inscriptions give ample evidence that this vast structure was the regular place for public meetings, especially in the case of a great crowd, which the theatre would accommodate.[32] The mob's insensate two-hour yell, "Great is Diana of the Ephesians!" (Acts 19:28), is not only psychologically amazingly accurate, but archaeologically corroborated as well. Not only was Diana intrinsically great at Ephesus, and a goddess "whom all Asia and the world" worshiped (Acts 19:27, 34), as is abundantly illustrated by the monuments, but the title "Great" for a deity was common in antiquity, and was not limited to Artemis. However, both literary references and numerous inscriptions from Ephesus attest to the custom of designating Artemis in this fashion.

The "town clerk" (*grammateus*) who was finally able to quiet the uprising by a common-sense appeal after the rioters had exhausted themselves, is known from evidence from Ephesus to have been a very important official and the dominant figure in the political administration of the city.[33] Leading men were chosen for this prominent post.

---

[28]About a century later the Artemis cult at Ephesus declined and the Ephesian Senate issued a decree (dated A.D. 160) aimed at restoring the goddess to her former prominence. For the decree, see Lily Ross Taylor, *op. cit.*, pp. 255-256.
[29]See *Forschungen in Ephesos* II, no. 27, line 266.
[30]For the social features of Ephesian life, see V. Chapot, *La province romaine proconsulaire d'Asie* (Paris, 1904).
[31]Guiseppe Ricciotti, *Paul the Apostle* (Milwaukee, 1953), p. 359. Such a representation of the temple and goddess occurs on a coin of Valentinian I.
[32]Filson, *op. cit.*, p. 79
[33]A. H. M. Jones, *The Greek City*, 1940, p. 239.

The incumbent of this office drafted decrees which were submitted to the popular assembly, sealed such documents with the public seal, acted as chairman of popular meetings which were often held in the theatre, had charge of money bequeathed to the people and was of such prominence that events were sometimes dated with reference to the year he held office.[34] When such an authoritative voice reproved Demetrius and his craftsmen and warned against incurring Roman wrath, the turmoil quieted down.

When the town clerk called the city of Ephesus the temple-keeper (neōkoros) of Diana (Acts 19:35), he was employing a term widely used of individuals. An inscription from Priene in Asia Minor refers to a man who was "temple-keeper" (temple official) of Artemis in Ephesus. A later papyrus mentions a man who was "temple-keeper of the great Serapis" (a famous Egyptian deity). Josephus refers to the Israelites as "temple-keeper" (guardian) of the shrine of their God.[35] This reference to a people as guardian of a temple is identical to the use by Luke where the people of Ephesus are called "temple-keeper of the great goddess Diana," as well as to various inscriptions where the city is spoken of as "temple-keeper of the divine emperor."

In the inscriptions Artemis is sometimes called the "savior goddess." Her image which, according to tradition, had fallen from heaven (Acts 19:35) was apparently a meteorite roughly shaped into a mummy form and regarded as *omphalos* or "naval of the earth," and in her many-breasted form adored as the mother of life and nourisher of all living things.[36]

The designation of the huge concourse in the theatre as "an assembly" (*ecclesia*) is interesting (Acts 19:32). The term may be employed of a regular legal assembly as it is used by the town clerk (verse 39) and frequently in inscriptions from Ephesus alluding to the meeting of the assembly in the theatre. One inscription notes a Roman official who donated silver images and other objects of Artemis to be placed on pedestals in the theatre at every "assembly."[37]

5. *The Asiarchs and the Imperial Cult in Ephesus*

Paul is said to have been urged not to venture into the crowd of rioters in the theatre by "certain Asiarchs, who were his friends" (Acts 19:31). These are officers like the "town clerk" and "temple-keeper," who are now well-known from the monuments. The Asiarchs, how-

[34]Coburn, *op. cit.*, pp. 466-467.
[35]*Wars of the Jews* V, 9, 4.
[36]Cf. Cobern, *op. cit.*, p. 468; Kraeling, *op. cit.*, p. 447.
[37]Filson, *op. cit.*, p. 80. In the New Testament the term *ekklesia* has the technical theological meaning of a local organized body of believers or more often as "the body of believers spiritually united to one another and to Christ," see Merrill F. Unger, *The Baptizing Work of the Holy Spirit* (1953), pp. 1-100.

ever, were provincial rather than municipal dignitaries, and were guardians of the rites of the Imperial Roman cult. They traveled in state accompanied by long-haired pages, and had special oversight of the great festival in adoration of the Emperor. Each Asiarch tried to outdo his predecessor in the spectacles and games he provided for the people.

There was only one Asiarch who held office at any one time, and the incumbent was changed every fourth year. There were naturally many ex-asiarchs, and there is little need now of seriously considering Sir William Ramsay's reference to the problem of a "council" of Asiarchs at Ephesus.[38]

The imperial cult early took hold at Ephesus, and it would be a mistake to think that this polytheistic city worshiped no deity but Artemis. Augustus Caesar permitted Ephesus, as the chief city of Asia, and Nicaea, as the capital of Bithynia, to dedicate areas sacred to Rome and the Emperor. When Paul preached at Ephesus, the city "was temple-keeper" of one edifice devoted to the worship of the Emperor. The city later added a second and a third temple for the Imperial Cult, and came finally to be styled "thrice temple-keeper" of Emperor worship. Although the new cult was overshadowed by the adoration of Diana in Paul's time, Emperor worship became prevalent by the end of the century as the Apocalypse and other evidence demonstrate.

[38]Cf. *Journal of Hellenic Studies* (1910), p. 261, also "Asiarchs" in *The Beginnings of Christianity*, ed. by F. J. Foakes-Jackson and Kirsopp Lake, Vol. V (1933), pp. 256-262.

Chapter 14

Gospel Progress and the Cities of the Lycus Valley

Of particular interest to students of the New Testament are the cities of the Roman province of Asia located in the Valley of the Lycus River, a tributary of the Maeander; namely Colossae, Laodicea, and Hierapolis. The Maeander (present-day Menderes) has it source in the Phrygian highlands and empties into the Aegean near the site of ancient Miletus. The Lycus (Churuk su) joins the Maeander near the modern town of Seraikoi, more than a hundred miles east of its mouth.

The Lycus Valley running southeast to northwest, a distance of about twenty-four miles, was a natural gateway to Caria, Lydia, and Phrygia. The area was the junction point of several important Roman roads connecting the Aegean coast to the hinterland of Anatolia. One highway left Ephesus via the Maeander Valley and connected with Magnesia, Tralles, and Laodicea, forking southeast and extending up the Lycus Valley to Apamaea, Pisidian Antioch, Tyana and through the Taurus range at the Cilician Gates to Tarsus. The second road traversed the Hermus Valley from Smyrna to Sardis and Philadelphia, climbing the mountains of Phrygia toward Ancyra (modern Ankara, capital of Turkey). The two principal roads connected by a road from Laodicea and Hierapolis to Tripolis and Philadelphia. Other roads ran south to the coast of Pamphylia connecting with Attalia and Perga and northeast across Phrygia to Lounda and Bouzos.[1]

I. Colossae, Seat of an Important Church

This town is famous in New Testament history because it had a church which was the recipient of one of Paul's later letters, the epistle to the Colossians. Colossae was situated in the upper part of the Lycus Valley less than a dozen miles in a southeasterly direction from Laodicea. It was built on a double hill just south of the Lycus River and not far distant from the Botzeli station of the modern railroad.

---

[1]W. M. Calder, 'The Royal Road in Herodotus," *Classical Review* XXXIX (1925), pp. 7-11; M. Cary, *The Geographic Background of Greek and Roman History* (Oxford, 1949), pp. 151-164; Sherman E. Johnson "Laodicea and Its Neighbors," in the *Biblical Archaeologist* XIII, 1 (Feb. 1950), p. 4.

To the south of it rose 8,000-foot Mt. Cadmus, whose melting snows formed streams that hemmed the site in on two sides.[2]

1. *History and Prosperity of Colossae*

Scant information is available concerning the city's early history, but according to both Herodotus[3] and Xenophon[4] it was a place of importance as early as the fifth century B.C. The nearby new towns, Laodicea and Hierapolis, later outstripped it in importance, but it must have been a strategic military base originally, dominating the road eastward toward Apamaea, Pisidian Antioch and the Cilician Gates.

Colossae was also a mart for the wool industry, its product called the *collossinus* being famous and attracting numbers of Jews. The Jewish and pagan portions of the population left their impress upon the curious perversion of Christianity that developed there which included worship of angels (Colossians 1:16; 2:15, 18), legal scruples concerning food and festal days (Colossians 2:16), and a form of asceticism (2:23; 3:5-10).

2. *Christianity and Pagan Cults at Colossae*

Coins from Colossae indicate that by the time Christianity came to the city, numerous pagan deities were adored there, including the old native Phrygian god Men, as well as Isis, Serapis, Helios, Artemis, Demeter, and Selene. The reference to pride in visions and "being puffed up without reason" by a sensuous mind (Colossians 2:18) is understandable in the light of the Phrygian background of the city and its interest in the mystery cult of Isis.

It is not certain that Paul never visited Colossae in person. The statement in Colossians 2:1 is not decisive. "For I want you to know how great a conflict I have on behalf of you and those in Laodicea and as many as have not seen my face in the flesh." There is nothing in this statement that would preclude the possibility that the Christians in Colossae and the Lycus Valley did not know Paul personally. Even though the establishment of the Colossian Church was due to the efforts of Epaphras and Timothy (Colossians 1:7, 8), and even if the majority of its members were later converts who had never seen Paul personally, the apostle nevertheless may well have passed through Colossae and the Lycus Valley cities on his third tour.

On this journey he is said to have passed through "the Galatic region and Phrygia" (Acts 18:23) and to have gone "through the upper country" on his journey to Ephesus (Acts 19:1). "The "upper coun-

---

[2]Victor Schultze, *Altchristliche Städte und Landschaften* II, *Kleinasien* (Gütersloh, 1922), pp. 445-49.
[3]VII:30.
[4]*Anabasis* I, 2, 6.

try" denotes the whole hinterland of Ephesus and comprehends "the Galatic region and Phrygia."[5] Many scholars, following Sir William Ramsay, interpret these data to indicate that Paul's itinerary embraced a westward trek from Pisidian Antioch just north of Hierapolis, where he pursued a hill road across Mt. Mesogis down to Ephesus.[6] Actually however, this route is unlikely. The most natural road led through Apamaea, Colossae, and Laodicea in the Lycus Valley and down the Maeander River to Ephesus.

3. Colossae and Archaeology

The name Epaphras borne by Paul's disciple, who had been active in introducing Christianity to the cities of the Lycus Valley, is an abbreviated form of the common name Epaphroditus. An inscription from Colossae mentions an individual named T. Asinius Epaphroditus.[7] The name was also found on a marble altar from Laodicea uncovered at Denizli, the modern successor of Laodicea, a few miles south of the ancient ruins.[8]

W. J. Hamilton visited and examined the site of ancient Colossae in 1835. At that time he reported extensive ruins in the form of columns, architraves, foundations, and large blocks of stone.[9] These have since largely disappeared, being quarried out and utilized for constructional purposes at Chonai (modern Honaz) south of the ancient site and in closer proximity to Mt. Cadmus.

Sometime toward the beginning of the eighth century A.D. Colossae was abandoned and the residents moved to Chonai. But Christianity took firm root, for Colossae became the center of a bishopric. Ephiphanius, a Colossian bishop, is known from his metropolitan, Nunechius of Laodicea, who signed the Chalcedonian decrees of 451.

The ruins of Colossae offer a challenging area for future archaeological research, since the site possesses "historical renown plus an accessible site completely unoccupied."[10] Future excavations will doubtless shed light on the historical background of the epistle to

---

[5]Kirsopp Lake and Henry J. Cadbury, *The Beginnings of Christianity* IV (London, 1933), pp. 235 f. Cf. Sherman E. Johnson, *op. cit.* p. 4.

[6]G. E. Wright and F. V. Filson, eds., *The Westminster Historical Atlas to the Bible* Rev. ed. (Philadelphia, 1956), plate XV, p. 99. *Hammond's Atlas of the Bible Lands* (New York, n.d.) plate B28.

[7]W. H. Buckler and W. M. Calder, *Monumenta Asiae Minoris Antiqua* Vol. VI *Monuments and Documents from Phrygia and Caria* (Manchester, 1939), p. 15. This work and Sir William Ramsay's *The Cities and Bishoprics of Phrygia* Vol. I (Oxford, 1895) collate the important archaeological material on Colossae and its neighbor Laodicea.

[8]Buckler and Calder, *op. cit.*, p. 1.

[9]W. J. Hamilton, *Researches in Asia Minor, Pontus and Armenia* (London, 1842), I, 509.

[10]Buckler and Calder, *op. cit.*, p. 15. For important inscriptional material on Colossae, in addition to Buckler and Calder, see Sir W. Ramsay, *The Cities and Bishoprics of Phrygia* Vol. I (Oxford, 1895).

the Colossians, which Paul penned about the middle of his two-year imprisonment in Rome about A.D. 60[11] and sent to the Colossian Church by Tychichus, who also carried with him the epistle to the Ephesians.

II. LAODICEA, THE OPULENT

Laodicea was situated on the River Lycus at the confluence of the Asopus and Caprus some ten miles northwest of Colossae and three miles north of modern Denizli. It lay at the crossroads of the great trade route from the East to Pergamum and Ephesus. In the pre-Seleucid period the city was first called Diospolis, then Rhoas. Antiochus II (261-246 B.C.) established it as a military base to guard the north frontier of his kingdom after the middle of the third century B.C. and rechristened it Laodicea in honor of his sister-wife Laodice.

1. Sources of the City's Wealth

Laodicea early became wealthy, especially in the Roman period. Its location on the important East-West trade routes gave it a brisk commerce. It had a prosperous live-stock trade, and a well-developed garment industry that produced the world-renowned black glossy wool of the region. The wool was woven directly into garments, and not into bolts of cloth, as in modern factories.

A special type of seamless outergarment called the *paenulae* (II Timothy 4:13) was rain-resistant and became popular in the Empire. Also well-known were the short cloaks (*chlamydes*) and the dalmatics (*paragaudae*) with purple borders. The dark wool seems to have been produced by a special breed of black sheep. However, it is possible it may have been dyed, since the water of the Lycus chemically is suited to dyeing.

Another source of wealth was a well-known eye remedy popularly known as "Phrygian powder" which apparently was compounded at Laodicea.[12] These industrial and commercial activities were factors in the city's financial prominence and helped it become a banking center. Cicero planned to take advantage of Laodicea's banking services by cashing drafts there on his travels through Asia Minor.

The affluence of the city is also reflected in the fact that its citizenry was enabled to rebuild without help from Rome or the provincial government after severe earthquakes, in the reign of Tiberius and particularly in that of Nero (A.D. 60), had laid waste much of the town.

Another bit of historical data demonstrating the city's prosperity

[11]Henry Thiessen, *Introduction to the New Testament* 3rd ed., (Grand Rapids, 1943), pp. 233.
[12]Cf. Sir William Ramsay, *Letters to the Seven Churches*, pp. 428f. and *Cities and Bishoprics of Phrygia* I, pp. 39f., 52.

is found in the indication that its population included a large colony of Jews. When Flaccus the pro-praetor seized the gold collected there for the temple in Jerusalem about 61 B.C., it proved to amount to more than twenty pounds in weight.

References to the city's natural opulence appear prominently in John's stern rebuke of the spiritual lapse of the church there toward the end of the first century when the Apocalypse was penned. "For you say, 'I am rich; I have grown wealthy; I need nothing . . . I advise you to buy fire-tested gold from Me, so that you may be wealthy . . .' " (Revelation 3:17, 18 Berkley Version).

Allusions to buy "white clothes to put on . . . and salve to put on your eyes . . ." (Revelation 3:18) doubtless have fuller meaning when viewed against the background of the fine glossy black woolen garments produced there and the Phrygian eye-powder compounded there, as Sir William Ramsay has pointed out.[13]

2. Christianity Established in Laodicea

The Christian evangel spread to Laodicea within a generation after Jesus' death, but little is known of the early history of Christianity there. Epaphras, a Colossian believer who had great zeal for the work in the Lycus Valley and signally for the cities of Laodicea and Hierapolis (Colossians 4:12, 13), evidently first introduced the Gospel, perhaps as a missionary project of the Colossian church. Paul's unusual success in Ephesus doubtless produced numerous converts and generated currents of influence that extended throughout Asia. A Christian church met in the house of Nymphus (Colossians 4:15) at an early period, apparently through the initial efforts of Epaphras. Philip and John may have preached there, and it is not impossible at least that Paul himself may have preached there on the third journey. At any rate, it was one of the centers in which his letter to the Colossians was to be read (Colossians 4:16) as well as his so-called epistle "to the Ephesians," since the latter was evidently a circular letter to various churches in Asia, one copy going to Laodicea and another to Colossae. Moreover, "the letter from Laodicea" (Colossians 4:16) has been construed by scholars to be in reality the Ephesian letter, since the latter apparently had no name in Ephesians 1:1 in the original, but only a blank space.[14]

[13]See preceding note 12.

[14]This is seen in Aleph, B, and Origen. Marcion was familiar with the copy in Laodicea. Most copies were made from the one in Ephesus, and hence came to be known as the epistle to the Ephesians. The general nature of the letter and absence of names in it furnish additional evidence that "the letter from Laodicea" was really the Ephesian Letter, cf. A. T. Robertson, Word Pictures in the New Testament IV, Epistles of Paul (New York, 1931), pp. 514f., 513. Cf. also Ernst Percy, Die Problems der Kolosser und Epheserbriefe (Lund, 1946), pp. 451-58; J. Rutherford, Int. St. Bible Encyl. III, pp. 1836-38. Other scholars believe the authentic Epistle to the Laodiceans was lost (Ricciotti, op. cit., p. 467), the apocryphal letter, however, surviving (op. cit. p. 83, note 1).

Besides Epaphras and Nymphas and the church which met in the latter's house, Paul evidently knew other believers in the city, for his salutation in a broader sense includes "the brethren who are in Laodicea" (Colossians 4:12). The Laodicean church naturally enjoyed the general material prosperity of the city and by the end of the first century had succumbed to apostasy and spiritual lukewarmness which are scathingly denounced by John the Revelator (Revelations 3:15-22).

Commentators have sought to illustrate the reference to the nauseating spiritual lukewarmness of the Laodicean church (Revelation 3:15, 16) by observations on the water supply of the ancient city, which has been supposed to be lukewarm and unpalatable. This could possibly be true if the supply came from the numerous hot springs in the vicinity. The water tower interestingly is one of the few extant monuments of the city, its terra cotta pipes being clogged with lime deposits. In the first half of the nineteenth century Hamilton saw these ruins, but modern railroad and road building have carried off most of the ruins of Laodicea as they have done in the case of Colossae.[15]

Some scholars are of the opinion that Paul's letter to Philemon was addressed to the assembly at Laodicea and intended also to be used in the church at Colossae. This hypothesis cannot be proved, but it seems probable that Laodicea was a natural place for a wealthy slave-owner like Philemon to live. Moreover, Ramsay found an inscription on a monument from Laodicea apparently set up by a freedman to one Marcus Sestius Philemon,[16] showing that at least one prominent Laodicean citizen by the name of Philemon owned slaves. If Apphia (Philemon 2) was Philemon's wife, it is interesting to note that the masculine form of this Phrygian name, Apphios or Apphianos, has been found at Hierapolis.[17]

Laodicea was also the seat of a medical school whose physicians prepared the Phrygian powder to treat ophthalmia. It is not impossible that Luke the physician, who joins in the salutations in Philemon (1:24) and Colossians (4:14) may have studied medicine in the school at Laodicea.

3. Later Christianity in Laodicea

The city early became the chief bishopric of Phrygia. About 166 A.D. its bishop, who bore a Phrygian name Segaris, suffered martyrdom.[18] The Synod of Laodicea, held in the city in 367, although only

---

[15]W. J. Hamilton, op. cit., p. 515
[16]Cities and Bishoprics of Phrygia, p. 72. Sherman E. Johnson, op. cit., p. 10.
[17]J. B. Lightfoot, Saint Paul's Epistle to the Colossians and to Philemon, 3rd ed. (London, 1879), p. 302.
[18]Eusebius, Ecclesiastical History IV, 26, 3.

regional in scope, nevertheless is highly significant in the history of New Testament canon and ecclesiastical law in general.[19]

The city continued in importance until taken by the Seljuks in 1071. In 1119 it was recovered to the Christians by John Commenus. In the thirteenth century it succumbed to Turkish domination. In the fourteenth century it was abandoned, and Denizli took its place.

4. Archaeological Remains of Laodicea

All that is left today of the ancient site are the dull ruins called Eski-Hissar ("old castle"), denuded by modern quarriers. Two theatres of uncertain date are still visible, as well as baths (or a gymnasium), a stadium, blocks of stone from the eastern gate, remnants of an aqueduct and traces of several early Christian churches. The area covers a small plateau about a square mile in area with peaks snow-capped much of the year dominating the horizon in every direction. The white travertine deposits of Hierapolis, a half-dozen miles distant, are plainly visible, with the Lycus Valley spreading out in the foreground.

III. HIERAPOLIS, OBJECT OF THE MISSIONARY ZEAL OF EPAPHRAS

This important city of the Lycus Valley is mentioned only once in the New Testament. The apostle signalizes it as the object of the prayers and evangelistic activities of Epaphras, a prominent exponent of Christianity in the Colossian church (Colossians 4:12, 13).

1. Name and Location of Hierapolis

The city was situated some six miles north of Laodicea on an elevated terrace which rises 564 feet above the Lycus plain, itself being 732 feet in elevation. Here were hot sulphur springs and a cave filled with noxious vapors, which from antiquity were apparently connected with nature gods and may have eventually resulted in the name Hierapolis ("holy city"), although the town may have got its name originally from Hiera, a mythical Amazon queen.

The deep cave with its sulphurous odors was called the Plutonium or Charonium, and its vapors were the object of much superstition. The city whose location was admirably fitted to excite the imagination became the center of the mysteries of the Phrygian divinity Leto, the native goddess of nature, corresponding to Cybele.[20]

2. Coins and History of the City

The earliest history of Hierapolis is obscure. Only after B.C. 190 when the town passed under the control of Pergamum is its existence

---

[19]Cf. C. J. Hefele, A History of the Councils of the Church (Edinburgh, 1876) II, 295-325.
[20]Article "Hierapolis" in Encyclopaedia Americana (New York, 1951) Vol. 14, p. 170.

authenticated by an inscription. After this, coins begin to appear. Rome came into control of the Lycus Valley and all Asia Minor when the realm of the Attalan dynasty of Pergamum was bequeathed to the power on the Tiber in 133 B.C.[21]

The original settlers of Hierapolis were Greeks from Macedonia and Pergamum with apparent admixture of native Phrygians. Numerous Romans also came in, as well as Jews. This complexion of the population is reflected in the religious situation. Apollo Archegetes was identified with the native divinity Lairbenos and had a temple in the vicinity of the Charonium, as well as a theatre dedicated to his honor. Phrygian Leto was identified with Cybele and was served with eunuch priests, who were considered immune to vapors of the Charonium. Greek and Roman elements are reflected in the adoration of Pluto and the worship of healing deities such as Hygeia and Asclepius, as well as in devotion to the imperial cult of Rome at least from Caracalla's reign (211-217 A.D.) on. Alongside of Greek and Roman gods, Men, Isis, and other Oriental divinities were supplicated.

The inscriptions attest to a sizeable Jewish segment in the population.[22] Such expressions as "the archives of the Jews" as well as "the community of the Jews who inhabit Hierapolis" and "the people of the Jews" occur on the monuments. This Jewish element apparently vanished as Christianity took root and grew.

Hierapolis has yielded a flow of coins from the Augustan to the Neronian period, when a severe earthquake levelled the city in A.D. 60, interrupting its history. In the Trajianic period (A.D. 98-117) coins again appear, attesting to the city's recovery by this time.

Christianity prospered in this city as well as in the other towns of the Lycus Valley. In the Byzantine era it was a prosperous episcopal see, and finally became the location of the seat of a metropolitan. The city survived until the Middle Ages, but suffered ruin and was eventually abandoned.

2. Archaeology and the Extant Ruins

The modern name of the site is Pamukkale ("cotton castle"), not because cotton is grown in the region, but because of the white chemical deposits formed on the ancient ruins by the calcareous springs in the vicinity. Remains of the Roman era appear in russet-brown structures set in a grassy meadow behind which is a mineral pool with flowing waters whose chemical-laden contents have deposited sediments that have covered the lower courses of the buildings.

Monolithic pillars forming some of the most striking ruins of the

[21]Carl Humann, Conrad Cichorius, etc., *Altertuemer von Hierapolis* (*Jahrbuch des Kaiserlich Deutschen Archaeologischen Instituts* IV, Berlin, 1898), pp. 22-27.
[22]Humann and Cichorius, *op. cit.*, pp. 42-44. Inscriptions 69, 212, 342.

ancient city apparently mark the site of a gymnasium. Next to these pillars on the cliff edge in the western sector of the town are the baths. These are built of beautifully cut and fitted stones, as stone cutting industries flourished here,[23] as well as metal working and woolen manufactures. The baths are spread over a considerable area. Some of the massive arches still remain, with a width reaching fifty-two feet, and contain stones that measure as much as 78 inches by 35 inches by 23 inches. The city not only was a religious mecca but a health resort as well.

Perhaps the most striking ruin of all is the great Roman theatre, with a width of over 325 feet at the front. Another theatre belonging to the Hellenistic period is smaller and much less impressive than the Roman structure which dominated a view of the city and the Lycus Valley and is remarkably well preserved.

The city shows evidence of Hellenistic planning. A main thoroughfare spans its length from northwest to southwest and streets cross at right angles. Some of the buildings date near the time when Christianity had taken hold of the city in the second half of the first century A.D. A basilica on the east side of the main street bears the Chi Rho monogram and may possibly be dedicated to St. Philip, although three other ruins are identifiable as Christian churches and one of these may turn out to be the edifice erected in his honor. Such a church is mentioned in an inscription.

3. Famous People From Hierapolis

Papias, a disciple of John, who suffered martyrdom about 155 A.D., was a native of the city. He collected much information about the apostolic age and wrote an *Exposition of the Lord's Discourses*. Irenaeus and Eusebius preserve fragments of this work.[24]

Perhaps the most renowned person from Hierapolis is Epictetus, the celebrated Stoic philosopher, who flourished in the first century. A slave like his older contemporary, the Christian Onesimus, he gave himself to the study of philosophy after obtaining his freedom. Although Christianity was a growing and virile faith in the Lycus Valley during Epictetus' adult life, he apparently was not sufficiently acquainted with it to be able to distinguish it trenchantly from Judaism, and he evidently is speaking of a Christian when he describes a man "who has been baptized and made a decision" as one who no longer vacillates but is in reality a "Jew," being so styled.[25] If such is the case of Epictetus' reference, it would not be surprising. Judaism and

[23]Victor Schultze, *op. cit.*, p. 413.
[24]Albert H. Newman, *A Manual of Church History* (Chicago, 1933), Vol. I, p. 237.
[25]II, 9, 20.

Christianity were in many localities not saliently differentiated, especially not among pagans. In the Jewish War (67-70 A.D.) in Palestine, Christians suffered indiscriminately alongside of Jews at the hands of Titus and the Roman armies.[26] Membership both in the synagogue and in the Christian community was practiced not only early as in the time of the gospel of John, when believers in the Messiah were being excommunicated from the synagogues (John 9:22, 34; 16:12), but later toward the end of the century when John wrote to the church in Philadelphia warning of "the synagogue of Satan" composed of those who said they were Jews, that is genuine believers in Christ, but who in reality constituted "the synagogue of Satan," or Jews who rejected Christ and demoniacally persecuted His followers.

Early in the second century the essence of Ignatius of Antioch's letter to the Church of Magnesia on the Maeander River was a warning against the peril of relapse into Judaism, and the Council of Laodicea (late fourth century) enjoins Christians not to "Judaize and be idle on Saturday," but rather to "work on that day."[27]

Besides Papias and Epictetus, Philip the Evangelist (Acts 21:8, 9) is connected with Hierapolis through a tradition handed down by Polycrates of Ephesus. However, this tradition does not differentiate between Philip the Evangelist and the Apostle.[28] Philip's four unmarried daughters are said to have been prophetesses, and women prophets are attested in Phrygia at a later period. Two of these who remained single were traditionally claimed to be buried at Hierapolis, while a third who later married was said to have been buried at Ephesus.

The Lycus Valley with its biblically significant sites of Colossae, Laodicea, and Hierapolis offers a promising area for future archaeological research. Someday future discoveries in this region will provide a clearer and more detailed picture of the progress of Christianity in this region.

---

[26]W. F. Albright, *Archaeology of Palestine* (Penguin Books, 1949), p. 240-243.
[27]*Canon* 29.
[28]Cf. Eusebius, *Ecclesiastical History* III, 31, 3.

Chapter 15

Gospel Progress in Other Cities of Proconsular Asia

Gospel penetration of proconsular Asia is in large measure hidden from view, but besides the labors of Paul in Ephesus and the work of others in the Lycus Valley, the Gospel was certainly carried to the approximately five hundred cities and towns of this wealthy and populous province by Paul's converts and others.

As early as the second century B.C., Roman power had begun to be extended over this profoundly Hellenized region. In accordance with the will of Attalus III, king of Pergamum, Rome inherited the territories of the Attalan dynasty in 133 B.C. and firmly established her dominion over this tableland of the Asiatic interior. Augustus elevated this rich and populous portion of the Empire to the status of a senatorial province, with the official designation, *Asia proconsularis.* The post of governor (proconsul) was filled by an ex-consul. Usually residing at Ephesus, the proconsul periodically visited the centers of the various judiciary districts to hold court. These judiciary assemblies, according to Pliny, were held in Laodicea, Sinda, Apamaea, Alabanda, Sardis, Smyrna, Ephesus, Adramyttium, and Pergamum.[1]

Taxes were collected by contract farmers who had a crowd of publicans operating under them and who often were guilty of abuses, as is known from inscriptions and literary sources.[2] Favored cities in Asia, as elsewhere in the Roman world, enjoyed immunity (exemption from property tax to the imperial treasury) and freedom (autonomy in electing local officials and passing of certain laws). Rome reserved the right to revoke these privileges in cases of insubmission.

The history of western Asia Minor is closely linked with its interesting geography. Four prominent river valleys give access to the interior. In the north is the Caicus Valley, the entrance of which in antiquity was dominated by Pergamum. South of the Caicus Valley lay the valley of the Hermus River, near the mouth of which lay Smyrna. Next came the Cayster with Ephesus near its mouth, and then the Maeander guarded over by Miletus.

---

[1]Pliny, *Natural History* V, 28-33.
[2]Cf. Cicero's *Pro Flacco;* Tacitus, *Annales* XII, 63; XIII, 33.

I. PERGAMUM, SEAT OF THE IMPERIAL CULT

Pergamum, like Ephesus, was a city of first-rate importance when Christianity came to proconsular Asia in the latter half of the first century. Although not as prominent as Ephesus in Apostolic Church history, it assumes significance to the New Testament student by virtue of its being the third church addressed by John in his message to the seven churches in the Revelation (Revelation 2:12-17).

1. Name and Location

The name Pergamum is the Latinized form of the Greek Pergamos, which was sometimes given the neuter form Pergamon by ancient writers. Situated about sixty miles north of Smyrna, it lay on the highway connecting this port with Adramyttium. Pergamum was located fifteen miles from the sea between two tributaries of the Caicus River, the Selinus and the Cetius, the former flowing through the city and the latter running along its walls. The Caicus was navigable for the smaller craft of antiquity, so the city's location commercially was not disadvantageous.

The modern town of Bergama (a Turkish corruption of the ancient name) is built among the ruins of the ancient metropolis, but it is far smaller in extent. Bergama has fifteen mosques, one of which is the early Byzantine church of St. Sophia.

The name of Pergamum has been perpetuated in the word "parchment" (Latin *pergamena*, Greek *pergamēnē* and *charta*) since the city developed the use of this writing material and excelled in its manufacture. The birth and development of this industry in Pergamum is said to have been due to the circumstance that Ptolemy Philadelphus of Egypt cut off the supply of papyrus to Pergamum because he was fearful that the great library located there, established by Eumenes II, would outstrip his own famed institution in Alexandria. Whether this tradition is legend or not, Pergamum became world-renowned in making a fine writing material from sheep or goat skin, highly polished with pumice stone and slit into sheets.

2. History and Brilliance of Pergamum

The town was founded by Greek colonists, and it soon became the chief city of Mysia. Lysimachos, one of Alexander's successors, chose it as the depository of his vast wealth, placing here 9,000 talents of gold under the guardianship of his lieutenant, Philetaerus. Upon Lysimachos' death, Philetaerus (283-263 B.C.) used this fortune to found the independent Greek dynasty of the Attalid kings. Under Eumenes I (263-241 B.C.) minted coins of the dynasty appear and the rapid expansion of Pergamum began.

Attalus I (241-197 B.C.) was a nephew of Philetaerus. By virtue of his victories over the barbarian Celts (who later became the Galatians), he distinguished himself not only as a defender of Hellenic culture but, by coming to the aid of the Romans in their contest with Hannibal, he signalized himself as a friend of Rome as well. He was consequently awarded the Seleucid dominions west of the Taurus Mountains, making Pergamum a powerful kingdom, comprising Mysia, Lydia, Caria, Pamphylia, and Phrygia. But Rome was somewhat dubious of his growing power and did not allow him to assimilate the Galatian kingdom.[3]

In addition to extending the kingdom, Attalus I adorned his capital city with architectural splendors that made Pergamum one of the most illustrious cities of the East.

Eumenes II (197-159 B.C.) brought the city to the apogee of its cultural prominence, establishing among other artistic accomplishments, the celebrated Pergamene library, containing 200,000 volumes, and second only in the Graeco-Roman world to that of Alexandria. More than a century later Mark Antony exappropriated the books, gave them to Cleopatra, and had them removed to Egypt to be added to the famed Alexandrian collection.

Upon his deathbed, Attalus III (159-133 B.C.) bequeathed his realm to Rome, from which was formed the province of proconsular Asia, with Pergamum as its capital. The Roman city continued and even surpassed the magnificence of the Hellenistic city, and a new series of coins were struck at Pergamum with the establishment of the province which continued until the third century A.D.

3. Christianity and Paganism at Pergamum

The Christian evangel reached Pergamum early in the second half of the first century, probably indirectly through the labors of Paul at Ephesus. A church was established in this pagan religious center which John denominates "the place where Satan's throne is" and where "Satan" himself "dwells" (Revelation 2:13). The reference is patently to the city's deeply intrenched and widely influential idolatry, which John naturally connects with evil supernaturalism, since the Bible posits demonism as the dynamic of heathen worship (Deuteronomy 32:17; Psalm 95:6; I Corinthians 10:20; Revelation 9:20, 21).

Two conditions are evidenced in the church in this pagan center toward the end of the first century A.D. One is fidelity to the faith despite severe persecuting pressures, resulting in the martyrdom of some. The other is infidelity manifested in doctrinal defection and compromise with paganism on the part of others.

The first condition is evidently connected with the Imperial Cult

[3]Emil G. Kraeling, *Rand McNally Bible Atlas* (New York, 1956), p. 468.

and the refusal of some to worship the Emperor. As a cultic center and especially as the capital of the province of Asia, Pergamum was naturally the place where the state religion was more thoroughly promoted. The specific citation of the Christian Antipas, who must have been well-known from the manner in which John alludes to him (Revelation 2:13), suggests that in all likelihood he was the first believer to suffer martyrdom in Asia under the persecuting policy established by Nero. In Pergamum, if anywhere, an example had to be made of those who refused to comply with emperor worship.[4]

As a religious mecca, Pergamum was styled "Thrice Neokoros," signifying that the city had three temples in which the Roman emperors were worshiped as gods. John the Revelator's allusion to Pergamum as the place where "Satan's throne is" may have specific reference to the temples dedicated to the Imperial Cult.

Other gods, however, were worshiped in the city, notably Zeus, Dionysus, Athena, and Asklepios, and John's reference conceivably could apply to them also. Popular in the Roman period was the healing god Asklepios, sometimes referred to as "the Pergamene god." The precincts of his temple were dedicated to the sick and afflicted, who came from all parts of the Graeco-Roman world to get both magical and medical aid from priest as well as god.

Athena was the patron goddess of the city as at Athens in Greece. Her magnificent temple occupied a dominant position and could be seen for many miles. Zeus was also adored by the populace. His gigantic altar, marvelously sculptured and portraying the god's struggle against primeval giants, was so superb that it was listed among the Seven Wonders of the World. Dionysus was also popularly adored and had a lavish temple west of Zeus' altar.

Alongside the fidelity of some in the church at Pergamos was the infidelity of others, who in yielding to the strong paganistic pressures of the city are severely censured by John the Revelator (Revelation 2:14, 15). Specifically, two doctrinal aberrations which were being taught in the Pergamene church are signalled out for castigation — Balaamism and Nicolaitanism. Both involve compromise with paganism in doctrine as well as in practice.

Balaamism was the teaching of Balaam the pagan prophet to corrupt the people of Israel who could not be cursed (Numbers 31:15, 16; 22:5; 23:8). This was accomplished by enticing them to marry women of pagan Moab, defile their separation to Yahweh, and surrender their pilgrim character. It constitutes union of the Church with the world and the admixture of Christianity with paganism.

Nicolaitanism is usually construed to be antinomian license and

[4]Kraeling, *loc. cit.*

committing the excesses of heathenism. But since no such a sect is attested historically before the third century, when a morally lax group of Gnostics appears by that name, the word is conceivably to be taken symbolically to describe the origin of an unscriptural clericalism in which the individual priesthood of the believer is violated by the usurpation of a human-constituted priesthood.[5] Whether this is the defection of the Pergamene church, the twin sins of conformity to worldliness and paganism and the early lapse of simple apostolic Christianity into hierarchial clericalism were two conspicuous reasons for apostasy in the history of the church.

4. *Archaeological Research and the Splendors of Pergamum*

Since 1878 excavations have been carried on at Pergamum by the Berlin Museum, with later work conducted under the auspices of the Imperial German Institute of Archaeology. The gorgeous artistic decorations of the Great Altar of Zeus vie with the famous frieze of the Parthenon in Athens. These and other lavish works of Pergamene art adorn the Pergamene Museum in Berlin. Fine plans and reproductions of the Altar of Zeus, the Temple of Athena, and the agora have been made on the basis of excavations.[6]

The ruins of the temple of Asklepios reflect the indescribable splendor of this mecca for the sick of the ancient world. W. Dörpfeld has given a comprehensive description of the excavations.[7]

Excavations of late years at Pergamum have been directed by Professor E. Boehringer (1955, and the years 1957 and 1958). The fall campaign of 1957 resumed the work interrupted after 1938.[8] The 1958 diggings were directed at the development of the Hellenistic Asklepieion, the south border of the precinct being defined.[9] Soundings were also made in the amphitheatre and in the Roman theatre. In the 1958 diggings, several phases of habitation belonging to the second century B.C. were discovered.

II. THYATIRA, CITY OF TRADE GUILDS

This ancient city, like Pergamum, was addressed by John among the churches of proconsular Asia (Revelation 2:18-29). It was situated in Lydia near the border of Mysia on the highroad from Pergamum to Sardis and on a tributary of the Hermus River. The town was located

---

[5] Greek *nikao,* "conquer," and *laos,* "people" or "laity."
[6] E. Pontremoli and M. Collignon, *Pergame* (Paris, 1900) especially *Koenigliche Museum, Altertuemer von Pergamon* I-III.
[7] *Die Ruinen von Pergamon* (Athens, 1902). Cf. also A. C. L. Conze (and others) *Stadt und Landschaft von Pergamon* (Koenigliche Museum zu Berlin, 3 vols., 1912-1913).
[8] Cf. H. Hanson in *Bericht uber den VI internationalen Kongress for Archäologie* (Berlin, 1940), pp. 473-77.
[9] E. Boehringer, *Neue deutsche Ausgrabungen* (Berlin, 1959).

so near Mysia that some ancient writers regarded it as a part of that country.

1. Present Site and Archaeology

The ancient city is occupied by the modern town of Ak-Hissar ("white-castle"), so named from the ruins of an old castle in the vicinity, which may still be seen. Here and there in the present-day town evidences appear of the antiquity of the place. In the higher part of the area are the ruins of pagan temples. In the walls of the houses are bits of sarcophagi, ancient broken columns, and inscribed stones. As a result of contemporary occupation, little can be ascertained about this town archaeologically.

2. General History of the City

Until it was refounded by Seleucus Nicator (301-281 B.C.), Thyatira was an insignificant town. It was originally established as a military base either as an outpost of Pergamum or of Sardis, according to which city had possession of it. Although not a strong fortress by natural location, it did command a strategic position guarding entrance from the Caicus Valley to the Hermus Valley or vice versa. As a fortress town it shifted from one power to another in the political upheavals of the Hellenistic era.

With the *pax Romana*, Thyatira's role as a garrison fort became obsolete, and it developed into a wealthy commercial city, being situated on the highway connecting with Sardis on the south and Pergamum and Troas on the northwest.

3. Jezebel's Teaching and the Thyatiran Trade Guilds

Saint John berates the church in Thyatira for permitting "the prophetess Jezebel" to teach doctrines of complicity and compromise with paganism (Revelation 2:20; cf. Acts 15:20). It is scarcely conceivable that this designation described an actual woman teacher named Jezebel,[10] but like the Nicolaitans had a symbolic reference to the propagation of very serious error fostering laxity concerning pagan customs and practices.

The meaning of this reference appears in clearer light against the background of the city's complex labor organizations. The ancient town was particularly noted for the number and organization of its trade guilds, more so apparently than in any other ancient city. Every skilled worker was a member of a union, which was an incorporated organization, possessing property in its own name, letting contracts, and exerting wide influence.

On Greek inscriptions are met woolworkers, linenmakers, tailors,

[10]Jezebel is patently a symbolic designation (cf. I Kings 16:31, 32; Proverbs 6:24) like Balaam (Revelation 2:14; cf. Numbers 31:15; 22:5, 23:8).

tanners, potters, bakers, and even slave-dealers. Among the larger guilds was that of the bronze workers, which represented one of the more famous industries of Thyatira (Revelation 2:18). Another was the guild of the dyers, who made a specially famous purple ("Turkish red") from the madder root of the region, rather than from the shell-fish, as the Phoenicians did. Lydia of Thyatira seems to have represented her guild at Philippi (Acts 16:14) where she sold her dyes and dye stuffs.

These commercial guilds in Thyatira were intricately connected with the pagan religions of the city, and involved participation in pagan feasts, pagan celebrations, and pagan ritual. The "prophetess Jezebel" represents a position of world-conformity and social adaptability to the popular beliefs and customs of the idolatrous society of the day. To many educated and cultured believers in the Thyatiran church, this doctrinal attitude seemed completely justified. But John saw the extreme danger. As Yahwism of ancient Israel had to be rigidly separated from the corrupt religion of the Canaanites if it was to survive, so Christianity had to be unsparing in its uncompromising separation from Graeco-Roman heathenism if it was not to be diluted with paganism, perverted into spiritual powerlessness, and eventually suffer extinction.

4. Other Gods of Thyatira

The particular patron of Thyatira was a deity by the name of Tyrimos, who appears riding on a horse and brandishing a battle-ax. This god was subsequently syncretized with Apollo and is portrayed on coins at a later time standing, rather than mounted on a horse, but still panoplied with his battle-ax. Artemis was the female deity most widely adored at Thyatira. It is an interesting circumstance that the high priest of Tyrimos-Apollo was the husband of the high priestess of Artemis. Other prominent gods of the Graeco-Roman world were also worshiped at Thyatira as in other cities of the Empire.

IV. SMYRNA, CITY OF SUFFERING AND CHRISTIAN PERSECUTION

The church at Smyrna appears second in the list of seven Christian assemblies enumerated in the second and third chapters of the Revelation (2:8-11).

1. The Ancient City of Smyrna

Lying on the Asiatic coastland at the sheltered head of a large gulf that extends thirty miles inland, this ancient metropolis was founded by Aeolic Greeks in the twelfth century B.C., and traces of the cyclopean masonry of the early city are still to be seen. In the early seventh century B.C. Smyrna passed under the control of the

Ionian Greeks and constituted one of the members of the Ionian Confederacy, but later was captured by the Lydians.

In Alexander's day the city had grown very wealthy on trade from the Orient and the West, and the Conqueror designed its reconstruction. One of his generals, Lysimachos, carried out the plans and entirely rebuilt the city on a new site to the southwest of the earlier location and enclosed it with a wall.

In the Roman period Smyrna reached a state of brilliance that made it a rival of Ephesus and Pergamum, especially in its handsome public buildings. Graced with wide and well-paved streets, it was so famous for its magnificence that it was called "The Golden," reminding one of the golden streets of the New Jerusalem (Revelation 21:21).

Smyrna was also noted for its institutions of learning and its schools of medicine. Coins of the city are found from every period, especially from the time of the Emperor Augustus and onward.

One of the evidences of the antiquity of the city was its claim to be the birthplace of the poet Homer. In commemoration of this honor, the citizenry erected a handsome memorial edifice called the Homerium.

2. The Modern City and Archaeological Remains

The modern city of Smyrna is called Izmir (a Turkish corruption of the ancient name), which consists of a Turkish vilayet (political division) with a population of almost a million and its seaport capital (ancient Smyrna) having a population of almost 200,000. By the thirteenth century A.D. Smyrna declined until it was only the ruins of its ancient splendor. But with the conquest of the country by the Turks in the fifteenth century the city began to revive until in modern times it has become the most flourishing city of Asia Minor. The harbor of Paul's day has been filled in and built up with modern bazaars. The ancient stadium and other constructions have been levelled to make room for modern buildings. Smyrna's ruins in large measure lie buried beneath the present-day city, though traces of the ancient walls and gates are still to be seen.

As a result of Turkey's defeat in World War I, the city was occupied by Greek forces, but restored to Turkish control in September, 1922, by the Treaty of Lausanne.

3. Smyrna and the Persecution of Christians

The conspicuous characteristic of the church located in Smyrna in the latter half of the first century A.D. was its fidelity in the midst of material poverty and tribulation (Revelation 2:8-11). Moreover the earlier persecutions of Christians there toward the end of the first century A.D. is reflected in the martyrdom of Polycarp, bishop of Smyrna, just after the middle of the second century (c. A.D. 155).

Likewise there was intense antagonism of the Jewish population of the city to the spread of Christianity indicated by John's reference to them as those "who say they are Jews and are not, but are of the synagogue of Satan" (Revelation 2:9). This pointed reference is illustrated by the fact that opposition to the spread of Christianity by the Jews of Smyrna was so fanatical that they willingly desecrated their Sabbath in order to bring wood to make the fire in which Polycarp was burned.

V. SARDIS, CITY WITH A GREAT PAST

The city is mentioned in the New Testament as the fifth of the seven cities of proconsular Asia to receive epistles addressed to the Christian churches established in them (Revelation 3:1-6).

1. *The Splendor of Ancient Sardis*

One of the oldest and most important cities of Asia Minor, Sardis had been the capital of the kingdom of Lydia until 549 B.C., and the imposing residence of the proverbially opulent King Croesus. It was built at the foot of the Mt. Tmolus (5,906 feet high), two and one-half miles south of the Hermus River. The Pactolus River traversed the city as it flowed on its course to empty into the Hermus a short distance to the north.

The ancient acropolis occupied an impregnable position perched on a spur of Mt. Tmolus 800 feet above the plain where the city proper was located. The elevated citadel was the bastion of the city's defense and the place of refuge in time of attack. A single road connected it with the residential area below.

Despite its apparent impregnability, a Median soldier successfully scaled the acropolis in 549 B.C. when it passed into Persian hands. Destroyed by the Ionians in B.C. 501, the city, however, was quickly rebuilt and soon regained its importance, being the home of the satraps during the Persian period.

Ancient Sardis derived much of its wealth from the gold found in the sand of the Pactolus River, and the city issued the first gold and silver coins struck in antiquity. A famous temple of Cybele, whose cult was identified with that of Artemis, was situated here. Important industries included the production of wool and woolen goods and the growing of fruits.

2. *Sardis of the Interbiblical and New Testament Era*

The city capitulated to Alexander the Great in 334 B.C., and the conqueror granted it independence. This brief period of autonomy lasted only for a dozen years when the city fell to Antigonus in B.C. 322. The Seleucid dynasty assumed control of Sardis in B.C. 301 and made it the residence of their governor. In B.C. 190 the city once more became autonomous, when it was constituted a part of the Pergamene empire under the Attalids until Attalus III (B.C. 139/8-133) willed his kingdom to Rome.

Under the Romans the city continued in splendor and importance. However, in 17 A.D., during the reign of Tiberius, it was destroyed by an earthquake. The emperor remitted the city's taxes and rebuilt it, but the city never regained its former glory. It had a name to live, but its previous splendor was dead, and toward the close of the apostolic era, it was exhorted by the apostle John "to strengthen the things which remain, that are ready to die" (Revelation 3:1, 2). Later at the end of the third century A.D. when the Roman province was broken up, the city became the capital of Lydia, and during the early Christian era was the home of Bishop Melito, one of the distinguished leaders in the early history of the church. The city survived until destroyed by the fierce Asiatic conqueror Tamerlane in A.D. 1402.

3. Sardis and Archaeology

A small village named Sert (a corruption of the ancient name) now exists among the ancient ruins which lie along the railroad route from Smyrna to Philadelphia. The hill where the acropolis was built rises 800 feet above the adjoining plain. The triple walls surrounding the acropolis are still to be seen. The lower slope of the hill, however, contains the more imposing extant ruins, including the temple of Cybele (Artemis), of which earthquake and man's depredations have left only two of the many columns standing. This great structure, measuring 327 feet by 163 feet, was situated west of the acropolis near the banks of the Pactolus. Crouching lions still flank the sacred way leading to the temple.

Excavation by the American expedition disclose how Christianity eventually supplanted the worship of Artemis. The sign of the cross has been found engraved on the pagan place of worship, indicating the new use to which the edifice was put.[11]

Early excavations at Sardis were conducted by H. C. Butler of Princeton University.[12] Latest campaigns began in 1958 as a joint operation of the Fogg Museum of Harvard University and Cornell University under Professors Hanfmann and Detweiler.[13] Finds include a large Christian house, a late Roman statue of a youthful god (perhaps Bacchus), a gymnasium from the second century and ad-

[11]Emil Kraeling, *The Rand McNally Bible Atlas* (New York, 1956), p. 471. *Bulletin of the American Schools of Oriental Research* 154 (1959), pp. 5-35.
[12]See *Sardis* I.
[13]*Archaeology* 12 (1959), pp. 53-61; *Bulletin of the Am. Schs. Oriental Research* 154 (1959), pp. 5-35; *Am. Journ. of Archaeology* 64 (Jan., 1960), pp. 67-68.

ditional discoveries in the vicinity of the temple of Artemis and in the sacred precincts. East of the precinct of Artemis one of the earliest Cybeles known from Sardis was found (dated to the fourth century B.C. by the excavators). It was recovered built into a Roman wall. Soundings into strata belonging to the Lydian period prove that the Lydian city is well preserved. It yielded Lydian ointment jars and a hoard of pottery. Numbers of coins from Sardis have been uncovered in the course of its various excavations, the latest dating from the rule of Heraklios (610-614 A.D.).[14] During the Roman era coins of Sardis form a beautiful series and have been found in considerable numbers by peasants who farm the surrounding areas.

VI. Philadelphia, the "Little Athens" of Asia

To the student of New Testament backgrounds, interest in the city of Philadelphia stems from the significant reference to it as the sixth of the seven churches addressed in the book of the Revelation (3:7-13). This church was apparently an ideal assembly and is highly commended.

1. Founding of the City

Founded by Attalus II of the Pergamene dynasty in 189 B.C., Philadelphia was a relatively young city when compared to similar cities of Asia Minor. It was built upon an elevated terrace above the Cogamus Valley, 105 miles distant from Smyrna. Behind the flat summit on which the city stood rose the volcanic cliffs of the mountain range which the Turks call *Devitt* or "ink-wells." Below the city stretched an exceedingly fertile plain, famous in antiquity for its vintage.

2. Naming of the City

Originally called Philadelphia in honor of its founder Attalus II, who was given the epithet "Philadelphus" or "brother-lover" because of his loyalty to his elder brother, Eumenes II king of Lydia,[15] the city was also called Decapolis, since it was considered as belonging to a group of ten nearby cities of the plain.

Apparently in commemoration of the kindness of Emperor Tiberius in rebuilding the city after the decimating earthquake of A.D. 17, the city changed its name to Neokaisareia or "New Caesar."[16] The new name, however, was not destined to remain. Although the original designation was at first abandoned, it began to reappear, and by A.D. 50 the Neokaisareia name had vanished from use.

[14]Machteld J. Mellink, "Archaeology in Asia Minor" in *American Journal of Archaeology* 64 (January, 1960), p. 68.
[15]William R. Ramsay, *The Letters to the Seven Churches of Asia*, p. 391.
[16]Ramsay, *op. cit.*, pp. 397-98. The epithet either honored Tiberius directly or indirectly by application to his son, Germanicus.

During Vespasian's reign (A.D. 70-79) the city once more assumed an imperial title, calling itself Flavia, which name remained in occasional use on coins throughout the second and third centuries A.D.[17] By the fifth century A.D. the temples and religious festivals of Philadelphia had so distinguished it that it was dubbed "Little Athens."[18] After the Turkish conquest in 1392 the city was called Alah-Shehir, "the city of God," the name by which it is known today.

3. The City and the Church of the First Century A.D.

The city of the first century was an important and wealthy commercial center, which recovered from several severe earthquakes. As such it contained a large Jewish population, as did other prosperous Asiatic cities. The church in the city was vigorously missionary[19] and apparently won many Jews to its fold. While those in Philadelphia who are described in the Apocalypse as of "the synagogue of Satan" (Revelation 3:9) were not members of the Philadelphian assembly, their implacable animosity toward the Jewish converts who were, suggests that the church had a substantial Jewish segment that had occasioned severe losses to the local synagogue.

These Jews were members of the Nationalistic Party and professed themselves to be the true Jews, the Chosen People, beloved and favored by God, who would one day be delivered and restored to Kingdom favor by the coming Messiah. The sender of the Apocalyptic letter had a different evaluation of them. Ramsay translates Revelation 3:9, "I will make them (who scorned you) to bow in reverence before you, and to know that you (and not they) are the true Jews whom I have loved."[20]

Interesting in the light of the first-century history of the city is the promise of Revelation 3:12. "Him that overcometh will I make a pillar in the temple of my God, and he shall go no more out . . . ." Ruined temples and broken pillars were a characteristic sight in this earthquake-ridden region, particularly after the fearful catastrophe of A.D. 17. The instability of the city furnishes eloquent background for the promise of eternal security to the faithful of that church amid the insecurity of the temporal scene.

Also meaningful in the context of Emperor Tiberius' rebuilding of the city after the earthquake of A.D. 17 is the added promise of Revelation 3:12, "And I will write upon him the name of my God, and the name of the city of my God, which is the new Jerusalem, which

[17]Ramsay, op. cit., p. 398.
[18]David Magie, Roman Rule in Asia Minor (2 vols., Princeton, 1950), I, p. 125.
[19]This is indicated by Revelation 3:8—"Behold, I have set before thee an open door and no man can shut it. . . ."
[20]Ramsay, op. cit., p. 409.

cometh down from heaven from my God: and I will write upon him my new name" (Revelation 3:12). As a show of gratitude, the city's assuming the name "Neokaisareia" by the Emperor's permission was in effect the Emperor's writing his name upon the city, since the imperial consent was necessary for this action according to Roman regulations. This was also evidence that emperor worship had achieved an entrance there. Ramsay is confident that a shrine of the *Neos Kaisar*, with a priest and ritual, was established shortly after A.D. 17 and not later than A.D. 19.[21]

In putting his name upon the city, the Emperor claimed possession of the town in a new way, although the new name had fallen into disuse by the time the Apocalyptic letter was sent to it. The church there is promised that upon it will be inscribed the name of the eternal God, not the name of a temporal ruler.

4. *Philadelphia and Archaeological Research*

Alah-Shehir is still a Christian town and the residence of a bishop. On the terrace where the ancient city was situated stand the ruins of a church dating to the late fourth century, which may still be seen. Few inscriptions are known and no significant archaeological diggings have been made. The site remains to be explored and its archaeological history elucidated.[22]

---

[21]Ramsay, *op. cit.*, p. 410.
[22]Cf. W. M. Calden, "Philadelphia and Montanism," *Bulletin of the Johns Rylands Library* 7:325 (1922).

CHAPTER 16

PAUL'S LAST JOURNEY TO JERUSALEM AND THE END OF HIS THIRD MISSIONARY TOUR

The story of Paul's travels is continued in Acts 20. Quitting Ephesus after the riot there, he returned first to Macedonia, revisiting the churches he had established in that region, and then went on to Greece, where he remained three months. Apparently from Corinth he wrote the epistle to the Romans, greeting many friends in the Imperial City in anticipation of a future visit (Romans 16:3-16).[1]

Paul's plan was to leave for Jerusalem as soon as navigation resumed around March 5 after the cessation of the winter storms. He intended to observe the Passover in Judaea and deliver the collection for the indigent Christians of Palestine (Romans 15:25). This was apparently in the year A.D. 58. At the last minute, however, probably as the ship was about to sail from Cenchreae, he was warned that the Jews had plotted to murder him (Acts 20:3), certainly not to rob him of the considerable sum he was taking to Jerusalem, but to vent their rage on a renegade Jew who had become the Apostle of the Messiah, Jesus of Nazareth.

Acts of violence of this sort were common among Zealots and Sicarii (Daggermen), "the assassins and cutthroats of the last sad years of Jerusalem and Judaism."[2] Among the crowds of Jews of the Diaspora headed for the Holy City to celebrate the Passover, it would be easier for the murderers to escape detection.

Paul quickly changed his plans and returned to Macedonia instead. At Philippi he celebrated the Passover and Feast of Unleavened Bread, and then sailed from its harbor Neapolis to Troas, a trip of some five days.

---

[1] Such an exceptionally long list of some twenty-five names has been held to have been derived from some other letter (Ephesians?) since it was unlikely Paul knew so many people in a city where he had never been. But this objection ignores the witness of the codices, all of which carry the list as a genuine part of the Roman epistle. It also fails to take into consideration the cosmopolitan character of the capital, as well as the authentic Roman origin of some of the names (attested to by the inscriptions), such as Ampliatus, Urbanus, and Junias.

[2] Edgar J. Goodspeed, *Paul* (Philadelphia, 1947), p. 165.

287

I. FROM TROAS TO PATARA

At Troas,[3] rich in spiritual reminiscences and historical lore, Paul and his party remained a week, ministering to the believers there. Only one event of the stay in the city is related by the historian Luke, who evidently had joined the group again. It is the episode of sleeping Eutychus who fell from an upper window and was revived by the apostle (Acts 20:7-12). Immediately, Paul left Troas by foot for Assos (a six- or eight-hour trip), likely following the road that approached the port via a valley from the north, rather than the longer route that skirted the entire peninsula, a few miles from the sea. However, if the apostle planned this trip for relaxing physical exercise and spiritual communion, mixed perhaps with sightseeing, it is not impossible that he might have intentionally chosen the longer route. The rest of the company embarked to sail around Cape Sminthium and eastward through the channel that skirted the northern shores of the island of Lesbos, planning to pick up Paul at Assos.

1. Assos the Beautiful

Built on a high conical-shaped eminence on the southern coast of the Troad with an admirable harbor sheltered by the island of Lesbos (which acted as a huge breakwater), Assos occupied one of the most scenic and imposing sites in proconsular Asia. As the apostle approached its superbly terraced heights, he must have been inspired by its magnificent view, after the quiet sylvan beauty of the approaching valley landscape.

The city from its alleged founding by the Aeolians had always been singularly Greek and had its own coinage from the fifth century B.C. to the third century A.D. Aristotle resided in the city from 348-345 B.C. and was related by marriage to the tyrant Hermeas, who ruled the town at that time. During the Pergamene period the city was called Apollonia. Its Byzantine name was Machramion, corrupted by the Turks to Behram, the modern name, which designates the inconsiderable village to which the former city has dwindled.

The ruins, covered only in part by the present-day village, are very imposing despite the fact that they have been for a long time used as a quarry for constructional operations at Constantinople. The Archaeological Institute of America carefully explored the site during the last two decades of the nineteenth century, and the entire plan of the ancient city is now clear. The double wall, the outer one protected with towers at sixty-foot intervals and originally sixty-five feet high, and dating mostly from the fourth century B.C., encircled the city for two miles.

[3]See Chapter XI. Under Augustus called officially *Colonia Alexandria Augusta Troas*, but designated Troas by the common people, as in the Acts.

Gracing the summit of the hill was the Doric temple of Athena, whose many splendid bas-reliefs now grace the Louvre in Paris and the Boston Museum of Fine Arts. Nestled among the natural terraces of the hill, which were enlarged by artificial means, lay the public buildings. On the northern side of the agora was a spacious stoa. On a lower level was the theatre commanding a panoramic view of the sea. Other important buildings were the treasury, the gymnasium, and the baths. The ancient road leading to Troas, and undoubtedly trod by the apostle, was well paved. The harbor from which Paul sailed has been filled in, but at its side the modern harbor protected by an artificial mole forms the hub of the present-day village.

2. From Assos to Mitylene

Probably taking advantage of the northerly wind that strikes up around daybreak, Paul's ship left Assos via the Gulf of Adramyttium and sailed into the channel of Mytilene, anchoring overnight at this town on the eastern coast of the island of Lesbos (Acts 20:14). The city was the most important town of Lesbos and originally was located on a separate small island, but it was subsequently joined to Lesbos by a causeway which gave it two fine harbors.

In B.C. 428 Lesbos, under the leadership of Mitylene, revolted from the Athenian Confederacy, but was later taken by the Athenians, who severely reduced its power, dismantling its walls. During this and later periods Mitylene was celebrated for its art and culture. It suffered under the Persian wars and was occupied by the Macedonians. In 39 B.C. it was given a free status by the Romans and was an important place when Paul visited its harbor.

From Mitylene the cargo freighter struck out past Chios through the picturesque channel that runs between the historic island and the peninsula that juts out of the Asiatic mainland west of the Gulf of Smyrna and northwest of Ephesus. Skirting the coast past Cape Argennum, the vessel headed for the narrow channel that brought them to the island of Samos.

Samos, situated at the mouth of the bay of Miletus between the cities of Ephesus and Miletus, was one of the most celebrated of the Ionian islands, third in size in the group including Lesbos, Chios, and Cos. Samos had enjoyed its greatest prosperity under the powerful tyrant Polycrates (533-522 B.C.), who built up an Aegean Empire. The island became a part of the Roman province of Asia in 84 B.C. Through the favor of Augustus it was granted the *civitas libera* in 17 B.C.[4]

According to Acts 20:15 in the Authorized Version and the mar-

---

[4]See "Samos" in *Encyclopaedia Britannica* (11th edition) for full bibliography both ancient and modern.

ginal reading of the American Revised Version,[5] Paul's ship put in at Trogyllium, which lay on the mainland opposite Samos, at the extremity of the ridge of Mycale, which projects into the sea, forming a narrow strait separating the mainland from the island by scarcely a mile. Here the famous battle of Mycale was fought in 479 B.C., when the Greeks met and conquered the Persian fleet.[6] Today the promontory is called Santa Maria and the place of anchorage Saint Paul's Port. Paul's vessel likely touched there, despite the doubt textual criticism throws on the reference to Trogyllium.

3. Paul's Visit to Miletus

Bypassing Ephesus because he was eager to be in Jerusalem for the Feast of Pentecost, Paul decided rather to send for the elders of the Ephesian church to meet with him at Miletus, where he reviewed his ministry among them and bade them a dramatic and moving farewell (Acts 20:17-38).

Miletus was one of the great cities of proconsular Asia vying with Ephesus in importance. Its long history reaches back to the eleventh century B.C. when it was founded by Ionians and became an important colonizing center. It had varying fortunes under Persian control and under the conquests of Alexander the Great. The Berlin Museum undertook excavations at the ancient site from 1900-1906, revealing the main topographical features of the metropolis. But discoveries disclosed principally remains which considerably antedate or postdate the time when Paul came to the city.

An important archaeological remain is the great theatre from Roman times, one of the largest in Asia Minor, which was erected in an open field instead of in the hollow of a hill, as in the case of most ancient structures of this kind. An interesting inscription in this pagan theatre shows the secularization of the Jews of the city. It reads, "Place of the Jews, who are also God-fearing."[7] Another magnificent structure was the temple of Apollo, which graced the city of Paul's day.

The topography of Miletus has radically changed since Pauline times. The Maeander River near which it was located has so filled with silt the Gulf into which it flows that it has transformed it into a marshy, malarial plain, and Palatia, the modern village on the ancient site, is now six miles from the coast. To journey to Ephesus, Paul's messenger probably took a boat across the gulf and continued by land

---

[5]Several of the best manuscripts omit the words "tarried at Trogyllium" as a gloss, as do Westcott and Hort, Nestle, etc. and the Revised Standard Version.
[6]Herodotus IX, pp. 100f.
[7]Camden Cobern, *The New Archaeological Discoveries* 4th ed., (New York, 1920) p. 555. Adolf Deissmann, *Light From the Ancient East*, pp. 446-455.

rather than to make a long detour around the gulf. Today, the direct journey may be made by land.

4. To Rhodes Via Cos

Quitting Miletus, Paul's vessel headed by a straight course to the island of Cos, off the coast of Caria, whose chief city bore the same name. This scenic paradise was one of the six Dorian colonies and like Corinth in Greece, became one of the commercial and financial centers of the eastern Mediterranean. It was famous for its wines, its hospital, its medical school, and as the birthplace of Hippocrates (the father of medicine). Asklepios, the god of healing, was its chief deity. From Cos the vessel steered south past Cnidus, a city of coastal Caria, and then southeast to Rhodes.

Rhodes was both the name of the island and its capital city, which was located at the northeastern extremity. The island was situated west of Caria and was rocky and mountainous in parts, but well-watered and productive in antiquity. The city founded in 408 B.C. was stoutly fortified. It had a fine double harbor, near the entrance of which stood a colossal bronze statue of Helios, the sun-god. This gigantic monument towering 105 feet, erected about 290 B.C., and toppled by an earthquake in 224 B.C., constituted one of the Seven Wonders of the World. The Romans restored it and when the ruins were sold by the Saracens in the seventh century A.D., the quantity of metal was so great that it made 900 camel loads and was sufficient to fill the cars of a modern freight train.

The island was a part of the Roman province of Asia when Paul visited it, and the Greek geographer, Strabo, declared he knew of no city so splendid in harbor, walls and streets. Built in the shape of an amphitheatre, the town commanded a magnificent view of the sea and had a most delightful climate. The apostle's brief visit here must have been restful and relaxing.

5. On to the Port of Patara

From Rhodes the coastal freighter sailed to Patara, a seaport of ancient Lycia, near the mouth of the Xanthos River (Acts 21:2). Because of its excellent harbor, Patara became a mecca for merchant ships, and grew into a wealthy port of entry for inland cities. The city was renowned not only as a trading emporium but particularly for its oracle of Apollo. As early as the fifth century B.C. the autonomous community struck its own coins and had a significant history.

In the modern ruins, called *Gelemish*, the ancient walls can still be traced, as well as the foundations of the temple and other public buildings. A triumphal arch, inscribed with the words "Patara the Metropolis of the Lycian nation," constitutes one of its most interesting and imposing ruins. Many sarcophagi are found outside the city ramparts, but time has choked with silt the superb ancient harbor, which once bustled with busy shipping when it welcomed the great apostle to the Gentiles, and reduced it to a reed-strewn swamp.

II. From Patara to Jerusalem

Leaving Patara, Paul's Phoenicia-bound ship headed for Tyre, for which its cargo was intended. The vessel passed Cyprus,[8] steering south of that island toward the coast of Phoenicia. The term (from the Greek *Phoinikē*) denoted "the land of dates or palm trees"[9] was apparently first applied to the coastal mainland opposite Cyprus, from Gabala (modern *Jebleh*) on the north to Aradus and Marathus on the south. However, since the date palm also flourished southward, the name came to denote more precisely the entire 150-mile stretch of coastline from Gabala to Mt. Carmel, the palm tree being common on the coinage of both Aradus and Tyre.

1. *The Stopover at Tyre*

At this ancient Phoenician port Paul and his company remained seven days with disciples who, being in touch with the explosive conditions in Judaea, solemnly warned him about the peril of going to Jerusalem. The apostle no doubt had passed through Tyre in his numerous earlier trips between Cilicia, Syria, and Palestine, but no evidence is available as to who founded the Tyrian church.

Until the time of Alexander the Great, Tyre was a magnificent and wealthy island city, which resisted the Conqueror. Alexander took it by constructing a mole and joining it to the mainland. The inhabitants were sold into slavery and its defenders killed in combat or executed after capture. But Tyre subsequently regained some of its splendor, and in 198 B.C. became a part of the Seleucid kingdom when Antiochus III expelled the Ptolemies from Syria. It was allowed the status of a free city by the Romans when in 65 B.C. it was annexed to the Empire.

Paul's visit gives a glimpse of how Christianity took hold in Tyre. The believers with their entire families conducted Paul and his party outside the city and knelt down on the shore and prayed before the apostle took ship (Acts 21:5). By the second century Christianity was so accepted by the Tyrians that it became the seat of a bishopric. In the fourth century a council convened in the city to hear charges brought against Athanasius by the Arians. But Tyre suffered in

[8]See Chapter IX.
[9]From *phoinix*, "the date palm." The term Phoenicia occurs biblically only in the book of Acts (11:19; 15:3; 21:2), the land being usually termed the "coast" or "borders of Tyre and Sidon" (Matthew 15:21; Mark 7:24, 31; Luke 6:17).

prestige by its condemnation of Athanasius, being already under suspicion as the home town of the anti-Christian philosopher Porphyry.

2. Trip to Ptolemais

A short voyage of about thirty miles brought the missionary party to Ptolemais, where the local church welcomed the visitors and where they remained one day. Ptolemais was superbly located on the finest bay and harbor on the entire coast with the exception of that of St. George at Beirut north of Sidon and of Alexandretta at Seleucia Pieria in the extreme north.

The ancient port lay a few miles north of Mt. Carmel on a small promontory on the north side of the bay, across which lies the prosperous present-day town of Haifa, which in modern times has supplanted Ptolemais in importance. Throughout Old Testament times the city, known as Accho (Judges 1:31), was coveted because it strategically commanded the approach from the sea to the fertile plain of Esdraelon as well as the trade routes running north and south. It fell within the territory of the tribe of Asher, but it remained too stout a fortress to be taken by the Israelites. Assyrian, Babylonian, and Persian conquerors dominated it, but it successfully endured many sieges.

Accho was occupied by the Ptolemies during the struggles subsequent to the death of Alexander the Great, and its name was changed to Ptolemais in honor of these rulers. This new name prevailed in the Graeco-Roman era. In the Maccabaean era the city was the most prominent town on the Phoenician coast (I Maccabee 5:15, 55; 10:1, 58; 12:48), reverting, however, to the Seleucids when the city was captured by Antiochus III in 219 B.C. Under the Romans it became a metropolis and a colony as indicated by its coins, and was thus a prominent port when Paul stopped there.

3. Paul at Caesarea

Paul's vessel left Ptolemais the next day and landed in the excellent harbor-city and capital of the Roman province comprising Judaea and contiguous regions. This magnificent Hellenistic town was at the height of its splendor with Herod's Palace, now the residence of the Roman procurator, and the Temple of Augustus and Rome, the Circus, the theatre and other buildings built by Herod the Great and subsequent rulers gracing the town and in full view from the harbor (Port of Herod), named after its founder, Herod the Great.

At Caesarea the apostle was entertained in the home of Philip the evangelist and his family (Acts 21:8, 9). Philip was one of the seven deacons who had been appointed by the church at Jerusalem to superintend its charitable and philanthropic works (Acts 7), who had evangelized the Samaritans (Acts 8:1-12), and prepared the way for the introduction of full gospel privilege through Peter and John (Acts 8:11-16). He was also the man whose casual encounter with an Ethiopian official on the highway to Gaza some years previously had resulted in the Ethiopian's conversion to Christianity and the entrance of the Gospel into that distant country.

Paul and his group remained in Caesarea for some days. During their stay a Christian prophet named Agabus[10] came down from Judaea, doubtlessly from Jerusalem, and performed a symbolic act like those commonly employed by ancient Hebrew prophets, especially Ezekiel, to warn the apostle that he was headed for trouble and imprisonment at Jerusalem.[11] But Paul, directed by a higher power, was firmly resolved to risk any personal peril or inconvenience to cement together Jewish and Gentile Christianity. Perhaps like Jesus, he felt that a prophet representing such a cause should die at Jerusalem.[12]

4. From Caesarea to Jerusalem

The trip from Caesarea to Jerusalem involved two full days' journey and had to be split up with an overnight stay at Antipatris, if the more inland route south were taken, or Joppa, if the road skirting the Mediterranean sea was used, midway points between Caesarea and Jerusalem. The stopover was spent at the home of Mnason, a citizen of Cyprus and an old disciple. After a night's lodging the brothers from Caesarea returned home, while Paul and the group set out on the forty miles of the last lap of their journey which would bring them to their destination after a dozen or so hours on horseback. Weary and travel-worn, the apostle must have been gripped by mixed emotions as he passed through the gates of the Holy City after an eight-year absence.

5. Paul at Jerusalem for the Last Time

This visit was probably in the year A.D. 56. Some eight years before, in A.D. 48, the situation under the Roman procurator Cumanus had been volatile, with violence breaking out between Jewish pilgrims and the Samaritans, and with political disorders and unrest resulting in Qadratus, legate of Syria at Tyre, intervening. Emperor Claudius (A.D. 41-54) had removed Cumanus, had taken the side of the Jews by executing the leading Samaritans, and had appointed a freedman Felix as the new procurator (A.D. 52). The new procurator had taken severe steps to deal with the revolutionary zealots (Sicarii) that in-

[10]Apparently the same person who came to Antioch from Jerusalem many years before (A.D. 44) and foretold the famine (Act 11:27, 28) (cf. Guiseppe Ricciotti, *Paul the Apostle* (Milwaukee, 1953), pp. 245, 406.
[11]Here Luke employs Jewish terminology rather than political.
[12]Cf. Luke 13:33; Goodspeed, *op. cit.*, p. 162.

fested the countryside and assassinated victims almost daily. But these daggermen, however, became bolder and bolder, with political Messianists arising and adding to the confusion.

Into such a volatile atmosphere the apostle entered Jerusalem, but it was farthest from his intention or that of James and the other leaders of the Jerusalem church to add to it. But circumstances were to work out otherwise. The apostle was under fire from the Christians of Judaea who were still zealous for the keeping of the minutiae of the law concerning circumcision, food, and the like. They suspected the apostle of teaching Jews in the West to abandon such practices, and Paul evidently saw nothing wrong with Jewish Christians of Judaea continuing their ancient social and religious practices.

To prove this point, the apostle consented to join a group of four men who were about to go through certain temple rituals, such as Jewish Christians still practiced. It was decided that he was to identify himself with four men who at that time were performing a Nazarite vow in the temple. While Paul held that no Gentile should observe the Mosaic law, and that no Christian Jew was bound to observe it, yet he saw no fault in Jews who chose to observe it. As far as he himself was concerned, he felt himself free to observe its regulations or not, as circumstances might seem to make expedient.

But the action proved ineffectual for the purpose for which it was intended. Paul was falsely charged with bringing Gentiles into the temple when he was spotted attending Pentecost by some Jews from Ephesus who regarded him as a renegade from Judaism and a man whose ministry was devoted to undermining the Jewish law, which they so venerated. They raised a cry against the apostle, which quickly incited a riot in the inflammable atmosphere of the city.

These Asian Jews recognized Trophimus among Paul's Gentile friends who had come with him to Jerusalem. Later when they chanced upon the apostle in the "court of Israel" in the inner precincts of the temple, to which only Jewish men who were not priests or Levites were admitted,[13] discharging the ritual obligations which he had assumed, they became obsessed with the notion that Trophimus was still with him.

Had the Jewish charge been true, it would have constituted a capital offense. On this point Roman authorities were so conciliatory

[13]The outer court of Herod's temple was open to Gentiles. After climbing a flight of stairs, however, the notices in Greek and Latin warned non-Jews to pass no farther on pain of death. The first court was the Court of the Women, because beyond it no Jewess might go. Jewish laymen could proceed farther into the Court of Israel. Beyond this was the Court of the Priests, reserved for the priests and Levites in the discharge of their respective duties. Within this court stood the sanctuary building itself, with its two compartments—the Holy Place and the Most Holy Place.

of Jewish religious scruples that they even condoned and permitted the death penalty for this offense when infracted by a Roman citizen. Moreover, the warning notices, two of which have been found, one in 1871 and the other in 1935,[14] were plainly visible and of course well known by Paul. It was unthinkable that he would have disobeyed these warnings. But the Asian Jews saw a way to trap him and destroy him whom they counted as a dangerous enemy, and so raised such a tumult that Paul would have been lynched on the spot had not the Roman garrison from the Castle Antonia, commanding the temple at the northwest corner, observed the disturbance and summoned the guard. Immediately the tribune Claudius Lysias with his soldiers came swiftly down the stairs that led from the Antonia right into the Court of the Gentiles, and thinking Paul some dangerous insurrectionist, placed him under arrest.

[14]See Chapter 5.

CHAPTER 17

PAUL THE PRISONER OF ROME

From the moment the Roman tribune intervened and rescued Paul from certain lynching at the hands of the mob in the temple area at Jerusalem (Acts 21:33) to the close of the book of Acts, the apostle was a prisoner of Rome. Interesting and significant as the legal aspects of this new turn of events are in affecting the rest of the apostle's ministry, two general difficulties preclude a full understanding of the problems involved. One is the limited knowledge of Roman law of this period, which however is alleviated along certain lines by the witness of the papyri from Egypt.[1] They shed light on such legal matters as arrests, imprisonment, examination by flogging, etc., and offer similar parallels to the Acts account. But since systematic codification of Roman legal procedure belongs to a later era, and then is more concerned with civil rather than criminal cases, knowledge of Roman law for this period is largely garnered from contemporary historians and orators such as Cicero.[2]

The other difficulty affecting the legal aspects of Paul's imprisonment under the Empire is the simple untechnical nature of Luke's account. He does not appear to have had access to official legal records such as appear in the Egyptian papyri and in later Christian *acta*. But the legal points touched upon by Luke have periodically been studied by scholars. Of special import is the standard work of Theodor Mommsen, which is an exhaustive study of Roman criminal procedure,[3] the results of which the author employs in relation to Luke's account.[4]

[1] R. Taubenschlag, *Das Strafrecht im Lichte der Papyri* (1916) and "Le procès de l'apôtre Paul en lumière des papyri," *Bulletin international de l'Académie polonaise des sciences et des lettres* (Krakow, 1922-1924), pp. 55-59.
[2] Cf. A. H. J. Greenridge, *The Legal Procedure of Cicero's Time* (1901); E. J. Urch, "Procedure in the Courts of the Roman Provincial Governors" in the *Classical Journal* XXV (1929), pp. 93-101.
[3] *Römisches Strafrecht* (1899), which has superseded the older standard work of Gustav Geib, *Geschichte des römischen Kriminalprocesses* (1842).
[4] "Die Rechtsverhältnisse des Apostels Paulus" in *Zeitschrift des Neuentestamentliche Wissenschaft* II, 1901, pp. 81f.; cf. also Theodor Mommsen's *Römisches Staatsrecht* (1887-1889), which sheds much light on the subject.

I. Paul's Arrest Under Claudius Lysias

The Roman guards stationed in the fortress of Antonia saw the riot instigated by the Jews against Paul in the temple precincts and took immediate steps to apprehend an apparent criminal and to quell a dangerous uprising.

1. *Claudius Lysias and the Procuratorial Government*

Lysias, who was in all probability Greek by nationality (Acts 31:37) and had evidently taken the Roman forename Claudius (Acts 23:26) when he purchased his citizenship (Acts 22:28), was the military tribune or chiliarch (i.e. leader of 1,000 men) in command of the local Roman garrison stationed in Antonia, the fortress commanding the Jerusalem temple.

Claudius Lysias bound Paul with two chains, thinking he was perhaps the Egyptian insurrectionist lately defeated by Felix.[5] Upon being assured by Paul that he was a "Jew of Tarsus," the tribune gave the apostle permission to address the people from the stairs connecting the Fortress of Antonia with the temple courts. As the speech had no pacifying effect, even though delivered in the native tongue, Lysias purposed to examine Paul by flogging.

The question raised by this action is whether it accords with knowledge of Roman legal procedure derived from historical and archaeological sources and whether it was consonant with the power of the procurator in a Roman province. To both of these questions an affirmative answer can be given. The procurator, as long as his own fitness for his office was above imperial suspicion, had no superior except the emperor himself, who personally appointed him.[6] Although the procurator was supreme in his own sphere of administration, it was of course impossible for him to deal directly with all cases of order. For this reason he had a considerable detachment of troops for police purposes, both at his official headquarters in Caesarea and at Jerusalem, stationed in the Fortress of Antonia. There was likely some sort of native police, purely Jewish and tolerated by the Romans, but definite knowledge exists from rabbinical writings of the Sagan or "Captain of the priests," with lesser officials subordinated to this of-

---

[5]Acts 21:38; Josephus, *Wars of the Jews* II, 13, 5; *Antiquities* XX, 8, 6.
[6]It is true that the legate of Syria twice intervened in the affairs of Judaea, according to Josephus, once when Vitellius dismissed Pilate (*Antiquities* XVIII, 4, 2; *Wars* II, 12, 3f.) and when Quadratus deposed Cumanus. But in each case special powers were bestowed upon the legate (Tacitus, *Annals*, VI, 32; XII, 5, 4). However, some scholars maintain that Judaea was not really a province but remained a client state to the time of Vespasian, whether ruled by a king, ethnarch, or procurator, who was subject to the legate of the province of Syria (Theodor Mommsen, *Gesammelte Schriften* Vol. III; *Juristische Schriften* (1907), p. 431, n. 1.

ficer in charge of the outer court of the temple and the temple itself.[7] The notices posted in both Greek and Latin at this parapet of the temple forbidding foreigners (even Roman citizens) on pain of death to enter the inner temple courts[8] imply strict authority resident in Jewish police forces to enforce such a ban. Moreover, the Sanhedrin and other Jewish courts would need some police arm to execute their decisions.

The duties of local authorities, whether Roman or native, were concerned with settling minor cases. Often, however, their duties were concerned with preparing information for disposition of a case to higher authority. This turned out to be Claudius Lysias' main role.

2. Paul's Arrest and the Sanhedrin

The tribune Claudius Lysias ordered a meeting of "the chief priests and all the council" to ascertain "the real reason" why the Jews accused Paul (Acts 22:30). This chief judicial council and supreme court of the Jews met in the chambers of hewn stone in the colonnade of the temple precincts. Its jurisdiction extended to matters of the Mosaic law, and it could decree capital punishment in instances of a major infraction, but the sentence had to be sanctioned by the Roman procurator, as in the case of Jesus (Matthew 25:59; Mark 14:55; 15:1; Luke 22:66; John 11:47). After its supreme act of injustice in the condemnation of Jesus, this body continued its policy of persecution of early Christians (Acts 4:5-21; 5:17-41), including the condemning of Stephen (Acts 6:12). Paul, however, outwitted the Sanhedrin's blind malignity (Acts 22:30; 23:15; 24:20). He, too, was apparently charged with a capital offense in the alleged crime of bringing a Gentile into the inner courts of the temple, which was so exceptionally treated by Rome that the Jewish court was competent to pronounce the death sentence and execute even a Roman citizen found guilty of sacrilegious intrusion into a forbidden holy precinct.[9] But since Paul was initially arrested by a Roman authority, the matter was clearly in the hands of Claudius Lysias, especially since the prisoner was subsequently found to be a Roman citizen.

3. Paul and the Tribune's Disposition of the Case

Claudius Lysias, either to dispose of the case himself or to refer it to the procurator, ordered Paul to be scourged. This was a legal

---

[7]Schürer, *Geschichte des jüdischen Volkes im Zeitalter Jesus Christi* II, pp. 320 ff.; cf. Luke 22:52; Acts 4:1; 5:24, 26; cf. also E. E. Briess, *Wiener Studien* XXXIV (1911), pp. 356f.

[8]The one in Greek is preserved. For a facsimile, see Adolf Deissmann, *Light From the Ancient East* (2nd edition, 1927), p. 80. For references to bilingual warnings, see Josephus *War* V, 5, 2; *Antiquities* XII, 3, 4. *Against Apion* II, 8; also Mishna (*Middot* II; 3; *Kelim* I:8).

[9]Cf. Josephus who plainly implies this fact (*Wars* VI, 2, 4).

method of examining slaves or aliens under Roman law, and the flogging was purely inquisitorial and not punitive, and from its wide use at the time was apparently effective. But flogging was distinctly forbidden to be inflicted upon a Roman citizen, as other testimony be-

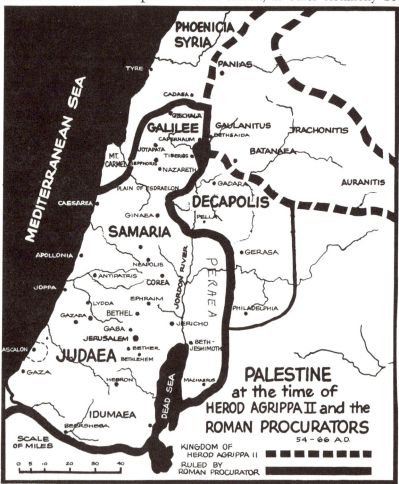

PALESTINE
at the time of
HEROD AGRIPPA II and the
ROMAN PROCURATORS
54 – 66 A.D.

KINGDOM OF
HEROD AGRIPPA II ■ ■ ■ ■ ■ ■ ■ ■ ■
RULED BY
ROMAN PROCURATOR

sides the book of Acts shows. A papyrus from Oxyrynchus (fourth century A.D.) is part of an edict against scourging free men and offers a striking parallel to the language and spirit of Acts 22:24-28.[10] Paul's declaration of his right as a citizen of the Empire promptly

[10]See Foakes Jackson and Kirsopp Lake, *The Beginnings of Christianity* IV, p. 283 for the Greek quotation. For the witness of the papyri on torture see U. Wilcken, *Archiv für Papyrusforschung* II, p. 119.

stopped the scourging. But the tribune wanted to be thorough in preparing the case for the procurator, and that is why he summoned the help of the Sanhedrin.

II. PAUL IN CUSTODY UNDER THE PROCURATORS

The discovery of the strong conspiracy to murder Paul by Paul's sister's son and the notification of the tribune to this effect led to the apostle's transferral to the capital city of Caesarea where Felix the procurator of Judaea "commanded him to be kept in Herod's Praetorium" (Acts 23:35). The Praetorium was the sumptuous palace erected by Herod the Great which was taken over by the Roman authorities and used as the headquarters of the Roman procurators in Palestine, just as the palace of Hiero at Syracuse became the *domus praetoria*.[11]

1. *Paul Before Felix*

Antonius Felix, the brother of Pallas, a court favorite of emperor Claudius, was immortalized by Tacitus who said, "He exercised the power of a king with the mind of a slave."[12] This trenchant analysis of Felix's character accords well with his conduct toward Paul as described in the Acts and his general evil career as recounted by Josephus.[13] He deferred the disposition of Paul's case interminably out of hope for personal gain, and his leaving Paul in bonds to please the Jews, notably his Jewish wife Drusilla, when he was succeeded in office by Porcius Festus, is a climaxing instance of one who sacrificed duty and justice for the sake of his own unscrupulous selfishness.

Although Felix suppressed the lawless bands of robbers and murderers (*Sicarii*) that harried Judaea, he did not hesitate to employ these same *Sicarii* on occasion for his own interests. Protected by the influence of his brother Pallas at Rome, Felix's cruelty and rapacity were notorious. During his regime, uprisings became more common and marked a distinct stage in the mounting unrest that was to culminate in the Jewish-Roman War of A.D. 67-70.

2. *Paul Before Festus*

Porcius Festus, succeeding Felix as procurator of Judaea under Nero, probably in A.D. 60 (Acts 24:27), is little known extrabiblically, except for casual mention by Josephus. In the Acts, however, Festus is brought into prominence in connection with the dispute between Paul and the Sanhedrin, which he inherited as a result of his predecessor's

[11]For a study of the praetorium, see Lightfoot in his *Commentary on Philippians*, pp. 99-102; M. Dibelius "Excursus on Philippians 1:13" in Lietzmann's *Handbuch zum N.T.*
[12]*History* V:9; *Annals* XII:54.
[13]*Wars* II, 13.

vacillation, selfishness, and incompetence. When Festus arrived in Jerusalem, the official capital of the province, the Jews made another attempt to persuade the Roman authorities to bring Paul there to appear before them, intending to murder him on the way (Acts 25:3). Festus' initial refusal and subsequent personal examination of Paul led the new procurator to suggest, however, that Paul go to Jerusalem to be tried before a more suitable court, since the charge concerned a point of Jewish law. To thwart this unwise suggestion Paul made his appeal, as a Roman citizen, to the Emperor himself.

3. Paul Before King Agrippa and Bernice

Sometime subsequent to Paul's decision to appeal his case to the Emperor, King Agrippa II and his sister Bernice came on an official visit to welcome Festus to his province. Since previous audiences with Paul and his accusers only served to confuse Festus, he enlisted the aid of Agrippa in attempting to get more precise information for the report he was required to send along with the prisoner to Rome (Acts 25:22-27).

Cornucopia drawn from a coin of Herod Agrippa II, dated A.D. 74

Drawing of coin of Herod Agrippa II (50-93 A.D.). Dated A.D. 74

The audience in the splendid hall of the praetorium at Caesarea, with military tribunes and prominent men of the city in attendance upon Agrippa, Bernice, and Festus, constituted a memorable scene as Paul was brought in to testify before this glittering array of the world's great. Festus' conclusion was that Paul was unbalanced but harmless. "Paul, you are mad; your great learning is turning you mad" (Acts 26:24). Agrippa's conclusion was in accord with Festus' view of Paul's case. "This man is doing nothing to deserve death or imprisonment" (Acts 26:30). Agrippa also said to Festus, "This man could have been set free if he had not appealed to Caesar" (Acts 26:31).

This monarch who uttered the notable words, "Almost thou persuadest me to be a Christian" (A.V.) or "In a short time do you think to make me a Christian?" (R.S.V. Acts 26:28) is known as Herod Agrippa II, son of Herod Agrippa I, the seventh and last ruler of the family of Herod the Great. Only seventeen years of age at the time

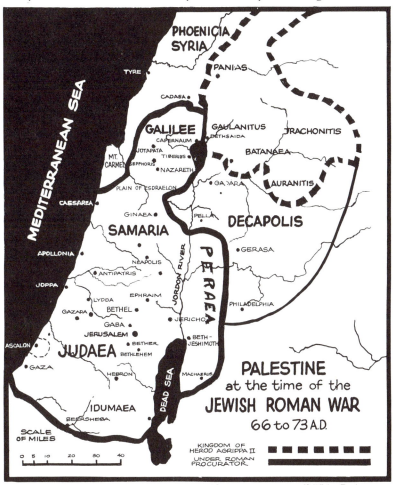

of the death of his father Agrippa I in A.D. 44, Agrippa II was not appointed by the Emperor Claudius to his father's throne on account of his youth, and Judaea was placed under a procurator. However, when Agrippa's Uncle Herod, king of Chalcis, died about A.D. 48, Claudius bestowed the small Antilebanon kingdom on Agrippa, from which in

A.D. 52 he was transferred to a larger kingdom forming the tetrarchy of Philip (Batanaea, Trachonitis, Gaulanitis, the tetrarcy of Lysanias and the province of Abilene).

About this time Agrippa's constant companionship with his sister Bernice, who appears with him so dramatically in the Acts narrative, began to create a scandal, according to Josephus.[14] Nero added the Galilean cities of Tiberias and Tarichaea and Julias in Peraea to his realm. Soon after Agrippa's contact with Paul, the prisoner at Caesarea, he enlarged the palace of the Hasmonaeans in Jerusalem and later beautified and enlarged Caesarea Philippi, instituting also theatrical exhibitions at Berytus. He tried to dissuade the Jews against useless opposition to the Romans and resistance against the procurator Fadus. When the Jewish-Roman conflict broke, he fought

ST. PAUL'S THIRD JOURNEY AND JOURNEY TO ROME

on the side of Vespasian. After Jerusalem's fall he removed to Rome, where he died in A.D. 100, enjoying the dignity of a praetor.

III. PAUL'S JOURNEY TO ROME

With Paul's case now out of the hands of the procurator of Judaea, Luke, evidently on hand, says, "And when it was decided that we should sail for Italy, they delivered Paul and some other prisoners to a centurion of the Augustan cohort, named Julius" (Acts 27:1). The term "Italy" by the first century A.D. was used to denote the entire Italian Peninsula from the Alps on the north to the heel of

[14]*Antiquities* XX, 7, 3.

the boot on the south, with the imperial city of Rome on the Tiber its governmental metropolis, from which practically the whole civilized world of that day was ruled and connected with it by a famous network of roads and sea lanes.

The centurion Julius, under whose custody Paul was placed, belonged to the "Augustan" band (*speira Augoustē*), i.e., the "imperial cohort," one of the five cohorts stationed at or near the provincial capital. Inscriptional attestations occur to the *Cohors Augusta I* in Syria during the reign of Augustus, the *speira Augoustē* in the same part of the empire several decades later, and the *Cohors III Augusta* at Rome.[15] The title "Augustan" was an honorable epithet often used to designate auxiliary troops, but Mommsen and Ramsay identify this particular cohort with the corps of officer-couriers, a kind of intelligence-liaison branch of the military service.[16] All sections of the Roman infantry army were divided into companies of approximately 100 men, each of which was commanded by a centurion.

1. *From Caesarea to Myra*

The port of embarkation was probably the splendid harbor of Caesarea. Paul's long stay in this beautiful Hellenistic city was at last terminated, and he, Luke, Aristarchus, and probably others looked forward to the sea journey to Rome. The day after setting sail, the ship docked at Sidon less than seventy miles northward. This ancient Phoenician emporium had a good double harbor and contained a Christian church and Christian friends, whom Paul was permitted to visit through the kindness of the centurion Julius.

Putting out to sea once more from Sidon, the vessel headed east and north of Cyprus, that is on the lee side of the island, since the westerly winds prevailed at that season. Memories of the early beginnings of his missionary career on the island (Acts 13:4-13) doubtlessly flooded Paul's mind as the ship headed for the Asia Minor coast at a point well to the east to enjoy the land breezes which would blow them westward as well as the steady westward current which would also aid them in their course. This was the normal route of the "ship of Adramyttium" (Acts 27:2) in which they were sailing.

Adramyttium was a very ancient town in the Roman province of Asia. It is only mentioned in the New Testament in connection with the ship on which Paul sailed part way to Rome. The city, with a good harbor, was situated at the head of the Gulf of Adramyttium,

---

[15]H. Dessau, *Inscriptiones Latinae Selectae* (Berlin, 1892), 2683; W. Dittenberger, *Orientis Graeci Inscriptiones Selectae* (Leipzig, 1903), 421; *Corpus Inscriptionum Latinarum* VI (Berlin, 1876), 3508.
[16]T. Mommsen, *Sitzungsbericht der Akademie der Wissenschaften zu Berlin*, 1895, pp. 495 ff., Sir W. M. Ramsay, *St. Paul the Traveller*, p. 315.

facing the island of Lesbos at the base of Mt. Ida. It was probably named or renamed after Adramys, the brother of the proverbially wealthy King Croesus of Lydia. In the heydey of Pergamum, Adramyttium was an important metropolis. Numerous coins have been found on the site, sometimes in connection with Ephesus, and dated as late as the third century A.D., some bearing the imprint of the deities Castor and Pollux, the constellation of the Twins (cf. Acts 28:11) supposed to be especially favorable to seamen and thus attesting to the commercial and maritime prominence of the seaport. The city with its harbor has disappeared.

By thus hugging the coast, the ship finally reached Myra, a city of Lycia, some two miles inland from the harbor village called Andriake. The city itself (present-day Dembre) was located upon a hill formed by the opening of two valleys. Myra gradually outstripped the neighboring city of Patara, where Paul had taken ship on his last voyage to Palestine (Acts 20:1), so that "a Christian of a later era held Myra to be the gate to the eastern Mediterranean in the same sense that Constantinople was the gate to the Aegean."[17] Here at the terminus of a long sea voyage sailors paid homage to an unknown deity, possibly Poseidon, who in Christian times when Myra grew in importance, was replaced by St. Nicholas, a bishop and patron saint of sailors, traditionally claimed to have been buried in a church on the road between Myra and its port Andriake.

The ruins of Dembre, the modern name of the site of Myra, are among the most imposing in that part of Asia Minor. Rock-cut tombs about the city bear bas-reliefs and inscriptions, and the decorations on the huge ancient theatre are particularly well preserved and attest to the wealth and importance of the place.

2. From Myra to Crete

At Myra the centurion Julius found a ship from Alexandria, Egypt, bound for Italy, to which Paul and his group were transferred. This ship undoubtedly was a grain freighter (cf. Acts 27:38), since Egypt was the bread basket of the Roman Empire and the wheat trade between Alexandria, the second city of the Empire, and Rome, the first city, was of the greatest importance. The Egyptian grain ships were of large size (cf. Acts 27:37) and were operated as a department of state,[18] the Roman government showing special favor to the corporation of owners of these boats, since they were actually its agents and concessionaires. Being on government service, these vessels could, as in the case of Paul, be used to transport prisoners under

---

[17]Emil Kraeling, *Rand McNally Bible Atlas*, p. 454.
[18]M. Rostovzeff, *Social and Economic History of the Roman Empire* (Oxford, 1926), p. 595. W. M. Ramsay, *St. Paul the Traveller*, p. 318.

imperial jurisdiction.[19] Rome-bound grain ships could not pursue a direct route, but had to take advantage of the prevailing west winds to get over to Myra, and then of the local coastal winds to travel westward, just as Paul's vessel had done, except that the latter deflected toward the Syrian coast by the winds shifting slightly to the north.[20]

Keeping close to the coast, the Alexandrian grain freighter slowly proceeded to Cnidus. The 130-mile trip could easily have been made in one day with favorable breezes, but because of adverse sailing conditions, it required "many days" (Acts 27:7). At the commodious harbor of Cnidus, the crew might have docked and waited for better weather, or if they chose to keep traveling, they could have struck out into the open sea and attempted to round Cape Salmone on the eastern extremity of Crete and sail under the lee of that island. This they decided to do, and accomplished their task with success (Acts 27:8) by the help of the northwest wind.

Sailing along the coast of Crete with difficulty, they finally reached Fair Havens in the vicinity of Lasea, a town five miles to the east. Ruins of the village still exist. The name of the small bay also still survives in the modern Greek form Limeonas Kalous. A short distance to the west at Cape Matala the Cretan coastline abruptly shoots northward, leaving seacraft at the mercy of a northwest or north gale.

The situation in which the Italy-bound travelers found themselves was becoming precarious, as a result of the delay caused by the unfavorable winds. Luke notes that "the Fast" (by which he means the great Day of Atonement) "had already gone by." Falling on October 5 in A.D. 59, and even earlier in neighboring years from 57-62, this meant that the danger season for sailing had set in from about September 14 on. Paul's advice in the exigency was to remain at Fair Havens, but the pilot and shipowner, the latter normally acting as captain of his own ship, were in favor of pushing on to a more commodious harbor along the Cretan coast. The centurion as the highest ranking official on board, and as such the commanding officer, since the ship belonged to the imperial service, ruled in favor of sailing on to Phoenix.

Phoenix has been commonly identified with Lutro, a harbor some thirty-four miles west of Cape Matala. But this is questionable, and the correct location is probably Phineka, a short distance west of Lutro on the other side of the peninsula of Muros. This port may have had a good harbor in Paul's day, although it does not in modern

[19]C. S. Williams, *A Commentary on the Acts of the Apostles* (1957), p. 270.
[20]Cf. James Smith, *The Voyage and Shipwreck of St. Paul* (London, 1880); H. Balmer, *Die Romfahrt des Apostels Paulus und die Seefahrskunde im römischen Kaiseralter* (Bern, 1905)

times. The two streams that enter the bay have undoubtedly silted it up in the course of centuries.[21]

The south wind that blew shortly after the decision to sail on was made bade fair to bring them to Phoenix in a few hours. But suddenly a violent northeast gale with typhonic fury rushed down from Mount Ida. This hurricane-like blast the sailors recognized as an ancient foe, and had dubbed it with a hybrid Greek-Latin name "Euraquilo."[22]

3. From Crete to Malta

Caught in the wild fury of the tempest, the ship was driven until it drifted under the shelter of a small island called Cauda, the modern Ghavdo, also known by its Italian name, Gozzo, some 23 miles southeast to the leeward. Frantically this brief period of protection was employed in pulling in the waterlogged dinghy, which was normally towed astern, except in rough weather, and in undergirding the ship.[23] This latter operation apparently involved trussing or "hogging" the boat, that is stretching a rope on props above decks from stem to stern to keep the vessel from breaking in two by holding it firmly together fore and aft.[24] An Egyptian drawing from an expedition of Queen Hatshepsut (sixteenth century B.C.) furnishes an illustration.[25]

Another grave danger which threatened the voyagers was that of being cast on the Greater Syrtis, the shallow quicksands off the coast of Africa, west of Cyrene. This hazard was not immediately to be faced, but if the violent northeaster continued its typhonic force, this was the direction in which the ship was relentlessly being driven about one and one half miles per hour. Since the distance from Cauda to Malta is 476 miles, the trip would have taken a little more than

[21]F. F. Bruce, *Commentary on the Book of Acts* (1954), p. 508. E. Kraeling wrongly identifying Phoenix with Lutro says, "But if the best manuscripts, as rendered by the Revised Standard Version, state that Phoenix looked northeast and southeast, this is erroneous; the harbor looks southwest and northwest" (*op. cit.*, p. 455).

[22]Derived from Greek *euros* ("east wind") and Latin *aquilo* ("north wind"), that is, "an east-by-north-east wind" (Smith, *The Voyage and Shipwreck of St. Paul*, pp. 103, 161), or nautically speaking, "north-one-third-east wind" (Bruce, *op. cit.*, p. 509, note 35). The word "Euraquilo" occurs only in Acts 27.

[23]For the various nautical terms used in this chapter and their historical and archaeological attestation and accuracy, see Smith, *op. cit.*; also A. Breusing, *Die Nautik der Alten* (1886); J. Vars, *L'Art nautique dans l'antiquité et specialle-ment en grèc* (1887); A. T. Robertson, *Luke the Historian in the Light of Historical Research* (1930), pp. 206-216; E. Smith "Last Voyage and Shipwreck of St. Paul" in the *Homiletical Review* (Aug., 1919).

[24]H. J. Cadbury, *The Beginnings of Christianity* V, note XXVIII; C. S. C. Williams, *A Commentary on the Acts of the Apostles*, p. 271. F. F. Bruce interprets the "undergirding" to mean passing cables around the ship "transversely underneath in order to hold the timbers together" *op. cit.*, p. 509.

[25]Cadbury, *The Book of Acts in History* (1955); *The Beginnings of Christianity*, p. 351.

thirteen days. Smith shows that "according to these calculations, a ship starting late in the evening from Cauda would by midnight on the fourteenth be less than three miles from the entrance of St. Paul's bay."[26] As A. T. Robertson says, "Luke has only a few disjointed allusions to these matters in his narrative, and yet they work out like a modern log-book the dead reckoning of the ship's course and speed."[27]

In addition the measurements of the water's depth as "twenty-seven fathoms" and "fifteen fathoms" (Acts 27:28) correspond to the coast at the place where "two seas" meet (Acts 27:41), which is still known as St. Paul's Bay.[28] These elements are but a few of many examples in the stirring narrative of Paul's shipwreck of Luke's

War galley drawn from a bronze coin of Ascalon dated A.D. 72

[26]*The Voyage and Shipwreck of St. Paul* (4th ed., 1880), p. 126. See also Edwin Smith in Tom Davin, ed., *The Rudder Treasury* (1953), pp. 55-66.
[27]*Op. cit.*, p. 209.
[28]Although numerous scholars favor St. Paul's Bay, Malta, as the place of Paul's shipwreck (this is the view of James Smith, *op. cit.*), recently W. Burridge argues that the site is rather Melliha Bay farther north, *Seeking the Site of St. Paul's Shipwreck* (Valletta, 1952).

graphic precision and accuracy. The story as told is a literary classic in its own right, as well as being what Holtzmann calls "one of the most instructive documents for the knowledge of ancient seamanship."[29]

The "sea of Adria" (Acts 27:27), through which the ship was tossed in the tempest, is a geographical designation of the central portion of the Mediterranean lying between the foot of Italy and Achaia (Greece) on the north, Cyrenaica (Africa) on the south, the island of Crete on the east and the island of Sicily on the west. The name took its origin from the town of Adria on the lower Po River and gradually had an expanded meaning, being referred to by such ancient writers as Ptolemy, Pausanias, and Procopius. Strabo in the first century calls it Hadria and says, "The Ionian Sea" (between the Peloponnesus and the foot of Italy) "is part of what is now called the sea of Hadria."[30] The Adriatic Sea so-called, between the leg of Italy and the Dalmatian Coast, was at that time known as "the gulf of Hadria" in distinction to the much larger entity "the sea of Hadria."

4. Paul in Malta

When the survivors of the wrecked ship escaped to land, Luke writes "then we knew that the island was called Melita" (Acts 28:1). This is the Greek name of Malta south of Sicily in the mid-Mediterranean, not Meleda off the Dalmatian coast. Such a "northeaster" could not have driven the ship in that direction, which before Smith wrote, was sometimes considered the scene of the shipwreck.[31] Doubtlessly some of the seasoned sailors knew Malta well, but were certainly unfamiliar with this part of the coast, customarily putting in at the harbor of Valletta, eight miles to the south.

The name Melita (Canaanite for the word meaning "escape" or "refuge") was given to the island originally by Phoenician sailors, doubtlessly because it frequently proved a haven of escape from similar storms such as that which harassed Paul and his fellow travelers.[32] The inhabitants of the island were to a large degree of Phoenician descent, and they spoke a Punic or Phoenician dialect, and so were looked upon by both Greeks and Romans as "barbarians" in the non-derogatory sense of "natives using a language not familiar to the hearer" (cf. I Corinthians 14:11), not necessarily wild or uncivilized.

Malta, the largest of a small group of islands, is about seventeen

[29]H. J. Holtzmann, *Handkommentar zum N.T.* (1889), p. 421.
[30]*Geography* II, 5, 20. Cf. Ptolemy III, 4, 1; III, 15, 1. See H. Treidler, "Das Ionische Meer im Altertum" in *Klio* XXII, 1928, pp. 86-91.
[31]C. S. C. Williams, *op. cit.*, p. 271. See Dissertation II, "On the Island of Melita" in Smith, *op. cit.*, pp. 162ff. This misidentification of Meleda with Melita is bound up with the misinterpretation of the "sea of Adria" (F. F. Bruce, *op. cit.*, p. 521).
[32]J. Rendel Harris in *Expository Times* XXI (1909-1910), p. 18; Williams, *op. cit.*, p. 520; Bruce, *op. cit.*, p. 521.

miles long and about eight miles wide. It was Roman by 218 B.C. and became part of the province of Sicily, only about sixty miles distant, which was under a propraetor. Publius, who is styled by Luke "the chief man of the island" (*protos*, "first man" in Acts 28:7, 8) is in all likelihood an official title of the propraetor's immediate subordinate in Malta. This official designation is archaeologically attested to, appearing on two inscriptions from Malta, one in Greek and the other in Latin.[33]

Luke refers to the official unceremoniously, simply as Publius, in the way the natives probably did, using only his *praenomen*, and not the more stilted full Roman nomenclature. In similar fashion Polybius, the Greek historian, customarily calls Publius Cornelius Scipio simply Publius. Luke says that Publius had an estate near the place of Paul's shipwreck and entertained the shipwrecked party for three days. This evidently was Publius' country villa, for certainly his official residence was at the capital Melite (Citta Vecchia). Paul had an opportunity to show his gratitude in healing Publius' father of fever and dysentery. "Maltese fever," due to an organism in goat's milk, has long been a notorious sickness in this region.

Both in the account of the viper biting Paul and in the terminology employed in connection with Publius' father's healing, a number of scholars have seen the influence of Luke, the physician. Harnack, for example, says "the whole story of the abode of the narrator in Malta is displayed in a medical light."[34] Such expressions as "fastened on," "swelling" (inflammation), "expected," "fevers," "dysentery" have been shown to have medical connotations and uses.[35] Even the expression, "honored us with many honors" (Acts 28:9, 10), may refer to "an honorarium or physician's fee."[36]

5. *From Malta to Puteoli*

Paul's shipwrecked company was not the only stranded group of sea-voyagers bound for Rome. Another ship of Alexandria, possibly also a grain-freighter, had been forced to winter at Malta, doubtless in the harbor at Valletta. After three months, the centurion Julius and his party sailed for Sicily on this vessel, sometime around the opening of the normal navigation season on March 5. A favorable wind may have tempted them to set out even before that date on the

[33]*Inscriptiones Graecae* XIV (Berlin, 1891), 601; *Corpus Inscriptionum Latinarum* X (Berlin, 1883), 7495.
[34]A. Harnack, *Luke the Physician* (1907), p. 179.
[35]A. T. Robertson, *op. cit.*, pp. 101-102; cf. Hobart, *Medical Language of St. Luke*, pp. 50-52; 288.
[36]"Honor a physician according to thy need of him with the honors due unto him" (Ecclesiasticus 38:1). Cf. also Cicero's use of *honos* in this sense (*Epist. ad Fam.* XVI, 9; cf. I Timothy 5:17).

short run to Syracuse, the chief city of the island located on the south-eastern coast, and the capital of the eastern half. Cicero described this ancient city, founded in the eighth century B.C., as "the greatest of the Greek cities and the most beautiful of all cities."[37] From its beginning it flourished and became very famous, particularly from the fifth to the third century B.C. It fell to the Romans in 212 B.C., and became the capital of the Roman province of Sicily. Here the ship put in for three days, possibly because the southerly breeze which brought the crew from Malta, died down. Julius no doubt gave Paul permission to see the city, including the celebrated Temple of Athena (fifth century B.C.), the great semicircular theatre hewn out of the rock, the Augustan amphitheatre, and other splendid structures of the city.

Women's hair styles in the Graeco-Roman world of Paul's day (cf. I Cor. 11:15, 16)

The Emperor Nero (54-68 A.D.), persecutor of the early Christians

As an interesting bit of local color, Luke mentions that the Alexandrian freighter in which the Malta-to-Puteoli leg of the sea journey was made carried the figurehead of "the Twin Brothers," Castor and Pollux, legendary sons of Zeus and Leda, called also Dioscuri, "lads of Zeus." These gods of Graeco-Roman mythology, worshiped by sea-

[37]*In Verrein* IV, 52.

farers, were considered the special friends and patrons of distressed mariners, and the constellation Gemini (the Twins) is called after the beneficent brothers. The two principal stars of this constellation are named Castor and Pollux, which when glimpsed in a storm were thought to be a sign of good fortune, as Seneca and other classical writers note.[38] Luke's reference to the ship's sign may have been suggested by the sad fate of the previous Alexandrian boat. Certainly his allusion to a very common Graeco-Roman custom carried with it no pagan superstitious element that the ship's figurehead augured a safe arrival in Italy.

Moulton and Milligan[39] in showing how common in Egypt were personal names derived from Castor and Pollux, at the same time point to the wide dissemination of Dioscuric worship in Egypt.

The vessel quitted the double harbor of Syracuse and "sailing round," probably indicating making progress by tacking, it arrived at Rhegium on the toe of the Italian peninsula (modern Reggio di Calabria) across the strait of Messina, some half-dozen miles from Messina on the Sicilian side. There they had to await favorable wind, which would blow them through the strait and on up the western coast of Italy. But only one day had been spent at Rhegium when a brisk south wind sprang up, which carried the freighter swiftly to Puteoli (Pozzuoli), near Neapolis (Naples). At this time Puteoli was the regular port of entry of Rome from the East, especially for large grain ships. Rome's own port, Ostia, was about this time being dredged to admit large ships, and thereafter largely supplanted the maritime importance of Puteoli.

At Puteoli the sea-going part of Paul's trip to Rome ended. The city as an important gateway port was not only the location of a group of Christian believers,[40] who entertained Paul for a week, but also was the site of the first Augusteum or temple of the imperial cult, which in the following centuries was destined to vie with the Christian faith for mastery of the Empire. Josephus also names an important Jewish community as residing at Puteoli.[41] Little remains of the ancient port-city except ruins of the ancient mole (where Paul first stepped on the soil of Italy), the amphitheatre where Nero played an actor's role, and the Serapeum.

[38]*Epistle* 77. Also Horace *Odes* I, 3, 2; III, 29, 64; see also F. L. Dolger in *Antike und Christentum* VI, 1950, p. 276.
[39]*Vocabulary*, p. 159.
[40]The Sator inscription may well point to the presence of Latin-speaking Christians at Pompeii before A.D. 79, A. D. McNeile, *Introduction to the Study of the New Testament* (2nd ed. 1953), p. 235.
[41]*Jewish War* II, 7, 1; *Antiquities* XVII, 12, 1.

6. *From Puteoli to Rome*

Not far from Puteoli at Capua, Paul and the group got on the Appian Way which connected with Rome via The Forum of Appius and The Three Taverns. Extensive sections of this well-paved road, planned by the censor Appius Claudius Caecus in 312 B.C., still exist, lined with tombs, sites of ancient Roman villas, and ruins of ancient aqueducts. In 1850-1853 a section of the road between the third and eleventh milestones near the St. Sebastian gate of Rome was uncovered by archaeologists, which the apostle walked as a prisoner of the

A view of the Appian Way as seen today   Section of a Roman road

Empire. From Capua it was 132 miles to Rome. By 244 B.C. the Via Appia was extended to Brundisium (modern Brindisi) on the heel of Italy, some 350 miles from Rome, where by ship across the Adriatic Sea, the Via Appia connected with the Egnatian Way across Macedonia to Appollonia, Amphipolis, Philippi, Asia Minor, and the East.

Since the Appian Way from Capua to Terracina Romeward skirted near the shore, picturesque vistas of land often combined with a magnificent view of the sea. Formiae was doubtlessly a stop-over place the first night, from which the party journeyed the next day past Cicero's country estate and on through the town of Fundi and through the road cut by Roman engineers through the pass of Lantulae and on to the town of Terracina, high over the Mediterranean. There perhaps the second night was spent.

At Terracina the Appian way ran through the Pontine marshes and skirted a canal built by Augustus for hauling passengers and freight on mule-drawn barges. At the Forum of Appius, 43 miles from the metropolis on the Tiber, Paul and the group had a pleasant surprise. Some of the believers at Rome, Luke writes, "came to meet us" (Acts 28:15), employing a word (*apantēsis*) technically used for the official welcome of a visiting dignitary by a deputation which went out of a city to greet him and conduct him on his way for the last part of his journey.[42]

Appii Forum was the terminus of the canal and an important stopover place for travelers. It was accordingly, a rendezvous for "knavish publicans and boatmen folk," as Horace satirizes.[43] In one of its busy inns, amid the bustle and confusion, Paul and his group had a happy meeting with those Roman Christians who were so eager to

The Arch of Titus, Rome

meet the apostle and the author of "The Epistle to the Romans" penned several years before, that they were willing to go the extra ten miles from Appii Forum to The Three Taverns (*Tres Tabernae*) where

[42]F. F. Bruce, *op. cit.*, p. 527; for a similar use, of Matthew 25:6; I Thessalonians 4:17.
[43]*Satire* I, 5, 3f.

the other part of the delegation awaited the apostle's arrival. Cicero mentions Tres Tabernae, 33 miles from Rome, as a well-known road-house in his day.[44] The site in the vicinity of present-day Cisterna was the scene of the joyful reunion of other of Paul's numerous con-verts over the Empire, who were now residing in Rome. Here the joyful party climbed the road as it led up the Albanian Mountains and past the Albanian Lake and on to the wide plain of the Cam-pagna with the city of Rome in the distance. Near the Appian Way at this point ran the immense aqueduct of Claudia completed by Em-peror Claudius in A.D. 50. Arches 110 feet high carried part of Rome's water supply across the Campagna from a source more than forty miles distant. Impressive ruins still remain of this great engineering construction, one of Rome's eight aqueducts of that period.

Now on both sides of the Appian Way were seen the tombs and funerary memorials of the generals, conquerors, and distinguished men who had raised an obscure Italian town to the position of the first city of the world, and surrounded it with a halo of martial glory unexcelled by any other metropolis. Many of these illustrious Romans had passed over this same road to enjoy a magnificent triumph in the city. But the prisoner who that day was surrounded by a retinue of converts and a few Roman soldiers was being led in a triumph far more memorable than that of any victorious Roman general.

III. PAUL AT ROME

Entering through the Porta Capena, the apostle was at last in the Eternal City. Paul, as a missionary statesman and strategist, had longed to visit the city on the Tiber, the hub and focal point of the Empire, for many years. At last his hopes and prayers were answered. Although a prisoner, he now awaited the divine opening of doors of access for gospel witness that would ra-diate to all parts of the far-flung Graeco-Roman world (cf. Romans 15:23-28; Acts 19:21).

1. Archaeology and the Size of Rome in Paul's Day

At Ostia, Rome's seaport, an inscription was discovered in 1941 with statistics for the year Ti-berius began to reign, indicating that in A.D. 14 the city of Rome had a population of 4,100,000.[45] This figure is about three times the population of the modern city, and more than three times the usual estimate of the ancient city. In any case,

Roman coins (c. A.D. 30)

[44]Ad Atticum II, 10.
[45]American Journal of Archaeology 41 (1945), p. 438.

Rome was a great metropolitan area, densely populated in the first century A.D. These teeming millions were housed in two types of construction, the *domus* of the wealthy with rooms opening on inner courts, and the *insula* or tenement house for the poor, as much as six or more stories in height and sometimes occupying a whole block. Two centuries and a half after Paul's day figures from the *Regionaires* containing statistics and descriptions of the city compiled probably in the early fourth century A.D. enumerate 1,797 *domi* and 46,602 *insulae* in the metropolis.[46] Although the city had good water brought in by aqueducts and an adequate sewage, the streets in the poorer section were unlighted and narrow and steep, and the tenements often ramshackle and unsafe for human occupancy.[47]

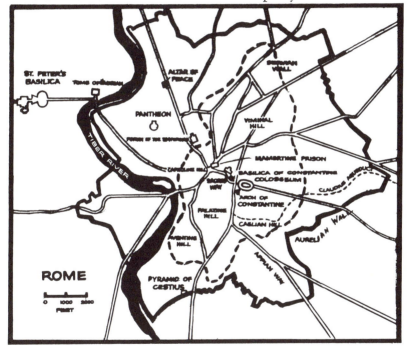

2. *Rome's Avenues and Hills*

Despite the crowded conditions and squalor of the teeming masses in the closely-packed tenement districts, Rome had many splendid features that made it a great imperial city. Foremost among these were its thoroughfares, giving access to the city from all directions and intertwining among the seven hills on which the main part

[46]Jerome Carcopino, *Daily Life in Ancient Rome*, p. 205.
[47]Cf. Juvenal's comments on this phase of Roman life (*Satire* III, 190-196).

The Colosseum at Rome viewed from the Forum. This great building at one time seated 50,000 spectators.

A view among the ruins of ancient Rome

A Roman table for reclining at meals (cf. John 13:23; Ps. 69:22)

of the city was built and past which the Tiber River flowed in a series of sweeping curves. Approaching from the southeast via the Appian Way, the Coelian Hill was passed on the right and the Aventine Hill on the left. Northwest of the Aventine across the Tiber lay the Palatine Hill. North of the Coelian Hill and south of the Via Tiburtina rose the Esquiline Hill. The Via Flaminia on the north connected with other streets and the Capitoline Hill. Other broad avenues leading from the north were the Via Nomentana, Via Salaria, and Via Pinciana.

On the south beside the Via Appia were the Via Ostiensis and the Via Latina. On the east was the Via Labicana and Via Tiburtina. Most of these thoroughfares were fifteen to twenty feet wide and opened up into the heart of the city in fine avenues.

3. Rome's Public Buildings and Parks.

The imperial city in the first century A.D. was given over to a large extent to pleasure, and was dotted with baths, amphitheatres, theatres, and circuses to entertain the blasé populace, whose innumerable holidays comprised more than half the days of the calendar year. With so much leisure, the state undertook to supply various kinds of amusement at public expense on 93 of the 159 holidays of the year.[48] Juvenal declared that the carefree people were concerned only about two things, "bread and circuses."[49] Among the famous Circuses where chariot races were held was the Circus Maximus, whose form is still traceable. It was enlarged until it seated a quarter-million spectators in Nero's time. Paul saw this huge structure between the Avenue and Palatine after entering the city proper through the Porta Capena. Other Circuses included the Circus of Caligula west of the Tiber, the Circus Flaminius at the site of the present Palazzo Caetani, and the so-called Circus of Nero in the Vatican.[50]

Famous theatres of Paul's day included Pompey's Theatre, built in 55 B.C., accommodating 10,000; the Theatre of Balbus, built in 13 B.C., seating less than 8,000; and the Theatre of Marcellus, erected in 11 B.C., seating 14,000.[51] The famous amphitheatres of Rome, except one in the Campus Martius, built in 29 B.C., date after Paul's day, such as the well-preserved Flavian amphitheatre or Colosseum, where gladiators massacred each other and Christians were later thrown to wild beasts. But both the main phase of the development of the

[48]Carcopino, op. cit., p. 205.
[49]Satire X, 77-81.
[50]See Samuel B. Platner and Thomas Ashby, A Topographical Dictionary of Ancient Rome (1929), 111-113; 370-371.
[51]Platner and Ashby, op. cit., pp. 513-517.

amphitheatre and its bloody orgies of barbarity were still in the future. The Colosseum completed by Titus was to become a somber symbol of Rome's cruelty and degeneration, as well as of her worldly grandeur.[52]

Besides numerous buildings for recreation and pleasure, Rome had beautiful gardens and public parks, adjoining spacious porticoes. In the Vatican district were imperial gardens and the lovely landscaped estates of Domitia, Nero's aunt. They became known as Nero's Gardens and after her death formed an entire district for the public enjoyment.

Ruins of the Roman Forum looking toward the Arch of Titus (center background). Courtesy Dr. John F. Walvoord

Rome was also distinguished by numerous baths or *thermae*. Many of these were sumptuous edifices whose ruins are still extant, such as the Thermae of Agrippa and the Thermae of Nero. The famous baths whose present-day ruins are most impressive date after Paul's time, such as the Thermae of Titus, the Thermae of Trajan, and the Thermae of Diocletian.

4. Rome's Palaces and Temples

Paul certainly saw the Palaces of the Emperors on the Palatine Hill and no doubt walked through the old Forum with its maze of

[52]Gladiatorial combats continued to the beginning of the fifth century A.D. Philip Schaff and Henry Ware, eds., *A Select Library of Nicene and Post-Nicene Fathers of the Christian Church* III (1890-1900), p. 151.

temples and altars. Extensive archaeological ruins remain of some of these structures, particularly of the house of Augustus' wife Livia on the Palatine with its fine murals. Nero's palace overflowed the Palatine onto the Esquiline, and was the acme of splendor and magnificence.

The Palatine was the seat also of two important temples – the Temple of Apollo and the Temple of Cybele. The Temple of Serapis adorned the Campus Martius near the Pantheon. The Temple of Castor and Pollux constitutes the most prominent ruin in the Forum. Many other temples adorned the city, such as the Temple to the Divine Julius, the Temple of Augustus, the Temple of Saturn, and the Temple of Jupiter.

Somewhat southwest of the Forum, near the Arch of Tiberius and in front of the Temple of Saturn, was the Militareum Aureum, a gilded shaft set up by Augustus as a sign-post listing names of places to which the Roman highroad system led, including far-distant cities such as Londinium (ancient London) on the west and Jerusalem on the east. Standing here, the great world-missionary and traveler was indeed at the center of the world at that time, where he was willing to lay down his life that the Gospel he preached might radiate to the ends of the earth.

IV. PAUL'S TRIAL AND THE OUTCOME

The book of Acts tells us nothing of Paul's trial at Rome, but it is known from the evidence of history and papyri that in the time of Claudius and Nero cases were heard by the emperor in person, assisted by a consilium of selected friends, but who, however, might delegate authority.[53] Philo was a member of a Jewish delegation of appeal to the emperor Caligula in A.D. 40 and his account of the proceedings sheds light on Paul's case,[54] as well as the inscription of Augustus from Cyrene. In the second of five edicts dated in the year 7-6 B.C., the emperor acquits from blame Publius Sextius Scaeva, apparently the provincial proconsul, for sending to him as prisoners three men who had professed knowledge of great import to the emperor, but proved to have had no such information. Augustus therefore released them from their custody and dismissed them, two of whom were Roman citizens.[55]

---

[53]See Henry Cadbury, "Roman Law and the Trial of Paul," *The Beginnings of Christianity* V, p. 321-325. For the papyri involved, see Cadbury, *op. cit.*, p. 323, note 5.
[54]*Legatio ad Gaium* 44
[55]J. G. C. Anderson, *Journal of Roman Studies* XVII, 1927, pp. 33ff.

1. *Possible Release of Paul*

Since no prosecuting Jews appeared in Rome against Paul (Acts 28:21), there is reason to conclude that the case against him came to nought and that after two years (Acts 28:30) he was released. During this two-year period his lodgings, doubtless in one of the *insulae* or large apartment houses of the city (such as those found at the suburban port of Ostia) were the scene of writing, preaching, and religious instruction. At this time the apostle evidently penned Philippians, Colossians, Philemon, and Ephesians. The two-year wait for his case to appear on the docket was due perhaps to the loss of official charges and papers in the shipwreck, failure of accusers to appear, or a crowded court calendar.

Modern sign on the Mamertine Prison, Rome. Courtesy Dr. John F. Walvoord

What was the outcome of the trial? One view is that when Paul was released he was enabled to realize his desire to evangelize Spain (Romans 15:24), which had a teeming population and a glamorous appeal in the apostle's day.[56] Then, according to this theory, Paul revisited the Near East, Crete (Titus 1:5), Asia (II Timothy 4:13), Macedonia (I Timothy 1:3), and Greece (II Timothy 4:20). This

[56]Cf. Clement of Rome who implies such a visit when he says concerning Paul's life "...and when he had reached the limits of the west, he gave his testimony before rulers..." (*Letter to the Corinthians* 5). Cf. Kraeling, *op. cit.* pp. 461-62. The *Canon Muratori* declare definitely that Paul went to Spain, as well as other second century sources.

position maintains that Paul was again arrested, probably at Nicopolis in Epirus (Titus 3:12), and then sent on to Rome where he was jailed in the Mamertine Prison, adjacent to the Roman Forum, and where he wrote the first and second epistles to Timothy and the epistle to Titus.

Another hypothesis is that Paul was imprisoned only once and that this ended in his execution, of which Luke does not write, in order not to have defeated his purpose of commending Christianity to the Roman world, which it is claimed he would have done by telling how the chief exponent of the Christian message was put to death, as an enemy of the Roman State. But this theory must assume that the epistles to Timothy and that to Titus are pseudonymous, but incorporate experiences that properly belong to Paul's earlier experiences.

The release of Paul from his first Roman imprisonment occurred probably in A.D. 63, and his subsequent activity lasted about four years. Eusebius says Paul's death occurred in A.D. 67. Jerome places it in A.D. 68. The circumstances of Paul's final arrest are unknown, but he was likely informed against as a leader of a now-outlawed sect, and finally condemned, probably because he was a prominent Christian and in accordance with the policy begun by Nero in A.D. 64. According to tradition, the apostle was beheaded with the sword on the Ostian Way, a method of execution consonant with his status as a Roman citizen.

When the church at Rome toward the end of the Apostolic Age (about A.D. 95) wrote the letter now known as I Clement, both Paul and Peter were already known and their memory revered as Christian martyrs. Dionysius of Corinth about the year 175 mentions Paul's martyrdom in Rome, and Tertullian of Carthage around 200 A.D. declared his execution was by beheading. Gaius of Rome, early in the third century, names the Ostian Way as the place, and Origen somewhat later names the time as under Nero (54-68). Eusebius (326), basing his ecclesiastical history on earlier authentic records, declares the same fact. As Goodspeed says, "On the whole, the testimony of antiquity on the subject is clear and unanimous."[57]

But the death of the great missionary evangelist and strategist was not to end his career. His numerous letters in dynamic fashion live on, and with the rest of the New Testament, together with the Old Testament Scriptures, which serve as their background, form a body of revealed truth constituting the supreme revelation of God to man, which archaeology is continually illuminating and illustrating on the human side.

[57]Edgar J. Goodspeed, *Paul* (1947), p. 211.

Chapter 18

Archaeology and the New Testament as Literature

As an ancient document of unparalleled importance, the Greek New Testament displays many elements of providential preparation. It did not come, of course, until the Old Testament to which it is vitally and inseparably connected, and which it unfolds, paved the way and opened up the need for it. It did not appear until the Saviour, whose Person and work it portrays, had first appeared. It was not given until the human instruments of its revelation were raised up, nor until the world was ready to receive its message, nor until a language which could be the fit vehicle for the clear and vigorous expression of its world-transforming truths was evolved. In short, the whole process of preparation for the appearance of this document bears the impress of divine providence at work.

Not least among the elements entering into this preparation was that of language. Not any language would do. Aramaic, the language of Jesus and the apostles, would not do. It was too provincial, too local, too uncosmopolitan. A religion destined to be world-wide needed a world-language. Aramaic would have seriously hindered the outreach of the Gospel. Classical Greek would not do. It was the language of the cultured, the wealthy, and the refined. Christianity came with a message of hope to the uneducated, the poor, and the oppressed. The masses could only be reached with a language of the masses.

Clearly providence was manifested in the preparation of such a language centuries before the New Testament was to be given. It was destined to be the Greek tongue, with its wealth of inflexion, wide range of vocabulary, richness of tense system, and qualities of clarity and grace. But what a miracle had to be performed! Ancient Greece was composed of autonomous city-states. These political entities were cut off from social intercourse with one another by rugged mountains. They vied with one another in maintaining their individuality. As might be imagined, they offered an amazing spectacle of dialectical diversity sheltered within narrow borders.

Greek, to be sure, was spoken in these states, but it was far from being a world language. In fact, it was just the opposite. There was the confusion of various dialects. The Attic, the speech of the Athenians, led as the language of culture and philosophy, but there were also others, such as the Ionic, the Doric, the Aeolic, and the Boeotian, as late as the early part of the fourth century B.C. Only a miracle could bring a universal language out of this hodge-podge.

Providence, however, is discernible in working out the miracle through the events of history. Philip of Macedon toward the middle of the fourth century B.C. effected the political unification of Greece. The isolationism of individual city-states was broken down. Dialectical peculiarities tended to vanish. Then came the lightning world conquests of Philip's son, Alexander the Great. Greek culture suddenly spread to the Mediterranean world, Asia Minor, and the East. Great impetus was given to the circulation of a common Greek. Boeotian, Spartan, and Athenian were herded together in camp and tent, with the inevitable result that dialectical differences disappeared. A common colloquial language emerged. Orthographically and basically, it was the standard literary model, the Attic. Orally, it preserved traces of its original dialectical diversity.

This universal language, extending, according to A. T. Robertson, from 300 B.C. to 330 A.D., was the current speech of the common people.[1] More important, it is the language of the New Testament, produced during the course of centuries, to be the medium for recording what Christianity holds to be the consummation of divine revelation.

It is this significant fact, that the New Testament is written in the ordinary language of the masses, of which critics have frequently lost sight. The result has been the rise of serious and perplexing questions concerning the estimate which is to be placed upon its language and its quality as literature.

I. THE PROBLEM OF THE EVALUATION OF THE NEW TESTAMENT

Is the Greek in which the New Testament is written pure Attic, or is it a kind of Hebraic-Greek, with every deviation and peculiarity to be accounted for as a Hebraism? In other words, is the Sacred Volume written in the best classical and artistic style, or is it a special biblical Greek, a sort of sacred and special "language of the Holy Spirit"?

1. *The Problem of Philological Evaluation*

The philological issues involved precipitated the once furious strife which raged between the so-called Purists and Hebraists. The Purists felt that revelation could only be given in the very "best"

[1]A. T. Robertson, *A Grammar of the Greek New Testament* (5th ed.) p. 43.

Greek, which they insisted had to be the classic Attic. In the seventeenth century various scholars labored relentlessly but futilely to prove that New Testament Greek was on a par with the literary Attic of the classical period. The Hebraists triumphed over them, however, and sought to demonstrate that it was a Hebraic Greek, a distinctive variety, if not a distinct dialect of biblical Greek.

This was the prevailing view even up to the opening years of the twentieth century. It was held in an extreme form by Guillemard[2] in 1879. Hatch,[3] in 1889, advocated a distinct biblical Greek of which he maintained the New Testament is a variety. Cremer,[4] about 1892, quotes with approval Rothe's remark:

> We may appropriately speak of a language of the Holy Ghost. For in the Bible it is evident that the Holy Spirit has been at work, moulding for itself a distinctively religious mode of expression out of the language of the country which it has chosen as its sphere, and transforming the linguistic elements which it found ready at hand, and even conceptions already existing, into a shape and form appropriate to itself, and all its own.[5]

Cremer adds to these remarks: "We have a very clear and striking proof of this in New Testament Greek."

Even Winer, though he had long seen that the vernacular Koine was "the special foundation of the diction of the New Testament," still held on to the idea of a "Jewish Greek, which native Greeks did not entirely understand."[6] Neither he nor Schmiedel saw the practical identity of New Testament Greek with the vernacular Koine. Blass[7] saw the dawn of a new day, but his work was published before it came.

With the turn of the century, such abundant light was shining from the ancient East as the result of archaeological research, that a new problem was opening up. Was not the whole philological approach to the New Testament wrong? Was it not just as erroneous to try to prove New Testament Greek a special Hebraistic variety, as to try to demonstrate it to be pure classical Attic? Could it not be that the truth of the whole matter lay in the practical identity of New Testament Greek with the lingua franca of the Graeco-Roman world? The problem of the philological appraisal of New Testament language was given an entirely new aspect.

[2]W. H. Guillemard, *Hebraisms in the Greek Testament,* 1879.
[3]E. Hatch, *Essays in Biblical Greek,* 1889, p. 34.
[4]H. Cremer, *Biblico-Theological Lexicon of New Testament Greek,* (tr. 1892).
[5]Rothe, *Dogmatik,* 1863, p. 238.
[6]Winer-Thayer, pp. 20, 27.
[7]F. Blass, *Grammar of New Testament Greek* (English trans. 1905).

2. The Problem of Literary Evaluation

How is the New Testament to be ranked as literature? Can it be favorably compared with the Greek classics? Does the New Testament possess literary quality? Did the New Testament begin as literature or did it become literature? These and kindred questions have occasioned great diversity of opinion among critics. One thing was evident. The philological problem was to be closely connected with the literary appraisal of the New Testament.

Many students of the Greek classics, imbued with Attic artistic molds and rules, have been prone to deny literary value and quality to the New Testament, and to look depreciatingly upon it from the literary standpoint. Comparing it with the ornate and florid classic style and finish, there was a tendency to despise it as literature. Freudenthal, hence, spoke of the Hellenistic Jews as "one of those societies without a mother-tongue which have never attained to any true excellence in literature."[8] And Mahaffy described the Greek spoken and written by the Jews as "the new and artificial idiom of the trading classes."[9]

But the question rather came to be, Was not the Atticistic revival artificial? Was it legitimate to evaluate the New Testament on the basis of the Attic regulations, and the rolling periods of Thucydides? Must the criterion of literary excellence consist in strict adherence to rigid rules and stilted regulations in straining after an antique Attic idiom? Had not the whole Purist controversy been needless, and the result of an entirely false basis of judgment of the language of the New Testament?

The question may also be raised whether the Hebraists did not likewise espouse an unsound criterion of criticism. Although their position seemed stronger and more tenable than the lost cause of the Puritan contention, and accordingly survived it, was it nevertheless fair to explain every puculiarity and deviation from classic Attic, or the literary Koine of the period, as a Hebraism, or as the special prerogative of an isolated sacred language? Was this to be the standard of evaluation?

As in the case of the philological problem, so in the case of the literary appraisal, the whole issue was directed into a new channel by momentous archaeological discoveries in the closing decades of the nineteenth century, and on into the twentieth century. New light was shed on the whole question. A new attack was made on the issue of literary evaluation. The problem was redirected and expanded.

The question was now asked, May not the language employed in

[8]Freudenthal *Hellenistic Studies*, 1875.
[9]J. P. Mahaffy, *Greek Life and Thought* (1896), p. 530.

the Sacred Volume on the whole be such as was spoken in the lower circles of society, and not such as was written in works of literature? Ought not the New Testament be evaluated as a book of the common people, written in the idiom of the masses? May it not be assigned a natural and beautiful intermediate position between the colloquial freedom of the populace and the studied style of the literateurs of the period?

II. THE NEW MATERIALS FOR EVALUATION OF THE NEW TESTAMENT

The new archaeological discoveries that were destined to revolutionize the philological and literary appraisal of the New Testament were the papyri, the ostraca, and the inscriptions.

1. *The Papyri*

These are inscribed bits of paper from antiquity, since papyrus was the paper of the ancient world. It was made from a reed cultivated in the marshy Delta of Egypt. The plant is now extinct in Lower Egypt. It is still found, however, in Upper Egypt and in the region of Abyssinia. Theophrastus, Herodotus, and other writers of antiquity enumerate the various uses of this plant in the manufacture of mats, cords, sails and for fuel and food, etc. But the most celebrated of all of its uses was the making of paper. It is as a writing material that papyrus is most significant in New Testament archaeology.

Manufacture of papyrus. Ancient paper was made by cutting the stem of the papyrus plant into longitudinal strips. These strips were placed side by side to form a layer. Across this another layer of shorter strips was woven. The resultant sheet was then soaked in the water of the Nile, hammered, and dried in the sun. Any ridges were removed by polishing with ivory or a smooth shell. The quality of the resultant product varied considerably according to the kind of strips used and the care taken in treating and polishing.

The widespread use of papyrus as a writing medium in the ancient world is abundantly attested to by archaeological evidence in the form of documents, paintings, and sculptures. The papyri discovered in Egypt have frequently been recovered in tombs, in the hands of the deceased, or as wrappings for the bodies of mummies. Funerary ritual is commonly the subject of Egyptian papyri but numerous also are the hieratic, civil, and literary documents, and the demotic and enchorial papyri, dealing with commercial transactions. Coptic papyri are concerned with biblical and religious texts or ecclesiastical matters.

Modern recovery of papyrus documents. Perhaps no other area of archaeological discovery has been so richly rewarding to New Testament students as the recovery of large quantities of papyri from the arid sands of Egypt, where the dry climate has preserved these price-less documents for the researches of the technical biblical scholar. Papyrology, the science or study of the papyri, is now an invaluable branch of scientific biblical inquiry, particularly in the case of New Testament historical and philological investigation.

Early finds of papyri. The first papyri to reach Europe were one Greek and two Latin fragments. These were donated to the library at Basel by Johann Jakob Grynaeus toward the end of the sixteenth century. The ruins of Herculanaeum in Italy, however, yielded the first substantial finds of Greek papyri. There in 1752 the charred remnants of a philosophical library were unearthed.[10] In Egypt Greek papyri made their debut in 1778, when a European merchant acquired one of a number of rolls reputedly unearthed at Gizeh. Evidence, however, furnished by the single surviving roll (the rest were burned by the natives because of the aromatic smell) suggests the Fayum as the real place of discovery, where later in the last quarter of the nineteenth century and on into the twentieth century rich stores of papyri were brought to light.

The last quarter of the nineteenth century yielded other substantial discoveries. From 1877 on, large finds were made in the ruins of Arsinoe and other places in the Fayum, a sandy depression in the Libyan desert west of the Nile and about eighty miles southwest of Cairo. In antiquity this district was a prosperous oasis graced by the well-known Lake Moeris, which the Egyptians named *Shei*, "the lake," and later *Piom*, "the sea." It is from the latter term the name Fayum is derived. Arsinoe was the capital city of the Fayum district and was called Crocodilopolis by the Greeks. It was the center of the worship of the crocodile god, Sebek, and its ruins consist of mounds situated north of the present Fayum capital, Medinet-el-Fayum.

Many of the Fayum yields were the accidental fruits of native *fellahin* digging in ancient mounds for *sebakh*, a nitrous soil used as a fertilizer. Other documents were the outcome of search on the part of dealers, and in some cases, were due to clandestine operations of plunderers. Combined activity of this sort insured an almost constant flow of papyri to the great museums of Europe.

In 1889-1890 Sir Flinders Petrie, digging at Gurob in the Fayum, came upon the mummies of the early Ptolemaic age, in the cartonnages of which papyrus had been employed. The British Museum and the Louvre about the same time acquired important literary papyri of Greek classics, including Aristotle's treatise on the Con-

[10]Edited by Walter Scott, *Fragmenta Herculanensia*, 1885.

stitution of Athens and the Mimes of Herondas, while the Louvre got a speech of Hyperides against Athenogenes.

Biblically significant finds of papyri. Scientific excavations in search of papyri began in the winter of 1895-96. In that year D. G. Hogarth, B. P. Grenfell, and A. S. Hunt undertook an expedition in the northern Fayum for the Egyptian Exploration Fund. The results were encouraging, and in the subsequent season an amazing find was made by Grenfell and Hunt at Behnesa, ancient Oxyrynchus, about ten miles from the Nile, and situated on the main canal (Bahr Yusef) which brought Nile water to the Fayum. This city in antiquity had been the capital of the Oxyrynchite nome. In the fourth and fifth centuries of the Christian era it was famous as a Christian community.

Grenfell and Hunt began to dig in the rubbish heaps of this ancient site on January 11, 1897. On the second day they unearthed a frayed papyrus piece four by six inches in size. The clearly discernible numeral in the upper righthand corner showed that it had been a page of a papyrus codex. The Greek word for "speck" *karphros*, gave the first inkling that here was a saying of Jesus concerning the "speck" and the "log" in the eye recorded in Matthew's gospel (7:3-5) and also in Luke's (6:41, 42). The entire fragment, dating evidently from the third century, proved to be a leaf inscribed with sayings of Jesus, which were published under the title of *Logia* in 1897.

". . . and then shalt thou see clearly to cast out the speck that is in thy brother's eye.

"Jesus says, Except ye fast to the world, ye shall in no wise find the kingdom of God; and except you make the Sabbath a true Sabbath, ye shall not see the Father.

"Jesus says, I stood in the midst of the world, and in the flesh was I seen by them, and I found all men drunk, and none did I find thirsty among them, and my soul is grieved over the sons of men, because they are blind in their heart, and do not see.

". . . poverty.

"(Jesus says) Whereas there are two, they are not without God, and wherever there is one alone, I say, I am with him. Raise the stone, and there thou shalt find me, cleave the wood, and there I am.

"Jesus says, A prophet is not acceptable in his own country, neither doth a physician work cures upon them that know him.

"Jesus says, A city built upon the top of a high hill and established can neither fall nor be hid.

"Jesus saith, Thou hearest with one ear (but the other ear thou hast closed)."

In 1903 Grenfell and Hunt uncovered a second papyrus fragment at Oxyrynchus containing other sayings of Jesus.[11] These documents recovered from the desert sands indicate how popular were the words of Jesus among Christians in Egypt and illustrate what sort of collections of the logia were being made.

At Tebtunis in the southern Fayum in 1899-1900, Grenfell and Hunt found papyri in a stranger place than Flinders Petrie had done in the human mummy cases at Gurob. Here in a sacred crocodile cemetery, where the deified animals had been mummified and interred ceremoniously, papyri turned up in profusion as wrappings for the crocodile mummies and, in some instances, as stuffings for their bodies. The discovery was made as one of the workmen, angered that nothing but mummified crocodiles appeared, hurled one of them on a rock. It split open, laying bare a greater treasure than a royal tomb — papyrus documents priceless to the student of ancient life and literature. There before the amazed eyes of the archaeologist were fragments of ancient classics, private letters, petitions, land surveys, accounts, contracts and royal ordinances. Each despised crocodile now yielded its wealth that formed the shroud of these bizarre deities which were reverently laid to rest two millenia ago.

Grenfell and Hunt carried forward work in various sites in the Fayum and elsewhere. They pursued excavations for some half-dozen seasons at Behnesa. French archaeologists worked in the Fayum (1901-1904), the Germans at Heracleopolis (1898-1899), Italians at Hermopolis (1903) and other groups labored at other places.

The extensive discovery and publications of papyri have continued practically unabated in the last half century. This ever-expanding field of research has had a growing significance for the study and interpretation of early Christianity and its literature. New evidence for the textual and historical evaluation of the New Testament has come to light in unexpected quantities. An estimated 25,000 or more papyri are now known. About half of these have been published.

More recent New Testament papyri discoveries. The most important New Testament documents discovered in recent decades are the Chester Beatty papyri.[12] These are numbered P45, 46, 47. Sir Frederic Kenyon published a facsimile and text edition of these in 1933-1941. Sixty other papyri are now known. These range in date from the third to the seventh centuries. Although these documents are fragmentary, they are valuable witnesses to the condition of the text during that period. Twenty-five are of the gospels, twelve of

[11]B. P. Grenfell and A. S. Hunt, *New Sayings of Jesus and Fragment of a Lost Gospel from Oxyrynchus* (London, 1904).
[12]Frederick G. Kenyon, *The Chester Beatty Biblical Papyri.* Fasciculus III Text 1934; Supplement Text 1936; Supplement Plates 1937; *Our Bible and the Ancient Manuscripts,* 1940.

Acts, sixteen of the Pauline epistles, four of Hebrews, four of the general epistles, four of the Apocalypse. These papyri are scattered in the museums of the world at New York, London, Paris, Cairo, Strasbourg, Oxford, Manchester, Florence, Glasgow, and Ann Arbor.

In addition to the original text, several papyri of the ancient versions have been recovered. Sahidic Acts of the fourth century (Sahidic and Akhmimic are Coptic dialects of Egypt), a Sahidic manuscript of Acts and the epistles of Paul (about A.D. 600) and a "sub-Akhmimic" text of John from the fourth century are the most significant. The last two were published by Sir Herbert Thompson in 1932 and 1924 respectively.

Papyri discoveries in the area of early Christian literature in the last several decades also have been amazing. The Greek text of the Shepherd of Hermas from the third century is contained in the Ann Arbor Codex. A hitherto missing conclusion of the Acts has come to light in a Hamburg papyrus of about A.D. 300, consisting of eleven pages. Among the Chester Beatty papyri in the University of Michigan has come the nearly complete text of a lost sermon of Melito of Sardis, "On the Passion." This was found in 1940. A Coptic text of the Epistle of the Apostles appeared in a Cairo manuscript. Of first-class importance are a dozen Coptic codices of over a thousand pages discovered in Upper Egypt in 1946. These contain forty-two Gnostic treatises, thirty-seven of which are complete.[13]

In addition, a large quantity of very fragmentary material has been recovered. This embraces portions of Irenaeus, Hippolytus, Gospel of Mary, the Abgar-Jesus letters, I Clement, Ignatius, Aristides, Acts of John, Protevangelium and a few hagiographa. An Oxyryhynchus papyrus of the fifth century contains a word of Jesus on healing the sick (numbered 1384).

About twenty-five "libelli" (certificates of loyalty), apparently dating from the persecution under the Emperor Decius, are now known. Other fragments contain hymns, prayers, sermons, letters and the like. Many preserve biblical quotations and allusions. All are interesting and valuable in their reflection of early Christian life and faith.

2. The Ostraca

Besides the papyri recovered so abundantly from the rubbish heaps, tombs, graves, and mummies of antiquity, other archaeological evidence having significant bearings on the study of the New Testament has also come to light in the modern era. This material consists of ostraca and inscriptions of a general nature.

[13]For discussion of these (especially the Gospel of Thomas) see Chapter IV.

The ostraca are broken pieces of clay and pottery used by the poorer classes as writing materials in the ancient world. Ostraca were so widely employed for this purpose because they were so cheap. Although ideal as a writing material, they were otherwise of little or no use. Greek ostraca in large numbers have been found in Egypt, preserving records of many kinds, chiefly tax receipts.

Ulrich Wilcken excelled all others in the collection and decipherment of the ostraca. By the end of the nineteenth century some two thousand of these inscribed potsherds already had been published, principally by Wilcken.[14] Adolf Deissmann gives a touch of local color when he mentions the stoic Cleanthes writing "on ostraca or on leather" because he could not afford papyrus.[15] W. E. Crum quotes the incident of a Christian apologizing for using a potsherd for a letter: "Excuse me that I cannot find papyrus, as I am in the country."[16] The chief value of the ostraca, accordingly, is in setting forth conditions among the lower classes of the people — the uneducated and poor — where the roots of Christianity first struck deep.

In some cases Christian biblical texts are preserved upon ostraca. Some twenty of them, dated commonly in the seventh century, are inscribed with the Greek texts of parts of the gospels. One extended passage (Luke 22:40-71) is recorded on ten of the ostraca. These potsherds contain from two to nine verses each, and are inscribed in three different hands. They cover Matthew 27:31, 32; Mark 5:40, 41; 9:17, 18, 22; 16:21; Luke 12:13-16; 22:40-71; John 1:1-9; 1:14-17; 18:19-25 and 19:15-17.

Coptic ostraca are also numerous, particularly from Byzantine times. These are even of more interest for the history of Christianity than the Greek. A Christian hymn to Mary, possessing similarity to the canticles of Luke and some Christian letters, have been found. W. E. Crum's studies on the Coptic ostraca have remained of paramount importance.[17]

3. The Inscriptions

The bulk of the ancient evidence from the Graeco-Roman world in this classification is engraved on stone. The ancients from very early times in Babylonia, Egypt, and throughout the Old Testament era on into Greek and Roman times and later set up slabs of marble, granite, or other type of rock. These inscribed pillars varied from simple milestones or grave-markers to formal monuments bearing im-

---

[14]*Grieschische Ostraka aus Aegypten und Nubien*, 2 vols., 1899
[15]*Light From the Ancient East* (1911), p. 46.
[16]*Coptic Ostraka*, p. 55.
[17]See note 6 above. Cf. also Adolf Deissmann, *Light From the Ancient East*, 1927.

portant laws or edicts of governors and kings. Frequently they were erected to commemorate some victory or extraordinary event.

Although the principal remains in this category are engraved on stone, examples are numerous in bronze, in lead or gold, in wax, in writings on walls, and in characters on coins and medals. Totalling hundreds of thousands, these inscriptions yield much information concerning the daily life of the world into which Christianity was born and bred. Since the Renaissance, travelers and scholars have noted and studied these epigraphical remains.

In the eighteenth century one scholar, Johann Walch,[18] employed Greek inscriptions in the exegesis of the New Testament. But the nineteenth century was distinctly the era of Graeco-Roman epigraphy. August Bockh is the important name in epigraphical research. His name is connected with *Corpus Inscriptionum Graecarum,* a definitive work. F. Blass, H. A. A. Kennedy, R. Helbing, H. St. Thackeray, J. H. Moulton, F. G. Kenyon and G. Milligan (as well as their successors in New Testament research to the present hour) were alive to the value of the inscriptions to New Testament study. The caution, however, to be observed in working with this type of evidence is that it rarely presents the vernacular, but the literary language. If the idiom of the common people is to be apprehended, the papyri must be studied. On the other hand, the inscriptions frequently give significant illustration of events or customs referred to in the New Testament, and in some cases furnish valuable authentication historically.[19]

III. Results of the New Material for Evaluation of the New Testament

The modern discovery of papyri, ostraca, and other epigraphic remains from the Graeco-Roman period has completely revolutionized New Testament philological study. Abundant new light, especially from the phenomenal finds of the non-literary papyri, has compelled abandonment of the old isolative method by which the Sacred Record was evaluated largely apart from its relation to the contemporary international Greek language. This mistaken procedure had been possible before the bulk of the new texts were discovered, or before they were studied historically and comparatively. With the new archaeological criteria available by the first decade of the twentieth century, this was no longer possible. The unsound isolation method had to give way to the sound historical method. The New Testament was now studied in the light of the new records, rather than dogmatically

---

[18]Johann E. I. Walch, *Observations,* Jena, 1770.
[19]Cf. the various works of W. M. Ramsay and A. T. Robertson, *Luke the Historian in the Light of Research* (1930), pp. 1-240.

separated from its historical and philological environment. The results were revolutionary.

1. *The Philological Results of the New Material for Evaluation*

The new texts make three important contributions to the philological appraisal of the language of the New Testament. First, *they prove the morphological identity of its idiom with that of the Koine of the same period.* The hundreds of morphological "oddities" in the New Testament which strike the reader of the classics will be found also in contemporary non-religious records of the everyday Greek of the period.

Among the first to set forth the real character of the Koine was the distinguished philologian, A Thumb.[20] Pioneering in applying the new knowledge directly to New Testament Greek was James Hope Moulton,[21] followed by Adolf Deissmann.[22] All subsequent scholarly research in New Testament language and literature in the twentieth century to our present day has had to deal with the ever-increasing fund of papyri and other epigraphic evidence. Such recent works as the *Greek-English Lexicon of the New Testament and Other Early Christian Literature,* translated and edited by Arndt and Gingrich and published in 1958 by the University of Chicago, as well as Gerhard Kittel's *Theologisches Woerterbuch zum Neuen Testament,* continued since 1948 by Gerhard Friedrich, have rendered obsolete such earlier lexicons as Moulton and Milligan, Thayer, and even Liddell and Scott.

Besides showing the morphological identity of New Testament Greek with the Koine, the new texts illustrate proper names[23] and in an amazing fashion elucidate vocabulary. Numbers of New Testament words, once considered strictly biblical, are now known to be common to the Koine of the period.[24] Even more important is the elucidation of the meaning of words. Words once thought to have special biblical or New Testament meanings in many instances have been found not to differ appreciably from their usage in the papyri. On the other hand, the larger context and usage of numerous words in the extra-biblical sources have invested the vocabulary of the New Testament with a much wider background for more accurate definition and illustration of meaning.

Other elements such as set phrases, peculiar idioms, and fixed formulas of expression have been clarified. In addition, the field of

[20]*Griechische Sprache in Zeitalter des Hellenismus. Beitrage zur Geschichte und Beurteilung der Koine* (1901).
[21]*Grammar of New Testament Greek,* I, *Prolegomena* (1906).
[22]*Light From the Ancient East* (1910).
[23]Adolf Deissmann, *Bibelstudien* (1895), p. 187.
[24]Cf. Deissmann, *Light From the Ancient East,* pp. 70-73.

syntax of the New Testament has been revolutionized. All grammars before the new archaeological finds were studied, such as Friedrich Blass',[25] as well as all grammars of New Testament Greek that have not been continuously revised in the light of the ever-increasing fund of new archaeological material, have become outdated.

The new archaeological evidence also sheds light on the style of the New Testament. For example, Johannine style used to be represented as being Semitic, notably for its paratactic ("and . . . and" style). Both Deissmann[26] and Brugmann[27] have demonstrated that parataxis was the original form of Greek speech and survived continuously in the language of the people, as the papyri prove.[28]

2. The Literary Results of the New Material of Evaluation

Not until scraps of papyri from the sands of Egypt and humble potsherds from the mud and silt of bygone civilizations were studied and compared with the New Testament was a correct criterion for appraising its literary quality supplied. Now it is obvious that the language of the New Testament is not to be depreciated on the basis of non-conformity with Atticistic standards nor to be adjudged a special "biblical" or "Hebraic" Greek. *It is patently the common, international language of the first century* A.D., *the popular Koine of the period, but with some literary elements.* This is the true view of the literary value of the New Testament supplied by archaeology.

The New Testament, although it employs the everyday language of the people, does so, as A. T. Robertson aptly points out, "with a dignity, restraint, and pathos far beyond the trivial nonentities in much of the papyri remains."[29]

It must not be forgotten that great diversity of culture existed among the writers of the New Testament. If Peter and John were "unlettered and unlearned" (Acts 4:13) and not men of the schools, this was far from the case with Luke, Paul, and the writer of Hebrews. Yet these writers were not Atticists, using an artificial idiom and straining after mere literary finish. They employed the popular tongue. But literary elements are discernible also.

Paul certainly does not deny that he could use the literary style in I Corinthians 2:1-4. He rather rejects the artificial and bombastic rhetoric so popular in the ancient world from Thucydides to Chrysostom.[30] He rejects it because artificiality and bombast have no legiti-

[25]*Grammatik des neutestamenlichen Griechisches,* 2 Aufl (1902).
[26]*Light From the Ancient East,* pp. 128, 129.
[27]Karl Brugmann, *Griechische Grammatik* (Muenchen, 1900).
[28]Cf. Deissmann, *op. cit.,* p. 164.
[29]*A Grammar of the Greek New Testament in the Light of Historical Research,* p. 84.
[30]W. H. Simcox, *Language of the New Testament* (1890), p. 15.

mate place in a true Christian. They may comport with heathen vanity, but not with Christian humility. The superlative characteristic of the New Testament is its freedom from artificiality and pedantry. The Spirit of God could never inspire bombast, even in a Luke or Paul.

The genius of the New Testament is its naturalness and simplicity. If the beauty of classical Greek literature has slain its thousands, the simple and moving narratives of the New Testament have slain their tens of thousands. The rolling periods of Thucydides may thrill the hearts of a learned few. But the heart of a whole universe leaps to the serene beauty and simple majesty of the words of Jesus or John or the impassioned exhortations of Paul. If classical Greek is like a garden made beautiful by the labor and ingenuity of man, the New Testament is like a flowering meadow carpeted by the wisdom of God. The beauty of one is man-made. The glory of the other is God-given.

J. C. Robertson in an article entitled, "Reasons for Teaching the Greek New Testament in Colleges," perceives the essential excellence of New Testament language, when he says:

> Take the parable of the Prodigal Son, for instance. In literary excellence this piece of narrative is unsurpassed. Nothing more simple, more direct, more forceful, can be adduced from among the famous passages of Greek literature. It is a moving tragedy of reconciliation. Yet its literary excellence is not accidental. The elements of that excellence can be analyzed.[31]

The New Testament is the Book of the people for the people. Archaeological evidence has aided this conclusion, and if one misses this essential point in evaluating the book as literature, he misses everything. God gives the lily to adorn every field and by-path. He gives a Solomon to adorn a palace. The classics may be had and known in the houses of the few rich and learned. But the Bible is read and known in the houses of the many poor and uneducated. It is at home anywhere there are human heartbreak and tears. It is lofty and sublime so that the mighty and the noble might rise to receive it. It is simple and humble that the lowly might be able to embrace it. It was born among the common people, written in the language of the common people, grew up among the common people, and is ever at home among the common people. Is it then to be thought strange that it is, in an age of books, still the world's best seller. It is accomplishing its divine mission when it reaches the heart of mankind.

---

[31] *The Classical Weekly,* March 9, 1912, p. 139.

BIBLIOGRAPHY

Abel, F. M. *Histoire de la Palestine depuis la conquéte d'Alexandre jusqu'à l'envasion arabe.* 2 Vols. Paris: 1952.

Adams, J. McKee. *Biblical Backgrounds.* Nashville: Broadman Press, 1934.

_____. *Ancient Records and the Bible.* Nashville: Broadman Press.

Albright, William F. *The Archaeology of Palestine and the Bible.* Westwood, N.J.: Fleming H. Revell, 1933.

_____. *From the Stone Age to Christianity.* Baltimore: John Hopkins Press, 1946; rev. ed., 1958.

_____. *Archaeology and the Religion of Israel.* Baltimore: John Hopkins Press, 1942.

_____. *The Archaeology of Palestine.* Hammondsworth, Middlesex, England: Penguin Books (Pelican Series), 1949.

Albright, and others. *The Haverford Symposium on Archaeology and the Bible.* New Haven: American Schools of Oriental Research, 1938.

Alouf, Michel M. *History of Baalbeck.* Beirut: American Press, 13th ed., 1925.

Avignad, Nahman and Yigael Yadin. *A Genesis Apocryphon: A Scroll from the Wilderness of Judah.* Jerusalem: Hebrew University, 1956.

Baly, Denis. *The Geography of the Bible.* New York: Harper & Brothers, 1957.

Barrett, C. Kingsley. *Luke the Historian in Recent Study.* London: Epworth Press, 1961.

_____. *The new Testament Background: Selected Documents.* New York: Harper & Brothers, 1961.

Barrois, A. G. *Manuel D'Archéologie Biblique.* Paris: Tome I, 1939; Tome II, 1953.

Barton, George A. *Archaeology and the Bible.* Philadelphia: American Sunday School Union, 7th ed., revised, 1937.

Benoit, P., J. T. Milik, R. de Vaux. *Discoveries in the Judaean Desert.* I, 1955; II, 1961. London: Clarendon Press, 1961.

Blaiklock, E. M. *Out of the Earth (The Witness of Archaeology to the New Testament).* Grand Rapids: Eerdmans, 1957.

Blunt, A. W. F. *The Acts of the Apostles.* Oxford: Clarendon Press, 1922.

Bouquet, A. C. *Everyday Life in the New Testament Times.* New York: Charles Scribner's Sons, 1954.

Brownlee, W. H. *The Dead Sea Manual of Discipline, Bulletin of the American School of Oriental Research, Supplementary Studies 10-12.* New Haven: American Schools of Oriental Research, 1951.

_____. *The Text of Habakkuk in the Ancient Commentary from Qumran,* Monograph series. Philadelphia: Society of Biblical Literature and Exegesis, 1959.

Bruce, F. F. *Biblical Exegesis in the Qumran Texts.* Grand Rapids: Wm. B. Eerdmans Publishing Co., 1958.

_____. *Commentary on the Book of Acts.* Grand Rapids: Wm. B. Eerdmans Publishing Co., 1954.

_____. *The Acts of the Apostles.* London: Tyndale Press, 1951.

Bultmann, Rudolf. *Theology of the New Testament.* Trans. by K. Grobel. New York: Charles Scribner's Sons, 1951.

Burrows, Millar. *The Dead Sea Scrolls.* New York: The Viking Press, 1955.

_____. *More Light on the Dead Sea Scrolls.* New York: The Viking Press, 1958.

_____. *What Mean These Stones?* New Haven: American Schools of Oriental Research, 1944.

Cadbury, Henry. *The Book of Acts in History.* New York: Harper & Brothers, 1955.

Caiger, Stephen. *The Bible and the Spade.* London: Oxford University Press, 1935.

_____. *Archaeology and the New Testament.* London: Cassell & Co., 2nd ed., 1948.

Carcopino, Jerome. *Daily Life in Ancient Rome.* New Haven: 1940.

Cobern, Camden M. *The New Archaeological Discoveries and Their Bearing Upon the New Testament.* New York: Funk and Wagnalls, 4th ed., 1920.

Cochrane, Charles Norris. *Christianity and Classical Culture*. New York: Oxford University Press, 1940.

Cowell, F. R. *Everyday Life in Ancient Rome*. Edinburgh: James Thin, 1961.

Craig, Clarence Tucker. *The Beginning of Christianity*. Nashville: Abingdon Press, 1943.

Cross, Frank M. *The Ancient Library at Qumran and Modern Biblical Studies*. Garden City, New York: Doubleday, 1958.

Crownfield, F. C. *A Historical Approach to the New Testament*. 1960.

Crowfoot, J. W., et. a. *The Buildings of Samaria*. London: Palestine Exploration Fund, 1942.

_____. *Samaria-Sebaste: Reports of the Work of the Joint Expedition in 1931-1933 and of the British Expedition in 1935*. London: Palestine Exploration Fund, 1957.

Cullmann, Oscar. *Peter: Disciple, Apostle, Martyr*. Trans. by Floyd Filson. Philadelphia: 1953.

_____. *The State in the New Testament*. New York: Charles Scribner's Sons, 1956.

Danielou, Jean. *The Dead Sea Scrolls and Primitive Christianity*. Baltimore: Helicon, 1958.

Daniel-Rops. *Jesus and His Times*. New York: Dutton and Co., 1954.

Davies, W. D. *Paul and Judaism*. London: Society for the Propagation of Christian Knowledge, 1948.

Deissmann, A. *Light from the Ancient East*. Trans. by L. R. M. Strahan. New York: Doran, 1927.

_____. *The New Testament in the Light of Modern Research*. London: Hodder and Stoughton, 1929.

_____. *Bible Studies*. Trans. by A. Grieve. Edinburgh: T. & T. Clark, 2nd ed., 1903.

Dodd, C. H. *The Apostolic Preaching and Its Development*. New York: Harper & Brothers, 1951.

Doresse, M. Jean. *Les livres secrets des Gnostiques d'Egypte*. Paris: Plon, 1958.

Dupont-Sommer. *Le Livre des Hymnes decouvert pres de la Mer Morte*. Paris: Adrien maison neuve, 1957.

Ehrlick, Ernst Ludwig. *Gescheichte Israels von den Angagen bis zur Zerstorung des Tempels 70 n. Chi*. Sammlung Goschen, Berlin: de Gruyter, 1958.

Eller, Meredith F. *The Beginnings of the Christian Religion*. New York: Bookman, 1958.

Elliger, Karl. *Studien zum Habakik-Kommentar vom Totem Meer*. Tubingin: J. C. B. Mohr, 1953.

Enslin, Morton Scott. *Christian Beginnings*. New York: Harper & Brothers, 1938.

Finegan, Jack. *Light from the Ancient Past*. Princeton, New Jersey: Princeton University Press, 1959.

Foakes-Jackson, F. J. K., Lake, H. J., Cadbury, et. al. *The Beginnings of Christianity*. 5 vols. London: The Macmillan Co., 1920-33.

Frank, Tenney, ed. *An Economic Survey of Ancient Rome*. 6 vols. Baltimore: 1933-40.

Free, Joseph P. *Archaeology and Bible History*. Wheaton, Ill.: Scripture Press, rev. ed., 1961.

Freedman, David Noel and G. Ernest Wright, eds. *The Biblical Archaeologist Reader*. Chicago: Quadrangle Books, 1961.

Friedlander, Ludwig. *Roman Life and Manners Under the Early Empire*. Vols. I-IV. Trans. by A. B. Gough. London: 7th ed., 1913.

Fritsch, Charles T. *The Qumran Community*. New York: The Macmillan Co., 1956.

Gartner, B. *The Theology of the Gospel According to Thoman*. Trans. by E. J. Sharpe. Leiden: E. J. Brill, 1961.

Gaster, Theodore H. *The Dead Sea Scriptures*. New York: Doubleday and Co., Inc., 1956.

Glueck, Nelson. *Rivers in the Desert*. New York: Farrar, Straus, and Cudahy, 1957.

_____. *The Other Side of the Jordan*. New Haven: American Schools of Oriental Research, 1940.

Goguel, M. *The Birth of Christianity*. New York: The Macmillan Co., 1954.

Goodspeed, Edgar J. *Paul*. Philadelphia: The John Winston Company, 1947.

_____. *Introduction to the New Testament*. Chicago: University of Chicago Press, 1937.

Grant, R. *The Sword and the Cross*. New York: The Macmillan Co., 1955.

Guignebert, C. *The Jewish World in the Time of Jesus*. London: Routledge and Kegan Paul, 1939.

Haefeli, L. *Caesaree und Meer*. Munster: 1923.

Harding, G. Lankester. *The Antiquities of Jordan.* Crowell: 1960.

Harnack, H. *The Mission and Expansion of Christianity in the First Three Centuries.* Trans. by J. Moffatt. Vol. I. New York: Putnam's, 1908.

Harrison, R. K. *The Dead Sea Scrolls.* New York: Harper & Brothers, 1961.

Heard, Richard. *An Introduction to the New Testament.* Harper & Brothers, 1951.

Howard, Wilbert F. *The Fourth Gospel in Recent Criticism.* Rev. by C. Kingsley Barrett. London: Epworth Press, 1955.

Howlett, Duncan. *The Essenes and Christianity.* New York: Harper & Brothers, 1958.

Hunter, A. M. *Interpreting the New Testament 1900-1950.* Philadelphia: Westminster Press, 1951.

Johnson, Sherman E. *Jesus in His Own Times.* New York: Charles Scribner's Sons.

Josephus, Flavius. The Antiquities of the Jews and The Jewish War. Trans. by H. St. J. Thackeray and R. Marcus. London: 1926-1943.

Kee, H. C. and F. W. Young. *Understanding the New Testament.* Englewood Cliffs, N. J.: Prentice-Hall, 1957.

Kelso, James. *Excavations at New Testament Jericho, Annual of the American Schools of Oriental Research.* Vol. CCCI. 1955.

Kenyon, Sir Frederic. *Our Bible and the Ancient Manuscripts.* Rev. by A. W. Adams. New York: Harper & Brothers, 1958.

_____. *The Bible and Archaeology.* New York: Harper & Brothers, 1949.

_____. *The Bible and Modern Scholarship.* Harper & Brothers, 1948.

Kosmola, H. *Hebraer-Essener-Christen.* Leiden, Netherlands: E. J. Brill, 1959.

Kraeling, C. H. ed. *Gerasa, City of the Decapolis.* New Haven: American Schools of Oriental Research, 1938.

_____. *John the Baptist.* New York: Charles Scribner's Sons, 1951.

Kraeling, Emil. *Rand McNally Bible Atlas.* Chicago: Rand McNally & Co.

_____. *Bible Lands.* Chicago: Rand McNally & Co., 1952.

Kuhn, Karl Gerog, ed. *Dictionary of the Qumran Texts.* Heidelberg: Qumran Research Institute, 1960.

_____. *Concordance of the Qumran Texts.* Gottingen: Vandenhoek and Ruprecht, 1959.

LaSor, William Sanford. *Bibliography of the Dead Sea Scrolls, 1947-1957.* Pasadena, Cal.: Fuller Seminary, 1959.

_____. *Amazing Dead Sea Scrolls and the Christian Faith.* Chicago: Moody Press, 1956.

Leary, Lewis G. *From the Pyramids to Paul.* New York: Thomas Nelson & Sons, 1935.

Licht, Jacob. *The Thanksgiving Scroll.* Jerusalem, Bialik Institute, 1957.

Lietzmann, J. *The Beginnings of the Christian Church.* London: Lutterworth Press, 1953.

Machen, J. Gresham. *The Virgin Birth of Christ.* New York: Harper & Brothers, 1930.

Mackinnon, A. G. *The Rome of St. Paul.* London: 1930.

_____. *The Rome of the Early Church.* London: 1933.

Mansoor, M. *The Thanksgiving Hymns.* Trans. and annotated with an introduction. Leiden: E. J. Brill, 1961.

_____. *Studies on the Topography of the Desert of Judaea III.*

Martin, M. *The Scribal Character of the Dead Sea Scrolls.* Louvain: Institute Orientaliste, 1958.

Mattingly, Harold. *Roman Coins.* Chicago: Quadrangle Books, Inc., 1961.

McCown, Chester C. *The Ladder of Progress in Palestine.* New York: Harpers & Brothers, 1943.

McNeile, A. J. *An Introduction to the Study of the New Testament.* Rev. ed. London: Oxford University Press, 1953.

Medico, Henri E. del. *The Riddle of the Scrolls.* Trans. by H. Garner. New York: McBride Co., 1959.

Metzger, Bruce M. *St. Paul's Journeys in the Greek Orient.* New York: Philosophical Library, 1956.

Milik, J. T. *Ten Years of Discovery in the Wilderness of Judaea.* London: and Naperville, Ill.: 1959.

_____. *Dix ans de decouvertes dans le desert de Juda.* Paris: Edition du Cerf, 1957.

Moe, Olaf. *The Apostle Paul.* Trans. by L. A. Vigness. Minneapolis: Augsburg Publishing House, 1950.

Moulton, James Hope. *Grammar of New Testament Greek.* Vol. II: Accidence and Word Formation. Edinburgh: T. & T. Clark, 1929.

Motscher, Friedrich. *Gotteswege und Menschenwege in der Bibel und in*

Qumran, Bonner Biblische Beitrage, No. 15. Bonn: Hanstein.

Olmstead, A. T. *Jesus in the Light of History*. New York: Charles Scribner's Sons, 1942.

Owen, G. Frederick. *Archaeology and the Bible*. Westwood, N. J.: Fleming H. Revell Co., 1961.

Parrot, A. *Le Temple de Jerusalem*. Neuchatel: 1954.

_____. *Golgotha et Saint-Sepulcre*. Neuchatel: 1955.

Perowne, Stewart. *The Later Herods*. Nashville: Abingdon Press, 1959.

_____. *Life and Times of Herod the Great*. London: Hodder & Stoughton, 1956.

Pfeiffer, Charles. *Baker's Bible Atlas*. Grand Rapids: Baker Book House, 1961.

_____. *Between the Testaments*. Grand Rapids: Baker Book House, 1959.

Pfeiffer, Henry. *History of New Testament Times*. New York: Harper & Brothers, 1949.

Ploeg, J. van der. *The Excavations at Qumran*. Trans. by K. Smith. Edinburgh: James Thin, 1957.

Pritchard, James B. *The Excavations at Herodian Jericho, Annual of the American Schools of Oriental Research, 1951*. Vol. XXXII-XXXIII for 1952-1954. New Haven: American Schools, 1958.

Purinton, Carl E. *Christianity and Its Judaic Heritage*. New York: The Ronald Press, 1961.

Ramsay, William M. *The Cities of St. Paul*. Baker Book House, reprint, 1960.

_____. *The Bearing of Recent Discovery on the Trustworthiness of the New Testament* (1911). Grand Rapids: Baker Book House, reprint, 1953.

_____. *St. Paul the Traveller and Roman Citizen*. Grand Rapids: Baker Book House, reprint, 1960.

_____. *Pauline and Other Studies*. London: Hodder and Stoughton, n.d.

_____. *Letters to the Seven Churches*. Grand Rapids: Baker Book House, reprint, 1962.

Ricciotti, Guiseppe. *Paul the Apostle*. Milwaukee: The Bruce Publishing Co., 1952.

Robertson, Anne. *Catalogue of Roman Imperial Coins*. Edinburgh: James Thin, 1961.

Rostovtzeff, M. I. *Dura-Europos and Its Art*. Oxford: 1938.

_____. and A. H. Detweiler, etc. *The Excavations at Dura-Europos, Preliminary Report of the ninth Season, 1935-1936, Part III*. New Haven: Yale University Press, 1952.

Roth, Cecil. *The Historical Background of the Dead Sea Scrolls*. New York: Philosophical Library, 1959.

Schlatter, Adolf. *The Church in the New Testament Period*. Trans. by Paul Levertoff. London: S.P.C.K., 1955.

Schreiden, J. *Les Enigmes des Manuscrits de la Mer Morte*. Leiden: E. J. Brill, 1956.

Schubert, Kurt. *The Dead Sea Community*. Trans. by J. W. Doberstein. London: A. & C. Black, 1959.

Simons, J. *Jerusalem in the Old Testament*. Leiden: 1952.

Stauffer, Ethelbert. *Christ and the Caesars*. Trans. by K. and R. Smith. Philadelphia: Westminster Press, 1955.

Stendahl, Krister, ed. *The Scrolls and the New Testament*. New York: Harper & Brothers, 1957.

Streeter, B. H. *The Primitive Church*. New York: The Macmillan Co., 1929.

Taylor, Vincent. *The Life and Ministry of Jesus*. New York: Abingdon, 1955.

Thompson, J. A. *Archaeology and the Pre-Christian Centuries*. Grand Rapids: Eerdmans Parkway Books, 1958.

Titus, Eric Lane. *Essentials of New Testament Study*. New York: The Ronald Press, 1958.

Toombs, Laurence E. *The Threshold of Christianity Between the Testaments*. Philadelphia: Westminster Press, 1957.

Vermes, Geza. *Discovery in the Judaean Desert*. New York: Desclee, 1956.

Vincent, L. H. *Jerusalem Antique*. Paris: 1912.

_____. and A. M. Steve, *Jerusalem de l'Ancien Testament*. 2 vols. Paris: Gabalda, 1954-1956.

_____. and F. M. Abel. *Jerusalem Nouvelle*. 4 Vols. Paris: 1914-1926.

Watzinger, C. *Denkmaler Palastinas II*. Chapter vi. Leipzig: 1935.

Wernberg-Moller, P. *The Manual of Discipline*. Grand Rapids: Eerdmans Publishing Co., 1958.

Williams, C. S. C. *Commentary on the Acts of the Apostles*. New York: Harper & Brothers, 1957.

Willoughby, H. R. *Pagan Regeneration.* Chicago: University of Chicago Press, 1929.

Wilson, Edmund. *The Dead Sea Scrolls.* New York: Oxford University Press, 1955.

Wiseman, Donald J. *Illustrations From Biblical Archaeology.* Grand Rapids: Eerdmans Publishing Co., 1958.

Wright, G. Ernest. *Biblical Archaeology.* Philadelphia: Westminster Press, 1957.

Yadin, Y. *The Qumran Cave I Scroll (War of the Sons of Light Against the Sons of Darkness).* Translation of the Hebrew Edition published in Jerusalem. Amsterdam: Erasmus, 1957.

Yeivin, S. *A Decade of Archaeology in Israel, 1948-1958.* Leiden: E. J. Brill, 1960.

GENERAL INDEX

A

Abel, 73
Abila, 73
Abilene, 66, 73, 304
Abraham's example, 212
    Israel, 32
Absalom('s)
    rebellion, 110
    tomb, 112
Abyssinians, 154
Accho, 119, 147, 293
Achaia, 211, 245
Acrocorinth, 243
Acropolis (Athens), 173, 176, 240-242
Acts of Apostles, 19, 25, 101-110, 121, 122, 138, 139, 146-336
Actium, 53, 65
Adams, J. McKee, 28
Adams, Pythian, 153
Adramythium, 213, 274, 275, 289, 305-306
Adria (Hadria), Sea of, 310
Aegean, 190, 213, 242, 249, 264
Aelia Capitolina, 82, 146
Aeneas, 163
Aenon, 117
Agabus, 294
Against Heresies, 92
Agora, 173, 233-237
Agrippa II, 136, 302-304
Agrippianon, 173
Ahasuerus, 28
Ahuramazda, 59
'Ain-et-Tabgha, 126
'Ain Feshka, 82, 84
'Ain Maryam, 121
Akeldama, 108
Ak-Hissar, 279
Alabanda, 274
Alah-Shehir, 285, 286
Aland, Kurt, 19
Albanian Lake, 316
Albright, W. F., 22, 25, 43, 48, 75, 91, 273
Alcimus, 43
Alexander Balas, 44
Alexander the Great
    career of conquest, 27-33
    results of his conquest, 33-36, 43, 158, 186, 214, 217, 226, 249, 251, 252, 282, 290, 292, 293, 325
Alexander, Jannaeus, 47, 48, 50, 51, 72, 141, 152
Alexandra, 48, 50
Alexandretta, 176
Alexandria, 32, 34, 38-40, 70, 158, 171, 214, 229, 249, 275, 276, 306, 311
Alexandrium, 117
Amarna Letters, 164
Amathus, 117, 184
Amazons, 249
Ambivius, Marcus, 67
American Journal of Archaeology, 178
American Philosophical Society, 166
American School of Classical Studies, 235, 236, 242, 246

American Schools of Oriental Research, 115, 142
Amman, 42, 78, 139
Amon, 33
Amorites, 134
Amorium, 209
Amphipolis, 218, 219, 226, 314
Amyntas, 34, 190
Anatolia, 264
Ancyra (Ankara), 210, 212, 264
    Inscription, 212, 213
Anderson, Bernhard W., 27
Anderson, J. G. C., 321
Andrew, 129
Andrews, H. T., 38
Andriake, 306
Androclus, 249
Anglo-Egyptian Sudan, 154
Ann Arbor Codex, 332
Annas, 66, 73-74
Anthios River, 192, 193
Antigonus, 51, 53, 81, 149, 213, 282
Antigonus Gonatus, 34
Antilebanon, 136, 303
Antioch-on-the-Orontes, 33, 34, 43, 44, 59,
    early history, 170-179
    171-172, under Rome
    172-173, in Paul's day
    174-176, Daphne
    176-178, excavations
    190
Antioch of Pisidia, 65, 186-195, 201, 204, 207, 208, 210, 248, 249, 250, 264, 265, 266
Antioch Gate, 180
Antiochus I Soter, 172
Antiochus II, 267
Antiochus III, 40, 292-293
Antiochus IV Epiphanes, 40, 41, 43, 45, 49, 158, 172, 177, 190, 200
Antiochus Eupator, 43
Antiochus Sidetes, 44
Antiochus, VII, 44
Antiochus of Commagene, 59
Antipater, 40
    I, 48, 51
    II, 51, 58, 60, 159
Antipatris, 59, 115, 163
Antiquities of the Jews, The, 85
Antonia, 103, 104, 106, 296, 298
    tower of, 98
Antonius Pius, 136
Antony Mark, 51, 53, 65, 98, 158, 190, 226, 276
Apamaea, 190, 250, 264, 265, 266, 274
Aphairema, 114
Aphrodite, 181, 184, 206, 243
Aphses, 129
Apis-bull cult, 32
Apocrypha, 27
Apocryphal gospels, 93
Apocryphon of John, 91
"Apology for the Jews," 85

Apollo, 222, 245, 280, 290
Apollo Archegetes, 271
Apollonia, 163, 213, 226, 288, 314
Apollonia Inscription, 191
Apollonius of Tyana, 240
Apollos, 258
Apphia, 269
Apphios, Apphianos, 269
Appian Way, 219, 314, 319
Appius Claudius Coecus, 314
Aqueology, 164
Aquila, 244, 248
Arabia, 96, 103, 153, 161, 166, 211
Aradus, 30, 31, 292
Aramaic Jewish-Christian gospel, 93
Araq el-Emir, 42
Aratus, 238
Araunah, 103
Arbela, 33
Archaeology
    definition, 13
    general, 13
    Biblical, 13
    how it facilitates N. T. study, 18-25
    expedites the scientific study of the N.T., 19-20
    balances critical study, 20-23
    illustrates and explains the N.T., 23-26
    authenticates the N.T., 25-26
    N.T. vs. O.T., 95
Archaeological Institute of America, 288
Archedemus, 159
Archelaus, 60, 67, 81, 114, 115, 148
Areopagus, 237
Ares, 236, 237
Aretas, 48, 72, 123, 139, 159-161
Aristarchus, 305
Aristeas, 38, 103
Aristobulus I, 47
    II, 48, 50, 51, 168
Aristotle, 35, 288, 329
Arkadianne, 255, 256
Armenia, 53
    sites, 112
Arnason, H. Harvard, 178
Arndt and Gingrich, 20, 144, 335
Arrian, 32, 38, 153, 188
Arsaces, 34
Arses, 28
Arsinoe, 249, 329
Artaxerxes, I, II, III, 28
Artemidonus, 159
Artemus, 24, 187, 193, 249, 250-253, 265, 280
    temple of, 24
Artemision, 250-253
Arundell, F. V., 192
Aryans, 28
"Ascent of Adummim," 115
Asclepius, 242, 271, 277, 278, 291
Ashby, Thomas, 319

Ashdod, 153
Asia, 29, 41, 211
Asia Minor, 34, 36, 40, 59, 156, 166, 170, 175, 186, 187, 190, 191, 207, 209, 214, 249, 250, 267, 274, 281, 282, 284, 290, 305, 306, 314, 325
Asiarch, 262, 263
Askar, 142
Askelon, 59
Asopus, 267
Assos, 213, 288-289
Assumption of Moses, 86
Assyrians, 148
Astarte, 181, 251
Astyages, 254, 257
Athanasius, 292-293
Athena (Nike), 240-242, 277
Athena Promachus, 240
Athenodonus, 159
Athens, 24, 59, 136, 158, 173, 232-242
    its idolatry, 233
    Paul's ministry there, 233-237, 242, 249
    his address at the Areopagus, 237-239
    its archaeology, 235-240
Attalia, 186, 187, 200, 264
Attalids, 34, 283
Attalus I, 275, 276
Attalus II Philadelphus, 200, 284
Attalus III, 34, 250, 275-278, 283
Attica, 232
Augusta, 149
Augustan Band, 305
Augusteum, 213
Augustine, 16, 53
Augustus, 53, 55, 57, 60, 66, 122, 136, 137, 148, 149, 150, 158-159, 173, 183, 190, 194, 213-214, 236, 263, 289, 314, 321
Auranitis, 72
Austrian Archaeological Institute, 253
Aventine Hill, 319
Avignad, Nahum, 77
Avi-Yonah, M., 130
Axum, 154
Ayasoluk, 250, 257
Azotus, 153

B
Baalamism, 277-278
Baalbek, 136, 137
Baal-Hermon, 134
Baal-Jupiter, 136
Baal sanctuaries, 134
Babylon, 28, 33
Babylonian Jew, 51
Bacchides, 43, 49
Baffo, 184
Bahr Yusef, 330
Balatah, 144
Baltimore Museum of Art, 176
Banias, 136
Banks, Florence A., 69
Baptism of the Spirit, 89
    of fire, 89
Barada River, 73
Baramki, Dimitri C., 115
Baris, 98
Bar-Jesus, 151, 185
Bar Kokhba, 80, 128
Barnabas, 156, 170-171, 173, 178-179, 181-186, 186-207

Barsabbas, 204
Barthelemy, D., 78
Bartimaeus, 115
Baruch II, 147
Batanaea, 72, 129, 304
Baucis, 198
Baur, F. C., 21
Beautiful Gate, 101, 102
Behnesa, 331
Behram, 288
Beirut (Berytus), 138, 293, 304
Beisan, 139
Beit Jibrin, 153
Belial, 89
Belshazzar, 28
Ben-Dor, Immanuel, 166
Benjamin, 147
ben Kosiba, Simeon, 80
Benndorf, O. H., 253
Bentzen, Aage, 27
Beqa, 136
Berea, 229-231
Bergama, 275
Bernice, 139, 302-304
Berlin Museum, 278, 290
Berytus, 304
Bethabarah, 117
Beth Alpha, 128
Bethany, 96, 109, 111-114, 117
Bethel, 44, 114
Bethesda, 22, 101, 118
Beth Gubrin, 40
Bethhoron, 44, 115
Bethlehem, 57, 58
Bethphage, 96, 109, 111-112
Bethsaida Julias, 72, 117-118, 126, 128-132
Bethshan, 116, 129-130, 139, 142, 159
Bethter, 153
Beth Yerah, 71
Bethzur, 43, 44, 48-49, 60, 153
Bewer, J., 27
Bezetha, 98
Biblical Archaeology, 13
Bibliotheque Nationale, 122
Bion of Soli, 154
Bir'im, 128
Bishop, F. F., 95
Bishop Melito, 283
Bishops, 92
Bithynia, 34, 213, 263
Black Obelisk, 158
Black Sea, 34
Blaiklock, E. M., 122
Blass, F., 326, 334, 336
Bockh, August, 334
Bodmer Paprus (Manuscript of John), 22
Boehringer, Prof. E., 278
Book of the Twelve Prophets, 79
Boston Museum of Fine Arts, 289
Botzeli (station), 264
Bouleterion, 236
Boulton, W. H., 26
Bouquet, A. C., 29, 30, 95
Bouzos, 264
Brested, James, 13, 29, 30, 181
British Museum, 253, 329
British School of Archaeology, 141
British War Cemetery, 110
Broneer, Oscar, 236
Broomall, Wick, 16
Broughton, T. R. S., 250

Brownlee, William H., 77, 87-90
Bruce, F. F., 21, 24, 64, 147, 162, 308, 315
Brugmann, Karl, 336
Brundisium, 216, 314
Brutus, 53, 226
Buddhism, 17
Bultmann, R., 21
Burkitt, F. C., 141
Burrows, Millar, 77, 104
Burton, Ernest De Witt, 229
Butler, H. C., 178, 283
Byblus, 30, 31
Byzantine
    Constructions, 121

C
Cadbury, Henry J., 26, 148, 154, 160, 308, 321
Caecus, Appius Claudius, 134
Caesar, Augustus, 61, 63, 67, 130, 134, 166
Caesar worship, 53
Caesarea (Palestine), 59, 67, 69, 82, 99, 103, 118, 156, 164-168, 248, 293-294, 302
Caesarea Philippi, 72, 132-137, 304-306
Caiaphas, 66, 73-74, 106
Caicus River, 257, 274-275, 279
Caiger, S., 144
Cairo Document of the Damascus Covenanters, The, 87
Calder, W. M., 264, 286
Caligula, 73, 159-161, 169, 176, 321
Calvary, 104
Cambyses II, 28, 183
Campbell, W. A., 180
Cana, 123
Canatha, 139
Candace, 153
Canonical gospels, 93
Canticles, 27
Cape Argennum, 289
Cape Malea, 243
Cape Matala, 307
Cape Salmone, 307
Cape Sminthium, 288
Cape Sunium, 232
Capernaum, 117-119, 123, 126-128, 131, 137
Cappadocia, 53, 103
Caprus, 267
Capua, 314
Caracalla, 137, 157, 271
Carbon 14 test, 76
Carcopino, J., 122, 317
Caria, 264, 291
Carter, Charles, 149
Cassander, 226
Cassius, 53, 226
Castle of Antonia (Fortress), 103, 104
Castor, 306, 312, 313
Catholic epistles, 92
Cauda, 308
Cave I at Qumran, 75-78
Caves II-VI at Qumran, 78-79
Cave of the Seven Sleepers, 256
Cayster River, 249, 250, 274
Cenchraea, 242, 246, 248, 282, 287
Census, 57
Centurion, 162-163
Cestros River, 187, 188

Cetius River, 275
Chaeronaea, 28
Chalcedon, 213
Chalcedonian decrees, 266
Chaldean Empire, 28
Chalice of Antioch, 178, 179
Charon, 177
Charonion, 177
Chenoboskion, 23, 91, 92
Chester Beatly Papyri, 19, 331
Chessuloth, 119
Cheyne, T. K., 112
Chios, 289
Chi Rho mongram, 272
Chonai (Honaz), 266
Chorazin, 118, 126-129
"Chrestos," 122
Christ, 16, 17ff., 50, 51, 63, 65, 70
Christian Church, 51, 81, 90
"Christian," origin of name, 171
Christianity vs. paganism, 276-277
Chronicles, 27, 97, 163
  II, 114
Chrysostom, 174, 336
Church of the Annunciation, 121
Church of Christ, 17
Church of the Council, 257
Church of the Forty Martyrs, 121
Church of St. John, 257
Church of the Tomb of the Virgin, 112
Church of the United Greeks, 121
Church of the Virgin Mary, 257
Churuk Su, 264
Cicero, 195, 206, 228, 297, 312, 314, 316
Cilicia, 156, 171, 186, 204, 248, 265
Cilician Gates, 30, 190, 207, 248, 265
Cilium, 156
Circuses, Roman, 319
Citium, 184
"City of the Sun, The," 136
Clapp, R. G., 141
Claudian Family, 66
Claudiconium, 196
Claudius, 73, 122, 169, 186, 196, 199, 244-245, 294
Claudius Lysias, 296, 298, 299, 301, 303, 316, 321
Claudio-Derbe, 199
Cleanthes, 237
Clement of Alexandria, 260
Clement I, 323
Cleopatra, 72
Clermont-Ganneau, C., 81, 84
Client king, 53
Cnidus, 291, 307
Cobern, Camden, 161, 191, 193, 256, 262, 290
Codex Bezae, 148
Codex Theta, 19
Codex Vaticanus, 148
Codex W, 19
Coelesyria, 123
Coelian Hill, 319
Coeur de Lion, Richard, 163
Cogamus Valley, 284
Coinage, 282
Collart, Paul, 224
Coloni, 192

Colony, 217-218
Colossae, 190, 250, 264-267
Colosseum, 66, 319-320
Colossians, 193, 265, 268, 269, 270, 322
Commagene, 53, 59, 200, 208
Commenus, John, 270
Community of the Covenant, 87
Compagna, 316
Coneybeare, W. J., 188
Confucianism, 17
Constantine, 137, 178
Constantinople, 214, 288, 306
Constitution of Athens, 330
Cook, A. B., 193
Cook, K., 85
Coponius, 64, 67
Coptic Church, 69
Coptic Codices, 92
Corban, 69
Cordylion, 159
Corinth, 24, 206, 227, 232, 240-248
  in Paul's day, 241-243
  his ministry there, 243-244
  Gallio's proconsulship, 244-245
  excavations, 245, 247
Corinthian Gate, 101
Corinthians
  I, 186, 205, 206, 208, 211, 221, 237, 247, 258, 276, 310, 336
  II, 159, 188, 210, 244
Cornelius, 162-164, 203
Cornell University, 283
Cos, 214, 289, 291
Council at Jerusalem, 169, 203-205, 207-208, 211-212
Council of Laodicea, 273
Council of Nicaea, 184
Court of Israel, 102
Court of the Gentiles, 102
Court of the Women, 102
Craig, C. T., 203
Crassus, 34
Cremer, H., 20, 326
Crete, 306-308
Crispus, 244
Crocodilopolis, 329
Croesus, 251, 254, 306
Cross, Frank M., 76, 79, 87-88
Crowfoot, J. W., 26, 42, 149
Crum, W. E., 333
Crusades, 112
Cumanus, 294
Curtius, 32
Cybele, 193-194, 251, 270-271, 282-284
Cyndus River, 158-159
Cypros, 58
Cyprus, 31, 151, 170, 181-186, 192, 202, 207, 292, 294, 305
Cyrene, 170, 308
Cyrus the Great, 28, 254

D

Dalman, G., 26, 81, 112-113, 116, 139
Dalmanutha, 131-132
Dalmatia, 211
Damaris, 242
Damascus, 59, 72, 73, 119, 126, 136, 139, 155-161, 195
Damascus Covenanters, 87
Daniel, book of, 27, 32
Daniel (Qumran), 78

Danielou, J., 90
Danube, 66
Daphne, 173-175
Dardanelles, 214
Darius, I, II, 28
  III, 28, 30, 33
David, 50, 97, 103
David, city of, 108
Davis, John, 73, 160
Day of atonement, 103
Dead Sea, 24, 71, 75, 96, 117, 125
Dead Sea Age, 92
Dead Sea Scrolls, 21, 22, 24, 47, 75, 94
  date, 75-76
  contents, 75-80
  Qumran Caves and the Essenes, 81-86
  Manual of Discipline and the Zadokite Fragment, 87
  John the Baptist, 87-90
  Jesus, 90
  the scrolls and the literary criticism of the N.T., 91-92
  Gospel of Thomas, 92-94
Deborah, 191
Decapolis, 48, 72, 117-118, 132, 137-142, 161, 284
Decius, 256
Dedication, feast of, 12, 42
Deissmann, Adolf, 20, 64, 238, 333, 335-336
Delitzsch, Franz, 184
Delphi, 23, 221, 245
Delphi Inscription, 244
Delphic seeress, 222
Delta, 32
Dembre, 306
Demeter, 265
Demetrius (image-maker), 262
Demetrius I, 43, 44
Demetrius II, 44
Demetrius Poliorcetes, 216
Demonism and paganism, 221, 259-260
Demosthenes, 234
Denizli, 266, 267, 270
Derbe, 190, 195, 197-200, 207-210
de Sion, Marie Aline, 104
Dessau, H., 163, 305
Detweiler, 283
Deuteronomy (Apocrophon), 78, 90, 128, 134, 154, 161, 221, 276
de Vaux, Robert, 78, 81, 83-84
Diana of the Ephesians, 187, 193, 250-253, 260-263
Diaspora, 35, 36, 39, 146
Diatessaron of Tatian, 19
Dibellius, Martin, 21, 209
Dinocrates, 251
Diocletian, 190, 226, 250, 256
Diodorus, 159
Dion, 139, 159, 232
Dionysia, 64
Dionysides, 159
Dionysius, 242, 277, 323
Dioscuri, 312-313
Diospolis, 267
Diplon Gate, 232
Divination, 222
Dome of the Rock, 103
Dominican Biblical School, 104
Domitian, 194

Dora (Dor), 82, 163
Dorcas, 164
Dorpfeld, W., 237, 278
Druse religion, 134
Drusilla, 301
Dupont-Sommer, A., 47, 78, 85, 86, 89
Dura, 19, 22, 178
Duumviri (duoviri), 65, 223
Dyrrachium (Durazzo), 216

E

Earle, Ralph 149
Eastern Hill, 97
Easton, Burton Scott, 222
Ecbatana, 33
Ecce Homo Arch, 103-104
Ecclesiastes, 27
Ecole Biblique, 80, 81
Ecole Francais d'Athene, 225
Edersheim, Alfred, 95, 129
Edomite settlement, 40, 45, 51
Egnatian Road, 216, 219, 226, 314
Egypt, 23, 30, 53, 60, 64, 119, 126, 153, 166, 171, 306 (census), 64
Eisen, G., 178-179
Eissfeldt Otto, 27
ej-Jish, 137
Ekistanbul, 214
el-'Azariyeh, 113
El Batila, 126
Elderkin, G. W., 176
Eleasa, 43
Eleusis, 242
Eleutheropolis, 40
Elijah, 162
el-Mekawer, 72
Elymas, 185
Emmaus, 44, 153
Emperor Decius, 332
Endor, 116, 125
Engedi, 85
Enoch, Book of, 86
En-Rogel, 97, 108
Enrolment, 63-65
Epaphras, 265, 270
Epaphroditus, 266
Ephesia grammata, 260
Ephesian Gallery, 253
Ephesians, 102, 322
Ephesus, 24, 190-196, 209, 248-263.
    early history, 249-250
    worship of Artemis, 250-252
    Artemision, 252-253
    Archaeological discoveries, 253-257
    Paul's ministry, 257-263, 265, 266
Ephiphanius, 266
Ephraim, 114
Ephron (Ephrain), 114
Epictetus, 272-273
Epicureans, 234-235
Epiphaneia, 172, 173
Epirus, 323
Epistle of the Apostles, 332
Erastus, 247
Erechtheum, 240-242
Esdraelon, 125
Eski-Hissar, 270
Essenes, 24, 27, 44, 47, 78, 80-81, 86
es-Suk, 73
Esther, 27
Ethiopian eunuch, 152-155, 168

et-Taiyibeh, 114
et-Tell, 130
et-Tur, 115
Euergetes, 39, 40
Eumenes I, 275
Eumenes II, 275, 276, 284
Euphrates, 13, 19, 33, 34, 158, 178
Euraquilo, 307
Europe, 67, 153, 214-215
Eurymedon, 188
Eusebius, 43, 85, 169, 272, 323
Eutychides, 178
Eutychus, 288
Exodus (Apocrophon), 78, 128, 161
Exodus (the), 134
Exorcists, 260
Ezekiel, 31, 110, 294
Ezra, 27, 148, 163

F

Fadus, 304
Fair Havens, 307
Famagusta, 183
Fasces, 223
"Fat Valley," 112
Fayum, 219, 329
Feast of Lights, 42
Felibedjik, 225
Felix, Antonius, 68, 294, 298, 301
Fertile Crescent, 162
Festus, 301-303
"Field of Blood," 108
Fifth Persian satrapy, 28
Filson, Floyd, 100, 103, 123, 141, 178, 250, 261
Finegan, Jack, 95, 97, 130, 132, 141, 194, 225
First Census, 65
First Century, 92
First Revolt, 25, 82
"Fisherton," 129
Flaccus, 268
Flavia, 285
Fogg Museum, 283
Form Criticism, 21
Forum, 320, 321
"Forum of Appius, The," 314
"Four Hundred Silent Years," 27
Franciscan Garden, 112
Franciscans, 128
Frank Mountain, 58, 60
Free cities, 218, 229
Free, Joseph P., 219, 229
Freebooters, 51
Friedrich, Gerhard, 20, 335
Fritsch, Charles, 80, 81, 83, 86, 87, 166
Fronto, Gaius Coristanius, 65
Funk, Robert, 49

G

Gabala, 292
Gabbatha, 103
Gabiniopolis, 149
Gabinius, 72, 149, 152
Gadara, 117, 139, 141, 159
Gadarenes, 134
Galasa, 139
Galatia, 34, 53, 65, 190, 194, 196, 197, 201, 202, 206, 209, 248
Galatian Regiment, 58
Galatians, 161, 188, 197, 204, 206, 209, 210, 211, 212
Galilean(s), 69, 72
    towns, 119

hills, 119
    capital, 123
Galilee, Lake of, 71, 72, 117-118, 123, 125-132, 134, 139, 141
Galilee, province, 51, 66, 72, 111, 114-118, 123-124, 137, 142, 144
Gallio, 23, 244-247
Gangites River, 217, 219, 225
Garden Tomb, 105
Gaster, Theodore, 77
Gate of the Essenes, 106
Gaius, 323
Gaugamela, 33
Gaul, 60, 72
Gaulonitis, 72, 118, 129, 137, 139
Gaza, 31, 32, 40, 152-153, 294
ge'e shemanim, 112
Gelemish, 291
Gemini, 313
Gemara, 131
Genesis Apocryphon, 78, 142, 205
Gennesaret, 125, 131
Gentiles, 36, 71
Gerasa, 115, 117, 141-142, 159
Gerasenes, 139
Gergesa, 139, 141
Gergasenes, 139
Gerhard Friedrich, 20
German Archaeological Institute, 242
German Regiment, 58
Gethsemane, 101, 109, 111-112
Gezer, 44, 48
Ghavdo, 308
Gibbon, 174
    (Decline and Fall of Roman Empire)
Gihon Spring, 97, 108
Gingrich, Walter, 20, 144
Ginnesar, Plain of, 131
Gischla, 137
Gitta (Jett), 148, 151
Gizeh, 329
Glueck, Nelson, 161
Gnostic Christology, 94
Gnostic literature, 23, 91-92
Gnostics, 21, 23
Gold, Victor, 91
Golden Gate, 101, 111
Golgotha, 104, 105
Good Samaritan, parable of, 114
Goodspeed, Edgar, 184, 187, 197, 202, 214-216, 230, 323
Gospel According to the Egyptians, 92, 93
Gospel According to Thomas, 22, 92, 93, 332
Gospel of the Hebrews, 92, 93
Gospel of Peter, 92
Gospel of Truth, 93
Gospel of the Twelve, 93
Gospel to Gentiles, 155
Gozzo, 308
Graeco-Roman Culture, 13
Graeco-Roman World, 23-25, 36, 115
Graffiti, 40
Granicus, 29, 31
Grant, Robert M., 92, 93, 94
Gratus, V., 67, 73
Gray, James M., 221

Greek Archaeological Society, 236, 242
Greek art and literature, 35
Greek Church, 69
Greek city states, 28
Greek colonists, 35
Greek conquest and culture, 30, 35, 99
Greek customs, 35
Greek language, 35, 50, 53
Greek speaking peoples, 39
Greek states, 35
Greek-English Lexicon of the New Testament and other Early Christian Literature, 20
Greek New Testament, 15, 18, 39
Greek Old Testament, 39
Grenfell, B. P., 330-331
Grollenberg, L. H., 100, 123
Grynaeus, Johann Jakob, 329
Gudelism, 199
Guillemand, 326
Gulek Bogaz, 207
Gulf of Issos, 156
Gulf of Salonika, 226
Gurob, 329, 331

H
Habakkuk Commentary, 77
Hadrian, 82, 103, 122, 142, 146, 196, 242
Hadrianic gateway, 200
Haifa, 163, 293
Hall, H. R., 193
Halys River, 34
Hamath, 71
Hamilton, W. J., 266, 269
Hanfmann, Prof., 283
Hannaniah, 73
Hanson, H., 278
Happizzez, 119
Haram esh-Sherif, 103
Harbor Gate, 256
Harding, G. Lankester, 78, 81
Harlot-priestesses, 206
Harnack, A., 311
Harris, Laird, 16
Harvard expedition, 43, 149, University, 283
Hasidim, 45
Hasmon, 42
Hasmonaean, 50
Hasmonaeans, 43, 44, 104, 106, 116
kingdom, 47, 48, 50, 51 (dynasty)
house, 53
zealots, 97
fortress, 117
Hasmonaean Palace, 106
Hatch, E., 326
Heberdey, Rudolph, 253
Hebraists, 325
Hebrew Scriptures, 36
Old Testament, 39
Bible, 77
Hebrews, Epistle to, 92
Hebrews, Gospel of the, 92
Hebrew University, 110
Hebron, 48, 60, 153
Hefele, C. J., 270
Helbing, R., 335
Heliopolis, 136
Helios, 265
Hellenists, 145
Hellenism, 36-44, 99
Hellespont, 29, 213

Hephaisteion, 236
Heraklios, 284
Hermeas, 288
Hermes, 198
Hermus River, 257, 278
Valley, 264, 274, 279, 282
Herod Agrippa I, 73, 98, 139, 160, 164, 168-169, 173, 303
Herod Agrippa II, 106, 122, 136, 302-304
Herod Antipas, 60, 66, 70, 71, 106, 117, 122-123, 130-131, 139, 160, 169, 277
Herod the Great, 24, 27, 40, 51-63, 70, 71, 80, 81, 97, 98, 114, 116, 117, 123, 134, 136, 148, 149, 160, 164, 166, 169, 173, 183, 293, 301
Herodian
line, 51
dynasty, 51
kingdom, 60
party, 61
Herodians, 61
Herodian Temple, 99-103, 104, 106, 111
Herodias, 71, 72, 160
Herodium, 58-60
Herod ('s)
court, 56
hog, 57
body, 58
will, 60
son, 67
winter capital, 114
"that fox," 117
"leaven of," 117
Hezekiah's Tunnel, 108
Hicks, E. L. 253
Hierapolis, 264, 266, 268, 270-274
Hill of Ares, 237
Hinnom, Valley of, 97, 106, 108
Hippicus, 98, 103
Hippocrates, 214, 291
Hippodrome, 99, 115
Hippos, 117, 139, 159
Hissardi, 65
Hissarlik, 214
Hodayot, 77
Hogarth, D. H., 186, 253, 330-331
Hollis, J., 103
Holtzmann, H. J., 310
Holy City, 96
Holy Family, 60
Holy of Holies, 103
Holy Place, 102
Holy Spirit, 17
Holy Writ, 15, 18
Homer, 281
Homerium (Smyrna), 281
Homonadensian Campaign, 65
Horace, 315
Horeb, 162
Horologium, 237
Hort, F. J. A., 219
Howard, W. F., 26
Howson, J. S., 188
Huha, 88
Hunt, A. S., 330-331
Hygeia, 271
Hyrcania, 80
Hyrcanus, John, 40, 42, 47, 81, 148
Hyrcanus II, 48, 50

I
Iconium, 191, 194-197, 208-210
Idolatry and Art, 233
Idumaea, 43, 48, 51
Idumaeans, 40, 51
Ignatius, 273
Ilissos River, 240
Illyricum, 21
Imperial Cult, 262-263, 276-277, 286, 313
Imperial German Institute of Archaeology, 278
India, 30, 33, 34
Indian Ocean, 33, 162
Indo-Europeans, 28
Indus, 33
"Inn of the Good Samaritan," 115
Inscriptions, 333-334
Inspiration of N. T., 15, 16
Iraq, 13
Irenaeus, 92, 272
Isaiah, 27, 88, 112, 153, 180
Isaiah Scroll, 76-78
Isaiah Scroll (Second), 78, 79
Isis Cult, 176, 177, 185, 265, 271
Israel, 17, 22
Israeli State, 108
Issachar (tribe of), 119
Issus, 30, 31, 33, 190
Iturea, 66, 72
Izmur, 281

J
Jabbok, 141
Jacob's Well, 142, 144
Jaddua, 32
Jaffa Gate, 98
James (St.), 168, 169, 204
tomb, 112
Japhia (Jopha), 98
Japho, 164
Jason, 227, 228
Jebel Duhy, 124
Jebel et-Tannur, 161
Jebel Fureidis, 58
Jebus, 97, 108
Jehoshaphat
tomb, 112
Jerash, 115, 117, 141, 142, 159
Jeremiah (Apocrophon), 78, 155
Jericho, 23, 24, 44, 58, 59, 101, 111, 114-117, 134
Jerome, 112, 139-140, 184, 240, 323
Jerusalem, 24, 25, 59, 67, 95-109
topography, 96-97
Herodian City, 97-99
Herodian temple, 99-103
other places in Jerusalem, 103-109, 112, 113, 294-296
Jerusalem Decree, 205-207
"Jerusalem Holy," 31
Jeshua (Jesus), 96
Jesus, 17, 24, 35, 45, 46, 60, 67, 69, 71, 75, 76, 81, 90, 94, 95
sayings of, 22
teachings of, 23, 24
Jesus' death, 69
Jett, 151
Jewish proselyte, 69
scruples, 69
Jewish autonomy, 50
coins, 48

communal life, 24, 25
Independence, 43, 50
parties, 48
people, 38
population, 25
rebels, 60
religion, 23
spies, 42
stock, 51
Talmud, 32
tombs, 25
writings, 23
Jewish-Roman War, 60, 68, 114, 116, 121, 123, 129, 301
Jewitt, Paul King, 16
Jews, 48, 51, 54, 57, 60
Jezebel, 279, 280
Jezreel, 125, 128
John (the disciple), 73, 74, 75, 152, 168, 169, 204, 268, 294
John's gospel, 21, 89, 90, 99, 101, 103, 104, 108, 110, 111, 112, 113, 114, 116, 117, 118, 123, 126, 129, 130, 132, 142, 144, 148, 273, 299, 333
John the Baptist, 24, 66, 70-71, 76, 81, 88-90, 117, 137, 161
Johnson, Sherman, 115
Jonah, 27, 164
Jonathan Maccabaeus, 43-44, 46, 163
Jones, A. H. M., 261
Joppa (Joffa, Japho), 44, 163-164, 294
Jordan Dept. of Antiquities, 81
Jordan Museum, 78
Jordan River, 72, 117-118, 125-126, 129-130, 139, 159
Jordan Valley, 85, 88, 95-96, 114-116, 134
Joseph, 60, 119
Joseph of Arimathaea, 104
Joseph, son of Antipater II, 51
Josephus, 32, 47, 51, 58, 60, 61, 63, 65, 70-71, 73, 81, 85-86, 100, 103, 116-117, 123, 130, 132, 142, 153, 155, 257, 262, 301, 313-314
Joshua, 119, 134, 164
Jubilees (Apocrophon), 78
Book of, 86
Judaea, 25, 28, 41, 43, 44, 48, 51, 53, 60, 65, 66, 67, 116, 130, 142, 168, 211, 293, 294
Judaea Capta, 82
Judaeans, 47
Judah, 40, 147
Judaism, 24, 32, 35, 36, 37, 39, 40, 45
Judaized Christianity, 202, 203
Judas, 49, 123
Judas (Barsabbas), 204
Judas Maccabaeus, 42-45
Judeich, Walter, 237
Judges (Apocrophon), 78, 134
Julia, 67, 130
Julian Basilica, 245
Julias, 304
Julius Caesar, 51, 61, 137, 172, 214, 217, 237, 243, 245
Julius the Centurion, 162, 304-305, 311, 312
Jupiter Capitolinus, 173
Justin Martyr, 149

Justus, 244
Juvenal, 174, 319

K
Kalir, Elegy of, 118
Kanatha, 159
Kantzer, Kenneth, 16
Kaoussie, 178
Karnak, 164
Katyn Serai, 197
Kefr Kenna, 123, 128
Kelso, James M., 83, 115
Kennedy, A. A., 334
Kenyon, Kathleen, 149
Kenyon, Sir Frederic, 19, 26, 64, 331, 334
Kerazeh, 128
Kersa, 141
Khan Minyeh, 126
Khartoum, 154
Khirbeh, 80
Khirbet Kana, 123
Khirbet el-Araj, 130
Khirbet Mird, 75, 80
Khirbet Qumran, 47, 75, 76, 81-86
Kidron
  brook, 112
  Valley of, 97, 101, 108, 111
King Croessus, 249, 282
Kingdom of Israel, 147
King-Priest, 90
Kings I, 47, 108, 155, 162, 177
  II, 109, 155
Kittel, Gerhardt, 20
Kittim, 77
Kohl, H., 128
Koine Greek, 324-326
Kolonos Agoraios, 236
Konia, 195
Kopp, Clemens, 121
Koran, 17
Koressos Gate, 256
Kraeling, Carl, 142
Kraeling, Emil, 71, 72, 115, 119, 130, 132, 144, 149, 153, 172, 180, 200, 244, 276, 306
Krenides, 217, 219
Ktima, 184

L
Lagidae, 38
Lairbenos, 271
Lake, Kirsopp, 65, 149, 153, 160, 266, 300
Lake Moeris, 329
Lantulae, 314
Laodicea, 190, 250, 264-270, 274
Larissa, 232, 250
Lasea, 307
Lassus, Jean, 176, 178
Last Supper, 90, 106, 111
Latin Church, 112
Law, 39, 45
Lazarus, 96, 113-114, 117
Leake, W. M., 197, 240
Lebanon, 31, 125, 134, 136, 171
Lechaeum, 243, 246
Lectionaries, 19
Lepidus, 53
Lesbos, 288, 289, 306
Leto, 270-271
Levi, 126
Levi, Doro, 177
Leviticus, 103, 155, 205
Leviticus (Apocrophon), 78
lex Porcia, 224

lex Valeria, 224
Libelli, 332
Lictors, 223
Liddell and Scott, 20, 335
Life Magazine, 166
Lightfoot, J. B., 269
Limeonas Kalaus, 307
lingua franca, 35, 39
Link Expedition, 166
Lithostraton, 104
Little Hermon, 124
Livia, 67
Livy, 233
Logia of Jesus, 330-331
Londinium, 321
Lounda, 264
Louvain, University of, 80
Louvre, 177, 216, 289, 329
Lower City, 108
Lower Galilee, 45
Lucius, 170
Lucius Sergius Paullus, 193
Luke, 25, 63, 66, 69-71, 88-89, 106-108, 110-128, 132-134, 138-142, 148, 168-169, 183-185, 195, 208, 213, 228-229, 240, 248, 299, 305, 311, 330, 333
Lustra, 198
Lutro, 307
Luxor, 91
Lycaonia, 190, 195, 197, 208, 209
Lycia, 186, 291, 306
Lycus Valley, 264-274
Lydda (Lod, Ludd), 115, 163-164
Lydia, 220, 280
Lydia (city), 264, 276, 278, 282, 306
Lysanias, 66, 73, 169, 304
Lysias, 49
Lysimachos, 249, 254, 275, 281
Lysippus, 178
Lystra, 190-191, 194-199, 208-210

M
Macalister, R. A. S., 161
Maccabaean age, 27, 40, 42, 45, 48
  suffering, 46
  struggles, 49
  kingdom, 50
  times, 72
  wars, 149, 175
Maccabaeus, Jonathan, 163
Maccabees, 41, 49, 99, 164
Maccabees, Rise of, 41
Maccabees I, 45, 49, 114, 293
  II, 45
Macedonia, 29, 34, 35, 211, 216-231, 271, 287, 314
Macedonian Vision, 212-215
Machaerus, 71-72, 116
Machramion, 288
Madeba, 117
Madeba Map, 153
Maeander River, 264, 273-274, 290
Magadan, 131
Magdal (Nuna), 131
Magdala, 125-126, 131-132
Magi, 56-58
Magie, David, 285
Magna Mater, 252
Magnesia, 190, 264, 273
Magnesian Gate, 252, 256
Mahaffey, J. P., 327
Malahas, John, 172, 177, 179

Malthace, 60, 70
Malta, 308-317
Maltese fever, 311
Mamertine Prison, 322-323
Manaean, 170
Manichaean, 23
Manual of Discipline, 17, 77, 81, 86-87, 92
Marathon, 28, 240
Marathus, 292
Marcellus, 67, 70
Marcus Cato, 159
Mariamne, 56-57, 98, 103, 169
Marisa, 40, 48
Mark, John, 181, 186, 207
Mark's gospel, 63, 71, 72, 88, 102, 103, 108, 111, 112, 113, 115, 116, 117, 120, 125, 126, 128, 129, 131, 132, 134, 137, 138, 139, 141, 181, 186, 299, 333
Mar Saba, 80
Martha, 113
Martin, Victor, 22
Mary of Bethany, 113, 132
Mary Magdalene, 131-132
Mary, mother of Jesus, 60, 119, 132
Mary, wife of Cleophas, 132
Mary's Spring, 121
Masada, 85
Masoretic Text, 77, 78, 131
Mattathias, 41, 42, 51, 53
Matthew's gospel, 56, 60, 102, 111, 112, 113, 116, 118, 119, 120, 121, 122, 125, 126, 128, 129, 132, 134, 137, 138, 139, 141, 151, 203, 299, 330, 333
Maximus, G. Vibius, 64
McDonald, W. A., 225, 232
Meander River, 257, 266
McGinley, L. J., 21
Mecca, 96, 103
Medina, 96, 103
Medinet-el-Fayum, 329
Mediterranean, 30, 45, 96, 120, 125, 158
  coast, 118, 137
Megabyzos, 252
Megora, 242
Meiron, 128
Meistermann, B., 128
Mejdel, 131
Meleda, 310
Melita (Malta), 310-311
Melito of Sardis, 332
Meekart, 31
Meelink, Machteld J., 284
Memphis, 32
Men, 193-194, 265, 271
Menderes, 264
Men's court, 102
Meroe, 154
Merom, Waters of, 118
Mesopotamia, 34, 166, 196
Messiah, 17, 46, 88, 89, 90, 92
Messiah of Aaron, 90
Messiah of Israel, 90
Messianism, 56
Messina, 313
Messoria, 181, 183-184
Metzger, Bruce, 19, 26, 170
Micah (Apocrophon), 78
Miles, George C., 115
Miletus, 214, 249, 257, 274, 289-291
Milik, J. T., 78

Militareum Aureum, 321
Miller, M. S. and J. Lane, 217
Milligan, G., 227, 313, 334
Mimes of Herondas, 330
Minuscule manuscripts, 18
Mishnah, 100, 131
Mithraeum, 23
Mithras, 59, 200
Mithridatis, 34
Mithridates I, 34
Mitylene, 289-290
Mnason, 294
Moab, 277
Modin, 41
Moe, Olaf, 183, 206
Moffatt, James, 197
Mohammed, 235
Mommsen, Theodore, 174, 211, 297, 305
Moore, G. F., 45
Mors, Voluntaria, 177
Mosaics (from Antioch), 176-177
Moses, 70, 161, 202, 258
"Moses' Seat," 129
Moslem
  world, 96
  chapel, 110
  shrine, 136
Moulton, James Hope, 229, 313, 334-335
Mount Amanus, 207
Mount Cadmus, 265, 266
Mount Carmel, 119, 163-164, 292-293
Mount Ebal, 142, 144
Mount Gerizim, 44, 69, 144, 148
Mount Hermon, 72, 119, 120, 125, 134, 136
Mt. Ida, 306, 308
Mount Koressos, 249, 250, 254
Mount Mesogis, 266
Mount of Offence, 109, 110
Mount of Olives, 96, 109-111, 112-113
Mount Pangaeus, 217
Mount Parnassus, 222
Mount Pion, 251, 254
Mount Scopus, 110
Mount Silpius, 171, 172, 173, 176
Mount Sion, 134
Mount Stauris, 176
Mount Tabor, 119-120, 125, 134
Mount Tmolus, 282
Mowrey, Lucetta, 91
Mugharet Ras en-Neba, 134
Muihlenberg, J., 79
Muros, 307
Murtana (Perga), 187
Musees Nationaux de France, 176
Muslims, 103
Mycale, 290
Myra, 305-307
Mysia, 213, 220, 275, 276
Mystery Religions, 22

N

Nabataea, 45, 139, 161
Nabataean
  prince, 48
  uprising, 55
Nabataeans, 72, 117, 123, 159, 161
Nablus, 144, 148, 149

Nabonidus, 28
Nacolta, 209
Nag-Hammadi, 23, 91-94
Nahr Sukner, 153
Nain (Nein), 124
Napata, 154
Naples, 313
Naphtali, 126
Nathanael, 123
Navigium Isidis, 177
Nazareth, 71, 116, 118-120, 121-125
Nazareth Inscription, 122
Nazareth Synagogue, 121
Neapolis, 144, 149, 287, 313
Neapolis (Kavalla), 216
Nebuchadnezzar, 31
Nehemiah, 27, 42, 148, 163
Nemrud Dagh, 59, 200
Neokaisareia, 284, 286
Nero, 56-58, 70, 82, 106, 136, 159, 243, 267, 277, 301, 304, 313, 321-323
Neronias, 136
Nestor, 159
Neubauer, 112
Newman, Albert H., 272
New Testament, 13, 15, 17, 34, 35, 36, 37, 38, 39
  conditions, 23
  scientific study of, 18, 19
  scholarship, 20, 21
  warnings, 23, 24, 25
  criticism, interpretation, 25
  political and cultural history foundations, 27
  world, 35
  literary criticism of, 90
  as literature, 324-337
  archaeological materials for evaluation
    (1) papyri, 328-332
    (2) ostraca, 332-333
    (3) inscriptions, 333-334
  results of archaeological materials for evaluation, 335-337
Nicaea, 213, 263
Nicolaus of Damascus, 55
Nicolaitanism, 277-279
Nicomedes I, III, 34
Nicomedia, 213
Nicopolis, 323
Niger (Simeon), 170
"Noble Sanctuary, The," 103
North Galatian Theory, 209-210
Northern Kingdom, 147
Nubians, 154
Numbers (Apocrophon), 78, 277
Nunechuis, 266
Nymphas, 268-270

O

Occidental cultures, 39
Octavian, 53, 217, 226
Odeion (Music Hall), 236, 240, 256
Oesterley, W. O. S., 40
Oesterreich, T. K., 220
Offal, 106
Old Testament, 13, 15, 16, 39, 47
  period, 28
  scholarship, 20, 25, 27
  Scriptures, 35, 38
  times, 36, 37
Oliver, J. H., 122
Olivet, 91, 102, 110, 111

Olmstead, A. T., 103
Olympia, 238
Olympic Games, 150
Olympieion, 240
Omri, 147
Onesimus, 272
Ophel, 98
Oralfi, G., 128
Orcistus, 209
"Ordinance of Caesar," 122
Oriental culture, 35, 39
Oriental people, 36
Origen, 139, 141, 323
Orontes, 33, 170-171, 174
Ossuary, 96
Ostia, 313, 316, 322
Ostraca, 19, 332-333
Ovid, 198
Oxyrynchus, 300, 330-331

P

Pactolus River, 282, 283
Palace of Herod, 103
Palatia, 290
Palatine Hill, 238, 319
Palaeographic, 75
Palestine, 13, 22, 23, 24, 25,
  28, 30, 31, 32, 34, 38, 39,
  40, 48, 50, 51, 53, 54, 66,
  67, 118-145, 292
Palestine Archaeological
  Museum, 79-80, 83
Palestinian coast, 33
Palestinian Syriac Gospel
  (text), 132
Pallas, 301
Pamukkale, 271
Pamphylia (n sea), 186, 187,
  264, 276
Pamphylus, 191
Pan, 132, 134
  worship of, 136
Panathenaeum Road, 236
Paneas, 72, 129, 136
Paneion grotto, 134
Pansa, 290
Paphos, 151, 184-186, 206
Papias, 272-273
Papyri, 19-20, 23, 64, 297,
  328-332
  early finds, 329-330
  Biblical finds, 330-331
  recent finds, 331-332
Papyrus, 328
Paris, 122
Parthenon, 136, 240-242
Parthia, 34
  (ans), 34
Parthian Invasion, 51, 53,
  148
Passover, 103, 287
Patara, 288, 291, 292, 306
Patas, 64
Paul, 17, 24, 35, 36, 139-319,
  173, 178, 181
  his arrest, 297-301
  before the Sanhedrin, 299
  before Felix and Festus,
    301-302
  before Agrippa and Ber-
    nice, 302-304
  journey to Rome, 304-316
  at Rome, 316-321
  trial and outcome, 321-323
Paul's citizenship, 158
Pausanias, 178, 232, 234,
  238, 310
Paul and Thekla, 191
Pauline Epistles, 19, 92
Pavement, 103-104

Pella, 25, 116, 117, 139, 159
Peloponnesus, 242
Pelusium, 32, 60
Pentecost, 106, 146, 203
Peraea, 111, 114, 116, 117,
  139, 144, 304
Perdiccas, 43
Perga, 11, 111, 187-188, 190,
  195, 200, 248, 264, 270-271,
  306
Pergamene Library (Berlin),
  276
Pergamene Museum, 278
Pergamum, 34, 209, 238, 250,
  257, 267, 275-278
Pericles, 35, 240
Perowne, Stewart, 53, 58
Persepolis, 33
Perseus, 34
Persia, 33, 158
Persian Empire, 183
Persian Gulf, 162
Persian royal road, 33
Persian army, 33
Persian kings, 33
Persians, 19
Pessinus, 209-210, 212
Peter, 17, 73, 74, 101, 126,
  129, 147, 151-155, 163, 164,
  168, 169, 204, 294
I Peter, 213
Petra, 48, 53, 161
Petrie, Sir Flinders, 329,
  331
Petronius Arbiter, 233
Pfeiffer, Henry, 27
Pfeiffer, R. H., 38, 45
Phaesalus, 59
Phaleron Bay, 238
Pharisees, 44-48, 57, 63, 80
Pharsalus, 232
Phasael, 51, 98, 103
Pheroras, 51
Phidias, 240
Philadelphia, 139, 159, 264,
  273, 283-286
Philadelphus, 38, 40
Philemon, 198, 269, 322
Philetaerus, 275
Philip I of Macedon, 28, 29,
  34, 35, 323
Philip II of Macedon, 216
Philippi, 24, 53, 216-225, 314
Philippians, 173, 211, 244,
  322
Philip the Evangelist, 147,
  151-155, 268, 273, 293
Philip the Tetrarch, 66, 71,
  72, 129, 130, 134, 136, 137,
  139, 169, 304
Philistia, 44
Philo, 47, 69, 70, 81, 85, 86,
  321
Philostratus, 240, 257
Phinehas, 175
Phineka, 307
Phocis, 222
Phoenicia, 31, 32, 39, 72, 118,
  137-139, 292-293
Phoenix, 308
Phrygia, 190, 192, 195, 209,
  248, 264, 265, 269, 273, 276
Pierene, 246
Pilate, 66-67, 69-71, 98, 104,
  106, 122, 130, 228
  ('s) praetorium, 103
Piraeus, 232
Pisidia, 209
Pisidian Antioch, 186, 194,
  209, 213

Pisistratus, 242
Pittsburgh-Xenia Theological
  Seminary, 115
"Place of Lazarus, The,"
  113
Plain of Achotis, 123
Plain of Esdraelon, 116, 118-
  120, 139
Plain of Shechem, 142
Platner, Samuel B., 319
Plato, 35, 258
Pliny, 47, 72, 81, 85, 86, 125,
  139, 141, 186, 195, 226, 274
Plutarch, 32
Pluto, 271
Plutonium, 270
Po River, 310
Politarchs, 223-224
Pollux, 306, 312, 313
Polybius, 188, 311
Polycarp, 281-282
Polycrates, 273, 289
Pompeii, 30, 115, 220, 313
Pompey, 48, 72, 141, 148,
  164, 172
Pontus, 34
Porta Capena, 316
Port of Herod, 293
Poseidon, 194, 306
Praeparatio Evangelica, 85
Praetorium, 103, 301
Praetorius, F., 154
Praetors, 223
Priene Inscription, 262
Princeton Theological Sem-
  inary, 166
  University, 176, 180
Priscilla, 244, 248
Prison Epistles, 322-323
Pritchard, James M., 115
Proconsular Asia, 274-286
Procopius, 310
Procurator, 67-70
Procuratorial government,
  298
Prophecy, 17
"Prophets, The," 110
Prophylaea, 240, 244
Proportis, 213
Proverbs, 27
Psalms (Apocrophon), 27,
  78, 90, 221, 276
Pseudepigrapha, 27
Ptolemaeus Lagus, 38
Ptolemaic
  period, 49
Ptolemais, 119, 137, 292
Ptolemies, 34, 36-40, 49, 310
Ptolemy I Soter, 38, 183
  II, 38, 39
  III, 39, 40
  IV, 40
  V, 40
Ptolemy Philadelphus, 275
Publius, 311
Publius Cornelius Sulla, 162
Publius Sextius Scaeva, 321
Puchstein, O., 137
Purists, 325
Puteoli, 311-315
Pydna, 232
Python, 221, 222
  —ess, 222

Q

"Q," 93
Qasr bint el melek, 71
Quadratus, 294, 298
Qubbet es-Sakhra, 103

"Queen of the East, The,"
173
Queen Hatshepsut, 308
Quirinius, 63-65, 73
Quispel, C., 93
Qumran, 21, 22, 24, 47, 75
Qumran Documents, 21
Qumran Manuel, 86
Qumran manuscripts, 76

R
Rabin, C., 87
Ramsay, Sir William, 25, 55,
63, 65, 151, 159, 188, 190-
193, 195, 199, 206, 210, 216,
263, 265, 268, 269, 285-286,
305
Raphana, 139, 159
Ras esh-Shiyah, 113
Red Sea, 162
Redeemer, 37
Regiments of the Line, 58
Reinisch, L., 154
Reisner, George A., 149, 154
Religionsgeschichtliche
Schule, 22
Repentance, 89
Republic of Lebanon, 138
Revelation, Book of, 19, 92,
268, 269, 275, 276, 277, 278,
279, 280, 281, 282, 283, 285,
286
Revett, Nicholas, 240
Rhegium, 313
Rhine, 66
Rhoas, 267
Rhode, E., 222
Rhodes, 291
Riciotti, G., 25, 55, 64, 160,
204-205, 209, 228, 238, 252,
261
River Styx, 177
Roberts, A., 92
Roberts, C. H., 21
Robertson, A. T., 185, 191,
208, 211, 217, 309, 311, 325,
336-337
Robinson, C. A., 29
Robinson, David, 194
Robinson, Edward, 58, 129
Robinson, George L., 161
Robinson, Henry S., 237
Robinson's arch, 106
Rodkinson, M., 117
Rogers, R. W., 30
Roman citizenship, 223-225,
300-301
Roman Epistle, 287
Roman Tenth legion, 81, 102,
162
Romans, 132, 205, 206, 247,
258, 287, 316, 322
Rome, 24, 34, 38, 50, 51, 53,
54, 55, 56, 57, 60, 86,
111, 114, 116, 122, 134,
297-323
size, 317
avenues and hills, 317-319
buildings, parks, 319-320
palaces, temples, 320-321
Rostovzeff, M., 306
Roth, Cecil, 82
Rowley, H. H., 47, 82, 85, 87
Royal Guard, 58
Royal Porch, 100, 102
Royal Road, 190
Rufus, Annius, 67
"Rule of the Community,"
77, 81, 90
Russian Cathedral, 99

Orthodox church, 110
site, 112
Ruth (Apocrophon), 78
Rylands, John
Library, 21

S
Sacred Oracles, 25, 26
Sacred Way, 256
Sadducees, 44-45, 47, 63, 80
Safed, 137
Sahidic Acts, 332
Sagan, 298
Saida, 138
Salamis, 28, 183-184
Salim, 117
Salonika, 226, 229
Salt Sea, 116
Samaria, 28, 43, 44, 51, 59,
99, 114, 142-144
district of, 147-148
city, 148-150
Samaritans, 60
religious enthusiasts, 69
Samos, 249, 289-290
Samothrace, 216
Samuel (Apocrophon), 78, 79
I, 155
II, 110
Sanballat, governor of Sa-
maria, 42, 148
Sanday, W., 212, 213
Sanders, Frank Knight, 27
Sanhedrin, 48, 103, 131, 147
Santa Maria, 290
Sardis, 33, 264, 274, 279,
282-284
Saturnius, 66
Saul, 147, 155-161, 170, 171
Sayce, A. H., 154
Schecter, S., 87
Schlatter, Adolph, 207
Schleimann, H., 214
Schmidt, Hans, 103
Schmiedel Paul, 209, 326
School of Tyrannus, 259
Schultze, Victor, 172, 265,
272
Scythopolis, 114, 116-117,
139, 142, 159
Sea of Galilee, 72
Sea Scrolls, 24
Sebaste, 59, 99, 144, 148-149,
150-151, 184
Sebastiyeh, 148
Sebastos, 53
Sebek, 329
"Second Isaiah," 27
Second Revolt, 80, 82
Second triumvirate, 53
Secundus, Aemilius, 65
Seetzen, 72
Segaris, 269
Sejanus, 69
Selene, 265
Seleucia, 156, 171, 172
Seleucia Pieria, 179, 180,
181, 293
Seleucid-Maccabaean Wars,
43
troubles, 49
Seleucids, 34, 40-44, 49, 158
Seleucus I Nicator, 172-173,
179, 190, 279
Seleucus II Collinicus, 172,
279
Selinus River, 275
Seljuk, 250, 270
Sellers, O. R., 19, 48, 49, 76
Sellin, E., 144
Semites, 28

Seneca, 244, 313
Sennabris, 71
Sepphoris, 71, 119, 122
Septimius Severus, 136
Septuagint, 39
Septuaginta, 38
Seraikai, 264
Serapion, 256
Serapis, 263, 265
Sergius Paulus, 185-186
Sermon on the Mount, 90
Sert, 283
Servilius, 65
Seutonics, 122, 214
"Seven Springs," 126
Shalmaneser, 158
Sharon, Plain of, 115, 163,
164
Shear, T. Leslie, 235
Shechem, 142, 144, 148, 149
Shekinah, 110
Sheep Gate, 101
Sheikh Khudr, 136
Sheneset-Chenoboskion, 23,
91
Shepherd of Hermas, 332
Shiloah, 109
Shomron, 147
Shrine of the Mother Gods,
236
Sicarii, 287, 294-296, 301
Sicily, 310-311
Sidon, 30, 59, 137-139, 293,
305
Silas, 204, 206, 209-215, 220,
223, 224, 227, 228, 229, 230-
231, 233, 234, 244
Silberman, L. H., 90
Siloam, Pool of, 108, 109
Tower of, 108
Silwan, 109
Simeon (Niger), 170
Simon a tanner, 164
Simon Maccabaeus, 44, 48
Simon the Leper, 113
Simon Magus, 149
Simcox, W. H., 335
Sinai, 161
Sinda, 274
Siwa, 33
"Skull," 104
Smith, George Adam, 153
Smith, James, 308-310
Smyrna, 192, 209, 257, 264,
274-275, 280-283, 289
Socrates, 35, 238
Soli, 184, 185
Solomon
his priest, 47
apostasy, 109
death, 147
Solomon's Porch, 101
"Solomon's Stables," 101
"Sons of Zadok," 87
Sosthenes, 246
South Galatian Theory, 211-
212
Spain, 322
Spinka, Matthew, 172, 179
Snons, Jacques, 240, 242
Square of Augustus, 194
Square of Tiberias, 194
Stauffer, Ethelbert, 26, 122
Steinmueller, J. F., 27
Steinspring, W. F., 174
Stephen, 299
Stephen ('s)
martyrdom, 146, 168, 170
Sterrett, J. R., Sitlington,
197, 199

Stillwell, Richard, 176, 246
Stoa of Attalos, 236
Stoa Poikile, 236
Stoa of Zeus Eleutherios, 236, 237
Stoics, 159, 234, 235
Strabo, 159, 172, 195, 199, 226, 250, 291, 310
Strato's Tower, 59, 166
Street Straight, 161
St. George, 136, 163, 293
St. John Thackeray, H., 103, 334
St. Paul's Bay, 309
St. Paul's Gate, 177
St. Sebastian Gate, 314
St. Sophia (Church), 275
St. Stephen's Gate, 102
Stuart, James, 242
Styger, Paul, 26
Subostrani, 228-229
Succoth, 117
Sukenik, E. L., 26, 77-78, 128-129, 149
Sulaiman II, 108
Sulla, 232
Sultan Dagh, 192, 193
Sunium, 240
Susa, 33
Sycamore, 115
Sychar, 115, 142-144
Syllaeus, 55
Synagogue of Satan, 272, 282, 285
Synod of Laodicea, 269-270
Syracuse, 312-313
Syria, 22, 23, 30, 32, 34, 36, 40, 53, 59, 63, 65, 136, 137, 141, 153, 196, 204, 292, 294
Syrian Antioch, 192, 202
Syrian Army, 42
Syrian Gates, 207
Synoptic Gospels, 91
Syrophoenician woman, 137
Syrtis, 308

T
Tabariya, 130
Tabgha, 129
Tacitus, 64, 70, 99, 185, 301
Tal 'at ed Damm, 115
Talmud, 32, 119, 131
Taoism, 17
Tamerlane, 137, 283
Tarichaea, 125, 132, 304
Tarn, W. W., 29
Tarshish, 164
Tarsus, 150, 156-159, 171, 190, 207, 234, 248, 250, 264
Tatian, 19
Taubenschlag, R., 297
Taurus Mountains, 59, 171, 196, 200, 207, 208, 264
Taylor, Lily Ross, 252, 261
"Teacher of Righteousness," 87
Tebtunis, 331
Teicher, J. L., 90
Tell Hum, 126, 128
Temple (Jerusalem), 40, 44, 61, 95, 97-98, 111, 148
Temple of Apollo, 246
Temple of Apollos Patroos, 236, 237
Temple of Bacchus, 136
Temple of Ares, 236
Temple of Diana, 260
Temple (Mt. Gerizim), 44
Temples of Rome, 321
"Temple-keeper," 262
Ten Tribes, 147

Tenth Legion, 82
Terracina, 314
Tertullian, 61, 323
Testament of the Twelve, 86
"Thanksgiving Psalm," 77
Theatre of Dionysos, 240
Thebes, 29, 232
Theodosius I, 126
Theodosius II, 256
Theologisches Woerterbuch zum Neuen Testament, 20
Thermaes, 320
Termaic Gulf, 226
Thermopylae, 28
Thessalonica, 218, 226, 229
Thessalonians I, 159, 227, 244
Thessalonians II, 159, 227, 244
Thiessen, Henry Clarence, 210-212, 267
Tholos, 236
Thomas, Apostle, 93
Thompson, Sir Herbert, 332
Thracian Regiment, 58
Three Taverns, 314
Throne of David, 61
Thucydides, 234, 327, 336
Thumb, A., 335
Thutmose III, 119, 164, 181
Thyatira, 220, 278-280
Tiber (river), 171, 174, 271, 314, 316, 319
Tiberias, 71, 117, 123, 125-126, 130-131, 175, 304
Tiberias, Sea of, 130
Tiberius (Emperor), 66-68, 70, 73, 122, 136, 159, 173, 252, 267, 283, 284, 285, 316
Tiburtinus, 65
Tigranes of Armenia, 172
Tigris, 13, 33
Till, W. T., 91, 93
Timothy, 206, 208, 215, 220, 231, 233, 234, 244, 265
Timothy I, 322
Timothy II, 200, 208, 211, 267, 322
Titus, 61, 82, 99, 102, 111, 136, 185, 206, 208, 320
Titus (Book of), 322, 323
Tobiads, 42
Tobiah, the Ammonite governor, 42
Tomb of St. Luke, 256
Torah, 38, 39, 89
Tower of David, 98
Tower of Siloam, 108
Tower of the Ascension, 110
Trachonitis, 66, 72, 129, 304
Tractate Middoth, 100
Trade Guilds, 279-280
Trajan, 214
Tralles, 264
Transfiguration, 134
Transjordan, 42, 44, 48, 116, 139
Translations, 19
Treaty of Lausanne, 281
Tres Tabernae, 314, 316
Tripoli, 59
Tripolis, 264
Tritons, 194
Triumphal Entry, 111, 113
Troas, 213-216, 244, 279, 287-289
Trogyllium, 290
Trophimus, 295
Troy-Illium, 213-214
Tuebingen School, 21
Tulul Abu el-'Alayiq, 115

Tyana, 264
Tychichus, 267
Tychi, 177
Tyrannus, 259
Tyre, 30, 59, 137-139, 292, 294
Tyrimos, 280
Tyropoean Valley, 96, 103, 106

U
Ulatha, 118
Umm Qeis, 141
Uncials, 19
Unger, M., 15, 21, 27, 39, 147
University of Chicago (publishers), 20
University of Cincinnati, 214
University of Louvain, 80
University of Michigan, 194
Upper City, 97, 103, 104, 106
Upper Egypt, 22, 23, 91, 92
Upper Room, 106, 111

V
Valletta, 310, 311
"Valley of Oils," 112
Valley of the Shadow of Death, 58
Vardar Gate Inscription, 229
Varus, 65
Vatican, 178
Vedas, 17
Verethragna, 59
Vespasian, 25, 114, 144, 164, 285, 298, 304
Versions, 19
Via Dolorosa, 104
Via Egnatia, 225, 226, 229, 230
Via Flaminia, 319
Via Labicana, 319
Via Latina, 319
Via Nomentana, 319
Via Ostiensis, 319
Via Pinciana, 319
Via Salaria, 319
Via Tiburtina, 319
Vienne, 60
Vincent, H., 104
Viri Galiloei, 110
Vitellius, 70, 74, 298
Von Dobschuetz, Ernest, 19

W
Wadi en Nar, 80
Wadi es-Semak, 141
Wadi Murabb'at, 75, 80
Wadi Quelt, 23, 58, 115
Wailing Wall, 98
Walch, Johann, 334
"War of the Sons of Light with the Sons of Darkness, The," 77
Warren, R. E., 106
Warren, Sir Charles, 100
Waterman, Leroy, 123
Waters of Merom, 118
Watzinger, Carl, 128
"Way of Sorrow," 104
Wernberg-Moeller, P., 77
Westcott and Hort, 18-19
Western Asia, 30
Western Hill, 97
Wheeler, Sir George, 242
Whiston, W., 32
Wilcken, Ulrich, 333
Wilderness of Judaea, 58

Williams, C. S. C., 160, 307, 310
Williams, Rev. G., 128
Wilson, Charles, 106
Wilson, R. M., 92
Wilson's Arch, 106
Winer, 326
Winged Victory, 216
Wisdom of Solomon (Apocrophon), 80
Wolfe Expedition, 197
Women in the Church, 220-221
Worcester Art Museum, 176
Wood, J. T., 252-253
Wright, G. E., 97, 100, 123, 141, 150, 160, 236

X

Xanthos River, 291
Xenophon, 71, 95, 158, 188, 265
Xerxes I, 28, 29
Xystus, 106

Y

Yale School of Forestry, 115
Yale University, 141
Yapu, 164
Yalovatch, 192
Yarmuk River, 141
Young, E. J., 27

Z

Zacchaeus, 115
Zachariah, 66
Zadok, 47

Zadokites, 47
Zadokite Document, 87
Zahns, Theodore, 139, 212, 227
Zealots, 82, 86, 287
Zebedee, 169
Zebulon (tribe of), 119
territory of, 126
Zechariah, 27, 90, 92, 110, 111
Zeiler, Jacques, 122
Zeno, 235, 236
Zephaniah (Apocrophon), 78
Zerubbabel, 148
Zeua Ammon, 33
Zeus (Kasios), 172, 183, 198, 277
Zeus (Olympian), 41, 193
Ziboetes, 34